Religion and
Global Politics

Religion and Global Politics

Paul S. Rowe

OXFORD
UNIVERSITY PRESS

OXFORD

UNIVERSITY PRESS

Oxford University Press is a department of the University of Oxford. It furthers the University's objective of excellence in research, scholarship, and education by publishing worldwide. Oxford is a registered trade mark of Oxford University Press in the UK and in certain other countries.

Published in Canada by
Oxford University Press
8 Sampson Mews, Suite 204, Don Mills, Ontario M3C 0H5 Canada

www.oupcanada.com

First Edition published in 2012

Library and Archives Canada Cataloguing in Publication

Rowe, Paul Stanley

Religion and global politics / Paul S. Rowe.

Includes bibliographical references and index.

ISBN 978-0-19-543812-3

1. Religion and politics. 2. Religion and state. I. Title.

BL65.P7R69 2012   201'.72   C2012-900058-2

Cover image: Jeff Hutchens/The Image Bank/Getty
Map on inside cover: Adapted from Encyclopedia Britannica

Oxford University Press is committed to our environment.
This book is printed on paper which has been certified by the Forest Stewardship Council®.

Printed and bound in Canada.

4 5 6 — 19 18 17

Contents

Preface

As this book goes into production, the radical actions of an otherwise unremarkable fundamentalist Baptist congregation in Florida have caused lethal riots in Afghanistan. The desecration of a holy book by self-appointed representatives of another world religion has had real and immediate consequences in the world of global politics. Not surprisingly, religion has become a central preoccupation of the world media, politicians, and scholars over the past several years, often displacing the forces of nationalism and ethnic politics, ideology, and culture. At this crucial juncture in a world frequently polarized by religious intolerance, the need for understanding can hardly be overemphasized.

This textbook is the product of several years of conceptualization and writing. It began as a project in support of a senior-level seminar in religion and global politics that I offered at the University of Western Ontario and Trinity Western University. In the wake of the events of 11 September 2001, the relationship between religion and politics became an important theme, yet there seemed to be no particularly suitable text that covered its many different permutations. Conversations with other professors confirmed this assessment. Over the years I have taught courses in religion and global politics with some measure of frustration over the absence of a text that combines insights from the most important case studies and themes in the field. In particular, I needed a text that would deal directly with theories and models rooted in political science while taking religion seriously as a motivator of action.

Religion and Global Politics is designed to fill this void. It combines insights from the empirical study of the politics of several nations and regions throughout the world, including the United States, Europe, India, South and East Asia, and Latin America. It also explores the roles that religion plays in the fields of human rights, international conflict and conflict resolution, and globalization. In each case, it draws on a wide variety of sources and introduces students to recent scholarship in the field.

Studies of religion and politics have been a growth industry throughout the past decade. When I completed graduate school, religion was rarely studied as an independent variable in political science. Rather it was viewed as a secondary phenomenon, often a contributing feature amid political culture, or a device in the hands of ruling elites or popular movements. Since that time, many excellent new works of scholarship have provided guidance in understanding this important causal variable. Indeed, the expansion of the literature on religion and politics added theoretical depth to this work even as it was being written.

The emergence of new case studies and themes in religion and politics speaks to the variability of the politics of religion. It is common to consider religion a static phenomenon, a set of doctrines and theologies in the hands of defenders of orthodoxy.

In practice, religious beliefs ebb and flow and their political impact changes with the tides of philosophic, doctrinal, and popular fads. There are strong generational effects in the development of religion worldwide. For example, two decades ago millenarian movements played a major role in the revival of evangelical Christianity in the United States, and their influence continues to be evident in the American religious right to this day. At the same time, growing recognition of the social justice and liberationist impulses of the Christian faith is beginning to refashion the evangelical perspective on politics in North America. The authoritarian crackdowns on Islamism and democracy that took place in the 1980s and 1990s helped to spark the radical movements of the past two decades. But the participation of Islamist groups in democratic societies such as Turkey and Indonesia has won many politically active Muslims over to the idea of democracy today. The seeds of the future are sown in the fertile bed of new ideas that transform the preoccupations of religious people, even as they remain rooted in age-old traditions that frame their basic worldview. Given the fluidity of religious belief, I urge caution to anyone who assumes that the details of the case studies and themes explored in this volume are immune to change. It is imperative to keep an eye on developments in each context with a view to remaining up to date.

Using this textbook in the classroom

In writing this textbook, I have deliberately sought to appeal to a wide variety of disciplines, including religious studies, sociology, anthropology, international studies, and history, in addition to my own field of political science. It is aimed at the level of the third- or fourth-year university student. Since this book was created to support an existing course, it corresponds well to the needs of a course in religion and global politics. Each chapter provides an introduction to a key theme that may be explored in a single week's session. The order of chapters is designed to expose students to the world of religious traditions before considering wider themes in religion and global politics. Students may thereby gain a strong grounding in examples that may later be used to illustrate themes in human rights, democratization, war, peace, and global order.

Of course instructors may choose to weave the empirical case studies and themes together or to assign the chapters out of sequence. The chapters have been designed to stand well on their own, so that the order may be altered to suit the instructor's own course plan. Conclusions and discussion questions at the end of each chapter direct students toward the key problems raised by scholars in the study of each religious tradition and theme. Each chapter also includes an extensive bibliography that can serve as both a useful resource and a starting point for research essays.

Understanding the diverse world of religion and global politics requires students (and professors!) to move outside their comfort zones and explore other worlds. For many students, the initial encounters with foreign cultures, practices, and ideas may be uncomfortable or even disturbing. To understand diverse religious views to the fullest extent may even require a certain change of lifestyle: openness to new worldviews, new smells and sensations, new cuisine, or new worship practices. It also requires learning new histories, cultures, and vocabularies. This text seeks to strike a balance between introducing new religious contexts and exploring their political implications. It assumes that the reader's understanding of comparative religion is limited. However, by necessity it stops short of explaining all the details of each religion, and external reading will certainly be required to gain a greater understanding of each religious tradition. I have made reference in most cases to the essential sacred texts. But to achieve a full grasp of a religious tradition, one needs to get to know its adherents and its practices in a place of worship or in normal everyday conversations. I recommend that this text be utilized in tandem with visits to local places of worship or in conversation with religious believers, clergy, and activists.

On a final and personal note, it should come as no surprise that this work reflects my own interest in journeys of faith. Religion is behind so many of the most important developments in history—from the greatest examples of human compassion and sacrifice to the worst depredations of intolerance and violence—precisely because human beings are innately religious. I concede that this conviction may be controversial in some quarters. But as I walk through my own journey of faith and converse with others who consciously or unconsciously struggle with matters spiritual and immanent, I am only more convinced that religion will be with us for some time to come. Learning to meet the political consequences of living with religious pluralism is therefore one of the greatest and most important challenges of the twenty-first century.

Acknowledgments

It was my father who first inspired me to a passion for faith and politics. Since those early formative years I have met many people of faith who have helped me to understand the perspectives and convictions they hold. I have been introduced to many Muslims, Hindus, Sikhs, and Christians in particular who have refined my knowledge of their beliefs and practice. Their names are too numerous to mention here. I am certain that there remains much to learn and explore together. In recent years, I have enjoyed the opportunities provided by the Multifaith Action Society of the lower mainland of British Columbia in getting to meet people of diverse faiths.

Early versions of the course that led to this textbook were offered at the University of Western Ontario and at Trinity Western University. In the past few years, students of my course in Religion and Global Politics have given me helpful feedback on the content of these chapters, for which I am most grateful. During the final revision of the manuscript, my research assistant Rebeca Besoiu provided valuable support in proofreading, editing, and suggesting changes from the perspective of an undergraduate student. I share my appreciation as well for my colleagues John Dyck and Jens Zimmermann, of the Religion, Culture, and Conflict Research Group as well as the Religion in Canada Institute based at Trinity Western University, for many discussions of the issues addressed in this work. Our research group benefits from a generous contribution from our media partners at JoyTV based in Langley, British Columbia. Thanks also go to Mary Wat and Kate Skene at Oxford University Press, who have provided me with several useful suggestions to improve the manuscript. Finally, I am grateful to the following reviewers (as well as one who wished to remain anonymous), who recommended specific additions and changes to the text:

Peter Beyer, University of Ottawa
Nathan Colborne, University of Nippissing
Irving Hexham, University of Calgary
Andrés Pérez, University of Western Ontario
Lucian Turcescu, Concordia University
John von Heyking, University of Lethbridge
Andrew M. Wender, University of Victoria

Though all of these people have contributed to the development of this textbook, I am responsible for any of its errors or shortcomings.

Chapter 1

Introduction and Theoretical Overview

A New Beginning?

On 4 June 2009, on one of his first trips as US President, Barack Obama made a point of visiting Egypt, a country that had been considered one of Washington's staunchest allies in the Middle East since the early 1980s. The administration of Obama's predecessor, George W. Bush, had been shaped by the infamous attacks of 11 September 2001, carried out by militants linked to al-Qaeda, the radical movement whose members cloaked their terrorist activity in the rhetoric of political Islam. Ever since 2001, US foreign policy had been focused on rooting out and pre-empting threats to US security, as enunciated in the 'Bush doctrine' of preventive war included in the 2002 National Security Strategy. The Bush doctrine had led the US first to invade Afghanistan and then Iraq, two nations that were held either to harbour or to support such terrorist efforts. Though President Bush emphasized that neither action represented a 'war on Islam', many **Muslims** around the world suspected that American intervention in the region was inspired by a barely veiled 'Islamophobia' or prejudice against Muslims. Consequently, popular opinion of the US had declined significantly in many Arab and Muslim states.

In a public speech at Cairo University, President Obama announced 'a new beginning' in the United States' relations with the Muslim world. Obama himself represented a sort of new beginning in the US, being the first African-American president, the descendent of Kenyan Muslims on his father's side. Although he had made a public declaration of his own Christian faith, his experience growing up in Indonesia—a predominantly Muslim country—and his multiracial background seemed to promise a new level of comfort with the concerns of the Islamic world:

> I have come here to seek a new beginning between the United States and Muslims around the world; one based on mutual interest and mutual respect; and one based upon the truth that America and Islam are not exclusive, and need not be in competition. Instead, they overlap, and share common principles—principles of justice and progress; tolerance and the dignity of human beings (Obama 2009).

Obama's speech represented a remarkable development in global politics. Religion was now something more than a private matter debated in **mosques** and cathedrals. It had assumed a central place in the discussions of international relations. More than two centuries after the modern world was supposed to have consigned it to the sidelines, religion remained important in public life, so much so that a US president made a point of reaching out not to states, organizations, or rival alliance blocs, but to the individual members of a worldwide faith community.

This book examines the interaction of religion and politics at the level both of individual societies and of the global community. In so doing, it takes seriously both the power of religion as a social force and the nature of global politics as the meeting point of domestic and international politics. It explores how religion works in specific states and societies as well as its impact at the level of international and global affairs. Rooted in case studies of the interactions between religion and politics in particular places and contexts, it also deals with some of the basic theoretical questions that modern scholars in political science have asked about how religion and politics can or should interact, although it does not attempt to survey all the normative philosophic questions that surround the relationship between **church** and state. In order to set the stage, we begin by looking at the background of this relationship.

Religion in the Premodern International System

The study of global politics typically begins in 1648, when the international states system as we know it today was created. In that year, the warring states of Europe met in Westphalia and agreed to a set of rules for state conduct that put an end to decades of conflict over religion and established a secular international system. For this reason the Peace of Westphalia is often seen as marking the conclusion of the medieval period, in which religion had a formative influence on affairs of state. To suggest that religious concerns disappeared from public life would be an oversimplification. However, their importance in political calculations began to decline at both the elite and mass levels. Just as public opinion on any issue changes over time, so does common wisdom about the relationship between religion and politics.

Before 1648 religion had always played an important role in global politics, both formally and informally. In ancient times, wars were often explained as originating in conflicts among the gods, and the success of a military campaign was often attributed to the intervention of patron deities. One of the earliest historical texts, the Sumerian 'Stele of the Vultures', casts the battle between the cities of Lagash and Umma in religious terms. Historical accounts from ancient Assyria, Egypt, and Greece do the same with their own battles. The Hebrew scripture describes how the ancient Israelites conquered the land of Canaan under the direct instruction of their God, Yahweh. Ancient Hindu texts such as the Vedas and the *Mahabharata* enshrined the notion that warfare and temporal rulership were the sacred duties of the Kshatriya **caste**. Deviation from a divine plan was the primary explanation for military defeat in many of these societies. Individual devotees of various pagan cults would continue to give the credit for victory to their divine patrons by dedicating important statues, buildings, and temples to them. The spread of first Greek and then Roman rule from southern Europe throughout the Mediterranean world and into the Near East in the first two centuries BCE created an integrated world of religion, where Eastern and Western traditions came to mix and spread.

Throughout antiquity, political leaders often espoused new religious doctrines. For example, the famous 'heretic' pharaoh Akhenaten attempted to transform the religion of Egypt but had no lasting success. In the second century CE, the Roman emperors Antoninus Pius and Marcus Aurelius introduced devotion to the community and stoicism into the governance of the empire, ushering in a sort of golden age of Roman prosperity and security. Five centuries later, toward the end of the Byzantine Empire, the Emperor Heraclius attempted to unite the Christian communities divided by a bitter dispute over the nature of Jesus **Christ** by proposing a theological compromise known as monothelitism, but the project came to an end with his death.

The growth of Christianity and the relative decline of Roman power in the late third and early fourth centuries set the stage for the establishment of a Christian civilization

Box 1.1: Major World Religions: Profiles

Judaism

Foundations The ancient religious beliefs of the Jewish people, including the belief that God made a sacred covenant with them, through Moses, and that the special obligations it imposed on them continue to govern Jewish life today, more than three thousand years later.

Sacred Texts The **Tanakh** (Law, Prophets, and Writings), composed between c. 1000 and 200 BCE, plus the Talmud (legal texts) and Midrash (commentaries) composed over many centuries.

Basic Teachings One God who intervenes in the affairs of His people; the covenant as a picture of the importance of the Jewish nation as an example of covenant faithfulness to the world; suffering as a divine calling for the people of God.

Practices Prayer; liturgical celebration of holy days; observance of the seventh day (the Sabbath; from sunset on Friday to sunset on Saturday) as a day of rest; obedience to Jewish legal traditions (Halakha), including dietary restrictions.

Major Divisions Conservative, Orthodox, Reconstructionist, Reform, 'Ultra-Orthodox'.

Christianity

Foundations Originated as a small Jewish sect centred on Jesus of Nazareth (c. 1–33 CE), whose followers believe him to be the expected **Messiah** or Christ. Adopted as the official religion of Rome following the conversion of the Emperor Constantine in the fourth century, Christianity became the most influential religion in Europe, a position it retains today.

Sacred Texts The **Bible**, consisting of two parts: the Old Testament (the texts that make up the Hebrew Bible or Tanakh in a different arrangement) and the New Testament, composed in the first century CE.

Basic Teachings The divinity of Jesus Christ as one of three persons of the divine Trinity; his death as a sacrificial atonement for human sins; his resurrection from the dead.

Practices Baptism, worship services on Sunday, the Eucharist or Lord's Supper.

Major Divisions Roman Catholic, Eastern Orthodox, Oriental Orthodox, Protestant, and Church of the East; each of these divisions is further divided by differences concerning doctrine and earthly authority.

Islam

Foundations Founded by the Prophet Muhammad (c. 570–632 CE), a religious and political reformer who established a community of Muslims in the Arabian city of Yathrib (Medina) in 622. The Prophet's successors, the **caliphs**, established an Islamic empire that at its height stretched from Spain to India; eventually, Muslims carried their faith around the world.

Sacred Texts The **Qur'an**, believed to be the word of Allah (the one God) as received directly by Muhammad and collated in the mid-seventh century. In addition, the sayings and traditions of the Prophet, known collectively as the Hadith, are considered authoritative. The collected legal texts and judgments, known as the **Shari'a**, form the legal code of Islam.

Basic Teachings The oneness of God (*tawhid*) and submission (*islam*) to God through spiritual practice.

Practices Recitation of the *shahada* (the creed or confession of faith), prayer, almsgiving, fasting, pilgrimage to Mecca at least once in one's life.

Major Divisions Sunni and Shi'i, each of which contains various sects and schools of thought.

Hinduism

Foundations The indigenous traditions of the Indian subcontinent, a broad and eclectic assortment of beliefs and practices handed down since ancient times. 'Hinduism' (from 'Hindu', 'Indian') is not so much the name of a belief system as a kind of umbrella term for a vast array of religious traditions originating in India.

Sacred Texts The Vedas (a collection of Sanskrit texts and hymns composed beginning with the Rig Veda c. 1500 BCE and concluding c. 600 BCE with the Upanishads), the epics (the *Ramayana* and **Mahabharata**, especially the section of the latter known as the **Bhagavad Gita**), and other sacred texts, all composed in ancient times.

Basic Teachings Hinduism can be understood as either a philosophy or a faith that sees and seeks out the presence of God in all. Central concepts include **dharma** ('faith', 'way of life', 'moral teaching', 'duty', etc.), **karma** (action and its consequences), **samsara** (rebirth/reincarnation of souls), and **moksha** (liberation from the cycle of rebirth). Hindus seek to attain moksha through the practice of various yogas (disciplines or paths of self-mastery).

Practices Diverse disciplines and devotions based on local customs or the advice of a guru (spiritual teacher). Historically, *dharma* was interpreted as reinforcing the four-part caste system, which is still informally recognized in Indian social life.

Major Divisions Innumerable local variations.

Buddhism

Foundations Rooted in the teachings of Siddhartha Gautama, a north Indian prince who lived c. 500 BCE who, after years of striving to reach enlightenment through extreme ascetic discipline, finally reached his goal when he embraced the moderate 'middle way' between the extremes of self-indulgence and self-mortification. Buddhists follow the example of the **Buddha** (the 'enlightened one').

Sacred Texts Numerous teachings attributed to the Buddha (transmitted orally until the first century CE), as well as many texts written by later devotees.

Basic Teachings *Nirvana* (liberation from the cycle of rebirth) is attained when all desires and attachments are extinguished. The merit ('good *karma*') earned in the course of each lifetime accumulates and, through many rebirths, helps the individual advance along the path to liberation.

Practices Moderation (the 'middle way'), compassion, non-violence (**ahimsa**). Monastic discipline includes meditation and chanting. Buddhists are committed to a life of moderation ('the middle way'), typically including a vegetarian diet. Some Buddhist traditions venerate celestial **bodhisattvas** ('enlightenment beings').

Major Divisions Three traditions or 'vehicles': **Theravada** (the earliest surviving tradition, centred in Southeast Asia), **Mahayana** (a first-century movement that diversified and eventually spread to East Asia), and **Vajrayana** (an esoteric school that emerged c. 500 CE and became the principal form of Buddhism in the Himalayan region; also known as Tibetan Buddhism).

in which religion was often inseparable from politics. In 312 CE, the Roman Emperor Constantine won a decisive battle after experiencing a vision of the cross, and although he did not accept baptism until just before his death in 337, the victory led to a dramatic improvement in the status of Christianity and, eventually, the adoption of Christianity as the official religion of the empire. From the death of Constantine until the 1600s (with a brief interlude under Julian the Apostate, 360–363), Roman and, later, European civilization was nominally Christian. In spite of early Christian traditions that clearly separated church and state, religion became closely associated with authority in Western civilization.

Various schisms in the Christian Church paralleled political developments within the Roman Empire. Over time, the eastern portion became increasingly alienated from both sacred and secular authority in Rome, and in 1054 the two bodies formally separated to form what would come to be known as the **Roman Catholic** and **Eastern Orthodox churches**. Although the rise of feudalism, which emphasized more local authority, eroded the political authority of the Roman Church in central Europe, the Christian faith remained the main unifying force for Europeans. European politics were dominated by rivalries between the Holy Roman Emperor—the supposed heir to the Roman Empire—and various **popes** who claimed the loyalty of Christian civilization.

The Holy Mosque of Mecca was built around the Kaaba: the black cube-like structure toward the top of this photo. The Kaaba is believed to have been built by the prophet Ibrahim (Abraham) as a house of monotheistic worship. Muslims around the world turn in the direction of the Kaaba to pray, and it is the focal point of the Hajj pilgrimage that all able-bodied Muslims are expected to perform at least once in their lives.
Source: © Kazuyoshi Nomachi/Corbis

A new pattern of relations between religion and politics came with the rapid rise of Islam following the death of the Prophet Muhammad (c. 570–632). Arab military expansion carried Islam throughout most of southwest Asia and north Africa within a few decades. Meanwhile, Christian unity had been so fractured that many of the subjects of the Eastern Orthodox Byzantine Empire welcomed their Muslim conquerors, believing that Muslim tolerance of other monotheists (or 'people of the book') would be preferable to the enforcement of Roman orthodoxy. The Muslim conquest created a new dynamic in the history of Europe and Asia, a political and religious division between the areas under Muslim control, known to Muslims as *dar al-Islam* ('the abode of Islam'), and the remaining Byzantine and European Christian kingdoms and principalities of the Holy Roman Empire, known as *dar al-harb* ('the region of war'). Islamic civilization was nominally united under the authority of the caliphs (the successors to the Prophet), but a minority called the **Shi'i** did not recognize the authority of the caliphate, and rival authorities among the **Sunni** mainstream also tended to ignore its temporal authority within their own domains.

Christian and Muslim societies, defined fundamentally by their embrace of divergent faiths, at times came into open political conflict, even though many Christians living in regions under Islamic control lived peacefully with their Muslim neighbours and governors. The westward spread of Islam was halted in Spain after Charles Martel defeated an attempted invasion of France in 732. In the east, however, the Christian Byzantine Empire, centred on Constantinople, would continue to fight a rearguard action against the encroachment of various Islamic empires for another seven centuries.

In 1009, the Fatimid caliph al-Hakim—an unorthodox Muslim of the minority Ismaili sect—ordered the destruction of the Christian Church of the Holy Sepulchre (known to the Orthodox as the Church of the Resurrection) in Jerusalem. The church was later rebuilt, but the incident revealed the vulnerability of Christian holy sites under Muslim control, especially after the '**Great Schism**' of 1054 left the Eastern Orthodox Church as sole custodian of the remaining Christian holy sites in the East. These political and religious developments increasingly disrupted the tradition of pilgrimage to the holy land by Christians from the West.

In an attempt to restore Roman Catholic authority over the Holy Land, in 1095 Pope Urban II called on Europe to undertake a '**crusade**'. Those who responded to the call—from landed gentry to mercenaries—were promised not only adventure, glory, and wealth but remission of their sins and guaranteed entry to heaven in the event of their death. The Crusaders established kingdoms in various parts of what are now Lebanon, Syria, Jordan, and Israel. But the Crusader kingdoms were internally divided by rivalries and therefore at risk when Muslim forces were united, as they were under the renowned Salah ad-Din (Saladin), who retook Jerusalem in 1187. By 1244 the Crusaders had been driven from Jerusalem for the last time, and less than a century later most of the Crusaders were driven out of Asia.

For all their differences, Islam and Christianity were both rooted in the Abrahamic tradition of the Middle East. This was not the case with the traditions that Muslims encountered as they pressed south and east into Asia. Military conquests in northern India beginning in the twelfth century brought the Muslims into contact with people whose social and political structures had developed under the influence of very

Box 1.2: Major events of the Crusades

1095	First Crusade declared by Pope Urban II
1099	Crusaders conquer Jerusalem
1145	Second Crusade declared by Pope Eugenius III
1187	Battle of Hattin; Salah ad-Din retakes Jerusalem
1187	Third Crusade declared by Pope Gregory VIII
1198	Fourth Crusade declared by Pope Innocent III
1204	Crusaders sack Constantinople
1213	Fifth Crusade declared by Pope Innocent III
1229	Emperor Frederick II negotiates the return of Jerusalem to the Crusaders
1244	Jerusalem retaken by Muslims for the last time
1291	Crusader city of Acre falls; Crusaders surrender lands in the Middle East

different religious beliefs. In both Hinduism and Buddhism, the term that most closely approximates 'religion' is *dharma*, but its meanings vary widely (see Box 1.1) and often have as much to do with life in society as with spiritual life.

In China as well, religious traditions differed significantly from their Western forms. For example, although it seems that Confucius (c. 500 BCE) probably did believe in a supreme deity, his teachings emphasized moral values and ethical conduct in this world. Confucianism made devotion to family (parents and ancestors) and community central to Chinese social and political philosophy. Between the seventh century and the tenth, Islam gradually spread eastward. By the sixteenth century much of the territory from Persia through Afghanistan to northern India was under Muslim rule, and by the latter part of the 1600s most of the Indian subcontinent had been incorporated into the Muslim Mughal Empire. Akbar (r. 1556–1605), widely considered the greatest of the Mughal emperors, extended royal support to all religions in India, laying down a model of public religion that sought to include both Hindus and Muslims and is still lauded by many scholars. Over the ensuing centuries, Muslim merchants and missionaries carried Islam to much of north India, Southeast Asia, and Indonesia.

Religious relations were tested in the areas abutting Europe where Muslims mixed with Christians and Jews. From 711 to 1492, most of the Iberian Peninsula was controlled by Muslim kingdoms. The Muslim policy of tolerance for Christians and Jews meant that relations between the various communities that made up Muslim Spain (Andalusia or Al-Andalus) were generally characterized by *convivencia* (peaceful coexistence). Nevertheless, a centuries-long campaign to return Spain to Christian rule (the *Reconquista*) finally succeeded in1492. With the restoration of Christian rule, Muslim and Jewish subjects were either forced to convert or expelled; many immigrated to North Africa to escape sectarian violence and the Spanish Inquisition of 1480–1530.

Meanwhile, the Ottoman Turks, having captured Constantinople in 1453, resumed the Muslim advance into Europe. That advance continued until 1683, when the Ottoman troops were defeated by the Austrians at Vienna. Relations between the Muslim Ottomans and Christian Europeans entered a new phase with the advent of the age of exploration and the expansion of trade between Christendom and Islam after 1453. Christian and Muslim nations alike maintained controls on the rights to citizenship and standing before legal courts of non-nationals—a category generally defined by religious adherence. However, the Ottomans responded to the growing numbers of European trade missions to the Near East and European expatriates living in Ottoman lands by granting European Christians special status under a series of agreements known as capitulations (Turkish *ahdnames*). Arguably these agreements were the first examples of international law. However, Christian lands recognized no special status for Muslims.

The division of Europe between Protestant and Roman Catholic states (and statelets) had begun in the early sixteenth century. Most popular histories trace the start of the Reformation to 1517, when a monk named Martin Luther posted 95 'theses'—basically, a series of propositions charging the Roman Catholic Church with corruption and false teaching—on the door of a church in Wittenberg, Germany. In fact, the Church's authority was already eroding as a consequence of cultural change (including new scientific discoveries and the spread of literacy) and political intrigue. Nor was Luther the only thinker calling for reform, both institutional and theological. Nevertheless, Luther's protest served as a catalyst for massive political as well as religious and cultural change.

Originally constructed as the greatest church in the Roman Empire, the Basilica of Hagia Sophia was converted into a mosque after the Turkish conquest of Constantinople in 1453. In 1935, as part of his campaign to modernize Turkey and make it a secular state, President Mustafa Kemal Ataturk ordered that the building be turned into a museum.
Source: © BL Images Ltd/Alamy

The Protestant Reformation called into question the notion of a single Christian civilization and brought new political divisions to Europe. The challenge that **Protestantism** posed to the Roman Catholic Church was also a challenge to the secular authority of Catholic monarchs across Europe. The Reformation led to a prolonged civil war in the German-speaking states that was brought to end only in 1555, when the Peace of Augsburg established official toleration of Lutheran Protestants in the Holy Roman (Hapsburg) Empire. Protestants in predominantly Roman Catholic France were guaranteed similar protection in 1598 under the Edict of Nantes.

For the next sixty years, Europe would be uneasily divided between Protestant and Roman Catholic powers as the Catholic Hapsburg emperors and their allies sought to regain their former supremacy across Europe. Conflict erupted into war in 1618, when Bohemian Protestants, with the support of the Protestant German states, sought to overthrow Hapsburg rule in their region. Over the next decade, the conflict spread throughout Europe and became the large-scale conflagration that we now call the Thirty Years' War. Every Hapsburg victory emboldened the Catholic forces but also pushed other Protestant states to go to the defence of the northern German states. Although the issue at stake may at first have appeared to be religion, it soon became clear that the war was above all a secular struggle for control of Europe. The strategic nature of the conflict was revealed in 1624, when Catholic France decided to ally itself with the Protestant states against its Hapsburg rivals. France's policy, motivated solely by *raisons d'état*, was a primary philosophical underpinning of the Peace of Westphalia: the treaty that finally brought an end to the war in 1648.

The Post-Westphalian System and the Secularization of Global Politics

The Peace of Westphalia marked a sea-change in the relationship between religion and politics. Many prominent scholars have observed that, with the erosion of the Christian social order in the period from the Reformation to the Enlightenment, man-made norms were increasingly emphasized over divine fiat. As Hedley Bull observed:

> The international society conceived by theorists of this period was identified as European rather than Christian in its values or culture. References to Christendom or to divine law as cementing the society of states declined and disappeared, as did religious oaths in treaties (Bull 1977: 33).

In the new international society, the religious concept of natural law was replaced by positive law codified in explicit treaties and international agreements. At the same time that the 'wars of religion' were pulling European society apart, political philosophers such as Thomas Hobbes (1588–1679) and Hugo Grotius (1583–1645) were beginning to articulate ways in which politics might be divorced from demands that all embrace the same religion.

The states that signed the Peace of Westphalia agreed to recognize that each monarch was sovereign in his own land. The principle of **cuius regio, eius religio** ('whose realm, his religion'), first introduced in 1555, was enshrined as a guiding philosophy, giving the monarch or government of each state the right to establish its religion and prohibiting interference on the part of other states. Foreign policy would be determined in the tradition of the medieval theorist Niccolo Machiavelli (1469-1527), on the principle that the most important objective was not the preservation of any particular religion but the survival of the state.

At the same time the signatories agreed to a set of rules that reflected the emergence of international social norms based on humanistic rather than explicitly Christian principles. In addition to the principle of *cuius regio, eius religio*, Westphalia introduced the notion of sovereignty as a territorial concept shared by the states of Europe. It ushered in a new period in which those states would pursue policies designed to ensure a balance of power, so that none of them would be able to gain political dominance over the continent. Thus Daniel Philpott argues that the '**Westphalian synthesis**' combined recognition of the sovereign state with recognition of the increasing secularization of the international order (Philpott 2002: 6–7). Elsewhere, William Cavanaugh suggests that the so-called 'wars of religion' that preceded the Peace of Westphalia were the birth-pangs of the modern state, which had already set religion aside in practice, if not in theory (Cavanaugh 1995).

The separation of religion from the state was reflected in domestic as well as foreign policy as it evolved through the eighteenth and nineteenth centuries. In France, for example, the revolutionaries saw organized religion as a prop for the *ancien régime* and strongly opposed any public role for the clergy. In July 1790 the French National Assembly passed the Civil Constitution of the Clergy, which severely limited the privileges and freedoms of the Roman Catholic Church in France. By the end of the Napoleonic Wars, more conservative regimes were anxious to re-entrench religion in its former place at the centre of political life. Among them were the monarchies of Russia, Austria, and Prussia, which in 1815 formed a pact against the threat of revolution under the name of the 'Holy Alliance'. But the pact was of little significance, either religious or political. Meanwhile, although the European states tended to treat the Ottoman Empire as a subordinate power outside their own society of equals, dealings with the Islamic world gradually took on all the features of interactions between Christian states, including formal diplomatic and trading relationships.

Religious bigotry and jealousies did not disappear from cultural and political life, of course. Religion played a central role in the peopling of the American colonies as well as British monarchy's various succession crises. Jewish minorities continued to be targeted for pogroms and persecution, and debates continued over the establishment of religion—the state's adoption of a particular faith as the national religion—in various places. The ideal of religious freedom did not truly emerge until the later 1700s as democratic regimes recognized the rights of free belief and assembly, and then it remained a generally western European notion. Still, the plurality of religious identification in Europe made it increasingly necessary for the international realm to operate without official reference to religion.

In the rush for colonies from the sixteenth to the early nineteenth century, Christian mission activity became closely associated with the expansion of European power. The mission enterprise sought to establish European cultural and religious norms in the developing world through education and social change. It reinforced the dominance of Christian Europe over the rest of the world while simultaneously seeking to improve the lives of the colonized by introducing them to European models of social organization, government regulation, law, and belief. In their groundbreaking work on the colonial period in South Africa, John and Jean Comaroff argue that missionary enterprise had an important influence in cultivating what have become the common notions of modernity. In the process it helped to spark anti-colonial resistance among indigenous peoples that prefigured the modern opposition to globalization (Comaroff and Comaroff 1997). In the developing world, then, religion has served both to reinforce Western dominance and to offer the most significant counterpoint to it.

Nevertheless, by the time the classical states system was restored following the Napoleonic Wars, most statesmen believed that religious viewpoints had no place in the making of either foreign or domestic policy. The two most influential diplomats of the nineteenth century, the reactionary Austrian Count von Metternich and the masterful Prussian politician Otto von Bismarck, each worked to preserve the international order without reference to religion except as a rhetorical device. Their rational, pragmatic approach, which came to be known as realism, was based on the assumption that the ethical principles associated with religious belief might be useful at the interpersonal level for a properly functioning society, but were counterproductive at the level of state decision-making (Waltz 1959), and it has dominated international relations almost ever since.

The only significant challenge to the received wisdom of realist theory developed in response to the First World War, and much of the impetus for it came from the liberal Protestant **social gospel** movement. Since the late nineteenth century, idealists inspired by the social gospel had devoted themselves mainly to reform of domestic social ills such as alcoholism and labour exploitation, but the horrors of the First World War led many of the same people to form the idealist movement, which called for an end to the global blight of war. US President Woodrow Wilson's '14 points' (among them the proposal to create the League of Nations) reflected the influence of the idealists. But efforts to deepen international acceptance of idealist norms, such as the 1928 Kellogg–Briand Pact (General Treaty for the Renunciation of War, or World Peace Act), proved futile. In the wake of the idealists' failure, realism regained its ascendency. The study of international politics subordinated religious impulses to the dispassionate pursuit of state interests.

Modernization and Secularization

The failure of the idealist movement appeared to vindicate the realist claim that religion was ineffective as a motivator of state action and had no place in the realm of public policy. This point was reinforced by the theologian Reinhold Niebuhr, whose

'Christian realism' argued that Christian moral principles (such as pacifism) could be set aside to achieve the greater moral good of preserving order in international affairs (Niebuhr 1960a, 1960b). Secular realists such as Hans Morgenthau and Kenneth Waltz described a world devoid of religion in which state action was determined by self-interest rather than any specific religious authority. This movement pervaded most of the social sciences (Morgenthau 1985, Waltz 1959). Scholars of sociology and political analysis argued that modern politics were secular, and that as the various members of the international system modernized, they would increasingly set aside religion in favour of secular rationalism.

The notion of the secularity of temporal authority has its roots in the Christian tradition of the separation of church and state. Although the line between the two was often infringed by religious authorities, the principle performed a legitimating function for those seeking to create international institutions and rules without reference to any religious authority. As early as the 1600s, political philosophers such as Grotius and Hobbes were describing law as a human endeavour, deliberately limiting the role of religious authority in modern politics. The **anticlerical** attitudes of political reformers and revolutionaries, beginning with the French Revolution, led to the Marxist critique of religion as a form of authority that hindered the progress of social institutions toward their modern form.

Early modern sociological and political thinkers tended to insist that modern political institutions were characterized by the absence of sacred authority. Auguste Comte, the nineteenth-century 'founder of sociology', predicted the eclipse of theological cultures by cultures grounded in science. Influential thinkers such as Emile Durkheim and Max Weber believed that with increasing rationalization and technological sophistication, the state would gradually dismiss religion from its public role and consign it to the private realm. This 'secularization thesis', in which secularization is defined as 'the process by which sectors of society and culture are removed from the domination of religious institutions and symbols' (Berger 1973: 113). The secularization thesis was a core assumption of a larger school of thought according to which the modern state was the product of a linear process of development from traditional agrarian societies governed by arbitrary authority toward more sophisticated urban societies with a complex division of labour, governed by the rule of law. Modern societies did not give credence to the traditional religious hierarchies and beliefs of the past. Therefore modernization was synonymous with secularization.

Some continue to present secularization as the wider guide for how religion affects world affairs. In a widely discussed assessment of religion and politics worldwide, Pippa Norris and Ronald Inglehart argue that levels of religiosity are directly related to perceptions of personal security at the individual level. They conclude that '[g]rowing up in societies in which survival is uncertain is conducive to a strong emphasis on religion; conversely, experiencing high levels of existential security through one's formative years reduces the subjective importance of religion in people's lives' (Norris and Inglehart 2004: 219). As a country develops the economic and political resources that make a more secure life possible, its people are less likely to feel the need to give religion a central role in public life. But this does not mean that religion is declining as a factor in world politics. Given the continuing population growth in developing

---

Box 1.3: Political Philosophers on Religion

And whereas some men have pretended for their disobedience to their Sovereign, a new Covenant, made not with men, but with God; this also is unjust: for there is no Covenant with God, but by meditation of some body that representeth God's Person; which none doth but Gods Lieutenant, who hath the Sovereignty under God.
— Thomas Hobbes, *Leviathan*, Chapter XVIII (1651)

Nobody therefore, … neither single persons, nor churches, nay, nor even commonwealths, have any just title to invade the civil rights and worldly goods of each other, upon pretence of religion. Those that are of another opinion, would do well to consider with themselves how pernicious a seed of discourse and war, how powerful a provocation to endless hatreds, rapines, and slaughters, they thereby furnish unto mankind.
— John Locke, *A Letter Concerning Toleration* (1689)

There is therefore a purely civil profession of faith of which the Sovereign should fix the articles, not exactly as religious dogmas, but as social sentiments without which a man cannot be a good citizen of a faithful subject. … The dogmas of civil religion ought to be few, simple, and exactly worded, without explanation or commentary.
— Jean-Jacques Rousseau, *On the Social Contract*, Book IV, Chapter 9 (1762)

The wretchedness of religion is at once an expression of and a protest against real wretchedness. Religion is the sigh of the oppressed creature, the heart of a heartless world and the soul of soulless conditions. It is the opium of the people.
— Karl Marx, *Introduction to a Contribution to a Critique of Hegel's 'Philosophy of Right'* (1844)

[Political liberalism] can be formulated independently of any particular comprehensive doctrine, religious, philosophical, or moral. While we suppose that it may be derived from, or supported by, or otherwise related to one or more comprehensive doctrines (indeed, we hope it can be thus related to many such doctrines), it is not presented as depending upon, or as presupposing, any such view.
— John Rawls, 'Reply to Habermas' (1995)

---

regions where life is anything but secure, Norris and Inglehart predict that religion will continue to be an important force in world politics for some time to come.

Critiques of Secularization

Scholars of sociology and politics today tend to dismiss the secularization thesis as an oversimplification that has not been proven true empirically. In fact, religion remains an important factor in the politics of many countries. It is not unusual for political parties to associate themselves directly with particular religious traditions, even in countries such as Germany (the Christian Democratic Union/Christian Socialist Union) and Japan (where the Komeito party was originally the political wing of the

Nichiren Buddhist organization called Soka Gakkai). In other countries, religion remains the primary or secondary basis of identity politics: in Lebanon, various religious confessional groups dominate political interactions; in Iraq, political unity is threatened by rivalry among Islamic sects; in Kashmir, political violence pits Muslims against Hindus. What's more, religion has been closely associated with many opposition and revolutionary movements. The South American left has strong associations with middle-ranking Christian leaders in the Roman Catholic Church. In 1979, the secular Iranian government was overthrown by a militantly religious opposition that created the Islamic Republic of Iran. The leadership of Pope John Paul II is often credited with helping to overthrow Communist regimes in Eastern Europe in the late 1980s. The potency of religion as a political force was amply demonstrated throughout the Cold War period—the 'golden age' of realism—and its public role in post-Communist states has only become more significant since the end of the Cold War.

Globalization has given religion a new relevance in the struggle against cultural homogenization. Friedman (1999) appeared to support secularization theory when he cast religious movements as residual elements of traditional societies struggling to hold back the inexorable movement of history. However, Lloyd and Susanne Hoeber Rudolph (1967) observe that religious movements have been adept at harnessing the technologies and innovations of the modern world. Certainly some religious movements seek to return to a past golden age (real or imagined) in which they believe that a purer form of religious devotion was the norm. But they also make full use of modern communications technologies and marketing strategies to take their message to a wider audience. Despite their professed desire for a 'return to the past', religious movements have adapted well enough to find a niche in most modern and even postmodern societies.

Some critics have observed that the association of secularization with modernization tends to be either an ideologically loaded assumption or a self-fulfilling prophecy. After gaining their independence, many former colonized societies set out to eliminate religion from public life as part of their effort to create a rational modern society. As a result, secularization came to resemble an ideological program. Thus secularization theory runs the risk of suggesting that because most modern societies are secular, all modern societies *should* or *must* be secularized. The Indian theorist T.N. Madan points out that it is important to differentiate between the simple observation that secularization has taken place in certain societies and the ideological insistence that secularization is the path toward modernization and institutional development (Madan 1998). It is also important to note that the Christian principle of church–state separation is not necessarily shared by other religious traditions; nor is it consistently practised in all Christian traditions.

In the end, secularization theory seems to sidestep the question of religion's value as a basis for judgments about policy and the way things *ought* to be. As Johnston and Cox argue:

Secularization theory's basic weakness is its assumption that ordinary decisions in public life should not be shaped by one's view of ultimate reality (i.e., issues of metaphysics). As this theory has begun to erode in many parts of the world—

often because of people's inability to deal with the strains of life apart from such a perspective—religion has recovered much of its salience (Johnston and Cox 2003: 14).

In short, it is not possible to engage in important debates over public policy and activism without reference to issues of religious import. In his recent work *A Secular Age* (2007), the Canadian political theorist Charles Taylor envisages modern **secularism** less as a principle demanding the total elimination of religious influences on public life than as a prevailing philosophy of modernity that might well include religious voices. This view is common to various streams of contemporary political theory and philosophy, and we will return to it in the conclusion of this book.

Still, the continuing dominance of secularity in international affairs, both in theory and in practice, demonstrates that these critiques have not had a strong impact at that level. The primacy of realism and the scarcity of strong religious or cultural alternatives to the prevailing terms of realist theory meant that religion was generally excluded from major discussions of international affairs until recent times. Two issues have brought religion back into global politics. One was the end of the Cold War and the resurgence of ethnic and religious groups in the politics of large parts of the globe. The second is the gradual evolution of international relations theory towards the recognition that non-state actors and cultural norms must be taken into serious account.

Perspectives on the Politics of Ethnicity and Religion

It was with the resurgence of the politics of identity after the end of the Cold War that religion was heralded as an important issue in world politics. The rise of sectarian violence in places such as the former Yugoslavia, Lebanon, and India raised the spectre of all-out war over religious identity. The resurgence of traditional religious movements in the countries of central Asia and Eastern Europe renewed interest in the relationship between religion and the consolidation of state institutions and their legitimization. Finally, the rise of important radical Islamist movements in places such as Algeria, Egypt, and Turkey drew attention to the way religion was transforming the politics of nations. The politics of religious pluralism, as a subset of cultural and ethnic pluralism, brought religion back into the foreground.

The collapse of the Cold War structure of international politics had an important impact on theories of international politics. Liberal arguments that the state was only one of many actors in international politics came to dominate and alter the field of study. No longer were international politics limited to the foreign policies of states and their interaction in the official organs of international politics such as the United Nations. It was obvious that non-governmental organizations, civil society groups, lobbies, resistance movements, and multinational corporations, among others, were likely to play increasingly central parts in the politics of the post-Cold War world. International politics gave way to 'transnational' politics: politics played out at the global level by a variety of players in both domestic and international environments. In an 'international' system, religion may influence major foreign policy preferences and decisions. In a 'transnational' system, religious forces may bring people together in a common cause, encourage lobbying across international borders, and even offer an alternative to the authority of the state (Rudolph and Piscatori 1997).

Increasing interest in ethnic and religious politics at the global level created opportunities for students of international politics to consider the issues of identity that had long been a subject of sociological and anthropological theorizing and of political study at the domestic level. Sociological analysts of the 1970s and 1980s tended to see religion as an expression of ethnic collective awareness. Among political scientists, religion was often understood as a political tool used to promote collective demands. Religious affinities were seen as offering various groups a way of defining themselves, a base on which to develop a sense of common interest and solidarity and to create an identity that would allow them to compete with other groups defined by their own distinctive religious beliefs or traditions. Religion in that context was used by some groups to frame their demands for representation, money, institutional change, resources, territory, and so on. This perspective, known as **instrumentalism**, suggested (among other things) that the actual content of religious belief was essentially unimportant in understanding the behaviour of a religious group or leader. Religious identification merely established the boundaries for the group and set it apart from competing groups. Anthropologists and sociologists, looking at the question from a different perspective, interpreted religion as a response to innate human needs for belonging and meaning. For them, human beings are social animals with a deep desire, either conditioned or biological, to find a place in a community of their peers. In the interdisciplinary realm, this broad perspective came to be known as primordialism.

However, many scholars found that they were not entirely satisfied with either the instrumental or the primordial perspective. For one thing, neither focused specifically on the content and nature of ethnic or religious political activism. Ethnicity and religion were not critically assessed: they were simply assumed to exist as natural realities. Thus a third perspective emerged to challenge received theories, a perspective known as **constructivism**, which deals with the construction of social phenomena over time. Constructivists tended to be historians and area specialists who were particularly interested in the development of nationalist movements around the world. The constructivist perspective developed in response to Benedict Anderson's groundbreaking work *Imagined Communities* (1991), in which he argued that nations are social constructions, creations of the mind that began to develop at particular points in history and used communication technologies such as the map and the printing press to present themselves as self-constituting philosophies of order.

The constructivist turn in studies of ethnic self-awareness has helped us to understand the politics of religious identity. It suggests (among other things) that the content of a group's religious convictions plays an important role in structuring its political interests. In other words, not all religious movements are alike. Islam's focus on communal devotion and submission led to the creation of unique structures to allow Muslims to deal with Jewish and Christian communities, who are tolerated but still stand outside the Islamic fold. North American **Evangelicals** have developed a more individualistic set of interests surrounding moral issues, such as government regulation of abortion or same-sex marriage. Since different religions apply morality in unique ways, there are naturally as many points of conflict among them as there are common causes that bring them together.

Taking Culture Seriously

Constructivism has had a different sort of impact in the field of international relations theory. Realist theory tended to focus on the state and consider religion only in its role as an instrument in the hands of state leaders. Liberal and neo-realist critiques of that approach arguably date back to the publication of Robert Keohane and Joseph Nye's important book *Power and Interdependence* in 1977 and the development of alternative critiques from neo-Marxist and feminist points of view. Each of these critiques took aim at different aspects of the reigning wisdom in political theory. Although few of them focused on the role of religion, liberal and alternative critics did give religious movements some consideration as societal actors.

From the mid-1980s on, the constructivist emphasis on ideas and norms of behaviour has had a significant impact on our understanding of world politics and world order. Recent scholarship in international relations has been strongly influenced by constructivist ideas, emerging from the British school of Realism, which emphasizes the role that international norms of state behaviour play in politics at the global level. Pioneers of this school include Hedley Bull and John G. Ruggie, but perhaps the best-known treatment of the subject is Alexander Wendt's *Social Theory of International Politics* (1999). Wendt suggests that we cannot understand international politics outside the social context in which states interact. Because the norms of international politics are created by the players within the international system, the meaning of terms such as 'anarchy', 'the state', or 'security' varies, depending on the players concerned, as does the perceived importance of those concepts. Thus it is vital for us to understand how actors (including the world as a whole) perceive the social conditions and ideas that exist around them. While religion is not central to Wendt's argument, clearly it has had an important influence on the social construction of ideas, from philosophy to the elaboration of basic ethics of right and wrong.

Social constructivist thought has found parallels among traditional scholars and popular commentators on world politics. Samuel Huntington's now famous 'Clash of Civilizations' article appeared in *Foreign Affairs* in 1993 and was followed up by his highly influential *The Clash of Civilizations and the Remaking of World Order* in 1996. Huntington's central idea was that the boundaries between major civilizational groupings, clustered around the religio-cultural metropoles of the modern world, would be the fault lines along which conflict would develop in the post-Cold War world. Ideological polarization between capitalism and communism might have come to an end, but conflict would continue in the form of disputes between the historic civilizations that have created distinctive norms and traditions to define themselves. Huntington pointed to several distinct civilizations, including those of Eastern and Western Christianity, Islam, Africa, and the Eastern/Confucian traditions. This idea was echoed in works such as Francis Fukuyama's *The End of History and the Last Man* (1992), which predicted warfare along the lines dividing competing ideologies of order, in this case between the democratic states and the states of the periphery that had not accepted liberal democracy. The resistance of Islamic societies in particular to liberal democratic principles seemed to confirm Huntington's view.

Responses to Globalization

The prospect of a world divided by religious and cultural particularisms seems to contradict the common notion that globalization creates a worldwide culture bolstered by freer trading principles and new information technologies, and dominated by a single power or hegemon in the form of the United States. But various scholars of globalization point to two contending forces that seem in some ways to parallel the democratic and undemocratic impulses observed by Fukuyama. Benjamin Barber (2001) coined the phrase '*Jihad* vs McWorld' to refer to the clash between a traditionalist revisionism that wants to turn back the clock and return to tribal or religious values of the past and the modernist dynamism that glorifies a new world economic and cultural order dominated by the West (or the US). An echo came from the prominent journalist Thomas Friedman, who suggested that the world is divided between people who would fight to preserve an ancient olive tree and those who just want a Lexus (hence *The Lexus and the Olive Tree*, 1999).

Amid all of this, it is clear that we cannot understand the modern world without reference to religion both as it adapts to globalization in the form of trans-national religious movements and (more popularly) as the modus vivendi behind religious revisionist movements worldwide. In this vein Juergensmeyer (1993) casts religious nationalist movements as a reaction to the perceived failure of the Western, secular nationalist movements that emerged in the period of modernization in the 1960s and 1970s.

An explosion of religious movements, both conservative and radicalized, appeared to dominate the politics of many countries in the 1990s. In North Africa, the cancellation of elections in Algeria in 1992 because of the impending victory of the Islamist *Front Islamique du Salut* (FIS) triggered a decade-long civil war between the military-backed government and the rebel *Gendarmerie Islamique Armée* (GIA). This emboldened similar movements whose participation in democratic politics was also limited by dictatorship and war, such as the Palestinian Hamas or the Egyptian *Gama'a al-Islamiya*. These groups also contributed to the creation of the al-Qaeda network of Osama bin Laden. Other radicalized groups also emerged to challenge governments and social stability: American forces engaged in a 51-day standoff with an apocalyptic movement known as the Branch Davidians, ending in a spectacular inferno, in 1993; Japan's Aum Shinrikyo cult staged sarin gas attacks against subway trains in 1994 and 1995.

Mainstream religious movements also gained ground throughout the 1990s. In India, the Hindu nationalist Bharatiya Janata Party became the main beneficiary of the erosion in support for the Congress party and of mass demonstrations in favour of reclaiming the land occupied by a mosque. In the United States, the impressive victory of Republicans in the 1994 congressional elections, based in part on alliances with the Christian Right and the 'Contract with the American Family', revealed that religion continued to play a significant role in that country's public policy. The alliance between cultural conservatives of a religious bent and the Republican Party remains solid today.

The religious dimensions of international conflict and cooperation also gained new recognition. The Israeli–Palestinian conflict, rooted at least in part in religiously justified debates over land and history, deepened as religious radicals attacked the basis of cooperative efforts enshrined in the 1993 Oslo Accords. In 1994, a radical Jewish settler opened fire on Palestinians praying at a mosque in Hebron in the West Bank. At the same time, the Palestinian Hamas movement increased its attacks on Israelis. Religious conservatives of many faiths spoke out against morally controversial methods of population control in response to the 1994 Cairo-based United Nations Conference on Population and Development. In South Africa, the appointment of Archbishop Desmond Tutu to head the Truth and Reconciliation Commission in 1995 symbolized the role that religion could play in providing guidance to the reconstruction of societies torn by conflict. Far from disappearing from the world as a result of modernization and globalization, religious networks and organizations assumed new importance in many arenas.

9/11 and After

The events of 11 September 2001 were a watershed in international politics comparable to the end of the Cold War. The fact that a non-state actor without any connection to the United Nations, major non-governmental organizations, or mainstream social movements was able to cause such damage to the infrastructure of the world's sole remaining superpower and reorient its foreign policy challenged prevailing notions of power in global politics. The attacks highlighted the growing relevance of the gap in global politics between the notional worlds of 'Christendom' and 'Islam'. They also indicated that religion has become an important part of world politics. As Daniel Philpott (2002) observed, Osama Bin Laden's al-Qaeda network, representing the pinnacle of a century and more of Islamist revivalism, presented a universal challenge to the authority of the secular international system. At a minimum, al-Qaeda's activities, to the extent that they represent a general dissatisfaction with the legitimacy of international politics (even if most would disapprove of the group's tactics), suggest that it is no longer realistic to insist that the international order remain uncontaminated by religion.

Religious movements are here, they are significant, and they must be studied and integrated into the practice of politics. To some extent, we ignore religion in international affairs at our own peril. It is not surprising that members of religious movements tend to feel isolated, alienated, and unfairly discounted. In the words of Douglas Johnston:

> The price of freedom is cultural engagement—taking the time to learn how others view the world, to understand what is important to them, and to

determine what can realistically be done to help them realize their legitimate aspirations (Johnston 2003: 9).

Certainly, given the decisive and deeply entrenched roles of religious movements for people around the world, they could become strategic partners in the quest for peace and development, for a truly functional international society.

But what role should religious movements play? To what extent does engagement with religious movements of any stripe, but especially radical and reactionary movements, signify acceptance of their goals or legitimization of their demands? Are religious movements inherently hostile one to another? Is there a risk that taking extremist movements seriously will encourage them? Questions like these give decision-makers and analysts pause. Nonetheless, this work proceeds on the presumption that greater understanding and consideration for religious movements and viewpoints will give us a broader understanding of international affairs, and quite possibly a more inclusive politics that will be beneficial for the world as a whole.

Understanding Religion: Definitions and Directions

Generally, this text will use 'religion' as a generic term for a system of belief or faith that in one way or another seeks to describe and define the immanent or transcendent spiritual realities that underlie the world we can detect with our five senses. The assumption that all faith traditions share enough in common that they may be compared is open to dispute: after all, the word 'religion' is a European invention used to differentiate systems of belief in ways that are foreign to many of those systems. The point is well taken, but today people around the world do commonly identify the major religious traditions as social forms that can indeed be compared one with another. The latter will be the basic assumption followed throughout this book.

It is also worth noting that this book concentrates on the more numerically significant religions: Christianity, Islam, Judaism, Buddhism, and Hinduism. Together these faiths claim the allegiance of more than half the world's people, and their distribution covers most of its inhabited land area. There remain many countries that are officially 'irreligious'—most notably the People's Republic of China—but this does not mean that religion (Confucian, Buddhist, even Christian) does not play a role in the construction of modern culture in those countries. In fact, the growth of Christianity in China, Korea, and southeast Asia and the renewed interest in Islam in central Asia suggest that many 'irreligious' states are becoming more culturally religious over time. There are also many countries where secularism has become more than a juridical-legal term: where religious belief is increasingly nominal and plays little (if any) role in public life. But even if traditional religion is ebbing as a force in western Europe or North America, it may indicate that what is changing is religiosity rather than religion per se, and that new forms of religion will arise to challenge the older forms that remain dominant in places such as Asia and the Middle East.

To delve into the nature of religion in any depth would be to engage in a philo-sophic and theoretical debate that is far beyond the scope of this work. Suffice it to

Table 1.1 Estimated Adherents of Selected World Religions, c. 2005

Christianity	2.1 billion
Islam	1.3 billion
Non-religious (agnostic, atheist, secular humanist, etc.)	1.1 billion
Hinduism	900 million
Buddhism	376 million
Sikhism	23 million
Judaism	14 million
Baha'i	7 million
Jainism	4.2 million
Shinto	4 million

Source: www.adherents.com

say that definitions of religion are a source of continual controversy. Scholars who study the interplay of religion and politics rarely approach their subject from the same perspective and therefore often find themselves speaking past one another. To some, religion is similar to ethnicity: a matter of simple 'ascription', whereby one is 'born into' one's parents' religious community. To others, a religion is another sort of 'imagined community' developed over time out of the ideas of people who believe themselves to belong to it. Many modern scholars see religious movements as essentially providers of ideas operating in a market where competition compels them to develop innovative responses to the felt needs of a particular population (Jelen and Wilcox 2002). Others emphasize the role that religion plays in constructing identity.

The basic thesis of this book is that in order to understand how religion affects global politics, we must take it seriously as a motivation for political–religious actors. To return to the important outcomes of social constructivist and cultural theorizing, this book proceeds on the assumption that 'content matters'. In other words, the beliefs that members of a religious group profess play an important role in shaping their behaviour. A pioneering effort to classify religious groups on the basis of their ethics was Ernst Troeltsch's *Social Teaching of the Christian Churches*. Originally published near the turn of the last century, it identified three basic types of Christianity: 'church', 'sect', and '**mysticism**' (Troeltsch 1976). More recently, Toft, Philpott, and Shah have argued that we should understand the many religious groups involved in politics based upon their 'political theology' (Toft, Philpott, and Shah 2011). Some analysts have focused on the distinctions within religious traditions between 'high church' organizations (associated with institutional and scholastic or 'formal' elements) and 'low church' organizations (associated with the informal and popular elements) (Rudolph 1997: 248–52). Others distinguish between 'prophetic' religious movements, which typically stand apart from political authorities or even oppose them, and 'priestly' movements, which stand with political authorities in a mutually supportive relationship (Jelen and Wilcox 2002).

Religion and Global Politics: A Survey

This survey of the interaction between religion and global politics follows two thematic tracks.

The first track is the relationship of religion to domestic and foreign policy in various states and regions of the world. Relating religion to state behaviour and the transnational politics of states around the globe, it focuses on specific religious traditions and contexts. Since the book is written for a Western audience, it begins with Western traditions and moves eastward. Here we explore the transnational significance of the Roman Catholic Church, the impact of religion on American politics and foreign policy, the influence of Jewish religious groups on Israeli politics and foreign policy, the various bases of Islamist activism as they have shaped politics in the Muslim world, and the various ways in which Hinduism and Buddhism have influenced politics in India and majority Buddhist states respectively.

The second track is the relationship of religion to world order. Here the focus is on the way religion affects various aspects of international politics, including conceptions and justifications of human rights, war and terror, conflict resolution and peace-building; the transnational politics of identity and belonging; and the interaction of larger 'communities of purpose' or 'civilizations'. Finally, we conclude with reflections on the politics of secularism around the world.

This book proceeds on the assumption that religion has a permanent and enduring influence on public affairs. As Max Weber, one of the greatest sociologists of religion, once wrote, 'The magical and religious forces, and the ethical ideas of duty based upon them, have in the past always been among the most important formative influences on conduct' (Weber 1958: 27). Though many have tried to consign those forces to the dustbin of history, for one reason or another they persist. To those magical and religious forces we now turn.

Review Questions

1. In what ways did religion function as a major political force in the premodern period?
2. What led to the gradual adoption of secularism in global politics?
3. How did the Peace of Westphalia (1648) alter religious and political notions of legitimacy and sovereignty?
5. What is the 'secularization thesis'?
6. How does religion constitute a form of cultural resistance to globalization in the modern age?
7. How might religion be used in politics according to the *instrumentalist* interpretation? How do *primordialists* and *constructivists* believe that religion affects political behaviour?
8. What developments have made religion such an important area of scholarly inquiry into politics in the twenty-first century?

Sources and Further Reading

Anderson, Benedict (1991). *Imagined Communities*. Revised edition. London: Verso.

Barber, Benjamin (2001). *Jihad vs. McWorld*. New York: Ballantine Books.

Berger, Peter (1973). *The Social Reality of Religion*. Harmondsworth: Penguin Books.

Bull, Hedley (1977). *The Anarchical Society: A Study of Order in World Politics*. London: Macmillan.

Cavanaugh, William (1995). "'A Fire Strong Enough to Consume the House': The Wars of Religion and the Rise of the State'. *Modern Theology* 11, 4: 397–420.

Comaroff, Jean, and John C. Comaroff (1991; 1997). *Of Revelation and Revolution*. 2 volumes. Chicago: University of Chicago Press.

Friedman, Thomas L. (1999). *The Lexus and the Olive Tree*. New York: Farrar, Strauss, and Giroux.

Fukuyama, Francis (1992). *The End of History and the Last Man*. New York: Avon Books.

Haynes, Jeffrey, ed. (2009). *The Routledge Handbook of Religion and Politics*. New York: Routledge.

Huntington, Samuel (1996). *The Clash of Civilizations and the Remaking of World Order*. New York: Simon and Schuster.

Jelen, Ted G. and Clyde Wilcox (2002). *Religion and Politics in Comparative Perspective: The One, the Few, and the Many*. Cambridge: Cambridge University Press.

Johnston, Douglas, ed. (2003). *Faith-based Diplomacy: Trumping Realpolitik*. Oxford: Oxford University Press.

————, and Brian Cox (2003). 'Faith-based Diplomacy and Preventive Engagement'. Pp. 11–31 in Johnston, ed. (2003).

Juergensmeyer, Mark (1993). *The New Cold War? Religious Nationalism Confronts the Secular State*. Berkeley: University of California Press.

Madan, T.N. (1998). *Modern Myths, Locked Minds: Secularism and Fundamentalism in India*. Delhi: Oxford University Press.

Morgenthau, Hans J. (1985). *Politics Among Nations*. 6th edition. New York: Knopf.

Niebuhr, Reinhold (1960a). *The Children of Light and the Children of Darkness*. New York: Scribner.

———— (1960b). *Moral Man and Immoral Society*. New York: Scribner.

Norris, Pippa, and Ronald Inglehart (2004). *Sacred and Secular: Religion and Politics Worldwide*. Cambridge: Cambridge University Press.

Obama, Barack (2009). 'Remarks by the President on a New Beginning'. *White House Speeches and Briefings* [online]. www.whitehouse.gov/the_press_office/Remarks-by-the-President-at-Cairo-University-6-04-09.

Philpott, Daniel (2000), 'The Religious Roots of Modern International Relations'. *World Politics* 52: 206–45.

———— (2002). 'The Challenge of September 11 to Secularism in International Relations'. *World Politics* 55: 66–95.

Rudolph, Lloyd I. and Susanne Hoeber Rudolph (1967). *The Modernity of Tradition: Political Development in India*. Chicago: University of Chicago Press.

Rudolph, Susanne Hoeber (1997). 'Dehomogenizing Religious Formations', in

Rudolph and Piscatori, eds. (1997).

Rudolph, Susanne Hoeber, and James Piscatori, eds. (1997). *Transnational Religion and Fading States*. Boulder: Westview Press.

Sampson, Cynthia, and Douglas Johnston (1994). *Religion, the Missing Dimension of Statecraft*. Oxford: Oxford University Press.

Taylor, Charles (2007). *A Secular Age*. Cambridge: Belknap Press.

Thomas, Scott M. (2005). *The Global Resurgence of Religion in International Relations: The Struggle for the Soul of the Twenty-First Century*. New York: Palgrave Macmillan.

Toft, Monica Duffy, Daniel Philpott, and Timothy Samuel Shah (2011). *God's Century: Resurgent Religion and Global Politics*. New York: W.W. Norton.

Troeltsch, Ernst (1976). *The Social Teaching of the Christian Churches*. Trans. Olive Wyon. Chicago: University of Chicago Press [1931].

Waltz, Kenneth (1959). *Man, the State, and War*. New York: Columbia University Press.

Weber, Max (1958). *The Protestant Ethic and the Spirit of Capitalism*. Trans. Talcott Parsons. New York: Scribners.

Wendt, Alexander (1999). *Social Theory of International Politics*. Cambridge: Cambridge University Press.

Web Resources

www.adherents.com – A collection of religious and geographical statistics about religious adherents around the world.

www.pbs.org/wnet/religionandethics – PBS Religion and Ethics Newsweekly.

www.pewforum.org – The Pew Forum on Religion and Public Life.

www.sacred-destinations.com – Profiles of sacred sites all over the world.

Part I

Religion and the Domestic Bases
of State and Foreign Policy

Chapter 2

The Roman
Catholic Church

As the foundational religion of Western Europe, Roman Catholicism had a formative influence on the development of Western thought, including modern interpretations and institutions of politics. Until the Protestant Reformation, all the statesmen and philosophers of Europe were steeped in Roman Catholic thought, and the critiques of the Church put forward by Reformers such as Luther helped to pave the way for the Enlightenment and the development of modern political theory. Furthermore, every state in Europe was to some degree subject to the authority of the Roman Catholic Church and therefore concerned with circumscribing its power.

In recent decades, a significant new element in the politics of religion was introduced in the form of the movement known as liberation theology, an alternative theology presented by Church leaders in the developing world in the 1970s and 1980s. Eminently political in both its tone and its application, liberation theology remains a subject of controversy within the Roman Catholic Church, but it has inspired similar movements in other religious traditions. In this chapter, we will explore both the established form of Roman Catholicism and the critiques levelled at it by proponents of liberation theology as influences on global politics.

The Roman Catholic Church is the largest organized religious institution in the world. While other religious traditions and philosophies may rival its numbers, none can match it in terms of geographic reach. Headquartered in Vatican City, an independent state ruled by the pope in his capacity as the Bishop of Rome, the Roman Catholic Church is also the only religious institution in the world with the diplomatic status of a state. This unique status enables the **Holy See** (the pope and his administration) to issue travel documents, to receive and dispatch ambassadors, and to conduct affairs of state with other nations.

But the power of the Roman Catholic Church goes much further. Together, the global community of Roman Catholics constitutes the world's largest social movement. The Church is therefore an important transnational actor (Vallier 1971). Much of its revenue comes from its assets and investments: it owns a massive number of properties in countries around the world. It also receives donations (known as **Peter's Pence**) from the faithful in nearly every nation. Revenues are used to support the Holy See as well as humanitarian and development work carried out by the *Caritas Internationalis* agency through its 162 member organizations. For these reasons, it is necessary to analyze the church both as a state and as an international non-governmental organization, albeit one that "to a far greater degree than other advocacy NGOs, is financially self-sufficient" (Ferrari 2006: 44).

The Church is institutionally diverse, encompassing scores of **monastic** orders and para-church organizations of various sorts. This diversity is both a strength and a challenge for an institution that is intensely hierarchical in its structure. Throughout the Church's history, competing forces have sought both to open the faith to new groups and to maintain the authority of the hierarchy. The Church has been flexible in embracing other religious traditions (as in the case of the Eastern Rite churches) but also critical of challenges to the authority of its teachings, as in the case of the liberation theology movement.

Box 2.1: Selected Organizations of the Roman Catholic Church

Augustinian Order Established in the thirteenth century and named for St Augustine of Hippo (354–430). The Augustinians are noted scholars and missionaries.

Benedictine Order A popular monastic movement, known for its moderation (as opposed to religious zeal or formally rigid religiosity) and its hospitality. Each Benedictine monastery is self-governing, following the Rule of St Benedict (the sixth-century monk who is widely considered to be the founder of the Western monastic tradition) without any external oversight.

Dominican Order An order of friars and sisters devoted to the tradition of St Dominic, founded in the thirteenth century. Dominicans are known for their dedication to learning and teaching.

Carmelite Order The Order of the Blessed Virgin Mary of Mount Carmel, a contemplative order of monks, nuns, and laypeople dedicated to prayer and supplication.

Franciscan Order Founded by St Francis of Assisi and dedicated to caring for creation, working for peace, and ministering to the poor, with whom they identify closely. The Franciscans have a special place in the Holy Land as custodians of the Roman Catholic sites located there.

Jesuits (Society of Jesus) A monastic order founded by St Ignatius Loyola during the sixteenth-century Counter-Reformation. The Jesuits became active missionaries and teachers throughout the world.

Cistercian Order Founded in the seventeenth century and known for the austerity of its rule, which emphasizes silence, solitude, and reflection; Trappists are Cistercians who follow a particularly strict rule.

Missionaries of Charity Order established by Mother Teresa of Calcutta in 1950, dedicated to caring for the poorest of the poor.

Caritas Internationalis An international network of Roman Catholic development and relief agencies, organized under its current name in 1954.

Opus Dei A strictly conservative organization founded by a Spanish priest named Josemaría Escrivá in 1928 and dedicated to integrating the spiritual dimension into daily life. Most members of Opus Dei are laypeople.

Order of St John of Jerusalem Originally known as the Knights Hospitaller for their medical work during the Crusades. The order became a religious and military organization during this period and eventually established its own state in Malta, where it became known as the Knights of Malta. The order disappeared in the nineteenth century.

Knights of Columbus A fraternal order established in New Haven, Connecticut, in 1881, dedicated to education, public service and aid to those in need. Today the Knights of Columbus have chapters throughout the world.

A Brief History of Christianity and the Roman Catholic Church

Christianity was founded in the first century of the Common Era by the followers of Jesus of Nazareth (c. 1–33 CE), a Jewish rabbi who is also known as the Christ (from the Greek for 'Messiah', the anointed one). According to tradition, his teachings and life story are recorded in the four gospels that begin the New Testament, the second part of the Christian Bible. His bold challenges to the religious leaders of his day eventually led to his arrest and trial for blasphemy. Found guilty, he was crucified by the Roman occupiers of Jerusalem, but Christians believe that he rose from his tomb three days later and continued to interact with his disciples for 40 days before ascending to heaven. His miraculous story is held as proof that he was the God of the Hebrew Old Testament incarnate on earth.

Jesus was a revolutionary ethical and moral philosopher, known for reinterpreting the Biblical traditions to emphasize the motivations of the heart rather than the letter of the religious law. Living as a peripatetic religious teacher, he set an example of humble service to others. His willingness to accept death at the hands of his enemies is widely revered as an example of his determination to live what he preached.

In addition to revering Jesus's teaching, Christians hold that his primary mission on earth was to provide a means by which sinful humanity might come to God. They believe that the death of Jesus Christ was a sacrifice that sufficed to achieve forgiveness of the sins of the world. The relevance of Jesus's death was elaborated by the **apostles** who were commissioned to spread the faith abroad, the first of whom were his original disciples. Among the latter was St Peter, said to have been one of Jesus's closest disciples during his earthly ministry. A later apostle, who never knew Jesus in life, was Paul, a Jewish scholar originally known as Saul, who began as an enemy of the Christian faith but became its greatest missionary after a dramatic conversion experience. The message that these men and others carried to the world is recorded in the later pages of the New Testament.

The gathering of Christians established by the apostles was known as the *ekklesia* (Greek for a public gathering of people). In English, this word was translated as 'church'. Roman Catholic tradition holds that St Peter founded the church in Rome and became its first bishop. According to a passage from the Gospel of Matthew (16:19) Jesus tells the apostle, 'I will give you the keys to the kingdom of heaven, and whatever you bind on earth will be bound in heaven, and whatever you loose on earth will be loosed in heaven'. The verse is interpreted as the basis for the heavenly authority of Peter's successors on earth. Based on this passage, the Roman Catholic Church defends the primacy of the office of the bishop of Rome.

Christians survived multiple persecutions in the early centuries, but their faith became the established religion of the Roman Empire following the Emperor Constantine's conversion in 337. Thereafter, although Rome was only one of four principal bishoprics, the bishop of Rome—as Peter's successor—became the head of the Church as a whole, which was organized geographically on the model of the Empire. Rome's primacy was by no means uncontested, however. Theological disputes and power struggles would come between the bishop of Rome and his counterpart in Constantinople, although the former continued to claim universal ('catholic') authority over the worldwide community of Christians as pope, or Holy Father.

As head of the Church, the pope inherited a growing collection of estates and properties through endowment by prominent parishioners. By the time of Pope Gregory I ('the Great'; r. 590–604), the Church was the largest single landowner in the Western Roman Empire (Duffy 2002: 64), and as a result of war neighbouring

Box 2.2: The Eastern Orthodox Church

In the early fourth century Constantine the Great relocated the capital of the Roman Empire from Rome to the ancient Greek city of Byzantium (later renamed Constantinople). After his death two rival poles of political leadership developed, one centred in Rome and one at the eastern end of the Mediterranean. In time the political rivalry between Rome and Constantinople came to be reflected in the development of two rival theological and ecclesial camps. The division between east and west was formalized in the **Great Schism** of 1054, when the bishops of Rome and Constantinople ceased to recognize one another's authority.

Since that time, the eastern churches have followed a distinctive religious tradition that we know as Eastern Orthodoxy. Although they affirm the same early creeds of the Church, the Eastern Orthodox churches are '**autocephalous**'—independent in authority—and are typically organized along national lines. Eastern Orthodoxy is the dominant Christian perspective across most of the countries of Eastern Europe (Russia, Belarus, Ukraine, Romania, Bulgaria, Serbia, Greece, Cyprus, and Georgia), many of which have their own national Orthodox churches. These churches are independent but are said to be in communion with one another.

Scholars of religion and politics often point out that the Eastern Orthodox tradition developed a unique view of church–state relations during the late Byzantine period (from the sixth century until the fall of Constantinople to the Ottoman Turks in 1453). In that era the Byzantine emperors and the Orthodox bishops of Constantinople coexisted in a relationship of mutual deference based on the principle of *symphonia*, which emphasized the harmony of interests of church and state (Stan and Turcescu 2007: 5–6). The principle of *symphonia* originated with the Byzantine Emperor Justinian I (483–565), who conceived of the church and the state as representing two complementary types of authority: while the emperor ruled the political realm, it was the role of the Orthodox Church to rule the spiritual realm, using its authority to legitimize the regime (Daniel 2006: 12). This model is an ideal, however, and in several periods, distortions of the principle of *symphonia* have either privileged state authorities or given the Orthodox Church undue influence in social affairs. Under communist systems, the Eastern Orthodox churches were largely brought under the control of state powers and their political role was limited. Even so, in many cases Eastern Orthodox clergy became prominent dissidents. Since the abandonment of state communism, Eastern Orthodoxy has experienced a resurgence as a political force both in tandem with state authorities and in opposition to them.

Kirill I, as bishop of Moscow and All Russia, is the current patriarch (head) of the Russian Orthodox Church. He was enthroned in February 2009 after the death of his predecessor Alexy II. Both Alexy and Kirill were compromise candidates between traditionalist and reformist elements in the Church. Even so, Kirill is noted for his commitment to ecumenical dialogue with other churches. Today the Orthodox patriarchs are widely respected and celebrated by the Russian government as representatives of the country's unique heritage and symbols of Russian nationalism.
Source: Sasha Mordovets/Getty Images

states were forced to accept the pope's rule over several territories (mostly in central Italy) known as the Papal States. This property gave the papacy considerable temporal power in addition to its spiritual authority, an authority that grew as the power of the Byzantine emperors and the rulers of various smaller kingdoms in Italy faded between the eighth century and the tenth.

At the same time, the decline and fall of Roman civilization in Europe had weakened the cultural authority of the papacy. In the late 700s, however, the Frankish king Charlemagne succeeded in re-establishing Christian control over much of the territory that had been lost. Thus in 800 Pope Leo III (r. 795–816) anointed Charlemagne as the temporal head of a new Roman Empire under the spiritual authority of the papacy. This relationship between the secular power of the Holy Roman emperors and the religious power of the popes would prove to be a source of continuing conflict through the centuries that followed.

Throughout the Middle Ages, Roman Catholic institutions were the primary preservers of knowledge and learning, and some of the most prominent contributions to the development of Christian political philosophy were made by scholars affiliated with the Church. Among them were St Augustine of Hippo (354–430), Isidore of Seville (c.560–636), Bernard of Clairvaux (1090–1153), and St Thomas Aquinas (1225–74)—the philosopher and theologian who laid the foundations of Roman Catholic theological and social teachings in his work *Summa Theologica*. Aquinas was strongly influenced by Aristotelian philosophy, which emphasized categorization of the natural world through empirical reasoning and discourse. The school of theology and philosophy that he founded, known as scholasticism, became the basis of Christian social and political commentary, and his works were to be cited frequently in theological and political treatises.

In the ninth and tenth centuries, the papacy was controlled by a succession of aristocrats and nepotistic rulers who contributed to the decline of the position of the pope. But internal reform led to a renaissance of both the papacy's spiritual authority and its political power in the eleventh and twelfth centuries. As a result, the papacy came into conflict with the kings of Europe, most importantly the German kings who, as occupants of the office of Holy Roman Emperor, insisted that they ruled by divine right. Debates over the right of monarchs to appoint the rulers of the church led to a prolonged conflict between the church and the kings of Europe, known as the Investiture Controversy. This conflict came to a head in 1075 when Pope Gregory IV asserted his authority over the Holy Roman Emperor Henry IV. Over the next several decades, the pope and his successors summoned allies in war against Henry IV and later his son Henry V, who arranged the appointment of rival popes ('antipopes'). The conflict came to an end in 1122 with the negotiation of an agreement between Pope Calixtus II and Henry V. Known as the **Concordat of Worms**, it laid out the distinctive powers of the king in granting the secular powers of the clergy but gave the church the power to appoint its own bishops and cardinals The Concordat is considered the first in a series of measures that gradually limited the role of the Church in secular affairs.

However, the process of persuading the Roman Catholic Church to give up its political or temporal role was long and arduous. For many centuries, the Church had conflated the pursuit of material wealth and political power with the exercise of its spiritual authority. Thus, for example, services to the Church—from donations of money or property to participation in military missions such as the Crusades—were encouraged by rewarding the providers of those services with 'indulgences': promises of reductions in the time that the individual would be required to spend in purgatory—an obligatory stop on the way to heaven after death. The practice of selling indulgences was the central issue raised by Martin Luther in 1517 and the most significant of all the complaints that led to the Protestant Reformation.

The Reformation was a broad social movement led by various religious leaders throughout Europe seeking change in the organization, practices, and doctrines of the Roman Catholic Church. Its earliest leaders, including Luther, were members of the clergy who began trying to reform the Church from within. In response to their criticisms, the Roman Catholic Church embarked on its own reform process, which came to be known as the Counter-Reformation. Lengthy discussions at the Council of Trent (1545–63) led to a prolonged political and social campaign to re-establish the authority of the Church, re-entrench the power of the Vatican, root out beliefs judged to be heretical, and bring new followers into the fold through missionary work and education.

In 1542, Pope Paul III founded the Sacred Congregation of the Universal Inquisition: an organization dedicated to eradicating doctrinal error, today known as the Congregation for the Doctrine of the Faith. The Congregation took an active role in opposing ideas that did not conform to Church teaching. This set the Church against the intellectual spirit of the age. Perhaps the most infamous example was the trial of Galileo Galilei in 1633 on charges of heresy for proposing—contrary to Church teaching—that the earth revolved around the sun. At the same time, missionaries and teachers set out to take Roman Catholicism to the widening colonial world and general education to the masses; the most prominent among the missionary/teaching orders was the Society of Jesus (the Jesuits), founded in 1534 by Ignatius of Loyola. The Vatican continued to enforce its central and unquestionable authority over the centuries that followed. The high point of that authority came in 1868 at what is now known as the First Vatican Council, a meeting of bishops from around the world at which the doctrine of Papal Infallibility was proclaimed: when the pope speaks authoritatively on matters of doctrine, there is no possibility that he is in error.

As ruler of the Papal States, the pope had been an important player in the politics of the Italian peninsula. By 1860, however, most of those states had joined the Kingdom of Italy, leaving the pope with a significantly diminished territory centred on Rome. The revolutionaries who achieved the unification of Italy in 1861 had tried to take that territory as well, but it was defended on behalf of the papacy by troops of the French Emperor Napoleon III until 1870. When those troops were withdrawn, the remaining papal territory was incorporated into the new Italian state. However, the papacy refused to recognize the legality of the annexation until 1929, when Pope Pius XI (r. 1922–39) and Italian Prime Minister Benito Mussolini signed the Lateran Treaty: an agreement laying out the boundaries of an independent city-state consisting of 108.6 acres of land within Rome, to be known as Vatican City. It also guaranteed special status for the Roman Catholic religion in Italian schools, the perpetuation of private Catholic education, and the inclusion of Roman Catholic family law in the legal code of the Italian state. As the head of state within the confines of the Vatican city-

St. Peter's Basilica, one of the grandest and most venerated sites in Christendom, is the most significant of several churches in Vatican City. Located on the site of a fourth-century basilica that had been erected (on the order of Constantine the Great) over the traditional site of the martyrdom of St Peter, the present structure was constructed during the fifteenth and sixteenth centuries.
Source: © Alinari Archives/Corbis

state, the pope is able to engage in debates in the United Nations, establish embassies abroad, and so on.

Over the next decade, both Germany and Spain would join Italy as predominantly Roman Catholic states that turned towards fascism. Almost a century later, the Vatican's conduct in that period remains a subject of controversy, for even though it opposed fascism in official statements, it continued to recognize the fascist governments of those countries. Hence many believe the Church was tainted by association (Cornwell, 1999). With the end of the Second World War, however, the Church began to encourage the growth of Christian democratic movements and speak out against communism.

The Modernizing Church: Changes under Vatican II

By the mid-twentieth century, new voices of change and reform were rising within the Church. Roman Catholic intellectual life was reinvigorated by numerous scholars. The

French philosopher Jacques Maritain (1882–1973), for example, revived the study of faith and reason begun by St Thomas Aquinas. Other prominent Roman Catholic activists challenged the Church to look beyond its traditional claim to be the unique path to salvation and open itself to religious pluralism. Perhaps most noteworthy among these was John Courtney Murray (1904–67), an American Jesuit who embraced a broader humanism. Murray was briefly silenced, but his views would prove influential in the mid-1960s. Among the religious and lay leaders who explored different paths was Thomas Merton (1915–68), an American Trappist monk and mystic who made an intensive study of Eastern religious traditions, especially Buddhism.

The convening of the Second Vatican Council (popularly known as Vatican II) by Pope John XXIII in 1962 marked a watershed in the history of the Roman Catholic Church. The Council entailed a complete reassessment of the Church's priorities and is generally considered the single most important development in the modernization of Roman Catholic institutions. In terms of practice, it provided for innovations in the liturgy of the Church. A public document known as the 'Dogmatic Constitution of the Church' (*Lumen Gentium*), published in 1964, challenged the traditional assumption that the promise of salvation was reserved exclusively for Roman Catholics. The council affirmed the place of Christians as a part of a wider society to which the Church should also minister. Another important product of the council was the 'Declaration on Religious Freedom' entitled *Dignitatus Humanae*, which reflected John Courtney Murray's understanding of the Church's role in the world with regard to secular authority by affirming the notion that the 'dignity of the human person as this dignity is known through the revealed word of God and by reason itself' (*Dignitatus Humanae* 2). This declaration would serve as a foundation for future leadership in the arena of human rights.

Vatican II is thus widely regarded as having pointed the Church toward a new way of relating to the rest of the world, including other branches of Christianity. One author asserts that 'the council disavowed a triumphal approach in favour of a dialogical partnership when engaging social questions' (Himes 2006: 22). It also altered the internal politics of the Roman Catholic Church. In the years following Vatican II, a new group of activist leaders emerged to give the Church vital new direction and helped to renew its authority and legitimacy among the faithful. Some of those people believed that Vatican II had opened the way for significant reform. Among them were people such as the Swiss theologian Hans Küng, whose work the Church disavowed in 1979 after he dared to reject the doctrine of papal infallibility, and the proponents of liberation theology such as Gustavo Gutierrez. Opponents of such innovations have suggested that Vatican II went too far in eroding the unique character and authority of the Church.

The conflict between modernists and traditionalists could have done serious damage, but so far the Church seems to have managed the strain reasonably well. Some of the credit for its resilience must go to the men who have held the office of pope in recent decades. When Pope John Paul I died only a month after his ascension to the papacy in 1978, a slightly younger and more vigorous leader was elected: this was the Polish bishop Karol Wojtyla, who took the name John Paul II and was the first non-Italian to hold the position since the sixteenth century. His background as both

The vigorous leadership of Pope John Paul II (r. 1978–2005) made him a towering figure in the revival of the Roman Catholic Church around the world.
Source: © Teodor Walczak/dpa/Corbis

a well-loved pastor and an active opponent of both fascism and communism gave him impressive spiritual and political credentials. He also stood as a mediating figure between the modernist and traditionalist movements in the Church. He was a natural communicator and his personal warmth contributed to his exceptional popularity inside and outside the Church.

John Paul II travelled ceaselessly, revivifying the Roman Catholic Church around the world. His visit to his homeland in the months after his election is widely credited with inspiring the pro-democracy movement that eventually brought about the demise of communism in Poland after a decade of struggle. His biographer argues that John Paul put into practice many of the innovations inspired by Vatican II: 'By lifting up the witness of hundreds of thousands of Christian confessors against communist tyranny, the pontificate of John Paul II demonstrated in action that Christian conviction can be the agent of human liberation' (Weigel 2005: 847). Indeed, the resistance of the Vatican to communism in Eastern Europe and abroad is often cited as a key factor both in the collapse of communism around the world and in the movement towards democracy of several states in eastern Europe and South America during the 1980s (Huntington 1991).

He remained engaged and committed to his public role even after sustaining a gunshot wound in an assassination attempt in May 1981. The motives behind the attack

Box 2.3: Some important terms in Roman Catholicism

bull An official document issued with the authority of the pope (from Latin *bulla*, an official seal).

cardinal One of the leading officers of the Roman Catholic Church. At the death of a pope, the College of Cardinals is responsible for choosing his successor.

catechism A summary of the Church's doctrines in the form of a series of questions and answers.

conclave The assembly of cardinals entrusted with the election of a pope.

Concordat An agreement or contract between the Holy See and a foreign government or authority.

Curia The collective name for the various offices, departments, and councils that govern the Roman Catholic Church.

diocese A territorial subdivision of Church authority, ruled by a bishop.

Ecumenical Council A 'universal' gathering of Church leaders (restricted to the Roman Catholic Church since the Great Schism of 1054) at which Church officials and prominent theologians discuss matters of practice and doctrine.

ecumenism The modern movement to bring unity to the various religious traditions of the world, especially the various Christian churches.

encyclical A papal letter on matters of doctrine addressed to Church leaders.

ex cathedra (Roman Catholicism) Latin phrase meaning 'from the chair', a designation applied to statements by the pope that carry the full authority of the office; the first Vatican Council (1868) ruled that teachings issued *ex cathedra* are infallible.

Holy See The pope and Curia, often used as a synonym for the papacy.

magisterium The teaching authority of the Church, handed down by the pope and bishops.

mass A service of worship in the Roman Catholic Church that includes the practice of Holy Communion, in which worshippers partake of bread and wine believed to be the body and blood of Jesus Christ. In the main body of the Church, the mass was conducted in Latin until after the Second Vatican Council, when permission was granted to use vernacular languages.

nuncio A permanent representative of the pope in a particular district; in effect, an ambassador of the Holy See, with authority in both ecclesial and political-diplomatic affairs.

Vatican The area within the city of Rome (now an independent state known as Vatican City) that is the home of the pope and his officials; often used as a synonym for 'the papacy'.

remain murky. The pope made a point of meeting with the would-be assassin, a Turk by the name of Mehmet Ali Agca, in 1983, in a widely publicized act of forgiveness. Nevertheless, the wound contributed to the pope's significant physical disabilities for the last two decades of his life. In seriously declining health by the late 1990s, he nevertheless kept up a demanding schedule of public appearances around the world.

Throughout the 1980s, John Paul II remained involved in diplomacy and public activism in a variety of places and at several levels. Under his administration, the Vatican acted as mediator between Argentina and Chile in their dispute over the Beagle Channel (Princen 1992: 133–85). Elsewhere, John Paul II was intimately involved in seeking reconciliation with Jewish people, and publicly expressed regret for the Roman

Catholic Church's timidity in resisting the Holocaust. As part of his commitment to ecumenical activism, he met with leaders representing most of the major world religions, including Islam.

John Paul II was equally noted for his conservative theology. He reinforced the Church's traditional opposition to abortion and contraception. He upheld the Roman Catholic insistence that the priesthood must be exclusively male and celibate. His appointment of Joseph Cardinal Ratzinger to the position of prefect of the Congregation for the Doctrine of the Faith signalled his support for Ratzinger's role in controlling the spread of liberal theological streams in the Church, which will be discussed below.

The Church and the Vatican Today

The Vatican stands at the centre of a vast complex of Church institutions organized in a hierarchy. In its most basic form, the hierarchy has three parts: parish priests report to their bishops, who in turn report to the pope. An archbishop is the senior bishop in a particular territory. Cardinals are bishops appointed by the pope specifically to serve as part of a special body called the College of Cardinals: in the event of the pope's death, the cardinals select his successor from among their own ranks. The initial organization of the Church owed much to the governing institutions of the Roman Empire, and the districts and divisions of the Church were modelled on the administrative divisions of the Empire. Monastic and lay orders operate in varying fashion under the authority of higher levels in the hierarchy, some reporting to bishops and others reporting directly to the pope himself. In the Western Church all priests and bishops are male.

This is not the case with all Catholic churches, however. In some parts of the world, Christians left their historic churches to form Roman Catholic churches that recognized their ancient rites. These Eastern Rite Catholic (sometimes called 'Oriental' or 'Uniate') churches, most of which operate under the authority of a patriarch, do allow priests to marry, although higher offices in the hierarchy are reserved for priests who remain celibate. Historically, they also differed from the Western Church in using local languages to conduct the mass. Through the Eastern Rite Churches, the Roman Catholic Church has a significant presence in places such as eastern Europe, the Middle East, and India.

All levels of the hierarchy are ultimately united in their dedication to the leadership of the pope. When a new pope must be chosen, the cardinals meet at the Vatican in a gathering known as a conclave. Over the course of several days, the conclave will vote several times, until the cardinals reach a consensus on one candidate. On election, the winning candidate is given the title of bishop of Rome and becomes both the bishop of the diocese of Rome and the reigning monarch of Vatican City (the last remnant of the medieval Papal States), as well as the head of the worldwide church. While his status as ruler of Vatican City makes the pope the last remaining absolute monarch in Europe, the Church takes care to explain that it 'does not consider its monarchical government a model for other nations. Rather, its purpose is to provide an internationally recognized territory where the Holy See can operate in total freedom, without political interference' (Reese 1996: 16).

The offices of the Holy See, the headquarters of the Roman Catholic Church, are called the Roman Curia, and include various councils and congregations known as dicasteries. These groups oversee policy on a wide variety of issues, from management of the clergy to matters of doctrine and ecumenical efforts. The central bureaucracy of the Holy See is the Secretariat of State, 'one of the least understood and yet one of the most important offices in the curia' (Reese 1996: 174). It is headed by the Secretary of State, who operates essentially as the prime minister of the Vatican. The Secretariat deals with the day-to-day operations of the government of the Vatican as well as the management of the pope's schedule, speeches, and correspondence.

Papal nuncios and pro-nuncios are the Holy See's diplomatic representatives. Dispatched to countries around the world, they serve a double function both as ambassadors to the governments of those countries and as the pope's representatives among their Roman Catholic populations. This arrangement occasionally gives rise to rivalries with the resident bishops and hierarchs, who may feel they are in a more legitimate position to speak for the Church than the papal delegate (Walsh 2000: 106–7). The papal state has diplomatic relations with at least 176 different states and it sits as a permanent representative in the United Nations, the African Union, and the Organization of American States (*The Economist* 2007: 58). Its interventions in world affairs are usually limited to issues that the Church deems to have a moral component, such as policy regarding family planning, prevention of war, and redistribution of wealth.

Liberation Theology

One of the principal challenges to the Roman Catholic Church's hierarchy and traditions of involvement in politics has been the movement known as 'liberation theology'. Developed in Latin America by a number of priests urgently concerned with social and economic justice, liberation theology proposes that it is the primary duty of the Church to support the poor and dispossessed. It has grown to have an influence outside the Roman Catholic Church through its adoption by other Christian denominations as well.

Liberation theology could be said to have its roots in the critical perspectives expressed by priests, theologians, and missionaries from the beginnings of the Spanish conquest of Latin America. The colonial enterprise that followed Columbus's discovery of America in 1492 was a brutal and bloody affair. The island of Hispaniola, one of the first to be discovered and colonized by the Spaniards, was a case in point. The European settlers quickly subdued and enslaved the indigenous Taino people and conducted a campaign of wanton killing and destruction, in the process introducing foreign diseases to which the native people had no immunity. Within a few decades, a thriving indigenous population of a few million had been wiped out.

One of the few colonial observers to document and protest against the brutality of the conquistadores was a Spanish Dominican monk named Bartolomé de Las Casas. In 1542, in a petition asking the King of Spain to intervene in favour of the indigenous people, he wrote that 'it would constitute a criminal neglect of my duty to remain silent about the enormous loss of life as well as the infinite number of human souls despatched to Hell in the course of such "conquests"' (Las Casas 1992 [1552], 6). Furthermore, he indicted the conquistadores for their venality: 'The reason the Christians have murdered on such a vast scale and killed anyone and everyone in their way is purely and simply greed. They have set out to line their pockets with gold and to amass private fortunes as quickly as possible. . . .' (Las Casas 1992: 3).

The sympathy and solidarity that Las Casas and others felt for the indigenous people of Latin America and the Caribbean were not shared by the Roman Catholic Church in the New World. In fact, the Church came to be an important part of the establishment, closely allied with the ruling elites from the initial conquest through the period of decolonization that began in the nineteenth century.

Decolonization, however, fractured the Church. While the hierarchy supported the elites in their opposition to revolt against Spain, some individual priests supported the various independence movements. And with the division in the Church, the people of the region became increasingly alienated from the European authorities. Christian organization in Latin America came to be characterized by two competing structures. On one side was the formal Church apparatus of the hierarchy and its properties, associated with the elite and wealthy. On the other was the 'popular' religion of the streets and rural areas where people practised their religion with little interest in formal rites and sacraments. The revolutions against the centralization of wealth and power in Latin American countries throughout the 1800s and early 1900s were often deliberately 'anticlerical', aimed at divesting the Church hierarchy of its assets because of its wealth and collusion with the previously ruling elites. These divisions in the Roman Catholic Church and in society at large served to weaken the political influence of the Church leadership even as it remained an important force in the everyday life of many Latin Americans.

In the late 1960s, in response to the spirit of renewal that stemmed from the Second Vatican Council, a number of Latin American priests and theologians set out to challenge the Church on its failure to identify with and promote the cause of the burgeoning numbers of the poor. Many of the priests involved had been ministering to communities on the fringes of Latin American society, in the rapidly growing shantytowns known as barrios lining the outskirts of major cities, and in the isolated rural villages where vocational and educational opportunities were severely limited. Here they created lay ministries that included the common folk, known as 'base communities'. Vatican II was both an opportunity and an impetus for these men, many of whom had already been actively involved in advocacy networks for the poor and vulnerable, in vaguely political organizations, and (in some cases) in revolutionary movements. They called on the Church to recognize a 'preferential option for the poor' that demanded active involvement in their temporal lives, including their political struggles. Roman Catholic priests began to work for structural change in their societies to foster social justice and equity.

In August 1968, Roman Catholic bishops from all over Latin America gathered in Medellin, Colombia. The discussions held at Medellin underlined the concern that the bishops felt for the economic conditions faced by the faithful in their dioceses as well as the necessity of creating institutions that would bring the Church closer to the people that it was seeking to serve. Among the more prominent voices at the conference was that of the Peruvian theologian Gustavo Gutierrez, who had passionately called for the development of a 'theology of liberation' a few weeks before the meeting. Following the conference, in 1970 and 1971, Gutierrez and a Brazilian, Hugo Assman, organized a flurry of conferences and published full-length monographs fleshing out this new theology of liberation. What these church leaders had in mind was liberation from oppressive economic and political structures that were sinful in themselves.

By the early 1970s the success of leftist political parties in South America, particularly the election of Salvador Allende in Chile in 1970, had created a highly charged political atmosphere. As fear of communist revolution spread throughout the Western hemisphere, the nascent liberation theology movement came under suspicion both within the Roman Catholic Church and in Western capitals on account of its apparent sympathy for Marxist-inspired revolutionary groups. The overthrow of Allende's socialist government in 1973 set the stage for a widespread challenge to leftist groups throughout the continent. The election in 1978 of Pope John Paul II—known to be both a critic of Communism and a theological conservative—ushered in a period in which the hierarchy of the Roman Catholic Church sought to limit the apparent extremes of the Latin American liberationists. The next gathering of Latin American bishops, held in Puebla, Mexico, in January 1979, was much more divided than its predecessor in Medellin had been.

What troubled the critics of liberation theology were its similarity to Marxist thinking regarding the place of the oppressed in world history and its reliance on materialist analysis of social realities. To be certain, there is much in liberation theology that recalls Marxist thought. It is essentially a critique of capitalist economics from a socialist standpoint, combining '[c]oncepts and categories like class, conflict, and exploitation . . . with general notions about dependence' (Levine 1992: 42). At the same time, liberation theology explicitly emphasizes the importance of praxis, calling for active engagement in the life of the world in addition to theological scholarship. To assume that liberation theology simply conveys Marxist theory in religious garb would be unfair in most cases: in the view of liberation theologians, 'conceptual borrowing does not require political alliance, and can be undertaken in any case without calling into question the religious roots of belief and commitment' (Levine 1992: 42).

Proponents of liberation theology draw on biblical traditions, such as the stories of Noah's ark, the exodus, or the healing stories of Jesus, to illustrate the active role that God has at times taken to liberate his people from structures of oppression. One might make the case that liberation theology is entirely consistent with the concern for the poor expressed in the 1891 papal encyclical *Rerum Novarum*. However, individual members of the movement have often engaged in radical activities, including violent protest and armed rebellion. Gutierrez did not embrace Marxist historical materialism, but some of his colleagues, such as Jose Comblin, borrowed quite heavily from it and other secular sources (Kee 1990: 164–69; Comblin 1998). While some liberationists concentrate on the Church's identification, in faith and in practice, with the plight of the poor, others have explicitly called for substantive if not revolutionary change in the apparatus of government.

By the mid-1980s, liberation theology was spreading from its home in Latin America to North America, Europe, and other parts of the developed world. In the process it has posed challenges to orthodoxy inside and outside the Roman Catholic tradition. Feminist and racial variations on its themes emerged in the late 1980s and 1990s, as in the work of the American feminist Rosemary Radford Ruether or of African-American leaders such as the Reverend Jeremiah Wright. The Orbis publishing house of the Roman Catholic mission society known as Maryknoll has played a central role in publishing and disseminating information on liberation theology.

Within the Church, the growing popularity of liberation theology elicited formal responses first from the bishops of the Latin American Church and eventually from the Vatican itself in the form of an *Instruction on Certain Aspects of the 'Theology of Liberation'* (1984) from Joseph Cardinal Ratzinger, then prefect of the Congregation for the Doctrine of the Faith. Ratzinger's response has been variously cast as anything from a strong rebuke to an attempt to silence and eliminate the dissenting voices of liberation theology. The text of his *Instruction* took direct aim at what he saw as an attempt to place temporal concerns above those of the spiritual. 'Liberation is first and foremost liberation from the radical slavery of sin,' he argued, going on to warn against

> the deviations, and risks of deviation, damaging to the faith and Christian living, that are brought about by certain forms of liberation theology which use, in an insufficiently critical manner, concepts borrowed from various currents of Marxist thought (Ratzinger 1984).

While the document was clearly aimed at controlling the application of liberation theology within the Church, it went on to state that the instruction 'should in no way be interpreted as a disavowal of all those who want to respond generously and with an authentic evangelical spirit to the "preferential option for the poor"'.

Two years later, a second *Instruction* focused specifically on the notions of freedom and liberation in the Christian tradition. This document was far more theological in tone. Questioning the premises of liberation, it suggested that the oppression liberation theology sought to relieve was hardly the only challenge facing humanity: 'new dangers, new forms of servitude and new terrors have arisen', and '[t]he salvific dimension of liberation cannot be reduced to the socio-ethical dimension, which is a consequence of it' (Ratzinger 1986, paras 10, 71). In his second instruction, Cardinal Ratzinger reflected the deep concern of the Church hierarchy that the liberation movement was simply playing into the hands of communist revolutionaries who would gladly use the support of lower levels in the Church hierarchy to undermine the freedoms and privileges of the Church in many states.

Not surprisingly, Western theologians have also criticized liberation theology for its single-minded condemnation of the capitalist economy as an inherently evil system. The American conservative commentator Michael Novak argued that what Gutierrez and his colleagues were criticizing was in fact not capitalism but a temporally and geographically specific economic system that was oppressive because it did not allow the 'free market' to operate as it should:

> Liberation theology says that Latin America is capitalist and needs a socialist revolution. Latin America does need a revolution. But its present system is

mercantilist and quasi-feudal, not capitalist, and the revolution it needs is both liberal and Catholic (Novak 1986: 5).

Responses to liberation theology in North America and Europe have tended to fall along the lines of denominational and doctrinal divisions. Mainline churches and liberal theologians have often embraced the liberationist perspective, while conservative denominations and theologians have condemned it for placing the material conditions of life over and above the spiritual dimension.

A Diversity of Political Movements

The theological debates that have arisen in the Roman Catholic Church have had a profound impact on politics in majority Roman Catholic states. In Europe, conservative movements have enjoyed the support of the Roman Catholic Church and have used it as a vehicle for their ambitions. In post-war Germany the Christian Democratic Party has enjoyed the support of the Christian Socialist Union, a like-minded movement rooted in the largely Roman Catholic state of Bavaria. The Church's tacit support for Christian Democratic parties in other states, such as Italy, also flowed out of the Church's staunch opposition to Communism throughout the Cold War and persists today in the tendency of religious conservatives to support right-of-centre parties. In the United States, Roman Catholic lay voters have traditionally been staunch supporters of the Democratic party, which cultivated its base among new immigrants from southern Europe and, later, Latin America. Nevertheless, the social conservatism of the clergy and Roman Catholic traditionalists has recently brought them closer to the Republican party.

In areas of the developing world, liberation theology has competed for ideological influence with the more conservative religious tradition defended by the Church hierarchy. A general increase in religiosity among average citizens in countries throughout Latin America has gone hand in hand with increases in the competition represented by **charismatic** Protestantism, which emphasizes 'gifts of the Holy Spirit' such as glossolalia ('speaking in tongues'), healing, and prophecy. In some Latin American societies, Pentecostalism has eclipsed traditional Roman Catholicism. Liberationist activism, where it was practised, offered a strong alternative to Pentecostalism, but more conservative movements have also taken on some of the characteristics of the evangelical Protestant denominations that seem to be better attuned to the temporal needs of the average churchgoer. As a result, some Roman Catholic groups have become 'Pentecostalized' in their organization and practice (Gooren 2010). Gill (1998) argues that contending Roman Catholic and evangelical voices of opposition to authoritarian regimes help to explain the success of both types of new religious movements in Chile and Argentina in gaining societal influence. This newly competitive environment has encouraged the Roman Catholic Church, among others, to take a more active role in social issues, which in some ways recalls the liberationists (Levine 2009).

Popular Catholic and Pentecostal movements alike tend to represent a syncretic mix of spiritual types. For example, Selka (2007) describes the diverse ways in which

Pentecostal and Roman Catholic social teachings have been combined with elements of traditional African religion as a political force in favour of racial equality in the state of Bahia, Brazil, in spite of their many contradictions. Betances (2007) argues that the strength of Roman Catholic religious forces in the Dominican Republic helps to explain the history of conservative politics in that country. By contrast, in Central American and South American contexts, revolutionary forces posed a significant threat to the government and consequently to the Church, weakening the authority of the Church hierarchy as a social force. In short, the areas of Latin America and the Caribbean that have endured the greatest social hardships have provided the most fertile ground for the liberationist movements that have divided the Church.

A case in point is the nation of Haiti. After the overthrow of the brutal Duvalier regime in 1986, popular religious movements emerged to represent the interests of the poor and downtrodden of Haitian society. A leading figure at the time was a Roman Catholic priest, Jean-Bertrand Aristide, who represented a major pole of opposition to the regime in the 1980s. Aristide's embrace of liberation theology as a weapon against the state brought him into conflict with the Church, and he eventually left the priesthood to become the first elected president of Haiti. Dedication to the cause of the poor gave Aristide immense popular appeal, but by 2004 he had become increasingly authoritarian. This, combined with his opposition to statist globalization strategies designed to open Haiti's economy up to neoliberalism, led to his downfall in 2004 (Dupuy 2007). Since that time the Roman Catholic Church has embraced charismatic renewal both as a way to reinforce its relevance among the Haitian people and to reduce the political impact of the liberation theology movement (Rey 2010).

In Southeast Asia, Roman Catholic leaders have often been at the forefront of political change. For example, in the late 1980s and again in the early 2000s, the ranking Roman Catholic leader in the Philippines, Jaime Cardinal Sin, was vocal in his support for opposition movements. His first interventions contributed to the success of the 'people power' movement that overthrew former dictator Ferdinand Marcos in 1986 and later forced the resignation of President Joseph Estrada in 2001. In 1996 Bishop Carlos Belo was awarded the Nobel Peace Prize for his work in promoting the peaceful independence of his home country of East Timor in the 1980s and 1990s.

Change, Continuity, and New Challenges

The effort to rein in the liberation theology movement has been relatively successful. The hierarchy of the Roman Catholic Church has largely followed Ratzinger's rebuke of the liberationists. Base communities continue to thrive and the theology of liberation continues to embolden the rank and file ministers in the rural areas. But it is unclear that liberation theology will provide guidance to the current generation of revolutionaries. Instead, it has informed less radical attempts to address justice, to come to peaceful conclusion of conflict, and to empower the disenfranchised. Liberation theology has become much more popular in Protestant and scholarly circles, where it is seen as a progressive attempt to ground the Christian message in temporal realities. For this reason, liberation theology lives on in a growing number of alternative theologies, even occasionally among those that share the Roman Catholic hierarchy's distaste for Marxism, as in the case of evangelical critics such as Tony Campolo or Ron Sider. It has likewise seen some revitalization in the work of more conservative thinkers such as Daniel M. Bell and William Cavanaugh (Bell 2001, Cavanaugh 1998).

The papacy has been vital in the resurgence of the Church as a worldwide force. In spite of failing health, Pope John Paul II continued to travel widely in the later years of his life. In January 1998, he became the first pope to visit Cuba. The visit gave the pope an opportunity to challenge publicly the limitations on freedom imposed by the Communist state even as he criticized the US embargo against Cuba that had been in place ever since the revolution of 1959. In the wake of the visit, the release of some political prisoners seemed to suggest that the pontiff's remarks were taken seriously.

In 2000, the pope embarked on a 'Millennium Pilgrimage' to holy sites in the Middle East. For many years, the diplomatic efforts of the Vatican to maintain strong ties to states and groups in the Middle East had been constrained by various ongoing conflicts in the Middle East. The fact that the Roman Catholic Church has numerous Arab adherents has been a particular strain on its relations with the state of Israel, especially since the Six-Day War of 1967. After the conclusion of the Oslo Agreements over the West Bank and Gaza Strip in September 1993, the way was cleared for the conclusion of agreements between the Vatican and the principals in the Israeli–Palestinian conflict. Having exchanged ambassadors and diplomatic staff with Israel

Joseph Cardinal Ratzinger, a German academic and assistant of John Paul II, became Pope Benedict XVI on 19 April 2005.
Source: © Andia/Alamy

in July 1994, in February 2000 the Vatican signed a set of understandings with the PLO. Then the pope set out for Egypt, where he conducted open-air meetings and met with representatives from the Eastern and Oriental Orthodox Churches. The following month he visited Israel and made a pilgrimage to the holy places, as well as a visit to the Yad Vashem memorial, where he communicated regret for the sins of the Holocaust.

Nevertheless, new challenges faced the Church in the early years of the twenty-first century. Cases involving child sexual abuse on the part of Roman Catholic clergy were coming to light in increasing numbers, and in 2001–2 it became clear that a number of American bishops had ignored allegations of abuse for many years, simply reassigning the priests in question to new parishes. Paying the financial compensation required by the courts in such cases has become a particularly serious problem for the Church. Meanwhile, *The Da Vinci Code*, an entirely fictional account of a Vatican-inspired conspiracy to hide ancient truths, rose to the top of the bestseller lists, further damaging the Church's popular image.

In early 2005, John Paul II's health declined rapidly. After his death in April, the College of Cardinals met to select his successor. Following a relatively brief period of deliberation, the best-known defender of doctrinal orthodoxy, the German Cardinal Ratzinger, was elected and took the name Benedict XVI. The new pope was well known as an important leader and a strong theological scholar, but he had neither the warmth nor the charisma of his predecessor. Many felt that he would have difficulty matching up to the stature of the man who had done so much to shape the nature of the Church for the past 25 years.

The Church under Benedict XVI

As was fitting for a man of Ratzinger's scholarly background, he quickly began to lay out the importance of reason in the elaboration of dogma. Thus on 12 September 2006, Benedict spoke at the University of Regensburg (where he had served as a professor) on the topic of 'Faith, Reason, and the University: Memories and Reflections'. In the course of the speech, the pontiff made a passing reference to the words of a fourteenth-century Byzantine emperor who criticized the role that violence had played in the spread of Islam: 'Show me just what Mohammad brought that was new and there you will find things only evil and inhuman, such as his command to spread by the sword the faith he preached.'

The quotation was merely an example used to prove a larger point, that religion and reason were complementary concepts, a premise that he felt created a firm foundation for interreligious dialogue. The message was directed not to the Muslim world but to the secular Europe that Benedict XVI knew very well. 'A reason which is deaf to the divine and which relegates religion into the realm of subcultures is incapable of entering into the dialogue of cultures' (Benedict XVI 2006). Nevertheless, earlier expressions of his concern regarding the expansion of the European Union to include Muslim-majority states in the Middle East (notably Turkey) had already made some Muslims suspicious that the pope was unfriendly towards their faith. Word of the controversial quotation spread quickly among media outlets in the Muslim world, provoking widespread rioting and threatening to derail the pope's planned visit to Turkey later that year. Benedict responded with a statement of regret for the effect the quotation had had, but refrained from apologizing for words that were not his own. However, many feared that the incident might only deepen the divisions in an increasingly polarized world, exacerbating what many have described as a 'clash of civilizations' between the Christian and Islamic worlds.

More damaging to the reputation of the Roman Catholic Church has been its lacklustre response to the charges of sexual abuse that had begun to emerge during the papacy of John Paul II. Bishop Bernard Law of Boston had been forced to resign in December 2002 for his role in covering up the crimes committed by priests (*Boston Globe* 2004). Concerns were renewed in 2010, when information came to light regarding allegations of sexual abuse within the Legionaries of Christ, a religious order whose leader, Father Marcial Maciel, had secretly fathered several children. Although the pope, as Cardinal Ratzinger, had removed the priest from his position in 2006, it was widely felt that the Church should have demanded redress, legal or otherwise, in such cases (Donadio 2010a).

Although the pope spoke to reporters with unprecedented frankness in May 2010, condemning 'the sin inside the church' and admitting that 'forgiveness is not justice', the scandal has not gone away (Donadio 2010b). Among other things, it has brought under criticism the age-old tradition of a celibate priesthood and undermined public trust in the administration of the Church. In July 2010 the Congregation for the Doctrine of the Faith issued a document entitled 'Norms concerning the most serious crimes', codifying the disciplinary measures required for priests involved in sexual abuse. At the same time, however, the document condemned the ordination of women as an equally serious 'crime'. The implication that a challenge to the male priesthood was equivalent to the sexual abuse of minors drew widespread criticism that the Church hierarchy was insensitive and myopic.

Conclusion

The Roman Catholic Church remains an important world player for a variety of reasons. Its membership is massive and it controls a vast array of organizations and properties. Through the Holy See it enjoys the status of a state and has the capacity to conduct official diplomacy. It has worldwide influence through the active application of its theology by priests, bishops, and laypeople involved in daily public life in Roman Catholic societies. In the case of liberation theology, the Church has struggled through the theological implications of inequality and oppression that beset world politics and has formed the battleground for theological defences of economic and political reform both in majority Catholic states and at the global level. The pope is an influential figure in world politics, who has variously been involved and implicated in struggles over fascism, communism, and the 'clash of civilizations' in his capacity as spokesman for the Church. Despite recent scandals and controversies, the Church seems likely to retain an important role in defining political interactions among the world's religions in the coming century.

Review Questions

1. What are the origins of the Roman Catholic Church and the Holy See?
2. What is the Lateran Treaty? What role did it play in establishing the official status of Vatican City?
3. What changes did the Second Vatican Council introduce to the Roman Catholic Church?
4. What were the contributions of Pope John Paul II to the revival of the Church?
5. What are the origins of liberation theology? In what respects does it resemble Marxist analysis?
6. How has the Roman Catholic hierarchy responded to the liberation theology movement?
7. What significant events have characterized the papacy of Pope Benedict XVI?

Sources and Further Reading

Bell, Daniel (2001). *Liberation Theology after the End of History: The Refusal to Cease Suffering*. London: Routledge.

Benedict XVI (2006). 'Faith, Reason and the University'. Lecture of the Holy Father, 12 September. www.vatican.va/holy_father/benedict_xvi/ speeches/2006/september/ documents/hf_ben-xvi_spe_20060912_university-regensburg_en.html

Berryman, Phillip (1987). *Liberation Theology: Essential Facts about the Revolutionary Movement in Latin America and Beyond*. London: I.B. Tauris.

Betances, Emilio (2007).*The Catholic Church and Power Politics in Latin America: The Dominican Case in Comparative Perspective*. Lanham, MD: Rowman & Littlefield.

Boston Globe (2004). *Spotlight Investigation: Abuse in the Catholic Church*. http://www. boston.com/globe/spotlight/abuse/

Cavanaugh, William T. (1998). *Torture and Eucharist*. Oxford: Blackwell Publishers.

Comblin, Jose (1998). *Called for Freedom: The Changing Context of Liberation Theology*. Maryknoll, NY: Orbis Books, 1998.

Cornwell, John (1999). *Hitler's Pope: The Secret History of Pius XII*. New York: Viking.

Coulombe, Charles A. (2003). *A History of the Popes: Vicars of Christ*. New York: MJF Books.

Daniel, Wallace L. (2006). *The Orthodox Church and Civil Society in Russia*. College Station: Texas A&M University Press.

De Rosa, Peter (1988). *Vicars of Christ: The Dark Side of the Papacy*. New York: Bantam.

Donadio, Rachel (2010a). 'Pope Reins in Catholic Order Tied to Abuse'. *New York Times*. 1 May.

———— (2010b). 'Pope Issues his Most Direct Words to Date on Abuse'. *New York Times*. 11 May.

Duffy, Eamon (2002). *Saints and Sinners: A History of the Popes*. New Haven: Yale Nota Bene.

Dupuy, Alex (2007). *The Prophet and Power: Jean-Bertrand Aristide, the International Community, and Haiti*. Lanham, MD: Rowman & Littlefield.

Economist, The (2007). 'God's Ambassadors'. 21 July: 58–60.

Ferrari, Lisa L (2006). 'The Vatican as a Transnational Actor', in Paul C. Manuel, Lawrence C. Reardon, and Clyde Wilcox, eds., *The Catholic Church and the Nation-State: Comparative Perspectives*. Washington, DC: Georgetown University Press.

Flannery, Austin, ed. (1996). *Vatican Council II: Constitutions, Decrees, Declarations*. Northport, NY: Costello Publishing Company.

Gill, Anthony (1998). *Rendering unto Caesar: The Catholic Church and the State in Latin America*. Chicago: University of Chicago Press.

Gooren, Henri (2010). 'The Pentecostalization of Religion and Society in Latin America', *Exchange* 39, 4: 355–76.

Himes, Kenneth R (2006). 'Vatican II and Contemporary Politics'. In Paul Christopher Manuel, Lawrence C. Reardon and Clyde Wilcox, eds., *The Catholic Church and the Nation-state: Comparative Perspectives*. Georgetown: Georgetown University Press.

Huntington, Samuel (1991). *The Third Wave: Democratization in the Late Twentieth Century*. Norman: University of Oklahoma Press.

Irani, George Emile (1986). *The Papacy and the Middle East: The Role of the Holy See in the Arab–Israeli Conflict, 1968–1984*. Notre Dame: University of Notre Dame Press.

Kee, Alistair (1990). *Marx and the Failure of Liberation Theology*. London: SCM Press.

Las Casas, Bartolomé de (1992 [1552]). *A Short Account of the Destruction of the Indies*. London: Penguin Books.

Levine, Daniel (1992). *Popular Voices in Latin American Catholicism*. Princeton: Princeton University Press.

——— (2009). 'The Future of Christianity in Latin America'. *Journal of Latin American Studies* 41, 1: 121–45.

Manuel, Paul C., Lawrence C. Reardon, and Clyde Wilcox, eds. (2006). *The Catholic Church and the Nation-State: Comparative Perspectives*. Washington, DC: Georgetown University Press.

McGovern, Arthur F. (1989). *Liberation Theology and its Critics*. Maryknoll, NY: Orbis Books, 1989.

Novak, Michael (1986). *Will It Liberate? Questions about Liberation Theology*. New York: Paulist Press.

Princen, Thomas (1992). *Intermediaries in International Conflict*. Princeton: Princeton University Press.

Ratzinger, Joseph Cardinal (1984). *Instruction on Certain Aspects of the 'Theology of Liberation'*. Vatican City: Congregation for the Doctrine of the Faith. www.vatican.va/roman_curia/congregations/cfaith/documents/ rc_con_cfaith_doc_19840806_theology-liberation_en.html

——— (1986). *Instruction on Christian Freedom and Liberation*. Vatican City: Congregation for the Doctrine of the Faith. www.vatican.va/roman_curia/congregations/cfaith/documents/rc_con_cfaith_doc_19860322_freedom-liberation_en.html

Reese, Thomas J. (1996). *Inside the Vatican*. Cambridge, MA: Harvard University Press.

Rey, Terry (2010). 'Catholic Pentecostalism in Haiti'. *Pneuma* 32, 1: 80–106.

Selka, Stephen (2007). *Religion and the Politics of Identity in Bahia, Brazil.* Gainesville: University Press of Florida.

Stan, Lavinia, and Lucian Turcescu (2007). *Religion and Politics in Post-Communist Romania.* Oxford: Oxford University Press.

Vallier, Ivan (1971). 'The Roman Catholic Church: A Transnational Actor', *International Organization*, 25, 3: 479–502.

Walsh, Michael (2000). 'Catholicism and International Relations: Papal Interventionism', in John L. Esposito and Michael Watson, eds, *Religion and Global Order.* Cardiff: University of Wales Press.

Weigel, George (2005). *Witness to Hope: The Biography of John Paul II.* New York: Harper Perennial.

——— (2005). *God's Choice: Pope Benedict XVI and the Future of the Catholic Church.* New York: Harper Collins.

Web Resources

www.vatican.va – The official website of the Holy See.

www.newadvent.org/cathen/index.html – The Catholic Encyclopedia.

www.liberationtheology.org – A web library of resources on liberation theology.

www.boston.com/globe/spotlight/abuse – The *Boston Globe*'s spotlight investigation on abuse in the Roman Catholic Church.

Chapter 3

Christianity and US Politics

The influence of religion in US foreign policy has attracted increasing attention over the past few decades. As is often the case with religion and politics at the level of the nation-state, there are significant contradictions in the United States. The US is an advanced capitalist country—the type of state that is least likely to retain a public role for religion, according to modernization theory. Yet religious perspectives have only become more influential as conservative Christians have come to feel that traditional American ways of life are threatened by modern technology, science, and globalization.

The United States was founded primarily by Christian minorities fleeing Britain and Europe in the wake of the Protestant Reformation. By the early 1600s, Protestantism had given birth to the Anglican and Presbyterian churches (the new national churches of England and Scotland respectively), as well as the Lutheran Church in northern Europe and various Calvinist Reformed Churches in central Europe. In addition, several newer churches were founded that differed more profoundly not only with the Roman Catholic Church but with the other Reformers. Members of these independent, nonconformist, or dissenting churches were often persecuted for their insistence on confessional autonomy.

First English minorities such as the Puritans and Quakers and later European groups such as the Amish and Mennonites migrated to the United States in search of a new society that would tolerate religious differences. Mixing with the broader population of Anglican (Episcopal), Presbyterian, and Roman Catholic settlers, they created a broadly Christian nation that encompassed many different sects and creeds. Freedom of religion created an open market of ideas that encouraged religious entrepreneurs to form new groups. Over time, dozens of new religious movements would emerge in the US and then move on to revolutionize the world of religion. The Church of Jesus Christ of Latter-day Saints (Mormons), Jehovah's Witnesses, Christian Science, and Pentecostalism, the social gospel, the prosperity gospel, and modern televangelism: all originated in the American religious marketplace.

In terms of religious participation and interest, the United States is generally considered to be one of the most religious nations in the world. Yet the constitution of the US government was deliberately designed to eliminate a public role for religion in hopes of avoiding the confessional politics that many early settlers had fled Europe to escape (Monsma and Soper 1997: 10–11). These contending forces make for a fascinating example of the interplay of religion and politics in a supposedly 'secular' state.

The 'City upon a Hill': Competing Themes in US Politics

Religious influences in US politics take a variety of forms, but three themes are particularly prominent. One is **disestablishmentarianism** and secularism, defined as the separation of 'church and state'. A basic principle of the United States constitution, enshrined in the first amendment (adopted in 1791), is that 'Congress shall make no law respecting an establishment of religion, or prohibiting the free exercise thereof.'

In addition to prohibiting the establishment of any faith as the 'official' religion of the United States, the constitution guaranteed that no member of the clergy would become an ex officio member of the federal government.

That secularism should be a guiding principle of American politics is not surprising. In Reformation-era Europe, state enforcement of religious orthodoxy was the norm; in Britain the head of state, the monarch, was also titular head of the Church of England, and members of the Church hierarchy held seats in the House of Lords. Having lived as dissenters in societies where the established church was inseparable from the state, the early settlers prized the freedom they found in the new world, and their sentiments were passed down through the generations of their descendants. The separation of church and state in America led to some paradoxical outcomes. For the founding fathers, the value of a secular state was not that it would be devoid of religion, but that it would allow all kinds of religious beliefs and practices to thrive. As a result, far from eradicating religious activity, the separation of church and state invigorated it. America became not the most irreligious nation in the world but one of the most religious. At the same time, instead of tying its legitimacy to any one religion, the state encouraged the proliferation of religious groups, many of which have had a significant impact on American public life over the centuries.

This brings us to a second theme: the competitive and activist nature of religious groups in US civil society. The absence of any official state church left the field open for an unlimited variety of religious movements to seek out a niche. The American reverence for personal freedom made it possible for people to evangelize, explore, and debate, to move from one faith to another or to claim no religion at all. Freedom of religion, coupled with freedom of association and a general proficiency in self-organization, created a wide-open market for religious ideas, entrepreneurship, and innovation.

This trend was remarked on as early as 1831, when the famous French observer of American life Alexis de Tocqueville (1805–59) noted that 'Religion in America takes no direct part in the government of society, but it must be regarded as the first of their political institutions; for if it does not impart a taste for freedom, it facilitates the use of it' (Tocqueville 1945 [1835–40]: 316). Together, freedom of religion and the general habit of forming small, self-constituting networks throughout the country have been credited for much of the vibrancy that American democracy still displays today. By the middle of the nineteenth century, the extension of foreign missions abroad reflected the democratic ideals of American civil society, concentrating on the free expression of religious convictions and persuasion.

This brings us to a third theme. Although the United States professes to be a state in which church and state were to be firmly separated, it has nonetheless developed a profound religious sensibility about both its role in the world and its public institutions. The earliest settlers sought to establish a new kind of society that would be a beacon to other nations. Perhaps the most famous statement of their ambition was a sermon delivered in 1630 by John Winthrop, the Puritan governor of the Massachusetts Bay Colony, in which he called on his fellow settlers to make their colony a 'model of Christian charity' that would be a 'city on a hill', an example to the world of God's work in action. These phrases have been echoed by numerous presidents throughout the history of the United States.

The separation of church and state notwithstanding, American policy-makers and citizens alike have tended to invoke the blessing of God on the nation and to understand American politics as an almost numinous endeavour. The significance of religion as a guiding force in American politics was noted in 1967 in a famous essay by the sociologist Robert Bellah:

> Although matters of personal religious belief, worship, and association are considered to be strictly private affairs, there are, at the same time, certain common elements of religious orientation that the great majority of Americans share. These have played a crucial role in the development of American institutions and still provide a religious dimension for the whole fabric of American life, including the political sphere (Bellah 1967: 3-4).

Regarding the tendency of American political rhetoric to use vague religious principles to justify US institutions and foreign policy, Bellah argued that the association of the nation with divine purposes was a uniquely American concept, an American 'civil religion'. He borrowed the latter term from *The Social Contract*, in which Jean-Jacques Rousseau had argued that the glue necessary to hold people together in a modern society was not a particular denomination or set of religious doctrines, but what he called a 'general will'. Along the same lines, Bellah suggested that American leaders had created an American civil religion that legitimized and justified US policy without reference to any particular set of religious doctrines. American leaders had forged a theology of American policy that could appeal to a wide variety of religious devotees. Throughout history, American civil religion had given US foreign policy a kind of missionary air, surrounding it with non-specific religious imagery that served to suggest that the United States had a special role in the world.

Religion in American Public Life: A Historic Perspective

The importance of religious movements in American politics has waxed and waned. The earliest colonies that would later form the United States were established by refugees from religious conflict in Europe. For some of them, the United States represented a new frontier, free of religious bigotry; for others, a place where they could live a communal religious life free of outside interference. Religious groups such as the Congregationalists and Methodists in particular played an important part in the growth of the movement for independence from Britain in the early 1700s. The 'great awakenings' of the 1730s–40s and 1820s–30s—periods of religious revival, charismatic preachers, and mass conversions—helped to sustain a strong, if informal, religious component in public life. Reform-minded Christians also played leading roles in the movement to abolish slavery in the period prior to the US Civil War (1861–65).

The second 'great awakening' in particular was characterized by a wave of millenarianism—the belief that the second coming of Christ (the 'second Advent') is imminent. A number of groups formed in and after this period have come to play a significant role in the politics of religion both domestically and abroad, among them the Seventh-day Adventists (founded in the 1860s), Jehovah's Witnesses (1870s), and Christian Scientists (1875). Perhaps most significant to the political life of the United States was the establishment of the Church of Jesus Christ of Latter-day Saints (in 1830. A series of incidents led its adherents—the Mormons—to move westward from New York to Missouri and then on to the region that is now the state of Utah, where they settled in such numbers that for some time they effectively governed the territory. They continue to be concentrated in the western United States, especially in Utah, but now claim converts around the world.

The explosion of American religion was characterized by evangelistic zeal and a vision of spreading American beliefs and values around the world. The Americas were of particular interest at a time when the US was proclaiming its 'manifest destiny' to become the leading power in the western hemisphere. But American missionaries, like their British counterparts, were active around the world. In the Middle East, Protestant missionaries founded modern universities that encouraged the development of the early Arab nationalist movement. Elsewhere, people such as Adoniram Judson (1788–1850), a Baptist missionary to Burma in the early nineteenth century, Dwight Lyman Moody (1837–99), an itinerant evangelist who travelled between America and Britain, and Wilfred Grenfell (1865–1940), the American-based British doctor whose Labrador mission inspired a whole generation of medical professionals, all embodied the American missionary impulse. Likewise, a succession of large and active mission societies, from denominational missions to groups devoted to the spread of Christianity in sub-Saharan Africa and South and Southeast Asia, were influential in projecting American values abroad. The missions followed the movement of American economic interests and scouted out new opportunities, driving American foreign policy to greater involvement in areas of the world that until then had been the preserve of the European colonial powers.

The Twentieth Century and 'Social Christianity'

Modern observers accustomed to the close links between the US Republican party and religious conservatives might be surprised to learn that the most important Christian social movements at the turn of the twentieth century tended to be bipartisan in their political sympathies, and that some had specific attachments to the Democratic party. The development of biblical text criticism—in which scholars examined the textual evidence to determine when, by whom, and for what purposes different parts of the Bible were composed—created major divisions between the 'liberal' mainstream and the more conservative church traditions of the period, which defended the literal inerrancy of biblical scriptures. Liberal Christians tended to champion what they called 'social Christianity', believing that it was up to human beings, working collectively, to transform the social order and solve problems such as poverty, violence, social discord, and war. While conservative Christian groups were no less interested in addressing social ills, they tended to believe that the individual pursuit of personal holiness and separation from the mainstream of society were more effective strategies.

Box 3.1: Families of Protestant Theology in America

'Liberal', 'mainline', 'fundamentalist', 'conservative', and 'evangelical' are terms commonly used to distinguish the main theological streams and groups among North American Christians. Their definitions are typically fluid, however. The word 'liberal' came to be used to describe the modern interpretations of scripture that were developed by nineteenth-century scholars. Liberal theology is most closely identified with **mainline** established churches (Roman Catholic, Anglican/Episcopal, Lutheran), although it is important to note that these churches themselves can be internally divided on matters of theology.

Those Christians who rejected the premises of textual criticism and insisted on a literal reading of scripture came to be known as **fundamentalists**. Fundamentalists have been defined by their firm belief in a fairly narrow set of Christian doctrines and literal interpretation of scripture. Fundamentalists regard those who do not share their dogmatic rigour as schismatic or heretical at best, and non-Christian at worst. Fundamentalists laid the foundations of modern 'conservative' Protestantism in America.

Among conservatives, the term evangelical has come to be applied to a wider range of believers who do not necessarily share the narrow dogmatism of fundamentalists: in other words, fundamentalists may well be evangelicals but not all evangelicals are fundamentalists. The word comes from a root meaning 'good news' or 'gospel', which emphasizes the active effort to convert others to the message of Christianity. In a widely cited study of the history of evangelicalism, Bebbington (1992) suggested four distinctive features of modern evangelicalism: biblicism (a high regard for scripture), crucicentrism (an emphasis on the salvific work of Jesus Christ on the cross), conversionism (the imperative that the individual must come to a moment of conversion to the message of Christianity), and activism (Christians are called to take an active role in spreading the gospel both individually and through collective social endeavours).

So it was that the liberal social gospel movement came to be associated with the internationalist and idealist vision of a more just world brought about through human effort. Closely associated with the idealist movement in international affairs were the movements for women's suffrage, prohibition, disarmament, and workers' rights. Their best-known leaders were also socialist or liberal internationalists seeking to bring Christian convictions about peace and justice to bear on the conduct of international relations. Among their more prominent leaders were Walter Rauschenbusch, a New York minister and the literary father of the 'social gospel' movement, as well as William Jennings Bryan, the unsuccessful Democratic candidate for the presidency in 1896, 1900, and 1908, who eventually became Woodrow Wilson's Secretary of State (1913–15).

The social gospel movement infused the liberal establishment with a socialized Christianity. Meanwhile, the fundamentalist Christians who represented the main opposition to the socially oriented liberal mainstream remained relatively apolitical for fear that their message would be tainted by involvement in politics. However, the disappointments of the Great Depression and the increasing menace of war in the early 1930s led many socially activist Christian groups to question the value of their idealism.

Most prominent among the disillusioned critics of idealism was Reinhold Niebuhr (1892–1971), a respected theologian and active socialist into the early 1930s who came to believe that the Christian Idealist movement was unrealistic in its expectations of human progress. He believed that human nature was essentially flawed, and that if Christians were to be effective in promoting international justice, they would have to use the morally dubious levers of state power. By the early 1940s, he was advocating the combination of self-interested state power with the moral project of the social gospel: a pragmatic combination of what he called the 'children of light' and the 'children of darkness'. 'If America achieves maturity,' he wrote, 'the primary mark of it must be the willingness to assume continuing responsibility in the world community of nations' (Niebuhr 1944: 185). His assessment was ample justification for linking US military power with a vision of moral leadership around the world.

Christianity and the US 'Mission' in the World: The Cold War

Sittser (1997) argues that four factors drove Christian groups to abandon the isolation-ism of the interwar years in favour of a new interventionism after 1945: the failure of the 1919 Versailles settlement to ensure a lasting peace; the lingering internationalism of the 1930s idealist movement; the growing influence of the international ecumenical movement; and the impact of Niebuhr's Christian realism. Niebuhr became one of the foremost defenders of realist approaches in American foreign policy, and his Christian Realism—combining hard-nosed moral relativism with implacable opposition to Communism at home and abroad—was effectively harnessed as a guide for foreign policy in the period following the Second World War. Christian realists, recognizing the limitations of the human capacity to address global problems, argued for the use of American power to defend national interests and ensure global security.

At the same time, after the end of the Second World War, US policy-makers and citizens alike came to identify Communism, and the Soviet Union in particular, in pseudo-religious terms as a real-world evil that the righteous West, led by the United States, was responsible to combat. The moral righteousness associated with the fight against Communism helped to justify widespread antagonism against the Eastern bloc, the excesses of anti-Communist campaigns, and the deepening of the Cold War throughout the 1950s.

According to Wald (1994), at least two factors contributed to the increasingly belligerent attitude taken by churches in particular against Communism. One was the obvious hostility of communist theory to the free practice of religion. In the minds of Americans, the communist philosophy was at once materialistic and atheistic: its determination to silence dissent was coupled with an inherently hostile attitude toward the free practice of religion. A second factor was the inherently conservative response of religious movements to revolutionary activity. Leftist revolutionaries had been associated with anticlericalism since the French Revolution. American Christianity continued to show both liberal internationalist and realist leanings, but a consensus emerged about the evils of communism:

The evolution of Reinhold Niebuhr's thinking between the 1930s and the 1950s illustrates the shift in American religion from idealist to realist views of US engagement in world politics. In works such as *Moral Man and Immoral Society* and *Children of Light and Children of Darkness*, Niebuhr presented a vision of a state that embraced the inevitability of war in defence of American security and values.
Source: Walter Sanders/Time Life Pictures/Getty Images

Where they differed, religious progressives and conservatives debated strategic premises about appropriate American responses to the Soviet challenge. That communism was a challenge to be resisted was not in question between the two camps (Wald 1994: 491).

Anti-communism became a common theme of fundamentalist and evangelical social action in the 1950s and 1960s. Fundamentalist populism arose as a prominent social movement during the 1950s. Religious conservatives made sophisticated use of new media technologies such as radio and television, as well as mass open-air spectacles organized around charismatic preachers. The most notable of the latter was Billy Graham, a South Carolina Baptist who became the first field evangelist of the Youth for Christ organization. Graham's 'crusades'—massive televised spectacles at which he

Billy Graham used his position as field evangelist for Youth for Christ to build a nationwide following for his open-air 'crusades'. He became a spiritual advisor to several presidents of both major political parties. By the 1960s, Graham was one of the most influential Christian leaders in the United States.
Source: David Hume Kennerly/Getty Images

preached the evangelical gospel of Christian conversion had a profound effect on public religion in America. His prominence also gave him a political role that he often publicly disavowed even as he called for the proper appreciation of Christian moral values in the halls of government. Martin (1996: 29) notes that 'warnings against communism began to be a regular feature of Graham's preaching' as early as 1947. Graham went on to have a close relationship with various presidents, including Eisenhower, Johnson, and Nixon, both as a confidant and as a sometime activist on their behalf.

Streams of Christian Activism

Christian activism took on a new character in the 1970s and 1980s, partly in response to the social changes that came with the various social and cultural revolutions of the 1960s.

As Americans increasingly questioned traditional authorities, values, and institutions, the courts began to take on controversial cases involving matters such as the civil rights of African-Americans, the place of prayer in public schools, and the constitutional right to abortion. In each instance the Supreme Court ruled in favour of the liberal option. At the same time, social movements came to challenge American policy and political culture: the peace movement protested against the war in Vietnam and the proliferation of nuclear arms, while the environmental movement challenged the unfettered pursuit of economic development regardless of the environmental consequences.

A second broad development, in many ways a response to the first, was a new willingness on the part of conservative Christian communities to engage with politics. These groups had been the social voice of conservative policy in sermons and publications denouncing atheistic Communism during the Cold War but had not been organized into a coherent political movement. Social change and the perceived erosion of American power encouraged the development of an organized network of lobby groups, churches, and para-church organizations opposed to the liberal social movements of the day. The election of Ronald Reagan to the presidency in 1980 was in part attributable to the mobilization of a conservative Christian constituency that came to be known as the 'religious right'.

The social changes that had taken place over the two previous decades had been profound. They began with an expansion of religious tolerance that was marked by the election of the country's first Roman Catholic president, John F. Kennedy, in 1960. Even more significant was the progress made towards the abolition of racial segregation and the achievement of full civil rights for African-Americans. Chappell (2004) argues that religious forces among African-Americans in particular were indispensable in this period to the development of a prophetic consciousness. This consciousness was employed in the struggle for abolition of racial segregation and full emancipation for Americans of all colours. The most prominent civil rights activists were Baptists, who used biblical imagery, themes, and scriptures to inspire the faithful in their struggle for justice. At their head was the Reverend Dr Martin Luther King, Jr (1929–68), the Baptist minister who, with his colleagues in the Southern Christian Leadership Conference (SCLC), was committed to the principles of non-violent civil disobedience and peaceful protest. Dr King won the Nobel Peace Prize in 1964 and remains a hero to supporters of racial justice and human rights around the world. The civil rights movement reaffirmed some of the progressive principles that had inspired the social gospel movement in the early 1900s.

The policy changes achieved under the Democratic administration of Lyndon Johnson had the effect of shaking up traditional political allegiances. In particular, many white social conservatives from the southern states who had traditionally supported the Democratic party came to find common cause with supporters of the Republican party's failed 1964 presidential candidate, Barry Goldwater. Social conservative leaders such as Phyllis Schlafly and Paul Weyrich brought a disparate collection of informal groups together to form a movement that would come of age over the following two decades.

The nomination of Jimmy Carter, a self-described evangelical Christian, as the Democratic candidate for the presidency in 1976 attracted some southern conservatives back to their old party. But they were disappointed, finding President Carter to be dovish in foreign policy and too quick to compromise with liberals on domestic social policy (Lindsay 2007: 52–6). In the next election, when the Republican Ronald Reagan promised to bring social conservatives into the mainstream of decision-making to reassert a public role for religion, he won in a landslide.

The contending forces that had emerged in American politics over the previous two decades had created new divisions among politically active Christian organizations. At the level of foreign policy, it polarized Christian movements in ways that paralleled the idealist and realist camps of the past, but with a difference. Wozniuk (1988) sought to update Niebuhr's distinction between Christian idealism and Christian realism for the late 1980s, arguing that a dichotomy had emerged among Christian political activists with regard to foreign policy between what he called Christian neo-realists and neo-idealists.

Similarly, Wuthnow (1988) proposed that there were two divergent interpretations of the national enterprise in American civil religion. He argued that the United States' 'virtual isolation from the rest of the world has resulted in the orientation of a segment of the bureaucratic state toward nationalistic concerns'. At the same time, 'America's rise to global power in the twentieth century has forced the state to act not only on behalf of narrow US interests, but also as a potential contributor to the common good in global terms' (Wuthnow 1988: 255). In other words, US foreign policy has meshed together and seesawed between two visions, both based on the notion of American exceptionalism (that the US is qualitatively different from other nations, and that it should operate accordingly) and a nearly sacred sense of the superiority of the US system. On one hand is the idea that such a country should remain in splendid isolation from the world, and on the other the idea that the country has a special mission to lead the world into the future. Christians active in the political sphere have reflected both of these visions, some attributing the country's superiority to its Christian moral compass, and others emphasizing the age-old understanding of the United States as a Christian nation with a mission to change the world for the better.

According to Wozniuk, Christian neo-realism was championed by conservative thinkers such as Michael Novak and Russell Kirk and at the popular level by leaders such as Moral Majority founder Jerry Falwell (1933–2007) and presidential hopeful Pat Robertson (b. 1930), both of whom were well known as conservative 'televangelists' due to their popular following based on radio and television. Neo-realists were most likely to come from conservative and fundamentalist religious backgrounds in denominations that were taking on a more activist role in response to what they perceived as a 'culture war' in American society between a Christian traditionalism under threat and a growing libertinism and secularism. Christian neo-realists were nationalists who argued that the United States must stand as a moral bulwark in the world. They saw the world in dualistic black and white terms, as a place in which dark forces were arrayed against the United States' freedom, democratic values, and the 'American way'. Whereas Niebuhr advised against an overtly moralistic or crusading American foreign policy, these groups emphasized America's role as a champion of Christian values and civilization and cast political antagonists of the United States as enemies of the good in world politics. Neo-realists had a strong attraction to millenarian and apocalyptic interpretations of world affairs, and a willingness to use armed force against what they perceived as the evil forces of the world. Understanding the creation of Israel in 1948 as a step towards the fulfillment of biblical prophecy (see p. 65), neo-realists were unyielding in their support for the Israeli state and held a critical attitude towards its Arab neighbours. Elsewhere, they denounced communism as a vehicle for atheism and denial of the right to religious freedom.

Christian neo-realism has had an important impact on US foreign policy, especially under Republican presidents from Ronald Reagan to George W. Bush. The extent of its influence at the elite level has been evident in presidential imagery, notably in Reagan's characterization of the Soviet Union as an 'evil empire' and the famous 2002 State of the Union address in which George W. Bush identified certain states as constituting an 'axis of evil'. The heirs of Christian neo-realism in the post–Cold War world have maintained close ties with the Republican party and administration. Although the theme of the communist menace has faded, other threats, such as so-called rogue states like Iran or North Korea, Islamist terrorism, and the prospect of new adversaries in the Middle East or East Asia have taken its place. The increasing radicalization of this wing of conservative Christianity is championed today by prominent religious conservative and fundamentalist personalities such as Rod Parsley and John Hagee.

Neo-idealists, by contrast, were represented in the mainline denominations, in the National Council of Churches, and in the evangelical pacifist community. They generally took a prophetic stance, criticizing traditional American foreign policy and calling for progressive change in the institutions of US democracy. Prominent leaders included the late Richard J. Barnet, the pacifist and Anabaptist scholar John Howard Yoder, and Jim Wallis, the leader of the *Sojourners* community (a critical network of theologians) in Washington, DC. Emboldened by liberation theology, which they applied to American politics, neo-idealists were united by their concern for justice and peace as a focal point in US foreign policy. They rejected the common assumption in American civil religion that the United States is at the centre of God's plan for the world. Instead, they perceived the US to be a flawed superpower in a fallen world in need of significant change. They sought structural transformation of the American economic and political systems and dismantling of the American nuclear arsenal.

At the level of political decision-makers, the Christian neo-idealist camp was represented mainly by a small group within the American left that included people such as former President Jimmy Carter. Christian neo-idealism survived the end of the Cold War, but the successes of the Reagan and Bush administrations in building bridges with the conservative and moderate Christian communities have depleted its ranks. In the later 1980s, with the polarization of American Christendom between the idealist and realist camps, a distinctive new centrist perspective emerged that Wozniuk described as the 'nexus' of those contrasting positions. Others have identified a modernizing movement within American conservative Christianity, often referred to as the 'New Evangelicalism' (Shibley 1998).

New Evangelicalism is a broad-based movement espoused by conservative Protestants and Roman Catholics alike. It includes organizations such as the National Conference of Catholic Bishops, but also the National Association of Evangelicals. Leaders of the movement would come to include a wide spectrum of modern Christian leaders, perhaps most notably the evangelist Billy Graham, the former presidential advisor Charles Colson, the late Roman Catholic priest Richard Neuhaus, megachurch leaders such as Bill Hybels and Rick Warren, and Philip Yancey, editor-at-large of *Christianity Today* magazine. Less ardently political than either the neo-idealists or the neo-realists, New Evangelicals have staked out a position in the territory between the two, characterized by support for a normative Just War tradition that embraces the cautious use of force abroad, a liberal internationalist concern for international development, advocacy of global human rights, and moderate positions on issues such as the Israeli–Palestinian dispute, the arms race, and environmental issues such as climate change.

The Rise of the 'Religious Right'

For all the distinctions among Christians with regard to American foreign policy, on domestic issues fundamentalist and evangelical voters alike favour the Republican Party; this consensus is typically referred to as the 'religious right' in American politics. Disappointed with the presidency of Jimmy Carter in the late 1980s, large numbers of Christian conservatives turned to an emerging right wing that came to be associated above all with two particularly charismatic televangelists and their respective organizations, Jerry Falwell's Moral Majority and Pat Robertson's political and media projects

The Moral Majority was a Christian lobby group founded in 1979 by the conservative Baptist minister and founder of Liberty University Jerry Falwell. The organization was explicitly non-confessional, seeking to bridge the divisions between social conservatives regardless of their specific religious traditions. In the course of the 1980 presidential campaign, the Moral Majority made clear its support for the candidacy of Republican Ronald Reagan, as did a number of traditionally apolitical churches. Though Reagan himself was not committed to the evangelical cause, he deliberately courted the religious lobby. In one particularly significant appearance at a 'religious roundtable' in Dallas on 21 August 1980, Reagan addressed an assembly of approximately 2500 pastors, telling them 'You can't endorse me, but I endorse you' (Martin 1996: 216–17). His public embrace of the growing conservative religious movement marked the beginning of a new era in the interplay of religion and politics. The Moral Majority and other like-minded groups were widely credited with mobilizing the religious conservative constituency for Ronald Reagan in both 1980 and 1984. After the Moral Majority organization closed its doors in 1986, many of its former members went to work for Pat Robertson in his campaign for the Republican nomination in the 1988 election and in so doing preserved some of the institutional strength of the religious conservative movement. Robertson was a businessman who had founded a large-scale media ministry featuring the first major Christian broadcasting outlet, CBN. His bid for the presidency foundered in the primaries, but not before demonstrating the growing organizational strength of the religious conservative movement. At the same time, other publicly oriented Christian organizations emerged that likewise captured much of the American religious community's concerns about social policy. Perhaps the most influential of these was led by Dr James Dobson, a psychologist and prolific author of Christian-oriented advice books on marriage, child-rearing, and family life, who in the late 1970s founded a group called Focus on the Family, based on the success of his pro-discipline child-rearing book *Dare to Discipline*. Despite Robertson's failure to move beyond the 1988 Republican primaries, his organization formed the basis for the creation of a new lobby group known as the Christian Coalition. In the 1990s the political movement of religious conservatives came to cluster around the Christian Coalition and the Washington-based Family Research Council.

The 'religious right' that emerged out of these parallel movements succeeded in mobilizing a key constituency for the Republican party. Together, first Ronald Reagan and then his vice-president, George H.W. Bush, captured strong majorities in three successive election campaigns (1980, 1984, and 1988) at least in part as a result of these alliances. The election of Bill Clinton in 1992 appeared to represent a setback. But the electoral power of religious conservatives was reaffirmed in the mid-term elections of 1994, when the Christian Coalition and allied groups mobilized so much support for conservative candidates that the Republicans gained a majority in Congress for the first time in 40 years. Following the successes of 1994, the 'Christian right' became a central component of the Republican party coalition.

Another part of the story is the cultivation of new relationships between American Protestants and Roman Catholics. Until the late 1970s and early 1980s, Roman Catholics remained outside the conservative movement in American politics. Not only were the majority of American conservatives Protestant, but in many cases their religious affiliation was combined with a militant anti-Catholicism that alienated Roman Catholics and reinforced their identification with the Democratic Party. Nevertheless, in the 1970s and 1980s the religious right began to embrace a more ecumenical spirit that gradually won over many traditionalist Catholics (Reidy 2006). As a result, Republicans running on socially conservative but economically centrist platforms, as both Ronald Reagan and George W. Bush did, have been able to mobilize strong support among Roman Catholics.

On foreign policy issues, the Christian right for the most part shared the positions of the secular 'new right'. These included staunch support for the state of Israel, suspicion of international institutions such as the United Nations and the International Monetary Fund, and promotion of religious freedom in non-Western nations (Martin 1999). In the cases of Israel and the United Nations, the Christian right's positions reflect the eschatological expectations of evangelical and fundamentalist Protestants in particular. Among those expectations is the idea that, according to biblical prophecies, Israel will play a key role in the future unfolding of God's plan and the 'second coming' of Jesus Christ (Weber 2004). The preservation of Israel is therefore seen as important for the unfolding of the divine plan.

Similarly, the 'Left Behind' novels—an astonishingly popular series of novels about the 'Rapture' that believers expect to be part of the second coming—reflect the Christian right's suspicion of multilateral institutions, which they perceive as instruments of demonic intervention in human affairs. These notions have combined with a longstanding tendency towards isolationism to create a realist bias among conservative Christian voters. However, international issues were less likely to mobilize

Box 3.2: The US Conference of Catholic Bishops (UCCB)

The leading formal vehicle for Catholic influence on US social policy is the US Conference of Catholic Bishops, based in Washington, DC. The Conference traces its origins to the National Catholic War Council, founded in 1917 to care for the spiritual needs of American soldiers. At the close of the First World War, a new group, the National Catholic Welfare Council (later Conference), was created in response to Pope Benedict XV's call for Catholics to pursue peace and social justice.

In 1966 the organization was split to separate the ecclesial and secular concerns of Roman Catholics in the US. This created what was called the National Conference of Catholic Bishops, charged with overseeing the affairs of the Church, and the United States Catholic Conference, which addressed a broader array of societal interests and involved lay Catholics as well as clergy and religious. These two organizations were amalgamated as the United States Conference of Catholic Bishops in 2001.

The stated purposes of the UCCB are 'to unify, coordinate, encourage, promote, and carry on Catholic activities in the United States; to organize and conduct religious, charitable and social welfare work at home and abroad; to aid in education; to care for immigrants; and generally to enter into and promote by education, publication and direction the objects of its being'. Over the years, the Conference of Catholic Bishops has been a focal point for Roman Catholic discussion and activism on many important national issues. Lawrence McAndrews (2010: 59–73) describes how the Roman Catholic leadership promoted civil rights through the institutions of the Conference even against some resistance, a stand that was vindicated by the wider support of most American Catholics. Its positions have typically been informed by Catholic teaching on social justice, so that it supports progressive causes such as social welfare programs while working with socially conservative groups on issues such as abortion and same-sex marriage. Reese (1992) argues that the Conference is limited organizationally by its inability to represent the concerns of all American Catholics and by its subordination to the Vatican. Nonetheless, the UCCB remains an important national voice for the Church in US politics.

the socially conservative Republican base than domestic issues such as abortion, school prayer, and (eventually) the public recognition of rights for homosexuals.

When the Republican Party gained control of Congress in the mid-1990s, it was partly because of its appeal to 'values voters'. The Christian Coalition, a political force led by Ralph Reed—a Republican activist who had been involved in Pat Robertson's unsuccessful nomination bid—echoed the Republicans' 'Contract with America' platform with a parallel 'Contract with the American Family'. The Contract included a ten-point plan that was embraced by many in the Republican congress, including support for 'restoring religious equality' through a constitutional amendment that would provide equality rights to religious people, 'school choice' (voucher-style funding for alternative and religious schools), restricting production of pornography, and curtailing federal funding for the arts. The apparent centrality of the Christian Coalition to the success of the Republican campaign in 1994 was a sign that the movement had significant clout and represented the rising force of the 'religious (or Christian) right'.

In 2000, the leaders of the Christian right endorsed the candidacy of George W. Bush partly because of his willingness to accept constraints on abortion and partly because of his overt religiosity. In power, the younger Bush appeared strongly favourable to the increased involvement of religious conservatives in public policy, embracing initiatives such as the funding of faith-based organizations working to rehabilitate inmates in correctional institutions and the provision of other public services. One of his first actions was to restore the so-called 'Mexico City policy' (cancelled by the Clinton administration) under which non-governmental organizations working abroad were ruled ineligible for funding from the United States Agency for International Development if they in any way promoted abortion as a method of family planning; reinstitution of this policy had been a key demand of Conservative religious groups. However, other areas of concern in foreign policy circles did not seem particularly affected by the prominence of religious conservatives in the Bush administration, which reflected the general tendency of the Republican Party to regard multilateral institutions with suspicion while stressing the United States' strategic role abroad.

Onward Christian Soldiers?

The influence of religious perspectives on American foreign policy seemed bound to increase following the terrorist attacks of September 2001. The motivations behind the attacks were primarily political: US support of Israel against Palestinians and the presence of American troops in Saudi Arabia were the main reasons cited. But those issues clearly had religious components, and the attacks themselves seemed to have been designed expressly to foment conflict between Christians and Muslims. Five days after the attacks, amid repeated protestations that individual Muslims had nothing to do with the actions of a radical fringe, President Bush announced that the United States was embarking on a long-term 'crusade' against terrorism. Many American observers were horrified at the choice of words, and the administration hastened to explain that the President's remarks were meant to underline the significance of the struggle against terrorism rather than its religious nature. One editorialist wrote that 'never before has America been brought deeper into a dynamite-wired holy of holies than in our President's war on terrorism' (Carroll 2004).

Through the next few years, the Republican party continued to enjoy strong support within the conservative religious establishment, and the invasion of Iraq in March 2003 was welcomed by many Christian leaders. But many observers were alarmed and disturbed by the prospect of thousands of troops from a majority Christian country occupying a Muslim nation. Some feared that the evangelical fervour of many American Christians would taint the military operation with an unacceptable flavour of colonial-style missionary activity. When an evangelical aid organization called Samaritan's Purse was reported to be joining the relief effort in Iraq, critics drew attention to the optics of a Christian nation seeking to impose a new order on its newly occupied dependency. The criticism only deepened when the organization's founder Franklin Graham (the son of Billy Graham) made cutting comments about Islam in the national media (Waldman 2003). Liberal critics of the relationship between Christian organizations and the presidency warned of 'theocracy and [a] new fascism' (Davidson and Harris 2006).

The Bush administration was re-elected with an increased margin of victory in 2004, and most Christian evangelicals supported the president. The rise of a class of neo-conservatives in power in the White House who differed from traditional conservatives in counselling expansion of a US foreign policy focused on the use of American power to bring about neoliberal economic reforms and democratic change abroad. As a result many saw close links between the 'culture war' rhetoric used by the religious right and the identification of external political opponents of the United States as 'evil' (Kline 2004). The expansive use of American power represented by the Bush Doctrine of preventive war and the increasing human cost of the war in Iraq were already raising concerns within more liberal denominations and even some in the evangelical Christian community in the United States (Avram 2004; Nelson-Pallmeyer 2005; Taylor 2005).

The religious right was entering a new and more radical era in which its leaders were seeking a revival of American religious values at a more foundational level. A series of books published in the wake of the Republicans' 2004 victory raised concern over the degree to which conservative Christian thinking was displacing the bland civil religion that had dominated US policy thinking for most of the country's history (Hedges 2006, Goldberg 2007). According to these perspectives, Christian neo-realist thinking was sliding toward a dangerous sort of theonomy (religious rule) in which the evangelical message of personal conversion was increasingly replaced by a rhetoric of war, fears of persecution by sinister forces that seek the destruction of believers, the demands of a warrior God promising blood and vengeance, and what Hedges (2006: 145) describes as 'a conspicuous and unapologetic infatuation with wealth, power and fame'. Other recent commentators, however, have found that the modern evangelical movement is far more diverse and multifaceted than the 'religious right' label would suggest. After extensive interviews with various evangelical leaders, D. Michael Lindsay argues that the movement attracts bipartisan support and is by no means monolithic. What's more, he suggests that the 'coalitions built by American evangelicals point to an elasticity in their faith that is at odds with conventional wisdom. In fact, this is one of the keys to evangelical influence' (Lindsay 2007: 57).

Seeds of a Middle Way

To a great degree, the successful integration of the religious right into the Washington policy community can be attributed to the movement's increasing sophistication, moderation, and breadth as a force in US politics. It also reflected religious conservatives' general agreement on matters of domestic policy. The situation was not so clear with respect to foreign policy. The divisions between Christian neo-realists, neo-idealists, and centrists remained, although certain concerns led to the formation of new alliances between and among them.

Christian conservatives are proving more likely to unite on the issue of human rights. Allen Hertzke (2003) traces the evolution of a coalition of conservative Christian,

Box 3.3: The US Commission
on International Religious Freedom (USCIRF)

The US Commission on International Religious Freedom was established under the IRFA 'to promote religious freedom as a US foreign policy goal and to combat religious persecution in other countries'. Its creation reflected bipartisan agreement on the importance of religious freedom to American concerns around the world.

The Commission has nine members: three of them appointed by the president, four appointed by the party that does not hold the presidency, and two nominated by the president's party in Congress. Its work is carried out by an ambassador-at-large stationed in the State Department. It is responsible for producing an annual report that identifies states around the world that are held to be 'of particular concern' in their treatment of religious groups, as well as a separate 'watch list' of countries that are judged to require specific monitoring. A list of the 'countries of particular concern' is forwarded to the president, who has the discretion to decide how the American government will respond to concerns expressed in the report. Commission members tend to be religious leaders, experts on religious rights, and scholars of religion.

The work of the Commission has been controversial since the beginning. Its investigation of religious freedom occasionally creates friction with US allies that find their way onto the lists, such as Egypt, Saudi Arabia, and Turkey. Yet, as critics point out, no president has ever chosen to undertake special action against a country 'of particular concern'.

For more information on the commission, consult its website at www.uscirf.gov

Jewish, and secular leaders in favour of religious freedoms in the later 1990s. By the late 1990s, this broad-based coalition was having an impact. It successfully lobbied Congress to adopt an International Religious Freedom Act (IRFA) in 1998. The IRFA mandated the creation of the US Commission on International Religious Freedom to elaborate on the US State Department's annual reportage on human rights practices throughout the globe and required it to advise the administration on how to deal with violations of religious rights.

In the wake of the passage of the IRFA, the coalition continued to pursue its interest in humanitarian action in the developing world. A campaign for action on human rights violations in the Sudan particularly dominated discussions in 2005 and 2006, pushing for presidential and congressional action that led to diplomatic initiatives to end the Darfur conflict. Likewise, the National Association of Evangelicals and various ad hoc groups in the evangelical Christian community called for a more active policy to control greenhouse gas emissions in 2006. While evangelicals are unlikely to challenge such basic principles of American foreign policy as support for the state of Israel, they are having an effect in the area of 'humanitarian and human rights policies, . . . altering priorities and methods while increasing overall support for both foreign aid and the defense of human rights' (Mead 2006).

Meanwhile, the long decline in Christian conservative support for the Democratic party that followed the Carter presidency appeared to be reversing to some degree in the years leading up to 2008. Both of the leading candidates for the Democratic nomination, Barack Obama and Hillary Clinton, made deliberate efforts to bridge the 'God gap', as did many evangelicals in the Democratic camp (Rosin 2007: 38–9). Furthermore, the absence of an obvious ally for the religious right among the main contenders suggested a certain erosion of their influence in presidential politics. One candidate for the Republican nomination, Mitt Romney, posed a problem for

Rick Warren, pastor of Saddleback Church, a 'megachurch' in Irvine, California, has become a leading figure in American evangelicalism based in part on the success of his bestselling book The Purpose-Driven Life. Warren's social and religious activism, which combines middle-class community and life ministry with global interest in problems such as AIDS in Africa, make him exemplary of new directions in American social Christianity.
Source: Alex Wong/Getty Images for Meet the Press

many social conservatives: as a member of the Church of Jesus Christ of Latter-day Saints (Mormons), he was considered suspect by mainstream Christians. Many social conservatives gathered around former Arkansas governor Mike Huckabee, but he was unable to attract sufficient support. Although Republican nominee John McCain deliberately sought to cultivate support among social conservatives, he was widely mistrusted, having referred to certain religious leaders as 'agents of intolerance' prior to the 2000 contest. However, his choice of Alaska governor Sarah Palin, a self-described 'hockey mom' and a very public evangelical, as his running mate provided the balance necessary and simultaneously reinvigorated the religious constituency's interest in the Republican party.

A growing sense that the concerns of Christian conservatives were broad enough to span the divide between the two leading political parties suggested that a new politics of religion might be emerging. A newly prominent figure in the evangelical camp, California megachurch pastor Rick Warren, made a point of hosting both presidential candidates for a 'civil forum' in August 2008 at which he engaged in fireside-style conversations with both men. Even though Warren later endorsed Republican candidate John McCain, President-elect Obama asked him to deliver the prayer at his inauguration in January 2009. In many ways Warren represents a new perspective in the evangelical community. He has been actively engaged in international initiatives to address the problem of AIDS in Africa and generally avoids the strident partisanship that characterized the politics of Christian conservatives of the 1980s and 1990s.

In addition, the growth of the Latino population in the United States is having an important impact on the relationship between religion and American political culture. While many Latino voters share the conservative social mores and theological views of their religious traditions (Roman Catholic and charismatic Protestant), this does not necessarily mean that they take conservative positions on either domestic or

Table 3.1 Americans by Religious Affiliation, 2007

Evangelical Protestant	26.3%
Roman Catholic	23.9%
Mainline Protestant	18.1%
Unaffiliated (incl. atheist/agnostic)	16.1%
'Historically Black' churches	6.9%
Mormon	1.7%
Jewish	1.7%
Buddhist	0.7%
Muslim	0.6%
Other/Don't know	4.0%

Source: U.S. Religious Landscape Survey, 2007. http://religions.pewforum.org/affiliations

foreign policy. Kelly and Morgan (2008) demonstrate that Latino voters behave quite differently from their Western European counterparts in this respect.

Barack Obama came to the presidency with a new interest in engaging American religious voters. Unlike many of his Democratic colleagues, he has not shied away from embracing American civil religion, and he openly described his experience of conversion to Christianity in his book *The Audacity of Hope* (2006). Obama's multicultural background and Muslim ancestors on his father's side have added to the complexity of religious politics in the United States. He has quietly courted a variety of religious groups by expressing a positive view of the public role that religion can play. At the same time, he has earned the opposition of the Christian right through his reversal of Bush-era initiatives such as the Mexico City policy. The rising tide of criticism surrounding the issue of public health insurance and the ongoing economic crisis in 2010 has encouraged the formation of new conservative groups, most significantly the 'Tea Party' movement, which combines fiscal and social libertarianism with a strongly Christian-nationalist streak.

Other Religions and US Politics

This chapter's focus on the influence of Christian groups in US politics reflects the fact that the vast majority of Americans identify themselves as Christians of one variety or another. Yet the United States is clearly a pluralist nation that has increasingly embraced people of other faith groups, especially in recent years.

Muslims have been a part of American public life since the beginning of immigration from areas such as South Asia and the Middle East, but they have also grown as a force within the African-American community. The events of 11 September 2001 were both a challenge to the rapidly growing numbers of US Muslims and a spur to more active involvement in American political life (Saeed 2002). Over the past decade, an increasingly devoted and influential network of Muslim lobby groups has developed. Among the more prominent organizations are the Islamic Society of North America and the Council on American–Islamic Relations. Founded in 1994, by 2011 the latter had 32 chapters across 20 states, dedicated primarily to responding to complaints regarding mistreatment of Muslim Americans and defending their civil rights. At the same time, Muslim Americans generally have been increasingly proactive in representing their community through dialogue and consciousness-raising. There have been no indications that Muslim Americans as a group identify themselves with any particular party (Barreto and Bozonelos 2009).

The history of Jewish American involvement in US politics reflects the diversity of US politics more broadly. Jewish Americans are by and large assimilated and are represented in both major political parties and display a variety of attitudes toward foreign policy (Wald and Williams 2006). Jewish Americans have frequently served as elected representatives at the state and congressional levels, and Senator Joseph Lieberman became the first Jewish American to run for the vice-presidency on the Democratic ticket in 2000. American-Jewish interest in Israel is obviously significant. One of the best-financed and best-organized lobbies in the United States is the conservative pro-Israel American Israel Public Affairs Committee (AIPAC), founded in the 1950s. A rival group, J Street, established in 2008, professes to be both pro-Israel and pro-peace. But support for Israel is hardly confined to Jewish Americans.

The clustering of ethnic and religious communities has meant that religious minorities have particular impact in specific areas of the United States. For example, the concentration of Arab Americans in southern Michigan, Jewish Americans in New York, and Latter-day Saints (Mormons) in the American southwest has given those communities considerable political influence in their respective regions. Mormons represent an interesting case in the sense that they are widely suspected by mainline and evangelical Christians. While Mormons are typically close to these groups in their positions on social and 'compassionate conservative' issues, Mormon candidates have not been widely embraced by the wider Christian conservative movement, as demonstrated by the case of Mitt Romney, the New England Mormon who ran for the Republican nomination in 2008 (Baker and Campbell 2010).

Thus the extent to which religious minorities have actually been embraced in the United States remains in question. During the 2008 Presidential campaign, Barack Obama was criticized not only for his association with a radical Christian minister, but also on the—mistaken—grounds that he was a Muslim (Hollander 2010: 64). As president, Obama has been forced to combat the misperception of his own religious faith. Nevertheless, he recognized the concern that US actions in the Middle East and South Asia have raised among Muslims worldwide in his 2009 Cairo speech announcing a 'new beginning' in relations with the Muslim world. While Obama's reluctance to be associated with Islam has occasionally grated on Muslim Americans, the administration's recent efforts at outreach have been appreciated (Elliott 2010).

Conclusion

It may be useful in conclusion to restate that the purpose of the constitutional separation of church and state in the US was to provide the greatest scope possible for religious freedom and diversity. Perhaps it is not surprising, then, that religion has come to play such a prominent role in American public life. The United States has embraced individualistic and entrepreneurial religion in such a way that churches, religious sects, and religious organizations and lobbies have managed to innovate and continue to claim the hearts and minds of individual Americans. The early development of an evangelical and democratic culture that came to be associated with the mission of the United States has created a moralistic and missionary civil religion that Americans have come to claim as a part of their national identity. This civil religion is based on broadly Christian beliefs that contribute to the contending demands of social justice and moral perfectionism, and often flow out of a linear view of history. American public religion has given a pluralistic religious community a shared sense of America's role in the world that is profoundly religious in nature. As a result, American politics combines official secularism with the active involvement of religious groups, and religion has remained important to American politics throughout the nation's history.

Review Questions

1. What three themes cited in this chapter help to explain the role that religion plays in US politics?
2. How has the concept of 'civil religion' been applied in the case of the United States?
3. What were the roots of the liberal and conservative political traditions among Christians in the United States?
4. In what ways did religious conservatives influence American politics in the 1980s?
5. How has the American religious right been criticized by observers and opponents?
6. How have the politics of American evangelicalism changed over the past few decades? In what respects have they stayed the same?
7. What minority religious groups have had an impact on American politics and what have they accomplished?

Sources and Further Reading

Avram, Wes, ed. (2004). *Anxious About Empire*. Grand Rapids: Brazos Press.

Baker, Sherry, and Joel Campbell (2010). 'Mitt Romney's Religion: A Five-Factor Model for Analysis of Media Representation of Mormon Identity'. *Journal of Media and Religion* 9, 2: 99–121.

Barreto, Matt A. and Dino N. Bozonelos (2009). 'Democrat, Republican, or None of the Above? The Role of Religiosity in Muslim American Party Identification'. *Politics and Religion* 2: 200–29.

Bebbington, David W. (1992). *Evangelicalism in Modern Britain: A History from 1730s to the 1980s*. Grand Rapids, MI: Baker Book House.

Bellah, Robert (1967). 'Civil Religion in America'. *Daedalus* 96: 1–21.

Carroll, James (2004). 'The Bush Crusade'. *The Nation*. September 20: 14–22.

Chaplin, Jonathan (2010). *God and Global Order: The Power of Religion in American Foreign Policy*. Waco, TX: Baylor University Press.

Chappell, David L. (2004). *A Stone of Hope: Prophetic Religion and the Death of Jim Crow*. Chapel Hill: UNC Press.

Davidson, Carl, and Jerry Harris (2006). 'Globalisation, Theocracy and the New Fascism: The US Right's Rise to Power'. *Race and Class* 47, 3: 47–67.

Dorrien, Gary (1995). *Soul in Society*. Minneapolis: Fortress Press.

Dyck, John, Paul Rowe, and Jens Zimmermann, eds. (2010). *Politics and the Religious Imagination*. London: Routledge.

Elliott, Andrea (2010). 'White House Quietly Courts Muslims in US'. *New York Times*. 18 April.

Goldberg, Michelle (2007). *Kingdom Coming: The Rise of Christian Nationalism*. New York: W.W. Norton.

Hedges, Chris (2006). *American Fascists: The Christian Right and the War on America*. New York: Free Press.

Hertzke, Allen (2004). *Freeing God's Children: The Unlikely Alliance for Global Human Rights*. Lanham, MD: Rowman & Littlefield.

Hollander, Barry A. (2010). 'Persistence in the Perception of Barack Obama as a Muslim in the 2008 Presidential Campaign'. *Journal of Media and Religion* 9, 2: 55–66.

Kelly, Nathan J., and Jana Morgan (2008). 'Religious Traditionalism and Latino Politics in the United States'. *American Politics Research* 36, 2: 236–63.

Kline, Scott (2004). 'The Culture War Gone Global: "Family Values" and the Shape of US Foreign Policy', *International Relations* 18, no.4, 453–66.

Lindsay, D. Michael (2007). *Faith in the Halls of Power*. Oxford: Oxford University Press.

MacAndrews, Lawrence (2010). 'Agents of Change: Lyndon Johnson, Catholics, and Civil Rights'. Pp. 59–73 in Dyck, Rowe, and Zimmermann, eds (2010).

Martin, William (1996). *With God on Our Side: The Rise of the Religious Right in America*. New York: Broadway Books.

———(1999). 'The Christian Right and American Foreign Policy'. *Foreign Policy* 114: 66–80.

Mead, Walter Russell (2006). 'God's Country?' *Foreign Affairs* 85, 5: 24–43.

Monsma, Stephen V. and J. Christopher Soper (1997). *The Challenge of Pluralism: Church and State in Five Democracies*. Lanham, MD: Rowman and Littlefield.

Nelson-Pallmeyer, Jack (2005). *Saving Christianity from Empire*. New York: Continuum.

Niebuhr, Reinhold (1944). *The Children of Light and Darkness: A Vindication of Democracy and a Critique of its Traditional Defense*. New York: Scribner.

———(1960). *Moral Man and Immoral Society*. New York: Scribner.

Reese, Thomas J. (1992). *A Flock of Shepherds: The National Conference of Catholic Bishops*. Lanham, MD: Rowman & Littlefield.

Reidy, Maurice Timothy (2006). 'Who Owns the "Catholic Vote"?', *Sojourners*, June.

Rosin, Hanna (2007). 'Closing the God Gap'. *The Atlantic*, January–February: 38–9.

Saeed, Agha (2002). 'The American Muslim Paradox'. In Yvonne Yazbeck Haddad and Jane I. Smith, eds. *Muslim Minorities in the West: Visible and Invisible*. Walnut Creek, CA; Altamira Press.

Shibley, Mark A. (1998). 'Contemporary Evangelicals: Born-Again and World Affirming'. In Wade Clark Roof, ed., *Americans and Religions in the Twenty-First Century: Annals of the American Academy of Political and Social Science*. Thousand Oaks: Sage, 67–87.

Sittser, Gerald L. (1997). *A Cautious Patriotism: the American Churches and the Second World War*. Chapel Hill, NC: University of North Carolina Press.

Taylor, Mark Lewis (2005). *Religion, Politics, and the Religious Right*. Minneapolis: Fortress Press.

Tocqueville, Alexis de (1945 [1835–40]). *Democracy in America*. New York: Vintage Books.

Wald, Kenneth (1994). 'The Religious Dimension of American Anti-Communism'. *Journal of Church and State* 36, 3: 483–506.

Wald, Kenneth, and Bryan D. Williams (2006). 'American Jews and Israel: the Sources of Politicized Ethnic Identity'. *Nationalism and Ethnic Politics* 12, 2: 205–37.
Waldman, Stephen (2003). 'Jesus in Baghdad'. *Slate*. 11 April: http://www.slate.com/id/2081432/
Weber, Timothy (2004). *On the Road to Armageddon*. Grand Rapids: Baker Academic.
Wozniuk, Vladimir (1988). 'The Contemporary Christian Debate Over America's "Mission" in World Affairs'. *Journal of Church and State* 30, 3: 493–514.
Wuthnow, Robert (1988). *The Restructuring of American Religion*. Princeton: Princeton University Press.

Web Resources

www.pewforum.org – The Pew Forum on Religion and Public Life.

www.religioninamerica.org – Religion in America collaborative blog.

www.sojo.net – Sojourners.

www.thearda.com – The Association of Religion Data Archives.

Chapter 4

Judaism, Zionism, and Israeli Politics

Israel today is a nominally secular, democratic, and pluralist state. Yet religion is in a sense the very reason for the state's existence, and the sacred significance of the land it claims means that religion plays an extremely important role both in the internal dynamics of Israeli politics and in Israeli foreign policy. In addition, Israeli foreign policy needs to respond to challenges that arise from religious movements inside the state. It also responds to religious pressures that influence foreign nations in their dealings with the Israeli state. The conflict that has developed over the past century between Israel and its Arab neighbours is rooted in conflicting and seemingly irreconcilable claims to a land that two peoples consider a divine gift to themselves alone.

At the same time, there is a danger that Israeli politics and the politics of the Arab–Israeli conflict may come to be 'overdetermined' by religion (Bunzl 2004: 2). The religious dimension is so central in the case of Israel that it is easy to underestimate the importance of other factors. The conflict over the land of Palestine, for instance, is in part a consequence of the incomplete process of decolonization after the British mandate dating back to the 1930s and 1940s. Another factor was the Nazi Holocaust, which killed six million Jews and turned many of the survivors into refugees. Finally, there is the essential problem of dividing a narrow strip of land with limited resources between two peoples. Still, even when the influence of other factors is recognized, we cannot fully understand Israeli foreign policy and the Israeli state's relations with its neighbours, friends, and foes if we do not take the religious dimension into account.

The most obvious reason that religion plays such a central role in Israeli foreign policy is the fact that the land the state occupies is holy to three of the world's great religious traditions. As one scholar puts it, 'the sacredness of the space is the subject and the object of the dispute [over land in Palestine] for millions of people' (Johnston 2003: 94). Discussions of the Israeli state, whether among Jews, Muslims, or Christians, are often fraught with religious memories, conflicting ideas of sacred terrain, and deep feeling for the holy land.

For the Jewish people, the land of Israel—*Eretz Yisrael* in Hebrew—has been at the centre of their religious tradition since biblical times, when God is said to have promised the Hebrew patriarch Abraham that his descendants would someday have that land for their own. When the idea of establishing a new state for the Jewish people of Europe was first proposed, in the late nineteenth century, the religious significance of the ancient land of Israel made it an obvious choice. Another important complication of the Israeli case is that Judaism is not just a religion: it is also an ethnic identity. Distinctive cultural traditions rooted in the religion—including holidays, dietary restrictions, and modes of dress—clearly distinguished Jewish society from others. At the same time, the egregious bias against Jews in those other societies gave them a strong sense of the need for solidarity within the Jewish community, as well as a deep suspicion that the world outside could not be trusted. The blurring of the boundaries between religious faith and ethnic community is rarely more instructive or problematic than in the modern state of Israel.

Finally, the structure of Israeli electoral institutions and the plurality of religious sects in the Israeli state mean that religious parties, both radical and mainstream, have significant power. Israeli elections are conducted according to a strict proportional representation scheme that allows even small parties representation in the **Knesset** (parliament). This has created a fractured and factionalized system in which mainstream parties of the left, right, or centre must seek out compromises and alliances with less popular parties in order to govern. Thus even though the modern Israeli state is largely secular in its orientation, small religious communities are able to have a far greater political impact than their numbers would appear to warrant.

A Brief History of Zionism

The quest for an Israeli state began in the context of the development of state nationalisms in nineteenth-century Europe. With the decline of the old Hapsburg and Ottoman empires, several newly independent countries emerged out of their constituent nationalities, from Hungary, Austria, and Czechoslovakia to the Arab states of the Middle East. At the same time, nations such as Germany and Italy were unifying under a single nationalist banner. These political developments stimulated nationalist sentiments in countries around the world, including the colonial dependencies of the Great Powers of Europe. In the case of the Jewish people of Europe and Asia, the early worldwide movement toward nationalism summoned up ancient memories of a time when they had their own homeland.

Over the centuries, Jewish people had more than once been forced out of their homeland in Palestine to form small communities in exile. The first diaspora (dispersion, scattering) followed the Babylonian conquest of Jerusalem in 586 BCE, when the leaders of the Israelites were sent as captives to Babylon. When Babylon in turn fell to the Persians, half a century later, the exiles were able to return home. But not all of them did. Many of them chose to remain in Babylon, and many other Jews willingly migrated in pursuit of trade and economic opportunities. In the early years of the Common Era, two failed rebellions against Palestine's Roman rulers, in 70 and 132, are believed to have led to massive outflows of Jews fleeing Roman persecution. Those who stayed in the Middle East, forming important Jewish communities in places such as Babylonia (modern Iraq) and Persia (Iran), came to be known as **Mizrahim** (from the Hebrew for 'east'). But many eventually moved west and north.

By the eleventh century, Jewish communities had been established throughout central Europe, but they often faced intense persecution; in 1096, for example, Jewish communities in the Rhineland region were attacked by crusaders on their way to the Holy Land. In time, those communities moved farther east and the people came to be known as **Ashkenazim** (from a Hebrew term referring to Europe). Meanwhile, numerous other Jews had settled in what are now Portugal and especially Spain. For centuries they lived under Muslim rule in relative peace and prosperity. With the completion of the Christian *reconquista* of Spain, however, these **Sephardim** (from the Hebrew for 'Spain') were expelled and forced into exile throughout the Mediterranean region. Although the Mizrahim share enough cultural and religious traditions with the Sephardim that the two are often treated as a single group under the 'Sephardim' name, the differences between them and the Ashkenazim are striking. The ethno-cultural divisions between the two groups can still be seen in the modern state of Israel.

Box 4.1: Historical Timeline

586 BCE Hebrew leaders exiled to Babylon. When return to Judea becomes possible, in 538, some Jews return and some do not.

66–70 CE The First Jewish Revolt against the Roman occupation of Palestine. The victorious Romans destroy the temple in Jerusalem and force many Jews to flee their homeland.

72 Masada falls. Jewish rebels under siege at the fortress of Masada take their own lives rather than surrender to Roman forces.

132–36 Second Jewish Revolt, led by Simon Bar Kokhba. Roman authorities expel all Jews from Jerusalem, driving many into exile.

1096 The First Crusade. Crusaders attack the Jewish people living in the Rhineland region of central Europe, beginning a long tradition of mob violence directed against European Jews.

1478 The Spanish Inquisition instituted. Jews and Muslims are compelled to convert to Christianity or leave Spain.

1880s Pogroms in Russia. Organized attacks on Jewish communities force growing numbers of Jews to leave.

1894 Dreyfus Affair. A French army captain of Jewish descent is framed and falsely convicted of treason.

1897 First Zionist Congress. Jewish nationalists meet to discuss the establishment of a Jewish state.

1917 The Balfour Declaration. The British government announces its interest in establishing a national home for the Jewish people in Palestine.

1938 Kristallnacht. On 9–10 November 1938, German authorities, paramilitaries, and civilians stage widespread attacks on Jews throughout the country. Many Jews are detained in concentration camps.

1939–45 The Second World War. Nazis dominate Europe and attempt to commit genocide against the Jewish people; six million are killed in the Holocaust (known in Hebrew as the **Shoah**).

1946 King David Hotel bombing. On 22 July, offices of the British Mandatory Authority in Palestine are bombed by the *Irgun Tsvai Leumi*, a radical Zionist movement.

1948 Israeli Declaration of Independence. Labour leader David Ben-Gurion declares the Israeli state on 14 May.

1967 Six Day War. Israel launches a pre-emptive attack on its Arab neighbours, taking the Sinai, the Gaza Strip, the West Bank, and the Golan Heights. The victory opens the way for the construction of Jewish settlements in the occupied territories.

1973 Yom Kippur War. Israel defends itself from attacks by neighbouring Arab states.

1982 War in Lebanon. Israeli forces invade Lebanon to root out the Palestine Liberation Organization.

1993 Oslo Accords. Israeli and Palestinian leaders sign the Declaration of Principles.

1994 Attack in Hebron. Israeli settler Baruch Goldstein murders 29 Palestinians at prayer in mosque on 25 February.

1995 Assassination of Yitzhak Rabin. The Prime Minister of Israel is killed by Yigal Amir, a religious radical, on 4 November.

Across Europe, the expansion of democratic suffrage and a general trend toward secularization in the 1800s led to the lifting of various legal restrictions that had prevented Jews from participating in the broader societies around them and in some cases had confined them to separate communities ('ghettos'). Official emancipation gave Jews access to modern education, literature, and travel. Not all embraced Western culture, but many did, becoming known as 'assimilated' Jews.

Yet within a few decades anti-Semitism became a major issue in France, when Alfred Dreyfus, an army captain of Jewish descent, was falsely accused of treason. Convicted in 1894, he spent six years in a penal colony and was not exonerated until 1906, even though the evidence proving that he was framed had been available 10 years earlier. Together, the anti-Semitism revealed by the Dreyfus affair and the injustice to which Dreyfus was subjected by the French courts persuaded many Jews that assimilation was no guarantee of freedom from persecution. Many were convinced that the only way to ensure security for their people was to establish a sanctuary in a state of their own.

Even prior to the Dreyfus Affair, some European Jews had begun discussing the possibility of establishing a state where Jewish people might thrive without fear of persecution. Many of these groups sought to achieve a centuries-old dream of returning to the historic land of Israel and so an increasing number of Jews settled in areas of

Theodor Herzl, a Jewish journalist of Austrian origin, is widely known as the founder of modern Zionism, though he built upon the work of prior Jewish nationalists. His book *Der Judenstaat*, published in 1896, proved the impetus for the convening of the first World Zionist Congress in Basel, Switzerland, in 1897.
Source: © Bettmann/Corbis

Galilee, Jerusalem, and other historic Jewish communities. Organized pogroms on Jews in Russia in 1881 and 1882 motivated large numbers of Jews to follow those early settlers in what is now referred to as the first *Aliya* (migration). Known collectively as the *Yishuv*, the early (pre-1948) settlers began the process of resurrecting the ancient Hebrew language under the leadership of Eliezer Ben-Yehuda. In 1896, a Viennese journalist by the name of Theodor Herzl published a book calling for a political solution to what was termed the 'Jewish problem': the inability of Western states to peacefully integrate Jewish people. This book, known by its German title *Der Judenstaat* ('The Jewish State'), stimulated a groundswell of support for the Zionist movement (named for the mount in Jerusalem where God was said to dwell). A network of Jewish political movements came together in 1897 to hold the First Zionist Congress in Basel, Switzerland, at which the World Zionist Organization was established with Herzl as its first president.

Over the next several years, leaders of the World Zionist Organization lobbied the imperial governments of the day to consider the Jewish desire for a homeland. Palestine was the preferred location, but early efforts to reach an agreement with the Ottoman Empire, which controlled the territory, were unsuccessful. As a result the Zionists focused their efforts on influencing the British government. With the outbreak of the First World War, British designs to occupy the territory of Palestine renewed the Zionists' hopes. As a result of Zionist lobbying, in the famous 'Balfour Declaration' of 1917 the British Cabinet assured Baron Rothschild (the major financier of Jewish settlement in Palestine) of its support for Jewish settlements in Palestine:

> His majesty's government views with favour the establishment in Palestine of a national home for the Jewish people, and will use their best endeavours to facilitate the achievement of this object, it being clearly understood that nothing shall be done which may prejudice the civil and religious rights of existing non-Jewish communities in Palestine or the rights and political status enjoyed by Jews in any other country.

Jews around the world embraced the Balfour Declaration as a sign of Britain's commitment to the future creation of a Jewish state. But the ambiguities suggested by the reference to a 'national home' rather than a 'state' and the promise not to prejudice the rights of non-Jewish communities were deliberate. Following the British conquest of Palestine at the end of the First World War, the League of Nations gave Britain a 'mandate' to administer the territory. Over the next two decades, the British authorities managed to infuriate both the Arab and the Jewish residents of Palestine by their obfuscation.

Meanwhile, the ranks of the *Yishuv* continued to grow. Beginning in the early 1900s, a second wave of Jewish settlers, motivated by socialist ideals, founded many collective farms known as *kibbutzim*, and agencies of the Zionist movement, in particular the Jewish National Fund, raised funds to purchase land in Palestine, in order to increase the amount of property under Jewish control. The British authorities provided varying levels of access to settlement, changing their policy from year to year, but throughout the 1920s and 1930s, Jewish residents of the mandate increased in number and created several political organizations, the most important of which was the Labour Zionist movement.

According to Lacquer, the Labour Zionists combined 'a strong romantic-mystical element' with 'a belief in historical materialism' (Lacquer 2003: 279). Its members were less interested in reviving ancient religious traditions than in promoting a nationalistic sense of Jewish belonging. On the other hand, more traditional and conservative religious Jews favoured compromise with the British authorities. Some of the more

Box 4.2: Jewish Religious Sects

Haredim
Haredim (literally, 'those who tremble in fear') are often described by outsiders as 'ultra-orthodox'. Internally divided into several sects (among them the Hasidim), Haredi Jews conform to specific types of dress, religiously follow the **Halakha** (Jewish legal code) as interpreted by their own rabbis, and tend to live in closed enclaves where they are able to enforce conservative traditions and strict Sabbath observance. They trace the origins of their tradition to a variety of messianic reformist groups that emerged mainly in Eastern Europe in the eighteenth and nineteenth centuries.

Orthodox
Modern Orthodox Jewish groups are diverse. They are united primarily by their rejection of the more modern and liberal forms of Judaism. They affirm the literal truth of the Hebrew scriptures and seek to live in fairly strict obedience to Halakha as defined by their rabbis. Conservative in their practice, the Orthodox are the religious establishment of Israel.

Reform
Reform Judaism is a liberal movement that accepts the validity of modern textual criticism and takes a philosophical view of the Torah as written by men rather than God. It embraces the modern world, including modern understandings of women's roles, and sees the Jewish way of life as a life of service to the world. Reform Judaism is the dominant form in the Americas.

Conservative
Conservative Judaism is a twentieth-century movement that developed as a middle way between the Orthodox and Reform schools. Conservatives preserve Jewish traditions relatively intact but do not subscribe to a fundamentalist or monolithic understanding of Halakha. In the Conservative interpretation, God remains interested in human affairs and the law should be adapted to modern needs. Although Conservatives reject some of the more liberal ideas of Reform Judaism, their approach is evolutionary.

Reconstructionist
Reconstructionism is a modern offshoot of Conservative Judaism that seeks to preserve elements of traditional Jewish culture but does not consider the Halakha to be binding and rejects the idea that the Jews are God's chosen people. Reconstructionists maintain that individual autonomy takes priority over the community. Reconstructionist theologies vary, but most tend towards the deist perspective, according to which God is not known through personal revelation but exists as a force outside the realm of human understanding.

assertive secular Zionists feared that the British would turn against the *Yishuv*. This group eventually broke away from the labour movement and formed what came to be known as the revisionist faction, a more aggressive and militant nationalist group. We will return to these political divisions later.

In the 1930s both the Zionists and the Arab population of Palestine began to demand independence from British rule. But the British authorities were unable to find a way of dividing power among the Jews and Arabs despite concerted efforts. Amid growing uncertainty over the future, Jewish factions formed paramilitary units in the late 1930s to defend Jewish settlements against both Arab Palestinians and British authorities.

In the wake of the Second World War, the experience of the Holocaust, known in Hebrew as the Shoah, had a galvanizing effect on world public opinion and on the urgency of the Zionist project. The existence of a huge Jewish refugee population in Europe and the widespread desire among Jews for a national home in Palestine put new pressure on the British authorities to come up with a solution that the Arab Palestinians—who feared they would be outnumbered by immigrants in their own homeland—could accept.

Increasingly unable to manage the conflict and impose a peaceful settlement, the British authorities submitted the question of the future governance of Palestine to a United Nations Special Commission (UNSCOP) in 1947. UNSCOP recommended that Palestine be divided into two states, one for the Jews and one for the Arab Palestinians. While the Zionists embraced the recommendation as their best hope, the Arabs would not accept the prospect of divided sovereignty over a land that had belonged to their own forefathers for many generations. In May 1948, with the departure of the British authorities, the Zionists declared the independence of the state of Israel and the first Arab–Israeli war began.

Dimensions of Zionism to 1948

As mentioned above, the Zionist movement was primarily secular and nationalist in nature, not religious. In fact, more ardently religious Jews were critical of the Zionist program from the beginning. Orthodox and Haredi Jews tended to see the Zionist movement as usurping the role that only the divine should play in restoring Jews to the land of Palestine. This did not prevent Orthodox Jews from settling in Palestine: large numbers of Haredi and Orthodox settlers arrived over the years, awaiting the fulfillment of divine providence. But the Haredim (those in Eastern Europe in particular) created a distinctive society of their own that rejected most of the nationalistic and political claims of the secular Zionists in the land of Israel. Today, many of these groups take an antagonistic view of the secular state and reject the idea that modern Israel is a fulfillment of religious prophecy.

Nevertheless, a small religious Zionist movement did develop in both Europe and Palestine in the early twentieth century. Known as *Mizrahi* (an acronym for 'spiritual centre', not to be confused with the term now used to identify Jews of eastern origin), it represented the Orthodox proponents of Zionism who sought to make Halakhic observances (e.g., kosher dietary restrictions) the law of the land in Israel. A rival organization known as *Agudat Israel* (Union of Israel) was formed by Haredi groups opposed to secular Zionism in 1912. Over the years, *Agudat Israel* walked a fine line between questioning the legitimacy of Israeli political institutions and participating in the politics of the *Yishuv*. Lacquer (2003) sketches the process by which the Haredi party gradually became a part of the wider politics of the new Zionist state as 'its leaders realised that the future of Judaism in Eretz Israel depended on Agudist support for the Jewish community and the extraction of maximal advantages for the faith in exchange for displays of solidarity' (413).

Outside the religious sector, secular Zionist leaders envisioned the state of Israel as a sanctuary for a persecuted people and deliberately avoided defining the nation in strictly theocratic terms. The largest and most dominant political faction of the Zionist movement was **Avodah**, the political party of the Labour Zionist movement. The Labour Zionist organization dominated the ranks of the Jewish defence forces known as the *hagana* and the political life of the Zionist movement. Its charismatic leader David Ben-Gurion (1886–1973) became the first prime minister of Israel. A second faction, the Revisionists, formed under the leadership of Ze'ev Jabotinsky (1880–1940) in 1925. The Revisionist faction sought the creation of an independent Israeli state through more aggressive means. It included a militant youth wing known as Betar and later created its own militia, the *Irgun Tsvai Leumi* or *Etzel* (National Military Organization). In the late 1930s and throughout the 1940s the *Irgun* led attacks against both Arab Palestinians and the British authorities. With the creation of the state of Israel in 1948 the Revisionist movement fragmented into a group of political parties that by 1973 had united to form the modern Likud party.

While neither of the two major Zionist factions envisioned a state that would be defined by its religion, the governing Labour movement sought to win the cooperation of religious Zionists by giving an Orthodox flavour to Israel's laws. Thus to this day, strict Sabbath closure laws prohibit most businesses from operating between sundown on Friday and sundown on Saturday. Orthodox rabbis were granted the right to control marriage and divorce laws. Civil marriage is not recognized by the state. Students in Orthodox seminaries, known as *yeshivot* (the plural of **yeshiva**), were exempted from the military service required of most citizens over the age of 18. By making these concessions to the Orthodox Jewish community, the Labour establishment gained their acquiescence to the Zionist project, and over the years this has contributed to a broader acceptance of the Israeli state. Today many of the most ardent Israeli nationalists are observant Orthodox Jews.

Political and Ethnic Divisions in the State of Israel

With the declaration of Israeli independence in 1948, the various strands of Zionism formed the basis for the political movements of the modern state of Israel. Each of the three general political perspectives outlined above (religious, labour, and revisionist) remained, but it is important to understand that Israeli politics continued to be strongly factionalized, with various groups representing smaller branches of the different Zionist movements. To this day, electoral politics in Israel is characterized by fluid factional movement between and among the larger families of political Zionism. This has been no less true of the religious Zionist factions than of the mainstream labour and revisionist factions, as we will see.

After leading the war for independence in 1948, the Labour movement forced the revisionist factions to acquiesce to the unification of the Israeli military under the banner of its **Hagana** militia, to eliminate rival military challengers to the state. Labour became the dominant party in post-independence Israel and remained the most popular stream of Zionism until the mid-1970s. Labour officially supported a secular and modernizing Israeli state, but it courted the religious constituency by providing a special place for Orthodox rabbis in determining marriage and citizenship rights. According to Rabkin, Labour Prime Minister David Ben-Gurion wanted to use the Haredi and Orthodox factions for the purposes of legitimization: 'religion could be made to serve the Zionist cause, preserving the Jewish people spread among the nations, but it certainly had no independent function' (Rabkin 2006:117). Nonetheless, as their support declined in favour of other factions, various Labour leaders sought to ensure the support of the religious parties. Opposition movements included the religious parties and the revisionists who were originally represented by the Herut Party.

The religious parties were divided by the ideological implications of their spiritual perspectives on the Israeli state. Ravitzky argues that the experience of the Shoah had had an important impact on the religious camp, reinforcing both positive and negative attitudes toward the Zionist project (1996: 38). Most of the religious Zionists of *Mizrahi* (later renamed the National Religious Party or *Mafdal*) believed that the hoped-for restoration of Israel as part of the messianic kingdom might be achieved through the auspices of the modern state. Haredi supporters of Agudat Israel, by contrast, held that the Israeli state had 'no particular Jewish significance', but favoured cooperating with other Jewish people over relying on the good will of other nations (Rabkin 2006: 53–4). A very small faction, including the group known as *Neturei Karta* ('guardians of the city [of Jerusalem]'), refused to recognize the Israeli state as legitimate, arguing that it was a satanic invention of the secular Zionists who dared to usurp the role of the hoped-for messiah in carrying out the act of national redemption.

Finally, in addition to the three basic Zionist strands, Israeli politics includes a fourth strand. The territorial partition of 1948 left many Palestinian Arabs in Israel. As citizens of the new state, they had the right to vote, and were represented politically by the Communist party and various Arab nationalist movements. Today these organizations are often referred to collectively as the Arab parties, although Jewish citizens equally have been active in the Communist movement (now represented by the Hadash party).

Throughout the post-independence period, the continuing arrival of Jewish immigrants from around the world created a multiethnic state with a broad range of religious perspectives. From the very earliest settlements, major distinctions existed between the Jewish groups based on their religious perspectives and areas of origin.

Another major distinction is the one between the historic *Yishuv* and newcomers. The early *Yishuv* consisted mostly of Ashkenazim from Europe and Mizrahim from the Middle East and North Africa. With the end of the Cold War, a new influx of Russian Jews arrived in Israel. At about the same time small minority communities such as the

Ethiopian Jewish Beta Israel immigrated to Israel, adding another ethnic flavour to the country. Today's Jewish state is an amalgam of these groups, and native-born Israelis (**sabras**) are increasingly of mixed descent. Nevertheless, ethnic divisions are revealed in Israeli politics through the strong identification of political parties with particular ethnic groups. This is no less true of religious parties, each of which tends to have a distinctive ethnic as well as sectarian character.

The religious Zionist movement revealed these divisions even prior to the establishment of the state of Israel. The Religious Zionist party among the Orthodox Jews (known as *Mizrahi*) formed the National Religious Party (NRP, Hebrew *Mafdal*) in 1956. Ashkenazi (European) Haredi groups formed the key constituency of Agudat Israel. By the 1980s, each of these groups had split along ethnic and religious lines: the NRP lost votes to Orthodox Mizrahis and the Agudat Israel divided among traditional Haredis and Hasids. In spite of schisms that have developed in the key constituencies of the religious parties, they have largely continued to cooperate in one way or another in Israeli government cabinets and through electoral alliances.

'Greater Israel'

The Arab states surrounding Israel had united against the newly created state in 1948. Refusing to recognize its legitimacy, they referred to it as the 'Zionist entity', rather than 'Israel', and threatened to fight a final war to eliminate it. After Israeli forces invaded Egypt's Sinai Peninsula in 1956 (as a pretext for intervention by British and French forces in the Suez Canal Zone), a multinational peacekeeping force was installed in the region. Despite their presence, however, war broke out again in 1967 when Egypt ordered them out of the Sinai and closed off Israel's access to the Red Sea. Israel staged a pre-emptive attack in June 1967 against Egypt and its Arab allies, in which it took control of the Gaza Strip, the Sinai Peninsula, the entire west bank of the Jordan River, and the Syrian Golan Heights in the space of six days. The dramatic victory of Israeli forces against its Arab neighbours in the 'Six Day War' allowed the state of Israel to occupy massive new tracts of territory.

It is not an overstatement to say that the 1967 war changed the character of religious political activism in Israel. In the eyes of many religious Jews, the victory was evidence of divine providence and an indication that the final restoration of the Jewish people to the land, promised in the Bible, had come. Even secular Jews tended to interpret Israel's victory as a vindication of the Zionists' struggle to re-establish the ancient homeland of the Jews. Israelis began to refer to the newly conquered areas of the West Bank by their biblical names, Judea and Samaria.

Both the religious rhetoric and the religious claims to the land became increasingly strident after 1967. Among the varied groups that supported Israel's claim to the totality of Palestine were the various Israeli governments, the National Religious Party, the *Gush Emunim* settler movement, and Christians around the world who saw the victory as a sign that the end-times envisioned by the prophets were at hand. Many historians and political scientists agree that religion has been used instrumentally to justify the actions of the Israeli state. At the same time, Israel's success in the Six

Day War led Jewish people to rediscover the scriptural background to the orthodox religious claims to the land of Israel (Akenson 1992).

In the wake of the war, the newly conquered areas of East Jerusalem were unilaterally added to the territory of Israel through municipal reorganization. The city thereafter came to be described in epic terms as the 'eternal, undivided capital' of the Israeli state, a phrase that is regularly used by politicians as a statement of policy. Territories in the Sinai, West Bank, and Gaza Strip came under military occupation. Under the terms of the 1978 Camp David Accords, Israel agreed to restore the Sinai to Egypt, but the West Bank and Gaza Strip remained under occupation pending negotiation of their status with Israel's Arab neighbours. Israeli occupation of the territories gave renewed impetus to the Palestinian nationalist movement, which by the mid-1970s was represented by the Palestine Liberation Organization (PLO), an umbrella organization led by the *Fatah* movement of Yasser Arafat. The Golan Heights, won from Syria, were officially annexed to Israel in 1981 over the objections of the Syrians, who continue to claim the land to the east of the pre-1967 borders.

Not all of the occupied territories were annexed by Israel following the 1967 war. Nevertheless, growing numbers of Israelis looked forward to the day when Jewish people would take possession of the land of their ancestors in its entirety. As mentioned above, Israelis started to refer to the northern and southern sections of the West Bank under the biblical names of Samaria and Judea. This verbal appropriation began to take physical form as growing numbers of Jewish Israelis moved to the conquered territories and began constructing homes or 'settlements' there, in the process creating a political constituency. The Likud bloc of revisionists became the main electoral beneficiaries of the victorious war effort. When Likud formed the government in 1977, the settlers took credit for the party's victory (Zertal and Eldar 2007: 53). The religious bloc, including the National Religious Party and Agudat Israel, also gained new influence as Labour declined. Israelis demanded a more assertive foreign policy in the hope of strengthening Israel's control over the occupied territories They felt that this would improve domestic security in the short term and in the long term might lead to the creation of a 'greater Israel' out of the occupied areas.

Box 4.3: What's in a Name?

The name of God is sacred in Judaism. For this reason, at some time after the composition of the Hebrew scriptures, the belief developed that it was disrespectful if not blasphemous to speak of God using his name. Thus the divine name represented in the written scriptures by the consonants YHWH was never pronounced: instead, those reading the texts aloud would substitute for YHWH either *adonai*, meaning 'Lord', or *hashem*, meaning 'the name'. Medieval scribes inserted two written vowels into YHWH, in order to indicate the pronunciation of *adonai*. Observant Jewish people today continue to replace the divine name with an alternative word.

In English the word God is used both as the proper name of the deity and as a generic term. For this reason, Orthodox Jews writing in English typically replace the vowels in both 'God' and 'Lord' with hyphens: 'G-d', 'L-rd'.

The Settler Movement and
the Rise of Israeli Revisionism

A small group of radical Israeli revisionists advocated consolidating Israel's 1967 gains in the West Bank by establishing settlements there. For some time, Orthodox *yeshivot* had been promoting a revival of the religious Zionist movement. The most prominent of these schools was the Merkaz Harav in Jerusalem, founded in 1924 by former Chief Rabbi Abraham Isaac Kook. The founder's son Tzvi Yehuda Kook (1891–82), who took over the school's direction in 1952, encouraged his students to work towards expanding Israeli settlement of the holy land. Many of those students saw Israel's victory in the 1967 war as clear evidence of God's desire to restore the conquered territory to his people. Israelis had lived in areas of the West Bank prior to the 1948 war and many hoped to rebuild the ancient settlements there described in the Hebrew scriptures. However, the Labour governments of the time were divided over the extent to which Israel should seek to formalize its control over the occupied territories. Gorenberg (2008) traces the birth of the settlement movement to the rivalry between two leading cabinet ministers of the day, Yigal Allon and Moshe Dayan, each of whom capitalized on the religious zeal that attended the victory in his own way, stressing either its cultural or strategic value.

In March 1968, a number of Jewish Israelis led by Rabbi Moshe Levinger, a former Merkaz Harav student and a young activist in the National Religious Party camp, travelled to the city of Hebron with the intention of establishing a permanent settlement there. They moved into a local hotel posing as Swiss tourists and began a public campaign to create a new Jewish home in the area of the Ibrahimi Mosque, a shrine venerated by both Jews and Muslims as the burial site of many of the biblical patriarchs. In the years that followed, increasing numbers of religious Zionists occupied key plots of land in the West Bank and Gaza Strip, in some cases sponsored directly by the Israeli government, and in other cases operating on their own. The pattern of settlement was seen as an extension of the original settlement pattern first established in the late Ottoman period and elaborated under the British mandate. The Israelis who created the new outposts called them *Yishuvim*, recalling the communities founded by the first and second *Aliyot*.

When the 1973 Arab–Israeli War (popularly known as the Yom Kippur War) ended in a virtual draw between the Israelis and their Arab neighbours, it only served to embolden the settler movement. Gorenberg (2008) argues that the strategic setback was cast as a victory by the religious movement, which saw Israel's eventual success as confirmation that Israel's redemption was under way (261–6). The next year, Israeli citizens living in the occupied territories created an organization to support their movement known as *Gush Emunim* ('bloc of the faithful'). Inspired by Rabbi Kook, the *Gush Emunim* was closely associated with the leadership of the National Religious Party and the Revisionist Likud bloc in the Knesset. When US Secretary of State Henry Kissinger arrived for a visit in August 1975, the settler movement greeted him with 'a festival of anarchic ferocity', and Jewish settlement spread to the northern West Bank with the establishment of a colony in Sebastia in the same year (Gorenberg 2008: 322–35).

The size and scale of the settlements increased dramatically with the formation of the first Likud government in 1977 (in a coalition including the NRP). This pattern persisted in spite of the decision to dismantle settlements in the Sinai under the Camp David Accords of 1978. (A similar decision would be enforced in 2005, when Likud

The Mercaz Harav Yeshiva in Jerusalem, where Rabbis Abraham Isaac and Tzvi Yehudah Kook served as chief rabbi. Rabbi Tzvi Yehuda Kook is widely considered the pivotal figure in the development of religious nationalism in Israel in the post-independence period. Born in Russia, he immigrated to Palestine in 1904 and became Rosh Yeshiva (chief rabbi) of the Merkaz Harav Yeshiva in Jerusalem in 1952. Many of the central figures in the post-1967 settlement movement had studied under Kook.
Source: © Rainer Kiedrowski/Arcaid/Corbis

party prime minister Ariel Sharon had Israeli settlers removed from the Gaza Strip.) The growth in the population of the settlements created a natural constituency for both the Likud and National Religious parties. Each of them enjoyed solid support from the settlements over the next few years.

Today many political activists, scholars, and foreign politicians believe the settlements to be among the greatest impediments to the conclusion of a peace treaty with the Palestinian population of the West Bank and Gaza Strip, though the settlers themselves disagree. Understanding the situation is complicated by the fact that not all the places identified as settlements share the same legal status; nor do all the settlers share the same motivations. Some of the places described as settlements are actually military outposts and army bases established by the Israel Defence Forces. Some are nothing more than small clusters of illegally situated trailers and prefabricated buildings. Others are large planned urban areas in central parts of the West Bank. The suburbs of Jerusalem, known to the Israelis as 'neighbourhoods', are considered settlements by the Palestinians because they are located inside the boundaries of the city of Jerusalem as they were unilaterally defined by Israel after the 1967 conquest. The motivations of the 'settlers' themselves also vary widely. Although some are devotees of the most radical religious nationalist movement, others are secular Israelis for whom the settlements represent nothing more than attractive, affordable places to live. Nonetheless, settlement construction has been largely spearheaded by the government and the *Gush Emunim* movement.

From the beginning, the religious nationalists saw themselves as following in the footsteps of the original Zionist settlers of Palestine. They would arrive in a spot, declare their intention to stay, and erect a shelter. Even a simple set of tents or a prefabricated home created a 'fact on the ground' that would eventually be approved by the government and put under military protection. They operated on the religious and ideological conviction that the whole of the ancient land of Israel belonged to the Jews in perpetuity, that others were only interlopers on Jewish land, and that whatever action might be necessary to claim the land was therefore justified. The movement was loosely organized and shunned traditional party politics (Zertal and Eldar 2007: 205–28).

As the settlements have become full-fledged towns and cities, they have required administration, services, and protection. Today the political administration of the settlements, in addition to their official representation to Israeli society, falls within the purview of an elected body known as the Yesha Council ('Yesha' is a Hebrew acronym formed from the names of the occupied territories—Judea, Samaria, and Gaza).

The early 1980s saw the emergence of a reactionary right wing that extended beyond the revisionist and religious right. In the early 1980s a small group of extremists developed an underground terror operation that targeted Palestinians in the West Bank and even developed an abortive plan to destroy the Dome of the Rock, an important Muslim shrine on the Temple Mount in Jerusalem. More notable was the establishment of the ultra-religious nationalist party Kach by Meir Kahane (1932–90), an American-born Orthodox rabbi who favoured the adoption of Halakha as law in the state of Israel and the subordination of the secular state to the dictates of Orthodox Judaism. He strongly denied the existence of a pre-existing Palestinian nationality and opposed the intermarriage of Jews and Arabs. In 1984 Kahane was elected to the

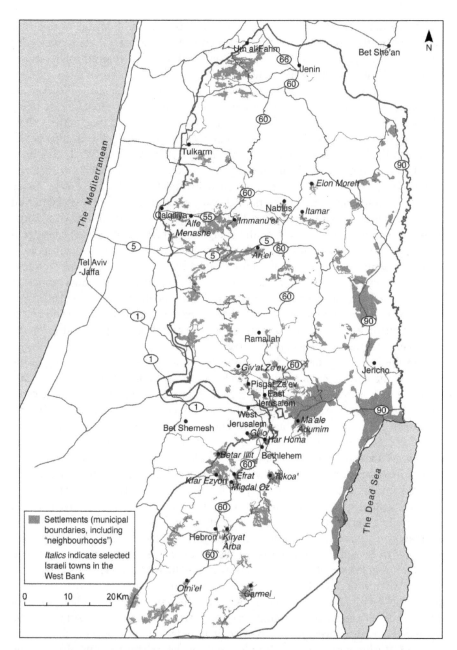

Map 4.1: Israeli Settlement Activity in the West Bank. The expansionist program sponsored by the Israeli government and the religiously-inspired *Gush Emunim* has led to the creation of dozens of Israeli settlements in the territories occupied by Israel in 1967. These settlements, shown in italics, include large suburbs and exurbs of Jerusalem such as Ma'ale Adumim, stand-alone religious settlements such as Kiryat Arba near Hebron, and small outposts established by independent activists. Many of the settlements stand alongside Palestinian communities, from which they are separated by security barriers and alternative transportation routes.

Knesset under the Kach banner, and although the party was banned from electoral politics under an anti-racist law promulgated in 1988, Kahane continued his political activity outside parliament. In 1990 he was assassinated by El Sayyid Nosair, an Arab-American terrorist, while visiting the United States. Thereafter the party split and in 1994 both factions were banned as terrorist organizations.

Paradoxically, the settler movement was strengthened in numbers and political influence despite a series of political developments that on the surface would suggest its marginalization. The first Palestinian *intifada* (uprising) of 1987–90 and strategic moves made by the Palestinians in its wake helped to set the stage for negotiations on Palestinian autonomy in the occupied territories. The Oslo Accords signed in 1993 ostensibly set Israel and the Palestinians on the road toward a two-state solution based on the assumption that Israel would exchange 'land for peace'. Yet even though that plan would likely require the dismantling of many settlements to make room for the creation of a new Palestinian state, since 1993 the settlements have continued to grow as ever greater numbers of Israelis have come to live in them. The period following the accords also saw intensification of the debate over how to deal with Palestinians living in the occupied territories, and led to the radicalization of many religious Zionists.

Two events in particular served to underline the radicalization of the National Religious community. On 25 February 1994, a settler from the Kiryat Arba settlement in Hebron named Baruch Goldstein entered the Ibrahimi Mosque in Hebron where numerous Muslims were at prayer. He opened fire on the worshippers, killing 29 and injuring many more, before he was killed by those who remained. The religious significance of the day that he chose to carry out the attack was not lost on Israelis, particularly members of religious communities. It was the holiday of Purim, during which Jewish people celebrate their deliverance from a murderous pogrom described in the biblical book of Esther through a reversal that allows them to kill their persecutors. The massacre evoked horror among the larger Israeli public, but galvanized a growing opposition to the peace process among the religious Zionists, some of whom venerated Goldstein as a martyr.

The second event occurred on 4 November 1995, when a religious nationalist and devotee of Kach named Yigal Amir assassinated Israeli Prime Minister Yitzhak Rabin at a rally in favour of the peace process. Amir was a law student from Bar-Ilan University, an educational bulwark of the National Religious community, and an admirer of Baruch Goldstein. In his testimony to police after he had been apprehended, Amir admitted that Goldstein's action had inspired his own decision to murder a person he deemed to be a traitor to the Jewish people (Zertal and Eldar 2007: 122; Shahak and Mezvinsky 2004: 137–8). These events introduced a new tension between the religious and secular factions in Israeli politics, but the polarization declined following the apparent failure of the peace process in 2000 and the eruption of violence in the second Palestinian *intifada* of 2000–3.

In the wake of the second *intifada*, the Israeli government adopted a strategy of 'unilateral disengagement'. Part of this strategy involved the dismantling of several settlements inside the Gaza Strip. The project was not completed until September 2005, when settlers who could not be persuaded to leave were forcefully evicted.

Meanwhile, settlements in the West Bank continued to grow. The ideology of the settler movement, as we have seen, is rooted in a religious nationalist interpretation of Jewish tradition popularized by the Rabbis Kook and their Orthodox followers. In the words of critics Shahak and Mezvinsky (2004), this

> ideology assumes the imminent triumph over the non-Jews and asserts that the Jews, aided by God, will thereafter triumph over the non-Jews and rule them forever. . . . All current political developments will either help bring this about sooner or will postpone it. (Shahak and Mezvinsky 2004: 65)

Advocates of this ideology understand the advance of Jewish settlers into Palestinian territory as a redemptive act: 'what appears to be the confiscation of Arab-owned land for subsequent settlement by Jews is in reality not an act of stealing but one of sanctification' (67). While the Haredim continue to regard the Israeli state with some degree of suspicion, the modern Orthodox followers of the National Religious Party and the religious settlers now accept the state as a stepping stone on the way to the future restoration of a truly religious Israel. Unlike Haredi dissidents, Orthodox conservatives participate enthusiastically in special units of the Israel Defence Forces called Hesder Yeshivot, which are known for their dedication and esprit de corps.

The centrality of settler consciousness both to religious Zionism and to Israeli policy regarding the Palestinian territories should not be underestimated. In the eyes of many observers, it represents the leading edge of Zionist ideology and practice, and it is embraced by the mainstream of Israeli society even though most Israelis remain secular in practice and outlook. Increasingly, then, the secular Zionism of the past is being challenged by the religious fringe. Menahem Klein writes:

> in an era in which classic Zionism has reached the limit of its abilities, religious fundamentalism has grown among extremist settlers, their reservations about the state are increasing, and the first signs of a messianic post-Zionism are appearing. (Klein 2007: 204)

Others believe that the settlement project could be the catalyst for a rupture at the very core of the Israeli state, pitting secular Israelis against the religious and hawkish elements that support the settlements (Taub 2010). Some Israelis, such as Shlomo Sand (2009), argue that the traditional definition of Israel as a religious community dating back to ancient times must be replaced by a post-national definition in which religion would be a marginal element. These debates continue to deepen the divide between religious and secular notions of the Israeli state.

Nonetheless, the political parties and movements of the religious sectors of Israeli society tend to have the greatest attachment to the notion of greater Israel and their numbers continue to increase. These groups have an ambiguous patriotism, supporting the Israeli state but condemning any attempt at a negotiated division of the land they view as a divine inheritance.

The Rise of Shas

While the various religious parties have assumed an important place in Israeli politics, they are also subject to significant internal political divisions. Among Orthodox Sephardim in particular, a feeling of alienation from the Ashkenazi-dominated Israeli institutions led to the erosion of public support for the established religious parties. In the early 1980s, Sephardi political leaders came together to form a party they called Shomrei Torah Sephardim (Sephardi Torah Guardians), or 'Shas', which won four seats in the national elections of 1984. Since that time Shas has continued to grow, attracting increasing support among Sephardim who are unhappy with the mainstream Likud and National Religious parties. Shas was originally founded out of the broader Haredi constituency and was approved by the Ashkenazi religious leaders as a rival to Agudat Israel. During the mid-1990s, Shas regularly won between six and ten seats, ensuring it an important voice in the formation of governing coalitions. Its founder and leader, Rabbi Ovadia Yosef, had become a widely popular figure in his own right. Shas has consistently been a member of the governing coalition since its first appearance in Israeli elections.

The party's electoral platforms generally focus on financial and moral support for Haredi religious institutions, especially those representing the Sephardic community. It also seeks generous social spending and special grants for the Orthodox *yeshivot* that make up its key constituency (Shahak and Mezvinsky 2004: 51). Rabbi Yosef himself was a former Chief Rabbi of the Israeli state, and the party's political leadership from the beginning operated under the authority of its spiritual leader. One of the most notable members of the Knesset (MKs) elected under the Shas banner was a young and charismatic leader by the name of Aryeh Deri. After serving as interior minister in the governments of Shimon Peres, Yitzhak Shamir, and Yitzhak Rabin, in March 1999, Deri was found guilty of accepting bribes of US$155,000.

Far from harming his party's electoral prospects, however, the conviction served as a rallying call for the Shas leadership, who denounced the verdict as ethnically biased against Sephardim. In the elections of May 1999, Shas won an unprecedented 17 seats, making it the third-largest party in the Knesset and a key coalition partner for Prime Minister Ehud Barak. The party's success was attributed mainly to the rise of disaffection among Sephardi Likud voters who interpreted the Likud government's upholding of the verdict against Deri as a slight to their community. The sudden rise in support for Shas alarmed a large proportion of the Israeli electorate who were concerned by the increasing influence of the Sephardi party. Widespread disgust with the clientelist politics of Shas and resentment against the influence of seminarians, most of whom managed to avoid national service because of their status as *yeshiva* students, came to dominate the politics of the urban secularists. In the 2003 elections, the Shinui ('change') party moved ahead of Shas, in a secular challenge to the clerics. Shinui imploded during the national elections of 2006. But the advocates of a secularist counterpoint to the influence of Shas and the other religious parties simply transferred their support to several other secular parties such as Ariel Sharon's Kadima ('forward') coalition, a pensioners' movement, and reactionary right-wing movements such as Avigdor Lieberman's Yisrael Beitenu ('Israel our home'). The seeds of a significant secular–religious divide had taken root.

Religious Parties and Coalition Politics

The intensification of the Arab–Israeli conflict that developed after 2000 has continued to buffet the Israeli political scene, with diverse implications for religious parties and their influence in the government. Nevertheless, it has receded in significance as Israel has faced the challenges of a second *intifada* in the occupied territories, a war with Lebanon's Hezbollah ('party of God'), and clashes with the Hamas movement in the Gaza Strip. In this context, today as in the past, parties tend to be gauged by their relative level of pugnacity in foreign policy, and the religious Zionist parties that court the votes of settlers in the West Bank have had a growing influence, as have other right-wing parties such as Likud and Yisrael Beitenu.

The influence of religious parties on Israeli politics can be largely attributed to the nature of Israel's electoral system and governing institutions. The prime minister chooses a government from among the individuals elected to the Knesset. The electoral system is based on strict proportional representation, so that the distribution of seats in the Knesset reflects the proportion of the popular vote won by each party. As a result, a single party rarely (if ever) wins a majority of the seats and the party with the most seats must cobble together a coalition in order to govern. The fragmentation of the party system over the past few decades has made the creation of stable parliamentary coalitions more problematic than ever.

The dramatic rise of Shas over the past two decades has demonstrated the growing importance of Israel's Sephardic population. Though it has meant an increase in the influence of the religious parties in government, it should not be understood simply as a sign of a rightward shift in Israeli politics. Shas does defend the role of religious leaders and religious identity in Israel, but its position on Israel's foreign policy regarding the West Bank and Gaza Strip has not been clearly defined. Initially it was not strongly committed to the maintenance of the settlements; however, as the numbers of Sephardim living in areas of settlement in East Jerusalem and the West Bank increase, the party has been adjusting its position accordingly.

The most stalwart defenders of the West Bank settlements for the last two decades have been the National Religious Party and its National Union allies as well as Agudat Israel, which eventually allied itself with an Ashkenazi Haredi party called Degel HaTorah under the name United Torah Judaism. The 2005 decision of Prime Minister Ariel Sharon to dismantle the Israeli settlements in the Gaza Strip broke his coalition with the religious parties. It also necessitated the creation of a new party known as Kadima ('forward'), a centrist and secularist grouping that drew support from former members of both Likud and Labour. Though Kadima harnessed some of the concern voiced by the secular mainstream of Israeli voters, many of its stalwarts, including Peres and Sharon himself, had been staunch allies of the settler movement in its earliest days.

Kadima won by far the largest number of seats in the 2006 elections, but its support eroded after Prime Minister Sharon suffered a massive brain haemorrhage and was replaced by the underperforming Ehud Olmert. In the 2009 elections, Kadima lost to a right-wing coalition led by Likud and the nationalist Yisrael Beitenu, a radical secular nationalist movement. At the same time, the formerly dominant Labour movement fell to fourth place in the polls. For the religious movements, the results of the past

Table 4.1 'Results of the Knesset Elections, 2000–2010'

February 2003			
Likud	38	Yahudat Hatorah	5
Labour-Meimad	19	Hadash (Socialist/Arab)	3
Shinui	15	Am Ehad	3
Shas	11	Balad (Arab)	3
National Union (Right-wing nationalist)	7	Yisrael B'Aliya	2
Meretz	6	United Arab List (Arab)	2
National Religious Party	6		

March 2006			
Kadima	29	Gil (National Pensioners' Party)	7
Labour-Meimad	19	Torah and Shabbat Judaism	6
Likud	12	Meretz	5
Shas	12	United Arab List	4
Yisrael Beitenu	11	Hadash (Socialist/Arab)	3
National Union/National Religious Party	9	National Democratic Assembly	3

February 2009			
Kadima	28	Ra'am Ta'al (Arab)	4
Likud	27	National Union	4
Yisrael Beitenu	15	Hadash (Socialist/Arab)	4
Labour	13	Meretz	4
Shas	11	Habayit Hayehudi	3
United Torah Judaism	5	NDA-Balad (Arab)	3

Source: Created from information gathered at www.knesset.gov.il/faction/eng/FactionListAll_eng.asp?view=1.

two elections have been ambiguous, suggesting that the average Israeli continues to support the foreign policies associated with the settler movement but is increasingly less supportive of the religious element in the Israeli state.

Reflecting on developments in Israeli public and religious life over the past few decades, the historian Colin Shindler (2008) has remarked that 'The Zionist national religious (*mafdalim*) have tended to become more religious while the non-Zionist ultra-orthodox (*haredim*) have become more nationalistic, producing an emerging hybrid, appropriately termed the *hardalim*'. Even though the numbers of Haredi schools and exemptions for military service have increased during this period, 'secular Jews and those who define themselves as "traditional, but not so religious" account for almost three-quarters of all Israelis' (Shindler 2008: 8). Though the Israeli people as a whole still define themselves as secular, the state continues to embrace religious rhetoric and support religious institutions. Paradoxically, then, Israel is a society that embraces secularism but reserves an important place in its political life for the religiously observant segment of the Jewish population.

The Wider Coalition: Christian Zionism

The Zionist project has attracted considerable support from religious perspectives outside the Jewish faith. Britain's decision to support the Zionist project from the beginning was at least in part a reflection of the desire among Christian members of the Cabinet as well as influential social movements to see the Jewish people restored to the historic land of Israel. Tuchman (1956) sketches the long history of British fascination with the land of Israel for both strategic and religious–sentimental reasons. Even before the period of the British mandate, British missionaries in Palestine had already begun proselytizing among the Jewish people there in hopes of ushering in the millennial kingdom they believed to be predicted in the Bible.

More recently, with the spread of certain brands of evangelical and fundamentalist Christianity in Western Europe and North America, Christian interest in supporting and partnering with the religious movements in Israel has been increasing. For those Christians, the declaration of the state of Israel in 1948 and its dramatic victory in the Six Day War of 1967 proved the imminence of the end times. Merkley (2001) follows the history of the modern evangelical movements that 'generally have generous or positive attitudes' toward the state of Israel (24). The theological bases of these groups are diverse, but a particularly significant base of support for Israel has been a movement called premillennial dispensationalism, whose members believe that we are now in the penultimate of several 'dispensations' or ages that began with the creation and will end with Christ's thousand-year reign on earth. At the time of its founding, around the turn of the last century, the movement maintained that the restoration of the Jewish people to the land of Israel was a precursor to the second coming of Jesus Christ; therefore modern dispensationalists argue that Christians should support Israeli Jews' efforts to re-establish themselves in the land of their ancestors, or at least not stand in their way. In the early 1970s, two books of prophetic commentary—Hal Lindsey's *The Late Great Planet Earth* and Billy Graham's *His Land*— had a profound impact in evangelical circles and stimulated American Christian interest in the restoration of the Jewish people to the Holy Land (Sizer 2004).

Today, American Christians are widely known as the most ardent supporters of the Israeli state. Large US lobbies dedicated to the cause include Christians United for Israel, led by the televangelist John Hagee, and the International Christian Embassy Jerusalem. Although the latter disavows the premillennial theology of the dispensationalists, it was founded in 1979 with the professed aim of offering 'comfort' to the Israeli state. It raises money for charitable projects in Israel, sponsors an annual gathering of Christians in Jerusalem during the Feast of Tabernacles, and provides financial support both for the settlements and for additional Jewish immigration to Israel (Clark 2007; Sizer 2004).

Conclusion

From the beginning, the Zionist project has combined two sometimes contradictory forces: Jewish nationalism and the religious drive to return to the historic *Eretz Yisrael*. Religious Jews originally regarded the Zionist movement with suspicion because of connections with socialism and the secular outlook of its champions. Since 1948, however, religious factions that originally refused to recognize the Israeli state have come to accept its existence; the National Religious Party and the settler movement have even embraced it as a part of the divine plan to redeem the land. The increasing importance of the religious parties over the past few decades has complicated Israeli politics. One scholar argues that even though the 'majority [of the population] supports secular principles in what has been termed the religious domain', they 'may not be in the majority much longer', and that in the 'sociological domain' Israelis are generally committed to preserving the Jewish character of the state (Tessler 2009: 216). As Israeli authorities continue to insist that a guarantee of this Jewish character be a precondition in any peace treaty, the religious–secular divide will be central to its relationship with its neighbours as well.

Box 4.4: Glossary of Terms: Judaism and Israeli Politics

Aliya 'Immigration'; a term commonly used to refer to the various waves of immigration to Palestine; plural Aliyot.

Ashkenazim Jews of northern, central, or eastern European descent.

Eretz Israel Hebrew, 'land of Israel'.

Gentiles, Goyim Terms for non-Jews.

Halakha The Jewish legal code and tradition, from a word meaning a way or path.

Haredi Literally, '[God]-fearing'; the preferred term for those Jews sometimes described as 'ultra-Orthodox'.

Hasidim A mystical sect of Orthodox Judaism, founded in Eastern Europe in the eighteenth century.

kibbutz A collective farm.

Knesset Hebrew for 'assembly', the name of the Israeli legislature.

Mizrahim Jews of non-European or 'oriental' descent (Egyptian, Iraqi, etc.); today often used synonymously with 'Sephardim'.

rabbi A Jewish religious leader.

Sabbath The Jewish day of rest, lasting from sundown on Friday to sundown on Saturday.

sabra A native-born Israeli (from the name of a cactus native to the Middle East).

Sephardim From the Hebrew word for 'Spain'; Jews of Spanish or Portuguese descent, many of whom settled around the Mediterranean region after they were displaced from Spain in the late fifteenth century; often used as a general term for non-Ashkenazi Jews in Israel, including Mizrahim.

Shoah Hebrew term for the Holocaust.

Yishuv Hebrew word meaning 'settlement'; used to describe the Jewish communities founded in Israel–Palestine beginning in the late nineteenth century.

yeshiva Jewish religious school or seminary; plural *yeshivot*.

Review Questions

1. What types of secular and religious groups brought about the restoration of the Jewish state in Israel in 1948?
2. What were the three political streams that characterized the early Zionist movement?
3. How does religion influence the internal politics of Israel?
4. In what ways is Israel divided on the basis of ethnic extraction?
5. What factors led to the establishment of Jewish settlements in the occupied territories following the 1967 war?
6. How does the Israeli electoral system contribute to the influence of religious parties in politics?
7. What is the Christian Zionist movement? Why does it support the state of Israel?

Sources and Further Reading

Akenson, Donald Harmon (1992). *God's Peoples: Covenant and Land in South Africa, Israel, and Ulster.* Ithaca, NY: Cornell University Press.

Amon, Moshe (2004). 'Can Israel Survive the West Bank Settlements?' *Terrorism and Political Violence* 16, 1 (Spring): 48–65.

Bunzl, John (2004). *Islam, Judaism, and the Political Role of Religions in the Middle East.* Gainesville, FL: University Press of Florida.

Clark, Victoria (2007). *Allies for Armageddon: The Rise of Christian Zionism.* New Haven: Yale University Press.

Gilbert, Martin (2008). *Israel: A History.* Revised English edition. New York: Harper Perennial.

Gorenberg, Gershom (2006). *The Accidental Empire: Israel and the Birth of the Settlements, 1967–1977.* New York: Times Books.

Herzl, Theodor (1988 [1896]). *The Jewish State.* New York: Dover Publications.

Johnston, Douglas, ed. (2003). *Faith-based Diplomacy: Trumping Realpolitik.* Oxford: Oxford University Press.

Klein, Menahem. (2007). *A Possible Peace between Israel and Palestine.* New York: Columbia University Press.

Lacquer, Walter (2003). *The History of Zionism.* London: Tauris Parke.

Lustick, Ian (1988). *For the Lord and the Land: Jewish Fundamentalism in Israel.* New York: Council on Foreign Relations.

Mayer, Arno (2008). *Ploughshares into Swords: From Zionism to Israel.* London: Verso.

Merkley, Paul Charles (2001). *Christian Attitudes towards the State of Israel.* Montreal and Kingston: McGill-Queens University Press.

Rabkin, Yakov M. (2006). *A Threat From Within: A Century of Jewish Opposition to Zionism* Trans. Red A. Reed. Black Point NS: Fernwood.

Ravitzky, Aviezer (1996). *Messianism, Zionism, and Jewish Religious Radicalism.* Trans. Michael Swirsky and Jonathan Chipman. Chicago: University of Chicago Press.

Reuveny, Rafael (2003). 'Fundamentalist Colonialism: The Geopolitics of Israeli–Palestinian Conflict'. *Political Geography* 22.

Ruether, Rosemary Radford and Herman J. Ruether (1989). *The Wrath of Jonah*. New York: Harper and Row.

Sand, Shlomo (2009). *The Invention of the Jewish People*. Trans. Yael Lotan. New York: Verso.

Shafir, Gershon (1996). 'Zionism and Colonialism: A Comparative Approach', in Michael N. Barnett, eds. *Israel in Comparative Perspective*. Albany, NY: SUNY Press.

Shindler, Colin (2008). *A History of Modern Israel*. Cambridge: Cambridge University Press.

Shahak, Israel, and Norton Mezvinsky (2004). *Jewish Fundamentalism in Israel*. New edition. London: Pluto Press.

Sizer, Stephen (2004). *Christian Zionism: Road-map to Armageddon?* Downer's Grove, IL: Intervarsity Press.

Sofer, Sasson (1988). *Zionism and the Foundations of Israeli Diplomacy*. Trans. Dorothea Shefet-Vanson, Cambridge: Cambridge University Press.

Sprinzak, Ehud (1991). *The Ascendance of Israel's Radical Right*. New York: Oxford University Press.

Taub, Gadi (2010). *The Settlers and the Struggle over the Meaning of Zionism*. New Haven: Yale University Press.

Tessler, Mark (2009). *A History of the Israeli-Palestinian Conflict*. 2nd edition. Bloomington, ID: Indiana University Press.

Tuchman, Barbara (1956). *Bible and Sword: England and Palestine from the Bronze Age to Balfour*. New York: New York University Press.

Zertal, Idith, and Akiva Eldar (2007). *Lords of the Land: The War over Israel's Settlements in the Occupied Territories, 1967–2007*, trans. Vivian Eden. New York: Nation Books.

Web Resources

www.btselem.org – Israeli Information Center for Human Rights in the Occupied Territories.

www.jewishvirtuallibrary.org – The Jewish Virtual Library.

www.gov.il – The Government of Israel.

www.knesset.gov.il – The Israeli Knesset (Parliament).

Chapter 5

Political Islam
and the State

The fastest growing religion in the world today is Islam, a religion with centuries of tradition and a cultural influence throughout vast reaches of the world. There are at least 40 countries in which the majority of the population is Muslim. The versions of Islam practised across those nations vary significantly, as do the official relations between Islam and politics. Muslim societies range from modern secular democracies such as Indonesia and Bangladesh, which have relatively few religiously oriented political movements, to societies in which religious authorities play a leading role, such as Saudi Arabia and the Islamic Republic of Iran. Yet even the most secular Muslim states do cultivate some public role for the religion, and most have at least one important political party or opposition group rooted in political Islam.

The worldwide emergence of movements seeking to combine Islam with politics has been noted in innumerable books and articles since the 1970s. It is nothing new for Muslims to discuss politics in the light of their theological and religious perspectives, but the rise of so many groups asserting in their own words that 'Islam is the solution' has given political analysts much to consider.

Over the years, many terms have been used to identify those who advocate the integration of Islam and politics. Among them is 'fundamentalists'; but 'fundamentalism' was coined in the United States to refer to a Christian religious phenomenon and is thus somewhat inaccurately applied to a political phenomenon of a very different nature. Most scholars today prefer to call proponents of political Islam 'Islamists' (this should be differentiated from mere followers of Islam, who are known as Muslims). Much of this chapter is dedicated to understanding the development of modern Islamism and its relationship to global politics. However, it is important to note that Islam may influence the political views of ordinary Muslims in many ways that do not demand that politics be driven by religion.

Muhammad, the Prophet of Islam, was both a religious and a political leader, so perhaps it is not surprising that Islam has always tended to play a dual role—political as well as religious—in Muslim societies. Traditions such as the extension of the Prophet's rule through a series of successors known as the caliphs, the pursuit of holy war (*jihad*) to spread and defend the faith, and the regulation of Muslims' behaviour have important political implications to this day. At the same time, Islam provides believers with a wide-ranging set of ethical and moral precepts that serve as a basis for opposition to societal injustice. These ideas are the central philosophic basis of Muslim groups that take a prophetic stance against state authorities that don't measure up to these expectations.

Introduction to Islam

Islam was founded in the early years of the seventh century near Mecca in Arabia. The society in which its prophet, Muhammad, grew up was largely polytheistic and pagan, but also included small numbers of Jews and Christians. Muhammad was a spiritual seeker and ascetic who one day experienced a vision of the angel Gabriel commanding him to 'recite' (or 'read') a message from God to his people.

A series of revelations followed, from which Muhammad understood that he was to take the religion of the one God, Allah, to his people and to reform their social as well as their spiritual life. But the people of Mecca resisted the message of Islam ('submission' in Arabic). Thus in 622 Muhammad and a small group of followers left Mecca for the city of Yathrib (later renamed Medina). This event, known as the *hijra* (migration), marks the beginning of the Muslim calendar. In Yathrib Muhammad became not only the spiritual leader of the Muslims ('those who submit') but the political leader of a new community based on the teachings transmitted to them by the Prophet. Eight years later, in 630, Muhammad led a larger band of followers back to Mecca, where they defeated the ruling tribes and established a new society. Although the Prophet himself died two years later, the Muslim society he created soon became an empire that eventually stretched across the Middle East and North Africa.

At the core of Islam is its insistence on *tawhid*, or the absolute oneness ('unicity') of God. As obedient servants of Allah (the Arabic word for God), Muslims seek to submit their entire lives to his demands, which are summarized in a set of rules known as the 'five pillars' of Islam (see Box 5.1).

In the years that followed the Prophet's death, the foundations were laid for the development of the Islamic tradition. Authoritative versions of the messages he had transmitted were promulgated by his successor Abu Bakr and collected in the holy Qur'an. In the early years after the *hijra,* sayings of or about the prophet and his practices were recorded in six collections that became the authoritative guides to Muslim practice, based on the example (*sunna*) of the Prophet himself. Together, these texts make up the collection called the **Hadith** (each individual text is a *hadith*).

Muhammad's successors quickly spread the temporal power of the Muslim community through force of arms. The geographic regions that came under Muslim rule were known as the *dar al-Islam* (household of Islam); those that did not were styled the *dar al-harb* (household of war). Within the *dar al-Islam* the religion of the Prophet became the basis of the legal order. Non-Muslim subjects such as Christians and Jews were tolerated as 'protected people' (***ahl al dhimma***) who had a portion of the Islamic message. They were exempted from military service on condition that they paid a poll-tax (the ***jizya***).

Because Islam was the basis of an entire civilization, the Qur'an and Hadith were interpreted with an eye to regulating the behaviour of Muslim societies. It was in this way that the traditions of Islamic 'jurisprudence' (*fiqh*) and commentary on the meaning of the Qur'an (*tafsir*) developed. Islamic *fiqh* took the form of individual judgments (*fatwas*) regarding behaviour and law. Collections of judicial precedents and their use as public and private law in judgments by local authorities (*qadis*, *mukhtars*, or **sheikhs**) have come to be known as the Shari'a (Esposito 2005).

Since the Shari'a is a central part of debates over the political role of Islam, it is important to understand the term. Shari'a means a path or way of life, and use of the term to describe Islamic law suggests that it is a set of principles according to which Muslims should live. In practice, both the content and the interpretation of Shari'a are fluid and open to debate. Although it is often said that the goal of political Islam is to impose the Shari'a—as if it were a single entity—in fact there are several schools (or *madhdhabs*) of Islamic legal thought, and disputes can arise over the proper interpretation of Shari'a even within an individual school. Some Muslims reject these interpretive schools, arguing that they have departed from the true and basic Islam. During the Middle Ages, legal discussions flourished as scholars pursued **ijtihad**, or independent reasoning.

In the years after the death of Muhammad, disputes arose over who should succeed him as leader of the Muslim community (the **umma**). The majority of Muslims— who called themselves **Sunni** (meaning followers of the **sunna**, the practice of the Prophet)—supported a system of political leadership in which various prominent Muslims would vie for power. However, a minority felt that the leadership should have remained within the family of the Prophet, passing to his son-in-law Ali ibn Abi Talib, because of his character and his close relationship with Muhammad. These people came to be known as the *shi'at Ali* (partisans of Ali), hence **Shi'i**. The dispute led to the first major division (*fitna*) in Islam.

In time Sunni and Shi'i Muslims developed distinctly different legal traditions and ritual observances, which have been handed down to the present. There are also some doctrinal differences, but these are relatively minor compared to the differences in historical interpretation. One example can be seen in the ways the two groups remember Ali's son Hussein, who died in 680 in a pitched battle against the Caliph Yezid I. Most Muslims remember Hussein as a hero and martyr, but among the Shi'i he became a central figure, and they believe that his descendants were the only rightful successors of the Prophet.

Among Sunni Muslims, the term '**imam**' refers to the person who leads the prayers at the mosque. Among the Shi'i, however, an **Imam** is one in a succession of divinely appointed leaders descended from Ali. Most Shi'i (the 'Twelvers') believe that the succession continued until the late ninth century, when the twelfth Imam disappeared into 'occultation'; they consider this Imam the Mahdi or messiah, and they expect his return at the end of history. But there are several other factions within the Shi'i family. Zaidis (sometimes known as 'Fivers') broke away because they recognized a different individual as the fifth Imam. Similarly, **Ismailis** ('Seveners') recognized a different seventh Imam; among the subsects within the Ismaili fold are Nizaris and **Druze**.

The division between Sunni and Shi'i is just one of multiple differences among Muslims. Some Muslims are strictly observant, and some hold only nominally to their traditions. Some embrace the mystical dimension of Islam known as Sufism; others reject it, asserting that it challenges the central doctrine of *tawhid*. Since Muslims are found in societies throughout the world, cultural practices may have an important role in differentiating one form of Islam from another. Islam is influential at official levels where it is discussed in major seats of learning and interpreted by state officials known as *muftis*. The influence of individual officials and the differences in their interpretations contribute to the variations in the flavour of Islam from one country to another.

Today Muslims make up the majority of the population in a belt that stretches from Morocco in the west to Indonesia in the east, including most of North Africa, all of the Middle East, and much of South Asia, including Pakistan and Bangladesh. There are also growing numbers of Muslims in Europe and North America, mostly as a result of immigration from their countries of origin. Individual Muslims gather for worship

Box 5.1: The Five Pillars of Islam

Shahada (Creed or confession) A person becomes a Muslim by reciting the creed or confession of Islam: *La ila illaha allah wa Muhammad al-rasul Allah* ('There is no god but God and Muhammad is his Prophet'). This creed is recited in the regular call to prayer issued from every mosque by the muezzin.

Salat (Prayer) Muslims are expected to pray at five intervals during the day, beginning before sunrise. Regular prayer times are based on the positions of the sun.

Zakat (Almsgiving) Muslims are expected to give generously to the poor, to charities, or to *da'wa* (propagation of the faith). The appropriate level of *zakat* is debated, but the most common figure is 2.5 per cent of one's income, based on passages in the Hadith.

Sawm (Fasting) During the month of Ramadan (when Muhammad is said to have received his first visions) Muslims engage in a daily fast. They refrain from both eating and drinking during the daylight hours and break their fast only after sundown, at a family or community gathering known as an *iftar*.

Hajj (Pilgrimage) All adult Muslims should undertake a pilgrimage to the holy city of Mecca at least once in their lives. The favoured time for the Hajj is the month of *dhul-hijja*, when millions of Muslims descend on Mecca. A Muslim who has completed the pilgrimage to Mecca becomes a *hajji*.

at mosques, where the prescribed prayers are offered five times each day under the leadership of the mosque's imam. Although there is no need to attend a mosque in order to perform prayers, Muslims typically gather at the mosque in large numbers on Fridays, when a learned Muslim, often the imam, will deliver a sermon (*khutbah*). Islam does not have a clergy as such; however, individual imams and learned scholars (**ulema**; singular *alim*) provide leadership to the community.

The Fusion of Islam and Politics: A Contentious Debate

It has often been observed that Islam is more naturally political than other religions because it is a totalizing tradition that demands specific observances and ways of life. For example, Islam forbids the use of alcohol, requires five daily prayers, creates rules for a just society, and was from its origins inseparable from the state. Throughout the centuries, Muslims have engaged in public discussions and debates over what is and is not acceptable, which practices are **halal** (permitted) and which **haram** (forbidden). Some would argue that the very practice of Islam necessitates a Muslim government, or a Muslim society, to regulate behaviour. This aspect of Islam has given a special place to the *ulema* in determining the proper role of government and the proper public application of Shari'a (Feldman 2008). According to Bernard Lewis, the 'notion of church and state as distinct institutions, each with its own laws, hierarchy, and jurisdiction, is characteristically Christian, with its origins in Christian scripture and history. It is alien to Islam' (Lewis 1993). The point is debated, but it is worth noting that from the Middle Ages until the twentieth century the dominant political force in the Middle East, the Ottoman Empire, was ruled by a sultan who was at the same time the caliph and the 'commander of the faithful'.

Among late twentieth-century specialists, the view developed that Islam was such an eminently political religion that it dominated the political culture of Middle Eastern and Islamic states, justifying Caesarism, dictatorship, the oppression of women, and the suppression of democratic dissent. According to Sadowski (1993), many scholars in the 1960s and 1970s argued that Islam's tradition of unquestioned authority, the legacy of the Islamic caliphate, and the very political nature of Islam itself demanded authoritarianism. By contrast, Edward Said (1979) criticized the tendency of Western scholars to reduce Islamic and eastern societies to simple stereotypes of romanticized barbarism, a perspective that he called Orientalism. To the Orientalists, Said wrote, 'Muslims were no more than fatalistic children tyrannized by their mind-set, their *ulama*, and their wild-eyed political leaders' (Said 1981: 28). In the wake of Said's criticism, later scholars argued that these arguments overstated the overall impact of Islam on such societies and for oversimplifying the impact of Islam on the Muslim imagination. Indeed, Islamic civil society became a force to be reckoned with in most Muslim majority states after the 1967 Middle East War. Islamist groups such as Egypt's Gama'a al-Islamiya, dissident groups in Saudi Arabia, and revolutionary groups in Iran all began to challenge the legitimacy and justice of those countries' political systems. With the success of the 1979 Islamic revolution in Iran, the idea that Islam silenced dissent needed to be re-evaluated.

Sadowski (1993) argues that the 'Neo-Orientalist' response was to turn the earlier image of Islam on its head, portraying the tradition as so perfectionistic in its expectations of rulers that it would always seek the overthrow of existing governments in favour of more radical alternatives. Thus Muslim societies would enter the modern age in a state of perpetual revolution and disorder. Since the 1980s, the idea of Islam's revolutionary and fanatical potential has been a central preoccupation of certain Western observers such as Wright (2001) and Pipes (2003). With the end of the Cold War, concern for the geopolitical challenges of the future increasingly focused on Islam and predictions of a 'clash of civilizations'. In 1993, the Spring issue of *Foreign Affairs* presented two opposing views of Islam's potential as a geopolitical threat (Hadar 1993; Miller 1993), and John Esposito, a respected scholar of Islam, published a book in which he called for a more balanced perspective on Islam and the threats it was perceived to pose (Esposito 1993). When the attacks of September 2001 were linked to Islamist militants, discussions of Islam's role in politics only became further polarized.

The Medieval and Colonial Ages

Islamic political philosophy developed with Islamic civilization across the Middle East, North Africa, and the portions of southeast Asia in which Muslims were politically dominant. The various legal schools gave rise to various streams of jurisprudence, and early philosophers explored the relationship between the religious and secular bases of Muslim societies. For example, Ibn Rushd (also known as Averroes; 1126–98) resurrected long-forgotten Greek political philosophies and Ibn Khaldoun (1332–1406) developed theories of urban cohesion in the face of barbarian threats for the Muslim *umma*. The basic notions concerning Islam and politics were established during the first few centuries after the Muslim conquest of the Middle East, a period of imperial stability and power. During this period and under the influence of Greek philosophy, Islamic theology evolved toward a more liberal style of philosophic reasoning. After the eleventh century, however, threats to Islamic civilization from both the west and the east motivated a turn toward conservatism and military defence.

Perhaps the most significant contribution to the future development of political Islam was made by Ibn Taymiyya (1263–1328), a prominent scholar and jurist in a period when Muslim societies generally were in decline. In the eleventh and twelfth centuries, repeated intrusions by European crusaders had disrupted life in the eastern Mediterranean. Then in 1258 the Mongols invaded and sacked the city of Baghdad. As a legal scholar in Damascus in the period after the fall of Baghdad, Ibn Taymiyya stood against the liberalizing current in Islamic theology at the time and called for Muslims to respond militarily to external threats. When the Mongols attacked Damascus in 1300, he himself took up arms in its defence. This experience turned his interest toward the subject of *jihad* ('struggle', often translated as 'holy war'). Ibn Taymiyya ruled that offensive *jihad* to spread the temporal power of the *umma* was a 'collective obligation' (*fard kifaya*) of the Muslim community in general, and that defensive *jihad* to protect Muslim communities against marauders was an 'individual obligation' (*fard ayn*) for all Muslims. This ruling is still cited today by many Islamists seeking to justify military action.

The restoration of Muslim civilization under the later Mamluks and Ottomans in the fourteenth to the seventeenth centuries reinvigorated the tradition of Islamic governance and in some ways deepened the conservative tone introduced by medieval jurists such as Ibn Taymiyya. For example, it reinforced the political division between Muslims and non-Muslims with the development of the *millet* system, which allowed non-Muslims to govern their own communities but left them as a separate class of citizen. On the other hand, increasing contact with European civilization was calling into question some of the more conservative aspects of Islamic society, such as constraints on dress or scientific inquiry. Over time, the increasing power and influence of the putatively Christian West became a preoccupation of Muslim scholars and political leaders, particularly as European colonialism reached its height in the mid-nineteenth century.

The beginnings of modern Islamist thinking can be traced to this period, when Muslim educators and political activists were anxious to demonstrate that Islamic civilization was no less dynamic than its Western Christian counterpart. In other quarters, the developing political discourse was strongly anti-modernist. As the former Ottoman Empire and its constituent parts moved toward modernization following the 1920s, this anti-modernist current began to gain political momentum.

From the time of the Prophet, the Sunni world had been governed by a succession of caliphs who represented the political power brokers of the day. The Ottomans had often justified their control of the Middle East on the grounds that it served as a uniting force for the Islamic *umma*. By the early 1900s, however, the Ottoman sultan had become the last recognized successor to the Prophet. The Ottoman Empire was formally dissolved in 1923 with the proclamation of the Republic of Turkey, and in 1924 the republic's first president, Mustafa Kemal Ataturk (1881–1938), declared an end to the caliphate. Now, for the first time in history, there was neither a recognized temporal successor to the Prophet nor a clear line of authority in the *umma*. Turkey embarked on a program of secularization and Western-style cultural and economic modernization in an attempt to emulate the West's power, as did former Ottoman dominions such as Egypt. By this time, the renaissance of Muslim political thought was already under way.

The Birth of Modern Islamic Activism

Islam has been used both by state authorities for their own purposes and by dissident groups opposed to the state. Ayubi (1991) stresses the role played by the state in cultivating Islamic jurisprudence rather than the role played by Islam in constituting an independent civil society. Nevertheless, it is clear that radical modern Islamism emerged in tandem with important social forces in the late colonial era. These social forces originated in different parts of the Muslim world, but they came to influence one another through social, cultural, and academic contacts.

In Arabia, a strictly conservative variety of Islam developed gradually over two centuries prior to the foundation of the modern state system in that part of the world in the mid-twentieth century. Muhammad Ibn Abd al Wahhab (or Muhammad Ibn Wahhab) (1703–92) was an Arabian sheikh who sought to unite Muslims in a renewed commitment to the original dictates of Islam. Wahhab called for the eradication of Sufi mysticism based on his interpretation of *shirk* (idolatry and improper veneration of God). He also insisted on the commendation of virtues and the condemnation of vice, enforced through the efforts of the governing authorities. Wahhab formed a close association with a chieftain named Muhammad Ibn Saud (d. 1765), who shared his vision of Islamic purity, and together they laid the foundations of an alliance that was to transform the culture of Arabia and continues in force today.

By 1924, the Saud family had taken control of most of what is now Saudi Arabia, including the holy cities of Mecca and Medina. In this way the Wahhabi school of thought became the guiding force for the modern Saudi state. Its ideas went on to inspire like-minded groups throughout the Muslim world, and resonated with other Islamic nationalists who were just beginning to debate how Muslims should respond to a modern world apparently dominated by the West.

In Egypt and South Asia in particular, Muslim scholars encouraged the development of political and social movements that would challenge both the colonial powers operating in their homelands and the secular anti-colonial movements that they perceived as emulating Western forms. For many of these scholars, the key was to rediscover the Islam of earlier ages and thereby reinvigorate Islamic civilization. The first of several scholars in this tradition was Jamal al-Din al-Afghani (1839–97), a peripatetic activist born in Persia who gained fame in Egypt and Europe. Afghani urged

Many of the debates that laid the foundations of Islamism were held at Al Azhar University in Cairo. Widely regarded as the centre of Sunni scholarship, it has been a source of official advice about public morality under successive Egyptian governments and today it remains an intellectual centre for political Islam.
Source: © Rainer Kiedrowski/Arcaid/Corbis

Muslims to demonstrate their intellectual and cultural superiority to Western society. Mandaville (2007) argues that Afghani sought to mobilize 'the best and brightest of his day around a vision of Islamic emancipation—but emancipation both from foreign rule and from internal religious stagnation'. Afghani's most notable disciple, Muhammad Abduh (1849–1905), thus sought the expansion of studies in the liberal arts as well as Islamic sciences as a way of reinvigorating the political potency of the *umma*. Later scholars working in the tradition of Afghani and Abduh developed a more critical attitude toward governance and the need for political reform along more conservative lines, most notably the Egyptian intellectual Rashid Rida (1865–35), who sought to motivate Muslim leaders to create institutions to replace the former caliphate.

Although Afghani, Abduh, and Rida were primarily scholars, their ideas were formative for a variety of political movements. By the late 1920s, several political groups were seeking to fill the vacuum left by the eclipse of the caliphate by reviving the political role that Islam had played in the days of the Prophet. Because this movement wanted to return to the 'pure' Islam of the earliest Muslims, or *Salafs*, it came to be known as Salafism. Salafism increased in salience over the course of the twentieth century with the expansion of Western power and culture in Muslim lands. The greatest threat to the Muslim world, according to the Salafists, was ignorance of the traditions and essential teachings of Islam: therefore Muslim rulers should enforce the Muslim way of life. The Salafists sought to develop an Islamist alternative to the modern liberal and secular state that would restore Islam's power as the guiding force in the governance of Muslim-majority societies.

The revivalist movements inspired by Salafism moved in fits and starts from social reform and social activism toward more direct political involvement. In 1941, a prominent journalist and social activist named Abul Ala Maududi (1903–79) founded a group called *Jamaat-e-Islami* (the Islamic society) in the region that was to become Pakistan. Combining religious revivalism with a religious nationalist ideology, this group served as a counterpoint to Muhammad Ali Jinna's secular Muslim League, which formed the first government of Pakistan. The ideological predecessor of today's radical movements in the region, the *Jamaat-e-Islami* remains one of Pakistan's leading opposition forces.

In Egypt, a community activist by the name of Hassan al-Banna (1906–49) founded a Salafist-minded reform group in 1928 that he called **Ikhwan** al-Muslimun, or the Muslim Brotherhood. By the 1960s it had become so influential that offshoots were formed in several other countries, including Jordan and Syria. Eventually a Palestinian branch was established, and the movement also inspired the intellectuals behind the National Islamic Front government in Sudan in the 1990s. The Muslim Brotherhood began as a social movement dedicated to reviving Islamic observance among ordinary Muslims by sponsoring community initiatives and sporting events, and cultivating religious discipline (prayer, fasting, and so on). Through the 1930s and 1940s, however, the group became increasingly involved in politics, publicly denouncing successive governments of Egypt (Mandaville 2007: 59–62). Matters came to a head in 1948, when an activist with the Brotherhood assassinated Egyptian Prime Minister Mahmoud al-Nuqrashi. The next year, Hassan al-Banna in turn was assassinated and

Sayyid Qutb (1906–66) was a pivotal figure in the development of political Islam. Originally a low-level functionary in the Egyptian government, he came to embrace an extremely critical attitude toward the secularized Muslim society of his day, which he condemned for its *jahiliya* (ignorance).
Source: LookLex

his movement was forced underground. Since that time, the organization has been intermittently tolerated and banned in the nation of its founding. Since the 2011 revolution, the Brotherhood has been an influential political force and its members have become leading politicians.

The leadership of the Brotherhood passed to Hassan al-Hudaybi, but it was Sayyid Qutb (1906–66), an Egyptian teacher and activist, who became the organization's most important ideological spokesman. To this day, Qutb is widely regarded as the most influential Islamist in radical circles, since his ideas laid the groundwork for the modern *jihadi* movements that combine Islamism with violent action against Western culture. Qutb wrote several monographs over the course of his life, including *Social Justice in Islam* in 1948 and *Milestones along the Way* (also translated as *Signposts on the Road*) in 1964. As an official in the education ministry, Qutb was dispatched to the United States in 1949–50 to study educational administration. He was both intrigued and horrified by American society, finding it to be technologically and intellectually sophisticated but morally bankrupt. It is widely believed that this trip played a major role in the development of his increasingly hostile attitude toward Western influence in Muslim societies.

With the formation of the Arab Republic of Egypt following the revolution of 1952, the Brotherhood came out of hiding and initially worked alongside the new government, but before long it became a major opposition force. Imprisoned from late 1954 until 1964, Qutb continued to write. Among the works smuggled out of prison was *Milestones*, in which he compared the state of Muslim societies under the influence of Western modernism to the condition of *jahiliya* (ignorance) in which the world existed before the revelation of the Qur'an to Muhammad (Qutb 1991). Qutb called for *jihad* against government authorities and the creation of an Islamic state that would restore the rulership of God on earth (*hakimiya*) (Ayubi 1991: 139–40). Later Islamists were to draw on Qutb's work to justify both rebellion against the governments of Muslim societies and attacks on the symbols of Western power and influence. They would also adapt his criticism of *jahiliya* to justify silencing or eliminating those believed to have defected from the true principles of Islamic governance, actions known as *takfir*. Qutb's revolutionary ideas were perceived as presenting a serious threat to the Egyptian government and he was executed in 1966.

Revolutions and Revivalism: Islamism to the 1980s

Two years later, the disillusionment that followed the massive defeat of Arab forces in the Six Day War gave new potency to Qutb's perspective. Pan-Arabism—the ideology of the Egyptian revolution of 1952—and secular nationalism both having failed, Islamic nationalist movements became the mainstream opposition to secular regimes throughout the Arab world (Haddad 1992). When the crisis deepened in the wake of an arson attack against the al Aqsa Mosque in Jerusalem in 1969, governments throughout the Muslim world came together at the first Islamic summit and formed the Organization of the Islamic Conference, an intergovernmental organization dedicated to promoting solidarity among Muslim countries. In Egypt, the Brotherhood thrived and inspired the formation of several underground movements in the military and in society at large that regarded the government as evil and idolatrous.

These groups became particularly aggressive after Egyptian President Anwar Sadat signed a peace treaty with Israel in 1978. Three years later one of them succeeded in murdering President Sadat. Nevertheless, most of them survived throughout the regime of his successor, Hosni Mubarak, though the more violent activists were brought to heel in the 1990s. Egyptian scholar Saad Eddin Ibrahim (1980) was surprised to find that the majority of the radical movement's members were well-educated middle-class university graduates.

The power of the Brotherhood in Syria provoked the government of Hafez al Assad to stage a bloody crackdown in the city of Hama in February 1982. Both indirect and direct influences link the ideology of the Brotherhood to the multitude of Islamist groups that emerged across the Muslim world in the 1970s and 1980s, some of which took violent action against the secular governments of their countries.

Finally, in 1979, Islamist activists managed to take control of the government of a state. Iran had embarked on a program of enforced modernization and secularization in the 1950s, and by the 1960s Shi'i religious leaders represented one of the key forces of opposition to the country's harsh and repressive monarch, the shah. Intellectuals such as Jalal Al-e Ahmed (1923–69) and Ali Shari'ati (1933–77) were also influential, however, helping to popularize the notion that Western culture had polluted traditional Iranian culture through '**westoxication**' (*gharbzadegi*). Revered Shi'i scholars known as ayatollahs and *hojjats al-Islam* called for political resistance to the shah in lectures and public denunciations.

The most famous of these men proved to be the Ayatollah Ruhollah Khomeini (1900–89). Although he spent much of the later 1960s and 1970s in exile, his teachings and philosophy were spread through the clandestine distribution of his lectures on cassette. Combining Marxist-style rhetoric with appeals to the Shi'i community's long-held feelings of marginalization, Khomeinism constituted a virulently anti-colonial, anti-Western, and conservative response to Iran's enforced Westernization and modernization. In 1979, amid widespread demonstrations and government instability in Iran, the Ayatollah returned from exile and took up the reins of the Islamist movement.

In late 1979 Khomeini drafted a new constitution that made Iran the world's first 'Islamic Republic'. Based on the unprecedented notion of **velayat i-faqih** ('guardianship of the jurist'), the constitution empowered Muslim scholars to oversee the governance of a truly Islamic state. Shi'is had traditionally held religious experts in much higher regard than their Sunni counterparts did, and Khomeini's constitution reflected the more hierarchical nature of Shi'i Islam, even if the most noted religious experts opposed it. Religious institutions such as the Assembly of Religious Experts and the Guardian Council, and religious foundations (large-scale business conglomerates) were established to support the religious establishment and reinforce its political influence. The Guardian Council in particular safeguards the purity of the revolution by inspecting and vetoing legislation and candidates for office to ensure that Islamist principles remained central to government operations. Khomeini appointed himself the Supreme Guide of the Islamic Republic, a position with almost unlimited power to overturn legislation and to confirm or reject candidates for public office.

Iran's revolutionary ideology did not stop at establishing the *velayat i-faqih* in the Islamic Republic. It also preached revolution abroad. By the mid-1980s Iran's Revolutionary Guards—an elite military unit under the control of the Supreme Guide—took the lead in extending Iranian influence via supporting proxy groups throughout the Middle East. Although few Shi'i outside Iran welcomed their efforts, the Shi'i of south Lebanon did prove receptive. When Israeli forces invaded Lebanon in 1982, Iranian-sponsored groups helped to establish a violent new resistance movement named Hezbollah, the 'party of God', dedicated to liberating the region from Israeli occupation and destroying the Jewish state.

For Sunni Islamists, the establishment of a Shi'i state in Iran was both a challenge and an inspiration. Sunni activists expanded their networks and influence in opposition to the predominantly secular and ideologically pan-Arab governments throughout the Middle East and elsewhere. In November 1979, a group of Islamist militants staged an armed takeover of the holy mosque in Mecca, preaching the advent of the Mahdi (the Islamic messiah). After a two-week standoff the Saudi military stormed the complex and killed or captured most of the insurgents. In response to the strident criticisms

Ayatollah Ruhollah Khomeini (1900–89) was the leading ideologue of the Iranian Revolution of 1979. Among his innovations was the principle of 'guardianship of the jurist', under which the governing institutions of the Islamic Republic of Iran are overseen by religious scholars.
Source: © Jacques Haillot/Corbis

levelled at the Saudi state by the militants and their supporters, the Saudi regime redoubled its efforts to demonstrate its conservative credentials.

Islamism also featured prominently in strategic and state politics throughout the 1980s and 1990s. In spite of the anti-Western rhetoric espoused by Pakistani and Afghan Islamists throughout the 1980s, the Islamist *mujahideen* militia fighting the

Soviet-backed government of Afghanistan was armed and supported by the United States as well as Saudi Arabia. Hundreds of volunteers went to Afghanistan to join the struggle, among them one named Osama bin Laden, a wealthy heir to a Saudi construction magnate. The conduit of funding to the *mujahideen* was the Pakistani government of Muhammad Zia ul-Haq, who legitimized his military regime by embarking upon a deliberate program of Islamization. Other states followed his example, perhaps most notably Sudan, where social divisions between northern Arabs and southern Africans were deepened by the implementation of an official Islamization policy under the National Islamic Front government of Omar Hassan al-Bashir. Throughout the 1990s, Bashir's government was defended by its chief ideologue, Hassan al-Turabi, who gave the regime a moderate face even as a strict brand of Islamic orthodoxy was being imposed in the school system and the public life of the state.

During the 1980s, the Muslim Brotherhood movement experienced a resurgence in several states, most importantly in Egypt and Jordan, as well as among the Palestinians and by extension throughout the Middle East and South Asia. In 1987 the Palestinian Muslim Brotherhood took up the banner of struggle against Israel by forming the militant resistance movement Hamas (an Arabic acronym for the Islamic Resistance Movement; also the Arabic word for 'zeal'). The Hamas Charter, promulgated in 1988, integrated nationalist resistance with Islamic ideals, enjoining both nationalism and Islamism as motivations for the defence of **waqf**, religious property. In the eyes of Hamas, Palestine itself was a *waqf* belonging to the Muslim *umma*:

> The Islamic Resistance Movement believes that the land of Palestine has been an Islamic Waqf throughout the generations and until the Day of Resurrection, no one can renounce it or part of it, abandon it or part of it. (Article 11)

Hamas also hearkened back to Ibn Taymiyya, asserting that *jihad* 'becomes an individual duty binding on every Muslim man and woman' (Article 12). Over the years of the first Palestinian *intifada* (uprising) from 1987 to 1990, Hamas became an important champion of the Palestinian cause and a powerful opponent of the secular nationalist Fatah movement.

By the early 1990s, Western and Middle Eastern governments were increasingly viewing Islamism with suspicion as a virulently anti-Western conservative movement. Leading Islamist networks such as Hezbollah, Hamas, and Islamic Jihad had joined the secular and left-wing radical groups on government lists of banned terrorist organizations. At the same time, a wave of democratization was sweeping the developing world. When the military government of Algeria consented to legislative elections in 1991, early local results appeared to indicate that the leading Islamist party, the *Front Islamique du Salut* (Islamic Salvation Front) was likely to win a resounding victory. Rather than allow an Islamist party to win at the polls, the military stepped in to cancel the second round of elections scheduled for that December. The suspended election served as a battle cry to the Islamists, and a radical militia called the *Gendarmerie Islamique Armée* (Armed Islamic Group) began a long and bloody civil war against the government. The events in Algeria had a chilling effect on Islamists elsewhere who had hoped to participate in democratic elections, and served to further radicalize the movement around the world.

Box 5.2: Prominent Leaders in the History of Political Islam

Muhammad Ibn Abd Al Wahhab (1703–92) Arabian fundamentalist reformer and iconoclast, whose political alliance with the family of Ibn Saud continues to shape the governing philosophy of Saudi Arabia to this day.

Jamal al-Din al-Afghani (1838–97) Father of pan-Islamism and an early intellectual proponent of Muslim unity in the face of modernization. Born in Persia, he travelled extensively, teaching and inspiring Muslims.

Muhammad Abduh (1849–05) Egyptian Islamic modernist and reformer, briefly rector of al Azhar University in Cairo. He was a pivotal figure in the Islamic renaissance that gave rise to both Arab nationalism and Salafism.

Rashid Rida (1865–1935) Syrian intellectual who worked in Egypt, a student of Abduh and one of the first scholars to address the political implications of the end of the caliphate.

Hassan al-Banna (1906–49) Egyptian popular activist, founder and supreme guide of the Egyptian Muslim Brotherhood. He is considered one of the chief founders of modern Islamist activism. Held to be a threat to the Egyptian government, he was assassinated in 1949.

Sayyid Qutb (1906–66) Activist and leading theorist of the Egyptian Muslim Brotherhood, radicalized in Egypt in the late 1940s. His work *Milestones along the Way* (1964) is widely considered a founding text of modern Islamic radicalism; he was executed by the Egyptian government in 1966.

Abul Ala Maududi (1903–79) Ideological theorist and founder of the Pakistani Islamist movement *Jamaat-e-Islami*.

Ali Shari'ati (1933–77) Iranian sociologist and journalist, one of the forerunners of the Iranian revolution.

Ayatollah Ruhollah Khomeini (1902–89) Charismatic Iranian Shi'i religious leader who became the chief ideologue of the Iranian revolution of 1979 and Iran's first Supreme Guide.

Sheikh Ahmed Yassin (1937–2004) Chief spiritual leader and founder of the Palestinian Hamas movement; assassinated by Israeli forces.

Abdullah Azzam (1941–89) Palestinian *jihadist* and mentor of Osama bin Laden during the *mujahideen* revolt of the 1980s.

Ayman Al Zawahiri Leading figure in Egyptian Islamic Jihad movement. He fought in Afghanistan and became the second in command in the al-Qaeda movement by 1998. He is now viewed as the leading figure in the international al-Qaeda network.

Osama bin Laden Saudi international financier and founder of the al-Qaeda terrorist organization who financed *jihad* in Afghanistan and commissioned the 9/11 hijacking plot. He was killed by American forces in a commando raid in Pakistan in May 2011.

Anwar Ibrahim Leading figure in the Malaysian opposition. He has championed dialogue as an alternative to a 'clash of civilizations' between Muslims and the West.

Tariq Ramadan Grandson of Hassan al-Banna, a leading intellectual voice in contemporary debates on the place of Islam in non-Muslim societies such as Europe.

The Crucible of Radicalization:
Afghanistan, bin Laden, and Militant *Jihad*

The forcible suppression of Islamist opposition movements in places such as Egypt, Algeria, and Saudi Arabia, together with the experience gained by foreigners who went to fight alongside the *mujahideen* of Afghanistan in the 1980s, laid the foundations for both the globalization and the radicalization of the Islamist movement. In a widely cited journalistic account of the history of the *jihadist* movement based in Afghanistan, Lawrence Wright describes how a number of foreign expatriates went to the border regions of Pakistan and Afghanistan to fight with the *mujahideen* throughout the 1980s (Wright 2006). Among them was a Palestinian Islamist by the name of Abdullah Azzam, who arrived in Pakistan in the early 1980s and worked for most of the next decade recruiting fighters from places such as Saudi Arabia. One of these recruits was Osama bin Laden.

Throughout the 1980s the *mujahideen* were supported by the governments of Pakistan and the United States as a counterforce to the Russian-backed communist regime in Afghanistan (Coll 2004). At the end of the Cold War, most of that support dried up. Although the *mujahideen* succeeded in dislodging the Afghan government, the factions among them soon came into conflict and began fighting one another. Meanwhile, the end of the Cold War provided an opportunity for the United States to attempt to end the Iraqi occupation of Kuwait in 1990. The government of Saudi Arabia provided the bases from which the Americans attacked. But the presence of non-Muslim forces in the state that guarded the 'two holy places' of Mecca and Medina was offensive to the *jihadis* who had fought the Russians in Afghanistan. For individuals such as Osama bin Laden, the American presence seemed to indicate that the threat posed by Western power—secular and putatively Judeo-Christian—was far deeper than the threat posed by the Russians in Afghanistan: it also encompassed a plot to expand Christian and Jewish power to the holiest sites of the Middle East, from Israel to Saudi Arabia and beyond. He thus began to denounce a worldwide conspiracy of 'Crusaders and Jews' against the *umma*, which all good Muslims should fight.

Bin Laden joined a growing number of Islamist radicals emboldened by the apparent success of the *jihad* in Afghanistan. Ramzi Yousef, who had spent some time in Pakistan under the influence of the group radicalized by the Afghan War, managed to set off a bomb in the World Trade Center in New York in February 1993. Yousef and an Islamist Egyptian sheikh, Omar Abd al-Rahman, were later arrested and imprisoned for the attack. Meanwhile, bin Laden's open embrace of radicals who called for the overthrow of the Saudi royal family led him into exile, first in Sudan and then in Afghanistan. In the wake of the *mujahideen* victory in Afghanistan, an even more repressive movement, reminiscent of the Saudi Wahhabi variety of political Islam, had come to power. Known as the **Taliban** ('students'), this faction rejected the usual approach to *ijtihad* (independent reasoning) that had developed since the time of Muhammad and embraced an extremely strict interpretation of Shari'a, enforcing harsh summary punishment for any offence against it. When the Sudanese government (under pressure from Saudi Arabia and the United States) ousted bin Laden in May 1996, he left for Afghanistan, where his campaign to create a subversive radical Islamist network began in earnest.

Over the next few years, bin Laden established the base for a global *jihad* against the West. In a self-styled *fatwa* issued in 1996, he opened with a litany of complaints against the United States and its allies in the Muslim world, concluding that Arabs living in the land of the two holy places (he would not name the state of Saudi Arabia because he considered it illegitimate) should fight both the regime and American soldiers stationed there. Two years later, a second *fatwa* extended the *jihad*, inveighing against the presence of American forces in Saudi Arabia, the sanctions regime then applying to Iraq, and American support for the state of Israel. Echoing Ibn Taymiyya, he announced that the 'ruling to kill the Americans and their allies—civilians and military—is an individual duty for every Muslim who can do it in any country in which it is possible to do it' (Donohue and Esposito 2007: 431). Over the next few years bin Laden's al-Qaeda organization led the *jihad*, bombing the US embassies in Nairobi, Kenya, and Dar Es Salaam, Tanzania, in August 1998 and claiming responsibility for a suicide bomb attack on an American destroyer, the USS *Cole*, in port at Aden, Yemen, in October 2000. US military responses, including missile attacks on targets in Sudan and Afghanistan in August 1998, proved ineffective.

Just over one year later, on 11 September ('9/11') 2001, four groups of hijackers took over four American flights bound for domestic destinations. Early that morning, two of the aircraft were flown into the New York World Trade Center towers and one into the Pentagon building; the fourth went down in Pennsylvania, apparently as a result of passengers' efforts to take control of the plane. Over the next few days, a conspiracy was revealed involving roughly two dozen men from the Middle East and North Africa, many of whom had travelled to Afghanistan and been in contact with al-Qaeda.

It would hardly be an exaggeration to say that 9/11 had a profound effect both on perceptions of Islam and on world politics. It proved a polarizing moment, leading the US to take an aggressive stance against 'global terrorism' and serving to justify first the invasion of Afghanistan in October 2001, which deposed the Taliban government, and later, in March and April 2003, the invasion of Iraq. Over the next several years, the battles in Afghanistan and Iraq continued without any clear indication of ultimate success. The assassination of Osama bin Laden by American forces in May 2011 was a breakthrough, but other groups appeared likely to take up the torch.

The *jihadism* espoused by groups like al-Qaeda is rooted in a particularly radical understanding of the idea of *jihad*. We will return to the topic of *jihad* in chapter 9, but at this point it may be useful to note that the offensive *jihad* advocated by radicals like bin Laden is an innovation, based on a controversial interpretation of Ibn Taymiyya that the vast majority of the world's Muslims reject. Nevertheless, its power was demonstrated in the lethal attacks carried out by small numbers of committed militants in Madrid, Spain, in March 2004 and London, England, in July 2005. In 2002 and 2005 radicals engaged in bombing campaigns against targets frequented by Western tourists in Bali, Indonesia. The American and allied military campaigns in Afghanistan in particular continue to meet fierce resistance from groups putatively allied to al-Qaeda and the Taliban. One particularly notable group is the Yemen-based al-Qaeda in the Arabian Peninsula, which attempted to bomb flights destined for the United States in 2009 and 2010.

The *jihadis'* call to violence against Western interests has inspired many anti-colonial and nationalist groups to claim that they share the ideals of the militants. Numerous otherwise unrelated violent opposition campaigns have proclaimed their solidarity with the cause of global *jihad*, from sub-Saharan Africa to East Asia. Chechen resistance against the central Russian government in the region of the Caucasus has often taken the form of *jihadi*-style terrorism. In the Philippines, radicals from the minority Muslim communities of the south have formed rebel groups such as Abu Sayyaf and the Moro Islamic Liberation Front, which have carried out numerous armed incursions and kidnappings over the past two decades. Groups critical of the more established Palestinian Islamist movements have periodically staged attacks to challenge the leadership of Hamas and Hezbollah in the Gaza Strip and Lebanon. In Somalia, factions such as the Shabab militia have often expressed sympathy with the purveyors of global *jihad*. These groups form a nebulous core of violent revolutionaries throughout the world who are difficult to identify and whose numbers are unknown. Although many have claimed allegiance to the al-Qaeda network, the solidity of those claims has often hinged solely on the words of the individuals involved. As a result, violent *jihadism* today appears to be more an idea than an organized movement.

Islamism Today: Democrats and Demagogues

Islamist movements have been condemned by Muslims and non-Muslims alike for their militant and typically violent behaviour. Since the radicalization of the Muslim Brotherhood of Egypt in the 1930s, the most powerful opposition forces in many Muslim societies have been Salafist movements. Over time, as these movements benefited from private and official Saudi funding and support, they increasingly embraced Wahhabi perspectives, to the point that today Salafism is synonymous with Wahhabism. The same societies have also typically denied Islamist groups the opportunity to participate in democratic politics, whether through a general policy of repression or through specific constraints on the participation of religion-based parties. The spread of *jihadi* ideology, bolstered by Islamism's condemnation of Western influence and support for the Palestinian cause, has expanded the scope of Islamist resistance throughout the world. Meanwhile, the dichotomous worldview championed by the *jihadi* movements encourages more violent and uncompromising militant activity.

Still, what is most notable today is the way the Islamist movement has expanded to include democratic-minded and accommodationist Muslims who accept the idea of compromise with other parties and governing authorities. Political Islam has become so central to the politics of majority Muslim states that it is difficult to envision any of them effecting a complete separation between the two. The contemporary association of Islamism with violence and revolution conceals the fact that Islamic renewal has taken place in many parts of the world without any bloodshed.

Islamist parties tend to emerge in societies where democratic participation is limited, but democratization promises to provide a wider array of opportunities to voice their concerns. Lisa Anderson (1997) argues that one should look to the 'institutional environment' in order to understand how Islamist parties participate in Muslim societies: some states are stronger than others, affording greater leeway for civil society to operate. Major changes have taken place in response to pressures for democratization and a more liberal civil society, perhaps most notably represented in the expansion of free media. For example, public acceptance of the freedom to critique and debate issues related to religion have changed as new media have transformed the cultural life of Muslim societies. On television, for example, the prominence of Islamic experts such as the Egyptian Yusuf al Qaradawi, a sometimes controversial commentator on al Jazeera's program *Shari'a and Life*, has encouraged a more public form of *ijtihad* than was typical in the past. Many of the political implications of these developments are as yet unclear.

Efforts to cultivate political Islam in Turkey began in the late 1990s under the *Refah* (Welfare) Party led by Necmettin Erbakan, which became the largest party in the

Recep Tayyip Erdogan, the prime minister of Turkey since 2003, has led the Justice and Development (AK) party to power. He has challenged the influence of the military, which seeks to preserve the secular republic against public recognition and display of religion. His activism led to a showdown with the military and opposition over his choice for the presidency of the republic in 2007 in which his candidate was eventually confirmed.
Source: © vario images GmbH & Co.KG/Alamy

Turkish parliament in 1996. Two years later, the party was banned on the grounds that it had violated the constitution, which demanded that Turkey remain a secular state. But the ban proved to be only a temporary setback. After 2002, a new party made up of many of the same Islamist activists, known as the *Adalet ve Kalkinma Partisi* ('Justice and Development' or AK Party), gradually moved into position as the governing party under Prime Minister Recep Tayyip Erdogan. AK has regularly contested elections, and although some of its policies challenge the secular principles of the Turkish state, it has continued to play by the rules of electoral politics.

The long-term intentions of Islamic political activists in Turkey is a matter of speculation. Some find the ultimate purposes of the AK Party suspect, pointing to some of the more radical proposals it has made in the past, such as criminalization of adultery or allowing seminary students to present applications for further study on par with secular university students (Hale and Ozbudun 2010: 149). Another concern involves the special privileges allegedly extended to a conservative Islamic movement known as the Gülen community, whose members have been given influential positions in the bureaucracy and public sector (Yavuz 2009: 250–2). However, most scholars believe that conservative elements are seeking fundamental reform of the secular assumptions that have underpinned the Turkish republic since the 1920s. Party activists shy away from the Islamist label and, instead of pressing for stricter enforcement of Islamic law, concentrate on addressing broader social issues from a conservative perspective. For example, party policy stances generally seek to cultivate support for releasing religious practice from state control and showing solidarity with other Muslim states (Yavuz 2009: 43). AK has also supported Kurdish demands for national recognition in Turkey.

The AK Party's challenge to the secular state came to a head in the election of 2007. After the party nominated long-time party politician Abdullah Gul for the presidency, the opposition and armed forces denounced the move, arguing that the openly religious Gul (whose wife wears a *hijab*) would challenge the secular premises on which the state was founded. Prime Minister Erdogan's response was to take the question to the people in a national election, in which the Turkish people gave his Party the largest mandate in Turkish history. AK's democratic credentials had clearly been burnished, marking a major break with Turkey's soft-authoritarian military past.

Parties inspired by Islamic themes were also a major factor in Indonesia's transition from an authoritarian to a democratic state beginning in 1998. Despite former President Suharto's efforts to use conservative Islamic rhetoric in defence of his authoritarian regime, more moderate groups undermined his Muslim credentials and supported demonstrations against his rule that year. Over the next few years, parties with roots in Muslim civil organizations became enthusiastic participants in Indonesian elections. Despite violent challenges by small groups of radicals, Jacques Bertrand argues that 'political Islam has only marginally been a hindrance to democracy in Indonesia.' (Saravanamuttu 2010: 61). Furthermore, according to Hefner (2000: 12–13) Indonesian Islam is a 'civil pluralist' variety that expects strong civil associations to check any authoritarian impulse on the part of the government. In today's democratic Indonesia, the Prosperous Justice Party (PKS) relies on Islamic themes but shies away from the direct state application of Shari'a.

Political Islam has also been an important theme in Malaysian politics, where a democratic system has been dominated by soft authoritarian control under the ruling National Front and its leading party, the United Malays National Organization (UMNO). UMNO occasionally plays on Islamic themes and has openly declared that Malaysia is an Islamic state, a position that privileges ethnic Malay Muslims over the Chinese and other minorities. Public morality and Islamic themes have often been used over the past two decades as a means of shaping the internal politics of UMNO and its party rivals (Saravanamuttu 2010: 26–41). In 1998, internal divisions in UMNO led to a split between a dominant faction led by Prime Minister Mahathir Mohamad and a smaller group led by his deputy, Anwar Ibrahim. Over the next several years, multiple charges of sodomy and corruption were raised against Anwar with the intention of sidelining him. Nonetheless, Anwar has taken up the cause of opposition to the regime, arguing for a moderate form of Islam that tolerates dialogue with Western civilization.

Amid the turbulence that moved across the Middle East in the period following the American invasion of Iraq in 2003, the pressure to democratize created new opportunities for Islamist parties. In Iraq, democratic elections gave new Islamist movements the chance to take part, some (though not all) of whom represented constituencies opposed to the American-backed regime. More controversially, the victory of the Islamist resistance movement Hamas in the Palestinian legislative elections of 2006 led to an ongoing crisis over power-sharing with the formerly dominant Fatah movement, which still controlled the presidency.

In non-democratic environments Islamists have often operated as social organizations, lobbies, underground movements, or tolerated participants in limited elections. For example, in Egypt the Muslim Brotherhood has been officially banned but unofficially tolerated since the 1980s. Although militants have often broken with the Brotherhood and staged violent attacks against the regime as well as 'soft targets' such as Christians and tourists, the Brotherhood has increasingly sought to present itself as a viable participant in general elections (Abed-Kotob 1995). An abortive attempt to develop a party with a moderate Islamist political tone known as *Wasat* was consistently stonewalled by the Egyptian regime from the late 1990s. When the government made known its plan to begin loosening its control over elections in 2005, Brotherhood candidates performed well, winning a large number of seats in the National Assembly.

In a groundbreaking work, Jillian Schwedler argues that Muslim parties' desire for peaceful political participation reflects a diverse set of influences (Schwedler 2006). Her exploration of the process of ideological moderation focused on the Jordanian Islamic Action Front, a political party linked to the Jordanian Muslim Brotherhood, and the Islah Party of Yemen, a looser coalition of conservative activists that has periodically cooperated with the ruling party over the past decades. Other scholars, such as Rutherford (2006), argue that the expanding scope of Islamist discussion in public forums and on television indicates a growing embrace of liberal democratic principles on the part of modern Arab Islamists.

Amid the dramatic protests that brought unprecedented political change to the Arab world in the early months of 2011, Muslims called for democratization and an end to authoritarian one-party rule in Tunisia and Egypt. While Islamist political parties took part in the revolutionary movements, they remained largely secondary players. The extent to which they will be able to follow the lead of increasingly influential Islamist and Islamically oriented political parties in places such as Turkey and Indonesia remains to be seen. A significant challenge to the mainstream Islamists of the Muslim Brotherhood has come from the Salafists, who now, under the influence of Wahhabism, call for even more dramatic application of Islamic law and disdain their rivals' calls for social justice.

Islamist efforts to gain power and institute reform have met with mixed success. Since 1979 the institutions and political processes of the Islamic Republic of Iran have become increasingly unpopular at home, as was made clear by the widespread demonstrations against the regime that followed the disputed elections of June 2009. Repressive regimes such as those of the National Islamic Front in Sudan and the Taliban in Afghanistan have been respectively weakened by defections and overthrown. Efforts to increase the power of Shari'a courts in northern Nigeria have sparked communal violence and attempts by the federal government to limit their authority. However, the influence of Saudi Arabia's Council of Senior Ulema and its 'religious police', the Society for the Preservation of Virtue and Prevention of Vice, has remained constant, maintaining strict controls on dress and public behaviour in the kingdom. Enforcement of a putatively Islamic dress code is legislated in states such as Iran and Saudi Arabia, but is also widely embraced in more liberal societies such as Egypt.

The expansion of Muslim minorities in Europe and elsewhere has increasingly turned scholars' attention to the ways in which Muslims participate in Western societies. This question is especially trenchant given that Islamism has generally been associated with criticism of Western society and its history of colonialism. Roy (2004) observes that such criticism has become globalized and deterritorialized, meaning that Muslim religious allegiances are less likely to be tied to a specific nation than to the worldwide *umma*, no matter where a Muslim happens to live. The early years of the twenty-first century saw the publication of numerous commentaries reflecting concern with the political implications of the expansion of the largely immigrant Muslim community in Europe (Bat Ye'or 2005, Phillips 2006, Caldwell 2009). In the wake of the terrorist incidents of the early 2000s, together with the high-profile debates over women's veiling in France, freedom of the press in Denmark, and the construction of minarets in Switzerland, political rhetoric in Europe (and occasionally elsewhere in the West) increasingly features allegations that Muslims threaten to erode Western civilization.

Muslims have responded with chagrin and often with constructive criticism directed inside as well as outside their community. Scholars such as Khaled Abou el Fadl, Abdullahi An-Naim, Tariq Ramadan, and Amina Wadud have criticized traditional Islamic thinking while suggesting ways in which Muslims might embrace Western-style rational discussion of their religious ideas without abandoning their essential traditions. As a result, Muslims have taken the lead in funding and establishing many academic think-tanks, community activist networks, and public interfaith discussions and seminars.

The Sunni-Shi'i Divide

One of the largely unforeseen consequences of the US invasion of Iraq in 2003 was a dramatic alteration of the relative political influence of Sunni and Shi'i Muslims in the Middle East. At least two factors have increased the tension surrounding religion and politics in and among majority Muslim states in the region. The first was the overthrow of the Baath party government in Iraq, which for close to 40 years had been dominated by the country's Sunni minority. The elections that followed the invasion brought to power a nascent Shi'i elite and at times during the violent years from 2003 to 2007 there was a significant threat of civil war between the Sunni and Shi'i Arab populations. A second factor was a shift in the strategic balance of the Middle East in favour of Iran, a Shi'i Islamic Republic. The revisionist policies of the Iranian state led US President George W. Bush to label it a member of the 'Axis of Evil' alongside Iraq and North Korea. Since the US interventions in the region that followed 9/11, the rising importance of Iran as a strategic player has served to increase the polarization of the politics of Islamic identity in both overt and implicit ways.

As was noted earlier, the division between Sunni and Shi'i Islam is rooted in the historic division over the succession of leadership after the death of the Prophet Muhammad. The defeat of the *shi'at Ali* in the late seventh century led the Shi'i to develop a theology of oppression that the Sunni tradition does not share. To this day, the Shi'i mark the day of Ashura—the annual commemoration of Hussein's death—with self-flagellation and ritual mourning. The Shi'i sense of historic injustice combined with an eschatological hope that in the end their resistance to Sunni authority would be vindicated. The more formalized understanding of religious leadership among the Shi'i gives both religious and lay leaders a ready-made form of political organization that has proven to be especially potent.

For many centuries, Shi'i were disempowered under Sunni rule. In states such as Iraq and Lebanon, where they came to be numerous, they remained largely disenfranchised and poor. However, several developments over the past decades have empowered the Shi'i clergy and religious parties, among them the Iranian Revolution of 1979, the Lebanese Civil War and resistance against Israel in the 1980s and 1990s, and the US invasion of Iraq. By the end of the first decade of the twenty-first century Shi'i parties were important actors in the region. In Iraq, several rival political alliances take an Islamist position among the Shi'i, including the Da'wa party, the Islamic Supreme Council of Iraq, and a variety of politicians allied with Moqtada al-Sadr, a populist revolutionary religious leader who rose quickly to prominence in post-invasion Iraq and represents a new generation of Shi'i resistance figures. In Lebanon, the Hezbollah and Amal parties represent Shi'i interests of in the National Assembly and frequently try to impose their will on other sectarian groupings. The Iranian government of Mahmoud Ahmedinejad dominated world headlines when it defied Security Council resolutions calling for his country to submit to nuclear inspections.

In a widely debated book, Vali Nasr argues that '[u]ltimately, the character of the region [of the Middle East] will be decided in the crucible of Shia revival and the Sunni response to it' (Nasr 2007: 22). In his view, the resurgence of Shi'i power throughout

Box 5.3: Some Leading Contemporary Islamist Movements and Parties

AK Party (Turkey) Known by the acronym of its Turkish name, which means 'Justice and Development', the AKP rose to form the government after the forced disbanding of an earlier party known as *Refah* ('Welfare'). The AKP is commonly described as a 'mildly Islamist' party that includes many religious activists. It has spent the last decade working against the formerly dominant secular parties and the secular establishment bolstered by the Turkish armed forces.

Muslim Brotherhood (Egypt, Jordan, Syria) The Brotherhood (*Ikhwan al-Muslimun*) was founded by Hassan al-Banna as a fraternal organization based loosely on the model of a Sufi order. Its informal revivalist approach inspired the formation of numerous branches throughout the Arab and Muslim world. It has also meant wide variations in the political methods preached by Muslim Brothers as they embrace diverse theologies and seek to address the needs of various societies. The Brotherhood has spawned political parties (in Jordan), engaged in unofficial electoral contestation (in Egypt), and formed illegal religious nationalist resistance movements (in Syria and among the Palestinians).

Hezbollah (Lebanon) A Shi'i national resistance movement organized during the Lebanese Civil War of the 1980s, Hezbollah is reviled in many Western states as a terrorist movement linked to Iran and aimed at the destruction of the state of Israel. It actively maintains an arsenal of weapons and its attack on Israeli soldiers led to open war with Israel in the summer of 2006. Hezbollah also operates as a leading political party and provides a wide array of social services for the people of Lebanon.

Afghan insurgency (Afghanistan/Pakistan) Often loosely identified as the Taliban, after the former government of Afghanistan, the insurgents also include numerous other individuals and groups who support a radical and repressive interpretation of Islam. These groups claim Islamist ideological motivations but are also united by common Pashtun ethnic ties and long-term enmity toward the governing coalition in Afghanistan.

Jamaat-e-Islami (Pakistan) The *Jamaat* is the leading Islamist faction in Pakistan. Founded by Abul Ala Maududi in 1941, it has been linked to various politicians and parties. It has also influenced the radical insurgent movements in Afghanistan and Kashmir.

Iraqi National Alliance (Iraq) An alliance of various Shi'i Islamist parties, including the Islamic Supreme Council of Iraq (ISCI) and political supporters of the revolutionary religious leader Moqtada al-Sadr, formed for the 2010 Iraqi national elections. The INA became the leading voice of Shi'i political Islam in the nation. It now participates in the governing coalition.

PAS (Malaysia) The Pan-Malaysian Islamic Party, or PAS, is a major Islamist voice in the Malaysian opposition. It calls for a more intentionally Islamic state in Malaysia based on the Shari'a.

PKS (Indonesia) The Prosperous Justice Party or PKS is one of numerous political parties that draw on Islamic sources to criticize social policy and government and bureaucratic corruption. In keeping with Indonesia's resistance to more militant forms of Islam, the PKS does not call for the application of Shari'a but advocates for a more moral society based on traditional Islamic teaching.

the Middle East and elsewhere constitutes a pivotal development for the politics of Muslim societies. Still, the implications are not clear-cut: for all the concern that the growth in Shi'i power would be destabilizing for the region, Nasr suggests that Shi'i are not likely to embrace the extremism and universalism of Sunni Islamism. The relative growth of Iranian power has not necessarily translated into a wider 'Shi'i axis' in the Middle East, even though local rivalries between Sunni and Shi'i have deepened in significance.

Conclusion

Hundreds of millions of people around the world embrace Islam as a way of life. Given the foundational role that Islam plays in the culture of Muslim societies, it is not surprising that it has always had a significant political role. In more recent times, the phenomenon of political Islam has developed as a response to Western colonization and globalization. It seeks to reverse modern innovations and revive what it considers to be the pure Islam of the first generations of Muslims, the *Salafs*. More radical and militant interpretations of Islam gave rise to the modern *jihadi* threats to Western societies and interests. Elsewhere, the influence of Islam has contributed to the development of opposition and mass political movements in majority Muslim societies. The growing political power of Shi'i Muslims has challenged the age-old dominance of their Sunni counterparts, but the overall political impact of these divisions remains a matter of some controversy. What is clear is that political Islam in its many manifestations is now a dominant political force throughout the world.

Review Questions

1. Why is Islam widely considered a more political religion than others?
2. How did the history of Islam contribute to its global political role?
3. What was the influence of Ibn Taymiyya on the development of militant political Islam?
4. What is Salafism and how did it become a political force in Muslim societies?
5. How did the Ayatollah Khomeini institutionalize Islamic government in Iran?
6. How was the ideology of the Islamist movement affected by (a) the Afghan War of the 1980s and (b) the suspension of elections in Algeria in 1991?
7. What are the bases and history of the global *jihadi* movement?
8. How have Islamist political parties and movements fared in democratic elections over the past few decades?
9. How does the division of the Muslim community between Shi'i and Sunni play out in global politics?

Sources and Further Reading

Abed-Kotob, Sana (1995). 'The Accommodationists Speak: Goals and Strategies of the Muslim Brotherhood of Egypt'. *International Journal of Middle East Studies* 27, 3: 321–39.

Anderson, Lisa (1997). 'Fulfilling Prophecies: State Policy and Islamist Radicalism'. In John L. Esposito, ed. *Political Islam: Revolution, Radicalism, or Reform?* Boulder: Lynne Rienner: 17–31.

Ayubi, Nazih (1991). *Political Islam*. London: Routledge.

Bat Ye'or (2005). *Eurabia: the Euro-Arab Axis*. Madison, NJ: Fairleigh Dickinson University Press.

Caldwell, Christopher (2009). *Reflections on the Revolution in Europe: Immigration, Islam, and the West*. New York: Doubleday.

Coll, Steve (2004). *Ghost Wars: The Secret History of the CIA, Afghanistan, and Bin Laden, from the Soviet Invasion to September 10, 2001*. New York: Penguin Books.

Eickelman, Dale F. and James Piscatori (1996). *Muslim Politics*. Princeton: Princeton University Press.

Donohue, John J., and John Esposito, eds. (2007) *Islam in Transition: Muslim Perspectives*. 2nd edition. New York: Oxford University Press.

Esposito, John L. (1993). *The Islamic Threat: Myth or Reality?* New York: Oxford University Press.

———. (2005). *Islam: The Straight Path*. Revised 3rd edition. New York: Oxford University Press.

Feldman, Noah (2008). *The Fall and Rise of the Islamic State*. Princeton: Princeton University Press.

Fuller, Graham E. (2003). *The Future of Political Islam*. New York: Palgrave.

Hadar, Leon T. (1993). 'What Green Peril?' *Foreign Affairs* 72, 2 (Spring 1993): 27–42.

Haddad, Yvonne Yazbeck (1992). 'Islamists and the "Problem of Israel": The 1967 Awakening', *Middle East Journal* 46, 2: 266–85.

Hale, William, and Ergun Ozbudun (2010). *Islamism, Democracy and Liberalism in Turkey*. London: Routledge.

Hefner, Robert W. (2000). *Civil Islam: Muslims and Democratization in Indonesia*. Princeton: Princeton University Press.

Ibrahim, Saad Eddin (1980). 'Anatomy of Egypt's Militant Islamic Groups: Methodological Note and Preliminary Findings'. *International Journal of Middle East Studies* 12,4: 423–53.

Kramer, Martin (1996). *Arab Awakening and Islamic Revival*. New Brunswick, NJ: Transaction Publishers.

Lewis, Bernard (1993). *Islam and the West*. Oxford: Oxford University Press.

Mandaville, Peter (2007). *Global Political Islam*. London: Routledge.

Miller, Judith (1993). 'The Challenge of Radical Islam'. *Foreign Affairs* 72, 2 (Spring 1993): 43–56.

Nasr, Vali (2007). *The Shia Revival*. New York: W.W. Norton.

Phillips, Melanie (2006). *Londonistan*. New York: Encounter Books.

Pipes, Daniel (2003). *Militant Islam Reaches America*. New York: W.W. Norton.

Qutb, Sayyid (1991). *Milestones*. Delhi: Markazi Maktaba Islami.

Ramadan, Tariq (2004). *Western Muslims and the Future of Islam*. Oxford: Oxford University Press.

Roy, Olivier (2004). *Globalized Islam: The Search for a New Ummah*. New York: Columbia University Press.

Rutherford, Bruce K. (2006). 'What Do Egypt's Islamists Want? Moderate Islam and the Rise of Islamic Constitutionalism'. *Middle East Journal* 60, 4: 707–31.

Ruthven, Malise (1997). *Islam: A Very Short Introduction*. Oxford: Oxford University Press.

Sadowski, Yahya (1993). 'The New Orientalism and the Democracy Debate'. *Middle East Report* 23, 4: 14–21, 40.

Said, Edward (1979). *Orientalism*. New York: Vintage Books.

———(1981). *Covering Islam*. New York: Pantheon Books.

Saravanamuttu, Johan, ed. (2010). *Islam and Politics in Southeast Asia*. London: Routledge.

Schwedler, Jillian (2006). *Faith in Moderation: Islamist Parties in Jordan and Yemen*. Cambridge: Cambridge University Press.

Wright, Lawrence (2006). *The Looming Tower: Al-Qaeda and the Road to 9/11*. New York: Vintage Books.

Wright, Robin (2001). *Sacred Rage: The Wrath of Militant Islam*. Revised ed. New York: Simon and Schuster.

Yavuz, M. Hakan (2009). *Secularism and Muslim Democracy in Turkey*. Cambridge: Cambridge University Press.

Web Resources

www.baylor.edu/church_state/index.php?id=35355 – The Islam and Democracy Project

islamonline.com – Islam Online: Islamic news and information.

www.cair.com – The Council on American-Islamic Relations; the leading Muslim lobby in the US.

Chapter 6

Religion and Politics in India

Indian history and society should be topics of significant interest to anyone who studies world politics. India is the world's largest functioning democracy, with frequent, heavily contested elections and a vibrant civil society. Democratic politics in India are extremely competitive, with a multitude of political parties representing different regional and ethnic identities, as well as different ideologies and religions. Although India is a professedly secular country, the influence of religion as a political force has increased dramatically in the years since the country gained its independence from Britain in 1947. Religion is so significant a force in Indian society that it would be very difficult to understand Indian public life without some notion of the religious traditions in play.

To the uninitiated, Indian religious traditions are exotic and the worldview that underpins them does not easily fit into the standard categories that define Western traditions. The most fundamental elements of Western religion—theology, orthodoxy, confessional identity, the norm of separation of church and state—are not applied in the same way in India. The very idea of religion as devotion to the idea of God, dogmatic teachings, and correct practice, is challenged by India's openness to the mixing of religious ideas and practices. Indian religions don't lend themselves to comparison with Judaism, Christianity, or Islam in particular. Likewise, even though India, like its Commonwealth counterparts, is a parliamentary democracy, Indian political movements do not always reflect the categories that divide civil society, political parties, and state institutions in other parts of the world. Indian religion's unique tolerance of **syncretism** lays the groundwork for an interesting study in the relationship between religion and global politics. Both India's relations with its neighbours and its internal politics have been affected by the politics of religion, as we shall see in this chapter's discussions of India's nuclear arsenal, its contested borders with Pakistan in the area of Kashmir, the attacks it has suffered at the hands of militant Islamists, and its continuing debate over the constitutional notion of secularism.

India is an emerging giant. With almost 1.2 billion people, it is the world's second-largest country by population and its most populous democracy. The strength of India's commitment to democratic governance is especially remarkable given that it is a developing country with high levels of both diversity and poverty. Except for a brief period in the 1970s when elections were suspended under a 'state of emergency' decree, India has experienced a regular democratic turnover of power at both the federal and state levels. The major political parties represent a wide variety of interests: secular, nationalist, socialist, and religious.

India is also a diverse and complicated country with an ancient history and entrenched traditions. A shared history and culture unite the countries of South Asia, including India, Pakistan, Afghanistan, Bangladesh, Nepal, and Sri Lanka. In part, this history has shaped the way religion affects Indian national identity, since the country has been defined in part by contrast with its neighbours. The modern states of Pakistan and Bangladesh were carved out of the former British India in 1947 as homelands for South Asian Muslims. Yet India itself is divided along multiple linguistic, ethnic, and religious lines. It is a federal state that encompasses 28 states and seven union territories, many of which are home to particular ethno-linguistic or religious groups. In 2001, approximately 80 per cent of Indians identified themselves as Hindus and 13 per cent as Muslims. Christians made up just over 2 per cent of the population and Sikhs just under 2, while Buddhists, Jains, and others together accounted for the rest.

What Is Hinduism?

The earliest Indian religious traditions have been practised literally since time immemorial. They were the foundations from which at least three other important traditions—Buddhism, Jainism, and Sikhism—developed, along with the yogic spirituality that has become popular in the West in recent times. But those traditions are not the only ones that have been practised in India. In the first few centuries of the present era, Christian missionaries introduced their beliefs and traditions to its coasts. The first Arab Muslims reached India as early as the seventh century, and by the sixteenth century much of the country had been incorporated into the Muslim Mughal Empire. Religion continues to pervade Indian culture in countless ways, from the legacy of the ancient caste system to the divisions that pit one community versus another in the northwest and the passionate contemporary debates over the influence of religious communities on the **personal status laws** that govern matters such as marriage and divorce. Indeed, few countries have been so shaped by religion as India.

Exploring the relationship between religion and politics in India is complicated by the fact that, strictly speaking, the word 'Hinduism' refers not so much to a particular religion as to the indigenous culture of the Indian subcontinent. In the same way, the term 'Hindu religion' refers not to a single, clearly defined set of beliefs and practices but to all aspects of indigenous Indian spirituality and philosophy. The very definition of Hinduism can therefore be understood as nationalistic: in that sense, any religion that is now indigenous to India is 'Hindu'. However, the term 'Hinduism' has come to mean something quite different among Westerners, and by the same token, among Indians. Between the sixteenth and twentieth centuries, different parts of India were colonized by several European powers, most importantly Great Britain. It was the European interest in studying Indian religion, and the colonizers' need to organize and control Indian society for their own benefit, that led to the categorization of Indians according to their religious traditions. In this way beliefs and practices that were distinct from Muslim and Christian traditions came to be identified as part of a larger system called 'Hinduism'. Today the term 'Hinduism' typically refers to the traditional polytheistic and deistic beliefs and practices dating back to the Vedas, the ancient Sanskrit writings held sacred by most Indians. Since they do not embrace these traditions, Indian Muslims, Christians, and even Sikhs and Jains generally reject the notion that they are 'Hindu'. In the past two decades, the lines surrounding the Hindu community in India have been more narrowly defined and have taken on a crucial political role. R. Sen (2010: 1–29) argues that over time the hardening of the boundaries of Hinduism has been interpreted in ways that conflate it with religious nationalism in the form of *hindutva*, a term to which we will return. This has had an important impact on both internal politics and Indian foreign policy.

It is important from the beginning to understand that Hinduism differs from most other religions both in its internal diversity and in its lack of a strong tradition of orthodoxy. Hindus practise many different forms of devotion and Hinduism does not impose any stringent requirements on either belief or practice. However, there are many unifying features of the Hindu tradition. Hindus recognize thousands of deities, but all of them are considered to be manifestations of one supreme being: Brahman, the consciousness of the universe. Brahman is represented in three forms: Brahma the creator, Vishnu the preserver, and Shiva the destroyer. Many Hindus worship just one of three principal deities: Vishnu, Shiva, and the Goddess Devi or Parvati, who is Shiva's consort. Hindu theology suggests that all people come to know the divine through their acts of devotion, no matter what they are. Hence it is often described as a universalist tradition that does not rule out the possibility that other religions could be valid.

Still, Hinduism also promotes broad concepts about the meaning and interpretation of life that challenge other religious viewpoints. For example, Hinduism tends to see each human life as a reflection of the individual's *karma* (action), either in this life or in previous lives, guided by the *dharma* that is his or her essential character, religious obligation, or destiny. Both of these concepts could be construed as fatalistic, interpreting life as the outcome of previous lives and one's place in the cosmos. This creates both commonalities and differences with other religious traditions. For example, in their affirmation of the unicity and transcendence of the divine, Hindus may find common cause with the Sufi mystics of Islam (the Hindu devotional tradition known as **bhakti** has had a profound influence on many Sufi orders, and vice versa). At the same time, they contradict basic Muslim and Christian teachings about the unique place of human beings in the world and the distinction between humans and the divine.

Hinduism has no single 'holy book', but there are several important religious texts. First among them are the **Vedas**, four ancient Sanskrit texts, the oldest of which contains material thought to have been composed before 1500 BCE. The Vedas are the most holy works of Hinduism and include hymns, rituals, and philosophic texts, most importantly the philosophic teachings known as the Upanishads. Many of the basic teachings of Hindu philosophy, such as *karma*, *dharma,* and *samsara* (the cycle of rebirth), come from the Vedas. Also fundamental to the tradition are the *Mahabharata* and the *Ramayana*, two pseudo-historical epic poems about great heroes who represent Hindu virtues. The best-known part of the *Mahabharata* is a section called the *Bhagavad Gita*, which takes the form of a conversation between the great hero Arjuna and his cousin Krishna (an avatar of the god Vishnu) about the right way of life (*dharma*). Today the most popular of the epics is likely the *Ramayana*, the story of Rama, a great warrior-king who is forced into exile and then returns to rule his people as the model of the righteous king.

Two other important collections are the *Puranas*, a set of mythological narratives of ancient times that have devotional application, and the *Dharmashastras*, codes of law and conduct that serve as guides to fulfilling *dharma*. The most important of the *Dharmashastra* texts, known in English as the *Laws of Manu,* sets out the positions and duties of the four major castes into which Hindu society was divided. In its original form, there were four **varnas** ('colours'): the priestly **Brahmins**, the royal warriors called **Kshatriyas**, the merchants or **Vaishyas**, and the servants or **Shudras**. Excluded even from the caste system were the 'untouchables', who today are generally known as **Dalits**. Within each *varna* were numerous smaller groups of people who in some ways functioned as tribes unto themselves, known as castes and subcastes (*jati*). The various castes of India add to the social complexity of an already very diverse society.

The caste system was abolished in 1950 and its influence has declined with increasing urbanization and Westernization. Still, the notion of caste remains significant in its cultural power even today, and in a classic study of Indian development, Lloyd and Susanne Hoeber Rudolph (1967) argued that caste was still an important social

Box 6.1: Religion and Caste in India

Westerners often misunderstand the nuances of caste in India. The origins of the castes are described in the *Laws of Manu* (c. second century CE), which describes the four castes as springing from Brahman's 'mouth, arms, thighs, and feet', but the system had its roots in the ancient Vedas.

It was the *dharma* of the highest *varna*, the Brahmins, to teach and study the Vedas. Next came the Kshatriyas, whose first priority was 'to protect the people', the Vaishyas, who would engage in agriculture and merchant commerce, and finally the Shudras, whose purpose was 'to serve meekly' the other castes (*Laws of Manu* 1: 87–91). The fact that each caste had its own specific *dharma* imposed occupational restrictions and created a hierarchy in which the Brahmins occupied the top rank. Members of the three highest castes were said to be 'twice-born', a status affirmed in a ritual initiation in adolescence.

The social roots of caste differentiation are a matter of conjecture, but they applied to the people of an ancient Indian civilization. Those who stood outside that civilization came to be understood as ritually impure outliers or 'outcastes'. Today these people call themselves Dalits, and they form a large underclass in Indian society. Non-Hindu and tribal groups as well generally stood outside the caste system. Since caste distinctions were not recognized among Muslims, Christians, Buddhists, or Sikhs, conversion to one of these religious traditions has often translated into upward mobility for the backward castes. Even though the caste system was officially abolished under the Indian constitution of 1950, the fact that one is born into a caste by virtue of descent in a particular tribal group or *jati* means that caste distinctions continue to have social weight.

The Indian government relies on a system of 'reservations' (quotas) to improve the social mobility of disadvantaged groups, of which it recognizes three types. By putting an end to caste distinctions while accepting affirmative action for caste groups, the constitution simultaneously eliminates and reinforces them. 'Scheduled castes' are the traditionally recognized lower castes of Hindu society. 'Scheduled tribes' are the non-Hindu peoples of the tribal areas of India. 'Other backward classes' are groups identified as underprivileged under government programs. The latter category is a fluid one that the government has interpreted in various ways since it was enshrined in the constitution.

Recent decades have seen several cases of mass conversion to other faiths by particular Hindu groups: Dalits to Christianity (Madhya Pradesh, 1952) and Buddhism (Nagpur, 1956); Tamils to Islam (Meenakshipuram, 1981). In addition, more gradual missionary work has won over converts among Dalit groups such as the Bhangis and Chamars. Such incidents have upset *hindutva* nationalist groups in the past (Frykenburg 2008: 473–8). They have also presented a complication for government officials trying to classify underprivileged groups according to Hindu caste. Finally, political parties of all stripes, from large brokerage parties (the Congress and BJP) to parties of the 'backward castes' (such as the Bahujan Samaj Party) regularly design their election platforms to appeal specifically to disadvantaged groups.

organizing feature that had been adapted to modernity in less than obvious ways (Rudolph and Rudolph 1967). Caste groups are not simply social strata analogous to socioeconomic classes: they also form tribal and political networks that mobilize at election season and lobby on behalf of group grievances. Government programs designed to alleviate the harm done by the caste system provide protection, affirmative action, and special resources for 'scheduled castes', 'scheduled tribes', and 'other backward castes'.

Two other distinctive features of Hindu society are its traditions regarding the status of women, married women in particular, and the sacredness of life. The ancient practice of *sati* (immolation of the widow on her husband's funeral pyre) was rooted in the belief that widows were ritually impure. Although *sati* was outlawed in the nineteenth century, many argue that women still face discrimination and abuse, even murder, because of Hindu conventions regarding matters such as inheritance and dowries (Agarwal 1994). By contrast, since the middle ages, Hindus have considered the cow a sacred animal that should not be harmed. As a result, cows wander the Indian countryside unmolested and the consumption of beef is strictly taboo, a custom that in recent times has been reinforced by law in most Indian states. In addition, many Hindu sects (as well as Sikhism and Jainism) either recommend or require that believers show their respect for the souls of all animals by following a vegetarian diet.

Hinduism, Islam, and Indian Independence

By the time British forces arrived in India beginning in the eighteenth century, the Muslim Mughal Empire, which had controlled most of the subcontinent since the early 1500s, was in decline. British colonial authorities consolidated their control over India through direct rule in some areas and in others through arrangements with local *maharajas* (princes) and large-scale landlords known as *zamindars*. After the 'Mutiny' of 1857, in which Indian soldiers in British employ led a rebellion against British rule, India came under direct administration as an overseas British colony. An extremely diverse and restive nation, still subject to the tensions that had existed under the former Mughal rulers, India was perceived by its new rulers as a hotbed of sectarian division in which the volatile tribes of Hindus and Muslims in particular needed to be pacified and managed.

Gyanendra Pandey (1990) argues that the colonial authorities classified all disturbances within the Hindu and Muslim communities of north India as religious and sectarian, regardless of their actual nature, and ignored the impact of colonial rule itself. Even disagreements over secular issues such as property were interpreted by the British merely as evidence of the warlike and collectivist tendencies of India's 'communal' groups. However, Pandey's argument that such 'communalism' was a construction of the colonial period does not mean that conflict between the religious communities disappeared in the post-colonial period. On the contrary, religious discord has contributed significantly to the breakdown of authority that Atul Kohli (1990) described as India's 'crisis of governability'. It has also motivated a large-scale effort on the part of Hindus to reinforce the Hindu character of the nation.

In 1947 the Indian subcontinent was partitioned to create the independent states of India and Pakistan. Prior to independence, the Indian nationalist movement had been divided along religious–communal lines. The early independence movement was led by the Indian National Congress, a secular nationalist movement of intellectuals, founded in 1885, that sought autonomy for all of British India. While its most prominent leaders, most notably Mohandas K. ('Mahatma') Gandhi (1869–1948), were Hindus, the Congress deliberately sought to include leaders from each of the major religious minorities (Muslims, Sikhs, and Christians). Gandhi, who by the 1920s was the movement's leader, had been educated in Britain and had led a movement for equality in South Africa before returning to India in 1915.

Deeply troubled by the potential for anti-colonial demonstrations to become violent, Gandhi developed a philosophy that stressed non-violent resistance, which he called *satyagraha* ('truth-seeking' or 'truth-force'). *Satyagraha* was strongly influenced by Hindu, Jain, and Christian concepts of pacifism, in addition to the work of Leo Tolstoy.

Mohandas K. Gandhi (1869–1948), known as the Mahatma ('great soul'), is an enduring figure in Indian national consciousness. Gandhi led the resistance to British occupation through his personal commitment to non-violence (ahimsa) and to the unity and dignity of India. Gandhi's generous attitude toward all religions was later challenged by Nehru's secular nationalism and the Hindu nationalist hindutva movement.
Source: Daily Herald Archive/SSPL/Getty Images

Gandhi believed that in essence all religions sought after the same goals of truth and peace. He thus combined a liberal and non-sectarian notion of Indian citizenship with a great enthusiasm for the moral force of religion. He spoke continually of the need to understand Truth as a divine notion, and emphasized that an individual's commitment to non-violent change would require a sacrifice no different from religious sacrifice. Thus *satyagraha* implied the acceptance of suffering in the pursuit of a greater, divine good, or 'vindication of Truth not by infliction of suffering on the opponent but on one's self' (Gandhi 2002: 86).

The application of *satyagraha* in his own life included non-violent resistance to British rule and led him to embrace a life of simplicity and asceticism. He became known for wearing simple clothes of his own making, both as a gesture to simplicity and as means of boycotting foreign-made clothing. Gandhi became the driving force behind the success of the Indian nationalist movement, and his philosophy was influential in the debates over the Indian constitution's provisions regarding religion. Gandhi's influence on India's history and on religious notions of non-violence worldwide is considerable, but his philosophy was not embraced by all Indians. In fact, as India's independence drew near, Gandhi was deeply disappointed by the growing violence within Indian society, especially the Hindu nationalist movement's chauvinistic attacks on Indian Muslims. He was assassinated by just such an extremist, a man named Nathuram Godse, in 1948.

The British colony of India was divided by previous arrangements between the Muslim majority areas of Pakistan and the Hindu majority areas of India. By the 1940s the Indian independence movement was divided between two major parties—the Indian National Congress, which sought a secular and non-sectarian India, and the Muslim League, which represented a broad majority of Muslims who desired separate political arrangements for Muslim-majority areas—and several smaller parties and movements. On the insistence of the Muslim League and the British authorities, the subcontinent was partitioned into a Hindu-majority area that formed the modern state of India, and two Muslim-majority regions known as East and West Pakistan. Today, West Pakistan is the country we know as Pakistan and East Pakistan has been the independent state of Bangladesh since a civil war it fought in 1971.

While Muslim-majority regions of colonial India were incorporated into the state of Pakistan, many millions of Muslims and others remained within India proper, particularly in areas of north India such as Kashmir, Gujarat, Rajasthan, and Uttar Pradesh. In the same way, many Hindus, Sikhs, and Christians found themselves inside the borders of Pakistan. The partition of colonial India was achieved at the cost of terrible violence, rape and abduction of women in certain areas, and massive displacement of population as Muslims and Hindus alike were uprooted and forced to start new lives in places far from their traditional homes. Portions of the boundary between India and Pakistan have remained in dispute ever since independence.

Amid the violence and chaos, new institutions and a new constitution were promulgated for India. The 1950 constitution laid out the structures of the Indian democratic state. It created a parliamentary system based generally on the Westminster model, run by a prime minister and cabinet drawn from the parties that are elected to the central legislature in New Delhi, known as the Sansad Bhavan. The parliament is bicameral, with a dominant lower house (the *Lok Sabha*).

It is important to note that while Pakistan was created as a homeland for Muslims, the designers of India's constitution envisioned a secular state that would be home to people of all religious backgrounds. Jawaharlal Nehru, Gandhi's successor as leader of the Indian National Congress, did not share his enthusiasm for spirituality and religion. In Nehru's view, religion was an atavistic diversion that hindered Indian development. In spite of his respect for Gandhi and people of religious faith, he was a modernist who felt that religion should play no part in public life. As a result, Nehru worked to enshrine secularism as a guiding political philosophy in India (Madan 1998: 233–47). The constitution that he helped to draw up was strongly influenced by the Enlightenment traditions that framed constitutionalism in countries like the United States. It included normal clauses guaranteeing freedom of religion and it did not enshrine any particular religion. In fact, the preamble to the Indian constitution was further amended in 1976 to describe India as a 'sovereign socialist secular democratic republic', a formula unique to India.

At the same time, the drafters of the constitution were deeply aware of the importance of religion in Indian public life, particularly in the way that religion affected citizens' lives through the caste system and personal status laws. Secularism as defined in the constitution was constrained by several articles that drove the courts to take an interventionist role with respect to the public practice and interpretation of religion. In particular, the courts have worked toward the constitutional goal of establishing a universal personal status code, which could be seen as favouring the Hindu majority over minority communities (Sen 2010: 201). The nature of Indian secularism has become a source of endless debate among Indian scholars. It is widely understood to require *neutrality* with regard to religion rather than strict European-style separation of church and state, but the application of this principle is a matter of some controversy. The state is expected not to eliminate religion from public life, but to arbitrate between religions. In the words of one analyst, 'secularism requires principled distance, not exclusion or equidistance' (Srinivasan 2007: 41). Proponents of Gandhian philosophy suggested that Indian secularism had to be understood in the context of a deeply religious society. Others argued that the Indian government should seek to preserve the traditional Hindu religious and philosophic ideals and defend the one Hindu state on the basis of Hindu values. Still others supported the Nehruvian modernist ideal of secularism (Srinivasan 2007). These divisions have become sources of severe friction in the Indian state.

While ensuring freedom of religion in articles 25 and 26, therefore, the constitution also allows the courts to pursue legislative change that is likely to trample on freedom of religion. For example, article 17 abolishes caste, specifically 'untouchability', which in itself could be argued to contradict a key doctrine of Hindu religious thought. One of the most controversial implications of the interplay of religion and secularism in India is the fact that religious authorities retain the right to rule over personal status law. The constitution announces the state's intention to create a single civil code (which would be used to judge in cases of family and personal status) in article 44: 'the State shall endeavour to secure for the citizens a uniform civil code throughout the territory

Table 6.1 Religions in India, 2001 (%)

Hindus	80.5	Buddhists	0.8
Muslims	13.4	Jains	0.4
Christians	2.3	Other	0.6
Sikhs	1.9	Not stated	0.1

Source: Indian Census, 2001. Available at: http://censusindia.gov.in/Census_Data_2001/India_at_glance/religion.aspx

of India'. Nevertheless, in an attempt to preserve national unity, neither Nehru nor his successors have made any attempt to overturn the Shari'a courts that have the right to rule on civil matters for Muslims. The result was a major crisis in the *Shah Bano* court case in the 1980s, to which we will return.

The Rise of Hindu Nationalism

Despite the religious diversity of its population and the contradictions implicit in its putatively secular constitution, India largely avoided serious crises over religion until the 1980s, when a religious nationalist movement became increasingly influential. The most likely explanation for this development was the strength of the Indian National Congress (popularly known as the Congress party), which maintained strong majorities in the parliament (the Lok Sabha) until 1976. The foundations of the Congress party's dominance were its clientelist approach and its ability to placate and balance the many different interests represented by the Indian populace. Congress worked to create a widely varied constituency, including religious and ethnic minorities, lower castes, and the Indian establishment. It generally followed the Nehruvian notion that modernization would eliminate religion from Indian public life. Martha Nussbaum (2007) argues that Nehru failed to appreciate the universal appeal of religion and thus left a vacuum that later Hindu nationalist movements could exploit (118). By the mid-1970s, the Congress coalition was fraying. The beneficiaries of Congress's decline were the nationalist parties of the right, who largely based their ideology on Hindu cultural and religious solidarity, and numerous smaller parties devoted to the political advance of various national identities in Indian society.

Since colonial days, a nationalist movement dedicated to reviving the Hindu traditional way of life and rediscovering ancient Hindu virtues had formed a counterpoint to the more inclusive philosophy of Congress. The roots of this movement were in the work of V.D. Savarkar (1883–1966), an outspoken critic of Congress throughout the late colonial period. In his most famous work, *Hindutva: Who Is a Hindu?* (written in 1923) Savarkar called for India to remain a united political entity (*akhand bharat*) and a Hindu nation (*hindu rashtra*). He coined the term **hindutva** ('Hinduness') that has come to be used as a label for a broad array of groups that have adopted his Hindu-nationalist message. While Savarkar himself was not motivated by religion, he believed that the Hindu, Jain, Buddhist, and Sikh traditions were all rooted in the

Indian subcontinent and therefore were all truly Hindu, whereas other religions, most notably Islam and Christianity, were not Hindu because they were originally imported to the subcontinent. He developed a political philosophy centred on the notion of a state dedicated to preserving the essential Hindu philosophies represented by these indigenous religions. This was the basic sense of *hindutva*.

The 1920s were a time of great nationalist activism and tumult in India. During that time a number of groups were formed that shared many of Savarkar's ideas. The most influential of these groups was the Rashtriya Swayamsevak Sangh ('National Volunteers Organization'), widely known as the RSS. The RSS was founded in 1925 by K.P. Hedgewar in an effort to create enthusiasm for traditional Hindu values among the youth of India and to respond to various social needs. In those respects it represented a parallel to various religious, nationalist, and socialist movements that were established both in Europe and in other parts of the developing world in that period. The RSS is represented at the local level in small community organizations known as *shakhas*, whose male members are easy to recognize by their uniform of khaki shorts and white shirts. Since 1925, a wide variety of other groups were founded on the political principle of *hindutva*; today these groups are represented by a loose organization known as the **sangh parivar**.

The political salience of these groups remained fairly marginal through the early post-independence period. An official ban on community activity on the part of the RSS was instituted in 1948 but lifted the following year. The RSS gradually grew in numbers and support, most notably under the charismatic leadership of its second supreme chief, M.S. Golwalkar (1906–73). In 1964, the *Vishva Hindu Parishad* or VHP (World Hindu Council) was formed as a global arm of the *hindutva* movement. The VHP joined forces with the RSS to become an influential political lobby.

Together, the various *hindutva* movements formed the most potent opposition to Congress during the 1970s. Among the *hindutva*-based political parties elected in this period, the most notable was the Jana Sangh, which took part in India's first coalition government following the defeat of Congress in 1977. The organizational strength of the RSS and the rest of the *sangh parivar* contributed to the increasing electoral success of the Jana Sangh's successor, the Bharatiya Janata Party (BJP), first elected to the Lok Sabha in 1984. Since that time, the BJP has become the leading *hindutva* party and the largest conservative brokerage party in Indian politics, building a supportive network among the various arms of the *sangh parivar*.

As Congress continued to decline through the 1980s, the expansion of mass media in India was helping Indians to rediscover their cultural roots and celebrate Hindu traditions. Meanwhile, Congress continued to resist structural adjustment, and developments in the world economy came to challenge the sustainability of India's socialist policies and Congress's traditional clientelist behaviour. The BJP promised to revivify Indian culture, oppose Westernization and cultural imperialism, and promote *swadeshi*, a term the BJP used for the search for self-sufficiency and protecting key markets. By the 1990s the BJP was the leading opposition to Congress. In 1996 it became the largest single grouping in the Lok Sabha and in 1998 it managed to form a coalition government. BJP leader Atal Bihari Vajpayee became prime minister and served for most of the period from 1998 to 2004.

Sikh and Hindu Nationalist Movements in the 1980s

The rising popularity of the BJP in the 1980s and 1990s is credited mainly to a series of sensational and controversial political crises. An ongoing problem in relations between religious groups in India has been the conversion of outcaste groups to other religions as a way of escaping the cultural status assigned to them by Hindu tradition. In the

Box 6.2: The Sikh Tradition

Sikhism arose as a distinctive religious tradition in India in the sixteenth century. The founder of Sikhism, Guru Nanak Dev (1469–1539), was born near Lahore in modern-day Pakistan. Around the age of 30, after a spiritual experience in which he said he had encountered the one Lord God, Guru Nanak set out to preach the irrelevance of religious distinctions between Hindus and Muslims. Over the next two centuries, the disciples ('Sikhs') of Guru Nanak and his nine successors established a community in the Punjab region of northern India. The holiest site in Sikhism today is the Golden Temple in Amritsar.

By the time of the tenth Guru, Gobind Singh (1666-1708), the Sikh community had become an important political force. Gobind Singh instituted a new set of regulations for the community leaders, who formed a military order known as the **Khalsa**. Today observant Sikh men who enter the order are said to be 'baptized' or *amrit-dhaari*. Male members of the Khalsa wear five distinctive items of dress (known as the five 'k's)—uncut hair and beard (*kes*), a comb worn in the hair (*kangha*), a small dagger (*kirpan*), a ring on the right wrist (kara) and shorts (*kachh*)—and are easily identified by their turbans (*dastaar*).

The Sikh population of India is concentrated in the state of Punjab, where Sikhs form the largest religious community, but many also live in various other Indian states as well as in diaspora communities around the world. Sikh worship takes place in a building known as a *gurudwara* and centres on the singing of hymns—many composed by Guru Nanak—and readings from the holy scripture known as the *Guru Granth Sahib* ('revered book'); before his death, Guru Gobind Singh decreed that the book itself was to be his only successor. The *gurudwara* also serves as a community meeting place, and every service is followed by a communal meal, prepared by members of the congregation, known as a langar. Offered to everyone who attends the *gurudwara*, the langar is an important symbol of the Sikh faith's emphasis on egalitarianism: everyone, regardless of social status, sits on the floor together and eats the same food.

The leading Sikh political party, the Shiromani Akali Dal, has played a major role in governing coalitions at both the state and federal levels. Sikhs are proud of their history of standing strong against discrimination and persecution. In the late 1970s, Sikh groups were among the many that resisted Prime Minister Indira Gandhi's imposition of emergency rule. The resulting clampdown on Sikh political movements led some Sikh nationalists to begin demanding an independent homeland to be called **Khalistan**, the 'land of the pure'. In 1984, after a number of armed militants had occupied the Golden Temple complex in Amritsar for several weeks, the government launched 'Operation Blue Star': a violent assault on the militants in which many innocent pilgrims were killed or wounded and the holy site itself was severely damaged. The tensions between the Indian state and Sikh militants intensified accordingly, exacerbating Sikh alienation from the national government (Mahmood 1996). Nevertheless, individual Sikhs have been influential in Indian politics; the current prime minister, Manmohan Singh of the Indian National Congress, is a Sikh.

early 1980s, several mass conversions led to clashes between Hindus and Christians, most notably in the Kanyakumari district of the state of Tamil Nadu in March 1982. A government commission (the Venugopal Commission) formed to inquire into the riots held the RSS accountable. But individual governments have struggled to find a balance between protecting religious freedom and protecting individuals from feeling coerced into conversion. Mass conversions tend to inflame Hindu nationalist sentiment and motivate governments to legislate against proselytization. Such incidents help to bolster support for the BJP and its associated groups.

The diversity of Indian religions has also contributed to conflict among the historic Indian religions. The early 1980s were a period of immense turmoil, much of it sparked by the Khalistan issue (see Box 6.2). Sikh nationalists were divided over the desirability of a separate state, some feeling that they ought to remain in India to defend the freedom of their co-religionists living in other parts of India, outside Punjab (Madan 1998: 86–97). Finally, in a bid to provoke a confrontation with the Indian government, increase their influence over the Khalsa, and thereby take control of the nationalist movement, a group of armed separatists led by Jarnail Singh Bhindranwale and Shabeg Singh moved into the Golden Temple complex in Amritsar, the most holy site in the Sikh religion. In early June 1984, on the orders of Prime Minister Indira Gandhi, the Indian armed forces laid siege to the compound. In addition to the militants, scores of ordinary Sikh pilgrims to the temple, including women and children, were killed or wounded.

The Golden Temple, a focal point of the Sikh faith, was the site of a deadly battle waged between Indian forces and Sikh separatist militants in June 1984.
Source: © iStockphoto.com/ppart

Outraged by the violence and the desecration of their most holy site, Sikhs in various parts of India demonstrated against the government. A few months later, in October 1984, Prime Minister Gandhi was assassinated by some of her own Sikh bodyguards. In the wake of her murder, Sikhs were deliberately targeted by Hindus across India, most notably in the capital city of New Delhi, where thousands were

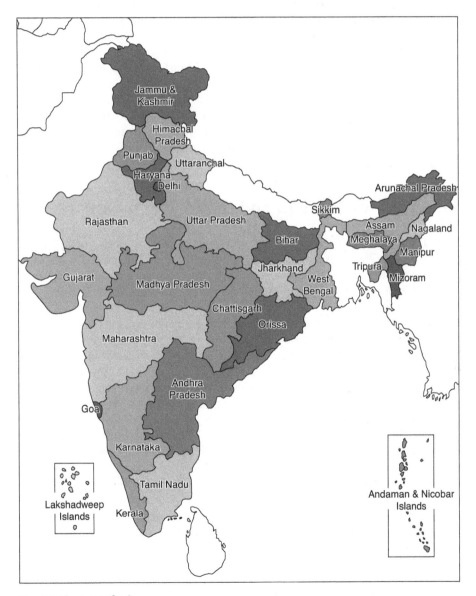

Map 6.1: The states of India
Source: © Embassy of India, Sofia (Bulgaria)

systematically killed. These tragedies led to further separatist violence, culminating in the June 1985 bombing of Air India flight 182, in which 329 people, most of them Canadian citizens, were killed. In addition to increasing nationalist sentiment among Sikhs, these events contributed to the growth of religious nationalism among Hindus.

Indian secularism also came under fire in 1986, when a controversial case involving the uneven application of personal status law made the headlines. A Muslim divorcee named Shah Bano was suing her ex-husband for regular alimony payments, but under Muslim status law her husband was required to pay her only a small lump sum. The Indian Supreme Court found that Shah Bano should receive alimony in contradiction to Islamic Shari'a law. The court's finding alarmed Muslims who felt that the ruling undermined their unique status in India and trampled on Muslim rights. In response, the Indian government led by Congress Prime Minister Rajiv Gandhi overruled the courts by passing a law that gave supremacy to the Islamic courts. This in turn caused resentment among Hindus who felt that the government was giving undue preference to religious minorities. The stridency of Hindu nationalist opposition to the ruling Congress party increased accordingly.

The Ayodhya Incident and the Rise of the BJP

These incidents and others contributed to a growing sense of siege among Hindus throughout India. Add to this the decline of central power, the gradual breakdown of state institutions amid local violence, and a worldwide turn toward postmodern rediscovery of religion, and the Hindu nationalist movements were largely the beneficiaries of political change. By the early 1990s, a Hindu revival was under way throughout India, focused on a movement to restore veneration of the birthplace of the Hindu god Ram, known as the *Ram Janmabhoomi*.

Lord Ram (or Rama) is the hero of the *Ramayana* epic, a legendary paragon of Hindu virtue and therefore a central figure in Hindu religion. His birthplace in the city of Ayodhya in the state of Uttar Pradesh was a traditional place of pilgrimage and veneration for Hindus, but in the sixteenth century a mosque was built on the site for the Mughal Emperor Babur I (for which reason it became known as the Babri mosque). The *sangh parivar* began cultivating the Ram cult as a symbol of the nation in the late 1980s, and in 1990 leaders of the RSS and VHP and politicians representing the BJP were among the participants in a cross-country march commemorating the ancient tradition of pilgrimage to the site. The fact that a television miniseries about the great hero had been broadcast in 1987–8 added to the popular interest in the event. Ram's commitment to *dharma* was associated with hypermasculine and military virtues and he was increasingly depicted carrying his bow and arrows as a defender of Indian soil and honour. Nussbaum (2007) argues that the Hindu nationalist movement appropriated the image of Ram as both a national figure and a newly militant nationalist hero (171).

The idea that the holy site of Ram's birthplace was covered by a mosque suddenly became a *cause célèbre* among Hindu nationalists. Resentment was stoked with references to ancient colonial oppression, creating a potent brew for public anger. Finally, on 6 December 1992, public demonstrations against the Islamic presence at the Hindu holy site culminated in violence and the mosque was destroyed. Communal riots throughout India resulted in the deaths of thousands of Muslims and Hindus alike (Vander Veer 1994a). The incident remains controversial, many Hindus maintaining that the presence of a mosque on sacred Hindu ground was an affront and Muslims feeling equally offended by the wanton destruction of a centuries-old place of worship.

Over the following years, Hindu extremists continued to use other religious groups, most notably the Muslim minority, as scapegoats for all sorts of political grievances. Vigilante movements under the rubric of the *sangh parivar* and *hindutva* ideology used minor provocations to launch public violence at various times. The Babri mosque episode raised the public profile of the BJP and moved it to the head of the pack of opposition parties vying to replace the Congress party. Until the 1990s the Congress had never had a truly national rival for political power. But as Hindu revivalism and religious nationalism became the leading social movements in India, the BJP moved into a position to challenge the Congress party's dominance. In the election of 1996, it adopted a strategy of catering to the interests of a variety of social and caste groups (Ghai 2010). The plan succeeded to the point of winning the BJP a plurality of seats, but the party was unable to persuade the other parties to work with it to form a lasting government. Two years later, however, the BJP did form a governing coalition with several other religious and nationalist parties as well as the Janata Dal, a party of the scheduled castes.

Ram-Prasad (2000) makes the argument that *hindutva* nationalism encompasses a range of variants from 'hard' to 'soft', providing a wide spectrum from which to mine political positions. The hard-edged *hindutva* radicals present Hinduism as a nationally bounded and rigid set of beliefs rooted in the traditional Indian religious context. But their softer-edged colleagues recall the inclusive Gandhian notion of Indian religion, accepting the presence of Christians and Muslims as fellow Hindus, on the ground that Hinduism is something similar to a national identity. These two perspectives mirror the divisions in the movement between programmatic radicals who encourage persecution of religious minorities (and former Hindus who convert to other faiths) as opposed to the more pragmatic politicians who set religion aside in order to benefit from the party's popularity.

Political power had provided an opportunity for the BJP to deliver on its hard-edged nationalist message. The BJP had run against Congress's increasing tendency to accept structural adjustment toward a neoliberal market economy and held that successive Congress governments had surrendered Indian sovereignty and potency through liberal and socialist reforms and through a passive foreign policy. BJP activists used strongly masculine imagery to boost their profile as the true defenders of *hindutva*. They promoted Indian self-sufficiency (*swadeshi*) through autarky as part of their *hindutva* program. However, in power the BJP moderated its tone. Far from reversing the structural adjustment policies adopted by the Congress government, the BJP accelerated the pace of neoliberal reform. Even though it had led the push to eliminate the Babri mosque in Ayodhya, the BJP left the issue to the Indian courts and prevented the construction of a Hindu shrine on the site until the court had its say.

Atal Bihari Vajpayee became the first BJP Prime Minister of India in 1998 and served in that role until 2004. Vajpayee was one of the founders of the party in 1980. He served many years as a member of parliament and became the elder statesman of the party. In power, Vajpayee confirmed his reputation as a moderate in the *hindutva* movement. Even so, he was often criticized for his tacit toleration of radicals involved in violent incidents such as those in Ayodhya in 1992 and Gujarat in 2002.
Source: © Pallava Bagla/Corbis

The BJP's time in government was thus marked by a significant move toward the centre, reflecting either ideological moderation or (more likely) the need to maintain the governing coalition. Moving towards the centre also gave the BJP an opportunity to become the alternative brokerage party to the Congress and India's pre-eminent conservative party. As it has come to be recognized as a governing alternative, the BJP's bases of support, originally among wealthier classes and the Brahmin caste have grown more and more broad. It now appeals to a broad spectrum of the electorate and relies on the ideological and strategic support of the *sangh parivar* at election time.

Even so, the BJP was ousted from power in 2004, partly because its reforms were unpopular and partly because of concern over the activities of radicals associated with the BJP in various regions. Perhaps most notable was the descent of the state of Gujarat into widespread communal violence after a fire erupted on a train carrying Hindu pilgrims in Godhra on 27 February 2002, killing 58 people. When Hindu nationalists blamed Muslims for the conflagration, riots broke out and hundreds of Muslim citizens were attacked, raped, and killed (Nussbaum 2007: 17–19). The state government of prominent BJP leader Narendra Modi was widely criticized for its limp reaction and public statements that sought to absolve the extremists. It was widely feared that the incidents indicated a radicalization of the BJP movement, but if this was the case, it proved to be unpopular among Indian citizens. In the 2004 general elections, the BJP's seats in the Lok Sabha were reduced, allowing Congress to form a coalition and return to power. Even so, the BJP has remained the major national opposition party, and it continues to rule alone or in coalition in several states.

At this point it should be noted that the BJP has not been the only nationalist or religious nationalist force in Indian politics over the past century. Other movements and political parties have also given a political voice to nationalist ideas, particularly among minorities and localized ethnic groups. Groups such as these may be small in relative numbers, but the need for coalition governments at the national level and the opportunity to form government at the level of the state can give them a great deal of clout. Like the BJP, other nationalist parties also cover the spectrum from radical militant groups like the Shiv Sena of Maharashtra state to more moderate brokerage parties such as the Dravidian parties of Tamil Nadu state.

The relative importance of *hindutva* religious nationalism and more secular forms of nationalism in these groups varies. Some groups, most notably the Shiv Sena, adopted *hindutva* when it became a popular ideology. The Shiv Sena is a particularly controversial group rooted in Marathi nationalism—Marathis being the dominant ethnic group in the populous state of Maharashtra. Its leader, Bal Thackeray, has close ties to organized crime and the party is well known for using coercion both during and between elections (Mehta 2004). However, the very name of the party (meaning 'army of Shiva'), its propensity for violence toward outsiders (often defined by religious sect), and its usual alignment with the BJP together provide ample reason to classify the Shiv Sena as one of the pillars of the Hindu nationalist movement.

Hindutva, Foreign Policy and the Issue of Kashmir

We have already noted that for two decades the BJP has tended to inflame public sentiment during electoral campaigns but has moderated its positions when in government. The BJP has sought to present policies that are a bold alternative to the universal disarmament and non-alignment movement championed by Nehru's post-independence governments. Yet it has also demonstrated continuity with Congress foreign policies and has at times shown itself to be more than willing to engage in negotiation over key strategic interests. Since the BJP is viewed as the political representative of the *hindutva* movement and has deep roots in the *sangh parivar*, one would expect it to be more militant about the defence of Hindu religion in the subcontinent. However, the looming threat of conflict with India's Muslim neighbour Pakistan means that religion always has a role to play in defining India's foreign policy objectives even under Congress governments, at least with regard to its neighbour to the west.

The BJP's ideological predecessor, the Jana Sangh, had long railed against the Congress party's strategic decisions on foreign policy. It advocated support for the Israeli state and a more pugnacious stand against India's neighbours China and Pakistan, with which India had fought border wars in the 1960s. From the late 1970s, the *sangh parivar* and the BJP have demanded a more confrontational position vis-à-vis India's neighbours, calling on the militant **himsa** tradition in Hindu theology. In the case of Pakistan, such demands are combined with militantly anti-Muslim rhetoric, especially at the level of local activists. The desire for a more assertive Indian foreign policy has thus increased Hindu–Muslim friction in India's domestic politics even as Muslim separatists, often supported by factions in the Pakistani government, have provided a convenient threat for *hindutva* movements to point to. At least two foreign policy issues have been strongly influenced by the religious nationalist movement over the past two decades: the internal and bilateral conflict with Pakistan over Kashmir and the development of an Indian nuclear arsenal.

Relations with Pakistan have typically been tense ever since partition, mainly because of unresolved questions regarding the shared frontier in Kashmir, a mountainous region in the Himalayas wedged between Pakistan, India, and China. For a century prior to independence, Kashmir had been ruled by a family of Hindu maharajas, even though the majority of its population was Muslim. (To this day the vast majority of Kashmiris are Muslims, although there are also populations of Hindus, Sikhs, and Buddhists in the region.) At the time of partition in 1947, regions of the Indian subcontinent ruled by hereditary monarchs could make the decision to join either India or Pakistan, but the last maharaja of Kashmir, Hari Singh, did not commit to either side for several months following independence in August 1947.

The events of August–November 1947 are a matter of dispute between Pakistan and India; however, it is clear that Singh's rule was threatened in September and October by Muslim insurgents sponsored by Pakistan. In late October 1947, the maharaja fled to India and asked for support in putting down the rebellion. The Indian government replied that it would help on condition that Kashmir acceded to India, and Hari Singh duly signed the agreement that brought his kingdom into the Indian orbit (Jha 2003). After several months of war involving Indian and Pakistani regular forces as well as militants supported by Pakistan, the two sides negotiated a ceasefire.

Since 1948 Kashmir has been divided between two spheres of influence. The southern portion, which includes the cities of Jammu and Srinigar, the Kashmir valley, and the mountainous region of Ladakh, has been attached to India and forms the Indian state of Jammu and Kashmir. The western and northern portions, however, remain under Pakistani control and are known in Pakistan as Azad ('free') Kashmir and the 'northern areas'. The far eastern region of Kashmir, a glaciated area known as Aksai Chin, is the subject of a separate dispute: it has been occupied by Chinese forces since the late 1950s, and although Pakistan recognizes China's claim to it, India does not.

The disputed region of Kashmir has been a locus of concern for Indian foreign policy since the first skirmishes with Pakistani and insurgent groups in 1947. Arif Jamal (2009) argues that 'Jihad, holy war, and diplomacy were . . . the first elements of Pakistan's foreign and defence policy—and they remain so more than sixty years later' (46). Over the years since 1948, Indian Kashmir has been the site of a continuing

Map 6.2: Kashmir
Source: Map Resources

insurgency promoted by Muslim extremists, many of whom are based in Azad Kashmir. Public interest in Kashmir within Pakistan has led the Pakistani government both to engage in armed incursions and to provide unofficial support to insurgent jihadist groups. In August and September 1965 Pakistan attacked targets in Indian Kashmir and was quickly repulsed. Since then, tensions over the stream of insurgents who pass over the ceasefire line (known as the 'line of control') have sparked threats of war between Pakistan and India on a regular basis. In the 1980s Pakistan's overtly Islamist President Zia ul-Haq began providing direct support to the *jihad* in Afghanistan and Kashmir. Since that time, Kashmiri insurgent groups such as the Lashkar e-Taiba and Jaish Muhammad have often been linked to the Pakistani Inter-services Intelligence Agency.

Indian religious nationalists have typically responded aggressively to the actions of Islamist militants based in Pakistan. *Hindutva* activists often depict the Indian Muslim population as a suspicious fifth column that might at any time be caught plotting against the nation. The BJP has both contributed to and benefited from such agitation. The defence of Indian prestige has always been an important part of its program. Its leaders regularly support the idea of *akhand bharat*, or 'greater India', arguing that Kashmir is an integral part of the Indian nation-state. The desire to present a threatening posture toward both Pakistan and China has motivated them to emphasize the need for a modern and well-equipped military.

So it was that one of the first actions of the government formed by the BJP in 1998 was to freely and publicly undertake an underground nuclear weapons test, demonstrating that India had a deliverable nuclear weapon. This test drew attention to India's rejection of the 1968 Nuclear Non-Proliferation Treaty (NPT), which the Indian government had refused to sign on the grounds that it stopped short of complete nuclear disarmament. Both external critics and the BJP itself referred to the nuclear weapon as 'the Hindu bomb'. Later that same month, Pakistan announced that it too had successfully detonated a nuclear weapon.

One might expect that a *hindutva*-inspired government would lead India toward more extreme foreign-policy decisions and deepen the divisions between the country's various religious groups. On the other hand, many argue that BJP foreign policy decisions were largely in line with the positions taken by other parties and governments in India. The 'Hindu bomb' was not intended to demonstrate India's power to Pakistan alone: it was also intended as a warning to China. What's more, the development of the nuclear weapon has given India a solid platform from which to negotiate a détente with China, a special arrangement with the United States for inclusion in the Nuclear Suppliers' Group, and some diplomatic openings with Pakistan.

For all its posturing in favour of an implacable Indian foreign policy and the development of an Indian nuclear capability, the BJP government also demonstrated willingness to deal with Pakistan. Prime Minister Atal Bihari Vajpayee negotiated a resumption of bus service between the two countries, reinstituting a transit connection that had been disrupted for forty years, in February 1999. And although Pakistani incursions over the line of control in Kashmir led to the brief Kargil War in May–July 1999, the two states backed down and have continued to seek diplomatic ways to avoid conflict since that time. Thus, according to Chaulia (2002) the BJP built on the work of its Congress rival throughout its time in office. The fact that Congress has continued to negotiate protections for the Indian nuclear weapons program under the India–US civilian nuclear agreement of July 2005 while pursuing diplomatic solutions with Pakistan reinforces this impression.

Flashpoints and Pressures:
The Continuing Problem of Interreligious Relations

In spite of the ebb and flow of party politics, religio-political strife remains a problem in the Indian context. The persistence of Islamist radicalism in South Asia is a barrier to the peaceful resolution of the Kashmir issue and an obstacle in Indo-Pakistani relations in general; and Hindu extremism continues to erupt from time to time despite the moderation of elected officials. In addition, since the events of 11 September 2001 the political calculations of dealing with extremism, particularly Indian demands that Pakistan crack down on militants based there, have added complexity to the problem of India-Pakistan relations. In December 2001 a brazen attack on the Indian Parliament left nine police officers dead. In July 2006 a series of bombs went off at various points on the Mumbai train station. Just over two years later, in November 2008, an intricately planned terrorist assault on targets throughout the city of Mumbai claimed the lives of almost two hundred people and continued for three days before government commandos were able to restore order. Thus the terrorist threat appears to have grown in significance. Each incident sparks new calls for the government of India to respond with sanctions or military action.

In each of the above attacks, the Kashmiri separatist group Lashkar e-Taiba was held responsible. Lashkar e-Taiba is an extremist group inspired by the Jamaat ud Dawa party of Pakistan, founded and led by Pakistani national Hafiz Muhammad Saeed. For many years the organization has been involved in supplying and supporting Kashmiri militants in their campaign against the Indian government. The movement of Lashkar e-Taiba personnel over the line of control in Kashmir suggests that the group has contacts within the Pakistani military and the powerful Pakistani Inter-services Intelligence Agency (ISI). Every time terrorists attack India, the Pakistani government condemns the action and disavows any foreknowledge of the plot, but such incidents continue to polarize relations between the two countries. The possibility that the latent conflict between India and Pakistan could escalate toward a nuclear standoff remains a strategic concern for both states and for the global community.

Frustration with the persistence of challenges to Indian security and the continuing politicization of religion in various parts of India continue to threaten communal peace. When Swami Laxmanananda Saraswati, a leading VHP activist in the state of Orissa, was murdered in August 2008, his followers blamed local Christians even though a Maoist insurgent group claimed responsibility. Christian settlements were destroyed in retaliation and at least three dozen Christians were killed. Thus despite the BJP's moderation when it has held power, and even though Indian politics has moved away from the polarized *hindutva* debates of the past decades, the potential for religion to be a flashpoint remains.

Conclusions

Diversity and pluralism establish a unique set of relationships between religious groups and the state in India. The breakdown of central authority, threats to security, the dynamics of former colonial rule, and an uneasy balance between secularism and sectarian politics have all created problems for religious tolerance in the subcontinent. Religious revivalism and the blatant politicization of religion for partisan gain have also introduced dangerous precedents over the past thirty years. Although India's founders attempted to constrain the divisive forces of religion, India has been internally polarized and divided from its neighbours on the basis of religion. Religion and radicalism are a particularly potent mix in an area of the world where several states, India included, boast large arsenals of both conventional and nuclear weapons. At the same time, India remains a vibrant democratic society that has succeeded in containing many of the factors that might tear apart similar systems in other parts of the developing world. India remains a vital and important case study in the interplay of religion and politics and will for some time to come.

Review Questions

1. How has Hinduism been defined by internal tradition, by the colonial powers, and by the *hindutva* movement?'
2. What are the institutional bases of the *hindutva* movement in India?
3. Who was Mahatma Gandhi, and how did he influence the relationship between religion and politics in India?
4. How is secularism defined in the Indian context?
5. How is India's religious diversity reflected in Indian politics?
6. How does religion affect the relationship between India and Pakistan, especially with regard to the disputed territory of Kashmir?

Sources and Further Reading

Agarwal, Bina (1994). *A Field of One's Own: Gender and Land Rights in South Asia.* Cambridge: Cambridge University Press.

Chaulia, Sreeram (2002). 'BJP, India's Foreign Policy, and the "Realist Alternative" to the Nehruvian Tradition'. *International Politics* 39: 215–34.

Frykenburg, Robert Eric (2008). *Christianity in India: From Beginnings to the Present.* Oxford: Oxford University Press.

Gandhi, Mohandas (2002). *Mohandas Gandhi: Essential Writings.* John Dear, ed. Maryknoll, NY: Orbis.

Ghai, Shelly (2010). 'Telling Multiple Stories: The BJP's Appeal to Group-specific Interests and the *Hindutva* Master Frame'. Pp. 160–75 in John Dyck, Paul Rowe, and Jens Zimmermann, eds. *Politics and the Religious Imagination.* London: Routledge.

Embree, Ainslee (1990). *Utopias in Conflict: Religion and Nationalism in Modern India.* Berkeley, CA: University of California Press.

Jaffrelot, Christophe, ed. (2005). *The Sangh Parivar: A Reader.* Oxford: Oxford University Press.

Jamal, Arif (2009). *Shadow War: The Untold Story of Jihad in Kashmir.* Brooklyn, NY: Melville House.

Jha, Rem Shankar (2003). *The Origins of a Dispute: Kashmir 1947.* New edition. London: Pluto Press.

Keay, John. *India: A History* (2000). New York: Grove Press.

Kohli, Atul (1990). *Democracy and Discontent: India's Growing Crisis of Governability.* Cambridge: Cambridge University Press.

Madan, T.N. (1998). *Modern Myths, Locked Minds: Secularism and Fundamentalism in India.* New Delhi: Oxford University Press.

Mahmood, Cynthia (1996). *Fighting for Faith and Nation: Dialogues with Sikh Militants.* Philadelphia: University of Pennsylvania Press.

Mehta, Suketu (2004). *Maximum City: Bombay Lost and Found.* New York: Vintage.

Nussbaum, Martha C. (2007). *The Clash Within: Democracy, Religious Violence, and India's Future.* Cambridge, MA: Belknap Press.

Pandey, Gyanendra (1990). *The Construction of Communalism in Colonial North India.* New Delhi: Oxford University Press.

Ram-Prasad, C. (2000). 'Hindu Nationalism and the International Relations of India'. Pp. 140–97 in K.R. Dark, ed. *Religion and International Relations.* New York: St. Martin's Press.

Rudolph, Lloyd I., and Susanne Hoeber Rudolph (1967). *The Modernity of Tradition: Political Development in India.* Chicago: University of Chicago Press.

Sen, Ronojoy (2010). *Articles of Faith: Religion, Secularism, and the Indian Supreme Court.* New Delhi: Oxford University Press.

Sidhu, Waheguru Pal Singh, Bushra Asif, and Cyrus Samii, eds (2006). *Kashmir: New Voices, New Approaches.* Boulder, CO: Lynne Rienner.

Srinivasan, T.N., ed. (2007). *The Future of Secularism.* New Delhi: Oxford University Press.

Vander Veer, Peter (1994a). *Religious Nationalism: Hindus and Muslims in India.* Berkeley: University of California Press.

——— (1994b). 'Hindu Nationalism and the Discourse of Modernity: The Vishva Hindu Parishad'. Pp. 653–68 in Martin Marty and R. Scott Appleby, eds., *Accounting for Fundamentalisms.* Chicago: University of Chicago Press.

Web Resources

www.bhagavad-gita.org – The *Bhagavad Gita*: online content and commentary on the great song of Hinduism.

www.hinduismtoday.com – *Hinduism Today*: quarterly magazine on Hinduism.

www.sikhs.org – The Sikhism Home Page: information on the Sikh faith.

Chapter 7

Buddhism
and Politics

Buddhism is one of the most ancient religious traditions in the world. It was originally founded around the same time that the ancient Greeks were fighting the Peloponnesian War and the ancient Israelites were returning from their Babylonian exile. To someone unfamiliar with the teachings of Buddhism, the tradition may seem esoteric and distant from the lived reality of public life, but the application of Buddhist teaching to social and political problems is common. Buddhist monastic practice has been introduced to Western societies through popular media on film, by popular writers who use Buddhist teachings to guide others to personal self-improvement, or as a foundational premise in speculative fiction. All of these applications of Buddhist teaching may distract from the fact that it provides a basic worldview for up to a sixth of the world's population in one form or another. As both a religious philosophy and a cultural touchstone, Buddhism has been a foundational guide to ethical conduct and spiritual enlightenment for many of the largest and most influential states in Asia, including China, Japan, Korea, Vietnam, Thailand, and Sri Lanka.

At the heart of Buddhism is the example of one individual, a man of royal descent who gave up his life of privilege to seek enlightenment. But that particular Buddha, the Buddha of the present age, is believed to be only one of many who, according to the tradition, have come in the past and will come in the future to guide humanity along the path to enlightenment. As it became a public tradition and worldview throughout Asia, the example of the Buddha, the message (*dharma*) that he preached, and the organization of the faithful who carry his message today have all demonstrated political potency.

Buddhism's Rise and Eclipse in India

The central figure in the history of Buddhism was a prince born in northern India sometime between the sixth and fourth centuries BCE. According to the legends, stories, and traditions that have been preserved in the sacred texts of Buddhism, Prince Siddhartha was the son of a wealthy local chief who provided him with all of life's pleasures and protected him from knowledge of life's suffering, so that he would not be distracted from the life of a royal prince. One day, however, while touring the royal gardens, Siddhartha came upon avatars of the gods who displayed to him the reality of suffering in the forms of disease, old age, and death. Shocked by his new insight into the nature of human life, the prince was then shown a fourth sight: an ascetic or monk whose air of calm detachment seemed to suggest that he had found a way to transcend suffering.

He abandoned his home and set out to become an ascetic, but even after six years of extreme self-mortification in the forest wilderness he had not reached the enlightenment he sought. Deciding to try the path of moderation instead, he went to a place now called Bodh Gaya, in the northern state of Bihar, sat under a tree, and began to meditate. In the course of his meditation he was visited by death in the form of an opponent named Mara, with whom he engaged in a difficult spiritual struggle, but he prevailed. Finally, following his victory over Mara, he was able to reach the highest level of meditative consciousness, *samadhi*, in which he laid aside the burdens of the mortal life. Having attained enlightenment, Siddhartha became the Buddha, meaning 'the enlightened one'.

The Buddha proceeded to Sarnath, a deer park near the holy city of Varanasi (now in the state of Uttar Pradesh,) to preach and share his message with others. In his first sermon he taught what have come to be known as 'the Four Noble Truths' of Buddhism. First, life is beset by suffering; second, the cause of suffering is craving, or attachment to the things of this world; third, suffering will end when craving ends; and fourth, it is possible to liberate oneself from suffering by following a set of principles known as the 'eightfold path'. For the remaining decades of his life the Buddha taught the way out of the world of suffering and the way of enlightenment. Following his death, or *parinirvana*, his followers spread his teachings throughout India and beyond.

Buddhism became established as a popular religion in India under the tolerant rulers of the Maurya dynasty (c. 321–185 BCE), especially Ashoka, who ruled from 261 to 226 BCE. Ashoka began his reign as a fairly typical monarch who regularly made war as a way of asserting his authority and extending his power over neighbours and rivals. After defeating the Kalinga people, however, Ashoka felt deep remorse for the bloodshed and suffering he had caused. He thus promised to embrace the true *dharma* and followed through by supporting religious institutions, treating his subjects with generosity, and insisting on religious tolerance throughout his kingdom. To that end he issued a series of 'edicts' that were inscribed on pillars and stones across India, in which he expressed his remorse for his former ways and set out the basic ethical principles of Buddhist *dharma*. It is widely conjectured that in doing so, Ashoka declared himself to be a Buddhist (Maguire 2001: 40–1). Whether or not that was the case, the tolerance and support of the Mauryan rulers, who also sponsored Buddhist missionary work, led to the rapid spread of Buddhism throughout India.

Over the next few centuries, Buddhism arrived in what is now Sri Lanka, Central and Southeast Asia, spread directly by missionaries and indirectly through commerce. Ashoka's own son is said to have taken the Buddhist *dharma* to Sri Lanka. Later, Sri Lankan devotees took Buddhism to modern-day Burma, Thailand, and Cambodia, where it became the dominant religious perspective in the first few centuries CE. Other followers took the message to Central Asia, from where it spread along the trade routes to the east to China, Korea, and Japan. By the third century, Buddhism was an influential force in China, and in the fourth century it reached Korea. The first Buddhists arrived in Japan about two hundred years later (Olson 2005: 9). At about the same time, the people of Tibet began to embrace their own form of Buddhism. In this way Buddhism became the dominant religious force in all of East Asia.

Although Buddhism was rooted in Indian culture and religion, it also developed in reaction against certain aspects of the Vedic religion taught by the Brahmin priests, notably veneration of the gods, sacrifice, and the caste system. Nevertheless, in the period following the Mauryan dynasty, the tradition of the Brahmins gradually regained its status as the common religion of the people of India. Invasions of north India by various groups, culminating in the Muslim invasions of the Middle Ages, also contributed to the disappearance of Buddhism. By the thirteenth century, Buddhism had become a very small minority tradition in the land of its origin. Instead, the vast majority of Buddhists lived in the countries surrounding India, in modern China and

The Lion Capital of Ashoka stood atop the Pillar of Ashoka in Sarnath and is preserved in the museum there. Ashoka caused similar pillars to be erected throughout the ancient Mauryan Empire announcing his commitment to Buddhist *dharma* and just rulership. The Lion Capital has become a symbol of India, featured on government documents and letterhead.

Source: © iStockphoto.com/eROMAZe

Box 7.1: The Many Names of the Buddha

The Buddha is known by many different names, each of which is linked to a particular stage in his development.

Siddhartha Gautama his birth name.
Buddha his epithet as one who has attained enlightenment.
Shakyamuni 'sage of the Shakya clan' (the clan of his family).
Tathagata 'come and gone', or 'thus perfected'; a reference to the Buddha's consciousness and role on earth.
Sugata 'the happy one'; describes the Buddha after his enlightenment.

Tibet, Korea, Japan, Southeast Asia, and Sri Lanka, as they do to this day. Thus the political impact of Buddhist *dharma* in India today is much less significant than it is in areas where the majority of the population are Buddhists. Even so, India remains an important centre of Buddhist pilgrimage, particularly to sacred locations such as Bodh Gaya and Sarnath. The northern Indian city of Dharamsala serves as the home of a large community of Tibetan Buddhists in exile, led by the Fourteenth Dalai Lama.

The Basic Tenets and Vehicles of Buddhism

The Four Noble Truths encapsulate the essential teachings of the Buddha: though life is full of suffering caused by attachment to the world, it is possible to liberate oneself from attachment by cultivating wisdom, ethical conduct, and self-discipline. Buddha Shakyamuni discovered through his pursuit first of worldly pleasure and then of extreme asceticism that neither could free one from the cycle. Instead, he preached the 'Middle Way' of moderation in all things.

It is worth repeating that Buddhism was rooted in an Indian worldview. Thus even though it challenged many of the pillars of Hindu religion, the basic concepts it built on reflect the way Hindus understood the world in the time of the Buddha. Thus the human problem to which the Buddha responded was cast in the vocabulary of Hindu belief. For example, according to the Hindu concept of *samsara* (rebirth), human beings on this earth are part of an ongoing cycle of reincarnation. Yet if life on earth is characterized by suffering, each reincarnation would merely represent another stage in an ongoing cycle of suffering. If it is a law of the universe that human beings will be reborn, achieving true liberation from suffering would require finding a way to transcend the cycle of rebirth. The Buddha responded to this problem by teaching humans to empty themselves of all desires and eliminate the ego, or **atman**. The state in which all desires are eradicated and the self is extinguished is called *nirvana*. *Nirvana* is the ultimate goal of the Buddhist.

Central to the cycle of rebirth is the principle of *karma*, which operates in conformity with a universal law of cause and effect. Meritorious conduct would improve one's lot in this life and the next. In the same way, unmeritorious conduct would harm one's ability to move ahead in the cycle of life. Karmic merit can be earned in a variety of ways: for example, by venerating past religious leaders, or the Buddha himself, by making a pilgrimage to a monument called a *stupa*, which holds a sacred relic, or by helping to support the monastic community. Monks are generally referred to by the Pali term **bhikku** (Sanskrit *bhikshu*), derived from a word meaning 'to beg', for Buddhist monks dedicate themselves to their spiritual discipline and rely primarily on donations from the lay community to survive. Giving with the right motivation to a monk increases the karmic merit of both the donor and the recipient. As a result, Buddhist societies develop a sort of symbiotic relationship between the communities of monks (the **sangha**) and laypeople. The *sangha* is thus central to Buddhism, although the tradition also recognizes the importance of Buddhist rulers because of their role in preserving order and promoting happiness.

The Buddha, his teaching (the *dharma*), and the gathering of his disciples (the *sangha*) are often referred to as the 'three jewels' or 'three refuges'. Buddhists revere the example of the Buddha as a model of enlightenment. They seek to follow the teachings he delivered to his disciples, which laid out the essential values of Buddhism, or *Buddhadharma*. Finally, they respect the gathering of his disciples, the *sangha*.

The Buddha himself did not leave any written record of his teachings; they were originally transmitted orally and were not written down until long after his death (probably sometime in the first century CE). The central texts were organized in three collections known as the **tripitaka** ('three baskets'). The texts of the **vinaya-pitaka** lay down the rules of order for Buddhist monks; the **sutra-pitaka** contains the general teachings of the Buddha, and the **abhidharma pitaka** consists of commentaries on the general teachings (Olson 2005: 16–18). The earliest texts were written in Sri Lanka in an ancient language (related to Sanskrit) called *Pali*. These scriptures became the basic texts of the oldest surviving school of Buddhist thought and they are known as the **Pali Canon**. It is useful to note here that the spelling of some Buddhist terms varies, depending on the context. Thus in discussions of the oldest tradition, Sanskrit words such as *dharma* and *nirvana* often appear in their Pali versions: *dhamma* and *nibbana*. Except for *bhikku*, however, this chapter will use the Sanskrit terms.

Soon after Buddha Shakyamuni's *parinirvana*, his followers met to recollect his teachings and, since memories differed, to decide which versions were authoritative. The decisions made at that First Council were reaffirmed at the Second Council, about a hundred years later. However, Buddhist teachers began to diverge on key matters such as the basic practices that lead to enlightenment, the role of Buddhist laypeople as opposed to monks, and various questions regarding authority (Maguire 2001: 36–7). Different interpretations were reflected in the gradual emergence of three major schools or 'vehicles' of Buddhist thought: Theravada, Mahayana, and Vajrayana.

The earliest and most conservative of the vehicles is Theravada, the 'teaching of the elders'. It is characterized by relatively rigid adherence to the traditions and teachings recorded in the Pali Canon. Theravada Buddhism focuses on education in monastic *sangha* and the individual search for *nirvana*. Therefore it tends more towards study and formalized ritual than towards spreading the Buddhist *dharma* to the world outside the monastery. Having originated in Sri Lanka, the Theravada tradition was taken by missionaries to Southeast Asia and took root in Burma, Thailand, and Cambodia. To this day, it remains the dominant religious tradition in all three of those lands.

The second school emerged around the first century BCE and came to be known as Mahayana ('great vehicle'). Mahayana thinkers set out deliberately to communicate the Buddha's message to the masses and help laypeople reach enlightenment or liberation. In particular, they sought to share the teachings of the Buddha in ways that would make sense to people in the context of their existing beliefs.

One important feature of Mahayana Buddhism is its reinterpretation of the *bodhisattva*. Whereas the Theravada tradition reserves the title for the few who, after countless previous lives, have been very close to attaining enlightenment, the Mahayana vehicle urges all Buddhists to take a *bodhisattva* vow and, while working towards their own liberation, to help others along the same path. In addition, the Mahayana school envisions a special group of celestial *bodhisattvas*: enlightened beings who, out of compassion, have chosen not to enter the final *nirvana*, but to remain available to help others towards liberation. The Mahayana tradition eventually produced a variety of branches, including Pure Land, Nichiren, and Zen Buddhism, each of which developed its own scriptural tradition. Today Mahayana in its various forms is the dominant Buddhist tradition in China, Korea, Japan, and Vietnam.

Mahayana Buddhism puts less emphasis on the disciplined life of the monk and more on making Buddhist *dharma* relevant to laypeople. Thus it typically focuses on teachings that can put into practice in the day-to-day life of the lay community. Its openness to a variety of cultural and spiritual traditions meant that it developed more syncretic practices. Mahayana Buddhism seamlessly combined with the cultural and religious traditions of China and Japan. The integration of Buddhist thought with Taoism, Confucian philosophy, and Japanese Shinto shaped the contours of religion in the societies of East Asia. Despite clearly discernible differences in religious practice, many people found themselves able to embrace both Buddhism and their own cultural traditions.

The same capacity for syncretism contributed to the development of a variant of Mahayana that came to be recognized as a third 'vehicle' in its own right. This is the Vajrayana ('diamond') tradition, sometimes described as esoteric or tantric and probably best known today as Tibetan Buddhism. Vajrayana thought emphasizes the integration of the temporal and spiritual realms through mystical or tantric practices. It teaches that the Buddhist may thus encounter the various *bodhisattvas*. The spiritual disciplines and practices employed to this end are intense and include dancing, the chanting of special mantras (passed from teacher to student), and various physical disciplines as well as meditation on mandalas (sacred designs or diagrams in the form of a circle). The importance of *bodhisattvas* and spiritual teachers in Vajrayana is reflected in the importance of the spiritual leaders of the *sangha*, or lamas. There have been numerous important lamas throughout history and many are venerated today, most notably the Dalai Lama, the leader of the Gelugpa sect of the Tibetan school. The fourteenth Dalai Lama, Tenzin Gyatso (b. 1935), is the most famous figure in Buddhism today, but it is important to understand that he is the head of just one sect within the Vajrayana tradition, which in turn is just one of three major vehicles of Buddhism. Vajrayana is the dominant Buddhist tradition throughout the Himalayas, from northern India, Nepal, and Bhutan to Mongolia; there is also one Vajrayana sect in Japan, known as Shingon.

Buddhism offers no directions for the construction of a political order or the proper application of political principles. Quite the opposite: it teaches that the temporal realm must be transcended by discovering its ultimate transitoriness. Even so, the Buddhist ruler is encouraged to take responsibility for the enhancement of *dharma* throughout his realm. An early Buddhist tradition describes the ideal ruler as a **chakravartin**, or 'turner of the wheel of *dharma*': one who ensures the righteous and consistent application of Buddhist ethical principles. Ashoka is often cited as the prototype of the ideal Buddhist king. Another important element of the Mahayana tradition is the idea that *bodhisattvas*, dedicated as they are to helping others, will use 'skillful means' (*upaya*) to communicate the *dharma* in a way that a given audience can understand. These ethical guidelines for authority contribute to Buddhist understandings of right leadership.

Sri Lanka: Buddhism Betrayed?

The island of Sri Lanka holds a central position both in the development of Buddhism and in its spread throughout South and East Asia. It was in Sri Lanka that the Pali Canon was first codified, some two thousand years ago, and Pali scripturalism is an important feature of Sri Lankan Buddhism. Several other texts include accounts of the history of the Theravada vehicle in Sri Lanka, the most important of which is a work known as the **Mahavamsa** ('the Great Chronicle'). Composed in the sixth century, it tells the story of the ancient founding of Sri Lanka and the spread of Buddhist *dharma* there. Among other details, the *Mahavamsa* describes the unique origins of the Sinhalese people of Sri Lanka and tells how a *bhikku* named Mahindra, the son of the Mauryan emperor Ashoka, brought Buddhism to the island in the third century BCE. As Buddhism declined in the Indian subcontinent and the Mahayana tradition developed in East Asia, Sri Lanka played the central role in the continuation of the Theravada tradition.

Modern Sri Lankan politics has been shaped by two struggles. The first was the struggle for independence from British colonial rule, which lasted from the foundation of the Ceylon National Congress's *swaraj* movement in 1926 to independence in 1948. The second was the post-independence struggle by the Sinhalese majority to consolidate its control over the institutions of the Sri Lankan state against the claims of various minority groups, in particular the Tamils concentrated in the northern and eastern portions of the island. In the late 1950s the government passed legislation that established Sinhalese as the official language of the state, and discrimination against the Tamils continued to deepen over the next several decades, leading to increasingly violent conflict.

The conflict is essentially rooted in the ethnic divide between the Sinhalese and Tamil populations. The Sinhalese people consider themselves the native inhabitants of the island, having arrived from India in the first few centuries before the common era. However, Tamils have also lived on the island for many centuries. They are linguistically related to the Tamil population that forms the majority in the Indian state of Tamil Nadu. During the colonial period, Sri Lanka's Tamil population was augmented by the arrival of large numbers of Indian Tamils who migrated to the island in search of work. The colonial authorities who permitted the expansion of the Tamil population were widely resented by the Sinhalese, who sought to limit the political clout of the Tamils. In response, a nationalist opposition developed among the Tamils, who increasingly sought recognition of their language and culture in Sri Lankan politics.

It is important to realize that there is also a religious dimension to the conflict. Today approximately 70 per cent of Sri Lankans are Buddhist, 8 per cent Muslim, 7 per cent Hindu, and 6 per cent Christian. The majority of the Sinhalese are Buddhists and almost all Buddhists are Sinhalese, while the majority of the Tamils are Hindu. Religion thus reinforces the ethnic divide.

By the late 1970s, many Tamils were calling for the creation of a national homeland and a separatist movement was developing, led by the Liberation Tigers of Tamil Eelam (LTTE). After more than two decades of civil conflict between the central government and the LTTE, the insurgency came to an end in May 2009 when government forces overran the Tamil enclaves.

Buddhism had played an important part in the resistance against the British colonial regime. By the late 1800s, the Buddhist *sangha* had embraced Western models in several areas: missionary work, a new emphasis on religious scriptures, organized monasticism, and the establishment of schools led by the *sangha* (Little 1994: 19–21). One of the leading figures in this revival was a young, educated Buddhist known as Anagarika Dharmapala (1864–1933), who had taken religious vows but did not enter the *sangha* until near the end of his life. Dharmapala's agitation for renewal of the Buddhist tradition mobilized laypeople, contributing to the modernization of the religious tradition while restoring its role in promoting social reform.

Buddhist monks were active as leaders in early nationalist projects. Among them was Walpola Rahula (1907–97), whose book *The Heritage of the Bhikku* (1946) helped to transform the image of the monk from that of a quiescent, apolitical figure to that of an activist fully engaged in the political life of his country. In 1956 a report entitled *The Betrayal of Buddhism* was published by the Buddhist Committee of Inquiry, a group established by a Sri Lankan political movement that included several monks. The report argued that the native Buddhist faith had been repressed throughout the colonial period. One leading monk from the Committee, D.C. Wijayawardena, went on to publish his own work describing the political role of the monk in resisting colonial repression of Sri Lankan culture (Tambiah 1992: 22–41).

In the wake of these developments in the early post-colonial period, the Buddhist religion has been mobilized as an important part of national consciousness among the Sinhalese of Sri Lanka. David Little writes that while religious beliefs have not typically been targeted in the midst of the conflict, 'there can be little doubt that religious belief has, for several reasons, functioned in an important way as a *warrant* for intolerance as far as the Sinhala Buddhists are concerned' (Little 1994: 104; emphasis in original) The combination of activism among Buddhist monks, the combination of Buddhism with Sri Lankan nationalism rooted in texts such as the *Mahavamsa*, and the narrative of victimization at the hands of the Tamil minority and the British colonial authorities have often been used to justify violent crackdowns on Tamils both by the government and by Sinhalese vigilantes. Sinhalese Buddhist nationalists also castigate Sri Lankan Christians as former allies of the colonial authorities who undermine national solidarity.

In his widely cited study of the relationship between Buddhist religious groups and Sri Lankan nationalism entitled *Buddhism Betrayed?* (1992), Stanley Tambiah criticizes the way monks and nationalists have cultivated Buddhism to serve their ends. During the 1980s, when Tamil nationalism sparked widespread violence against the state, Buddhists actively supported the major Sinhalese political parties. Tambiah highlights the efforts of two leading political monks, Pannasiha Thero and Gnanasiha Thero, on behalf of an ethnic state that would protect and cultivate the Buddhist heritage of Sri Lanka (Tambiah 1992: 102–28). It is important to note, however, that the Sri Lankan *sangha* is large and diverse, and that not all monks support the more radical nationalist vision. Daniel Kent (2010: 157–77) reports that Buddhist monks during the war steered clear of either condoning or condemning the war against Tamil separatists; instead they focused on ministering to the people and nation of Sri Lanka. Thus they would bless soldiers as they would anyone else and preach the general protection of the nation as a priority for Buddhists, regardless of their personal sentiments.

Buddhism in East and Southeast Asia: Protest and Peace

The political impact of Buddhism in East Asian societies has been limited both by the rapid secularization of those societies and by the Mahayana tradition's inherent openness to syncretism. Since the formation of the People's Republic in 1949, the public role of Buddhism in China has been subordinated to the state's Communist ideology, and Buddhist orders have been permitted to exist only under tight regulation. Taiwan and Hong Kong imposed fewer controls, but the rapid modernization of these societies led the *sangha* to adopt a more philosophic and less traditionally religious form of Buddhism, open to innovations from the outside world, which has had a declining role in politics despite periods of revived public interest (Chandler 2004). Elsewhere, in societies such as Korea and Japan, capitalist modernization has also contributed to the marginalization of Buddhism as a force in public life. In Vietnam, both Theravada and Mahayana in the form of the Zen and Pure Land schools are practised, but Buddhism's political role has been diminished by the diversity of the traditions represented in the *sangha* and four centuries of Confucian governance (1500–1900) (Harris 1999: 254–83). Although the concept of 'engaged Buddhism' (see Box 7.2) was first introduced in Vietnam, it came under attack from both left and right, and the prominent Buddhist dissident who proposed it, Thich Nhat Hanh, was forced into exile in the 1970s.

One might be able to detect Buddhist themes in the national ideology of *juche* (self-sufficiency) in the People's Democratic Republic of Korea (North Korea) in that it emphasizes centralized direction under an enlightened ruler and self-abnegation for the good of the state. By and large, however, Buddhist practice has been stamped

Box 7.2: Engaged Buddhism

'Engaged Buddhism' is a term coined by the Vietnamese Zen monk Thich Nhat Hanh in a work published in 1963, during the Vietnam War. Thich Nhat Hanh linked a peaceful world to a peaceful mind, arguing for Zen meditation as a way of cultivating peace. This challenged the traditional interpretation of Zen as an individualistic and isolationist practice. The concept of engaged Buddhism has spread to other Mahayana schools and has been embraced by many Theravada and Vajrayana Buddhists as well. It has often been described as a Buddhist form of Liberation Theology.

Other leading figures in the movement include the Thai monk Sulak Sivaraksa, who founded the International Network of Engaged Buddhists in 1989; the Cambodian monk Maha Ghosananda (1929–2007), and the Fourteenth Dalai Lama, Tenzin Gyatso. The US-based Buddhist Peace Fellowship based in Berkeley, California, has also applied Zen practice to the cultivation of peace in North America.

out under the Kim regime. In South Korea, the association of Buddhism with the colonial rule of Japan until the mid-twentieth century meant that the *sangha* emerged from the Second World War without clear ties to the newly independent South Korean government. Authoritarian rulers cajoled and harassed the Buddhist orders into supporting the regime. Some attempts to dismantle Buddhist organizations in the 1980s elicited public demonstrations by the monks (Harris 1999: 137–40). The increasing political power and influence of Korean Christians has frequently put the two major religious traditions at odds with one another. The overall trend has been toward the declining influence of Buddhism as a political force.

In Japan, Zen monks cooperated with the national Shinto religion to encourage the pursuit of traditional Bushido (the 'way of the warrior', or 'code of the Samurai') and nationalism during the Second World War (Victoria 1997). Since that time, Buddhism's public role has receded. The Nichiren Buddhist Soka Gakkai, a largely lay society devoted to cultivating peace and harmony, sparked the development of a political party, the Komeito, or 'Clean Government' Party, in 1964 (Queen and King 1996: 265–400). The party has been reorganized as 'New Komeito' since 1999 and generally distances itself from a strictly religious ideology or program.

In Southeast Asia, Theravada Buddhism is a cultural force that has provided important guidance to the construction of politics. While Buddhism guides the *bhikku* to seek his own self-abnegation, Buddhist texts also enjoin the ruler to embrace his *dharma* and serve his subjects well as a *chakravartin*. Many scholars point out that this contributes to strong identification between Buddhism and nationalism in both positive and negative ways. Suksamran (1982) and Swearer (1995) describe how Buddhist symbology and royal patronage of the Buddhist *stupas* and **wats** (temples), as well as land donations and the granting of honorific titles to leading monks were common throughout Southeast Asia in past centuries, as indicated in Burma, Thailand, and Cambodia. These practices reflected both the Buddhist teachings about divine kingship and the relationship between support for royalty and the cultic devotion to

Buddha as a semi-divine entity upholding world order (Swearer 1995: 63–95) and offering good *karma* to the donor (Suksamran 1982: 13–24).

The first prime minister of Burma, U Nu, cultivated support for the regime through an ideological program that he characterized as Buddhist socialism. General Ne Win, who overthrew U Nu in 1962, sought to eliminate religious influences in government circles, but in 1980 the military regime began cultivating its own supporters in the *sangha* (Swearer 1995: 99). The Burmese junta has regularly sought to deepen this support through patronage and propaganda, defending its own claim to stewardship of the country in the tradition of the *chakravartin*. Ne Win's successors formed the State Law and Order Restoration Council, (later the State Peace and Development Council) led by General Than Shwe have consolidated a draconian regime over the country, which they renamed Myanmar. They have worked together with the *sangha* to repress the Muslim minority: monks participated in widespread anti-Muslim riots throughout the country in 2001 in response to the Taliban's destruction of Buddhist statues in Bamiyan, Afghanistan (Florida 2005: 107). Members of the military junta regularly seek to burnish their reputations as patrons of the *sangha*.

On the other hand, Buddhist philosophy and the *sangha* have periodically been mobilized in opposition to the military regime. The Burmese *sangha* boasts a huge number of monks, drawn from across Burmese society. It has been estimated that the number of Burmese who belong to the Buddhist *sangha* rivals the number serving in the military (Rogers 2008: 116). On certain occasions, the *sangha* presents a united force representing the citizen population of Burma and forms a respected opposition force in a country that brooks very little dissent. In the late summer and autumn of 2007, widespread protests against the regime were embraced by the Burmese *sangha*, which began taking part in public demonstrations and street marches in mid-September 2007. Chanting slogans from the **sutras** of the Pali Canon, the monks marched past the home of the leader of the opposition National League for Democracy, Aung San Suu Kyi, publicly bestowing blessings on her. The unequivocal disavowal of the government by the Alliance of All Burma Buddhist Monks was unprecedented. The leadership of the monks in the midst of the street protests led the international media to label the uprising the 'Saffron Revolution', after the colour of the monks' robes. In spite of the social power of the *sangha*, the Burmese military clamped down in force, imprisoning, punishing, and defrocking many monks in an apparently successful effort to silence their dissent. The long-term implications of the Saffron Revolution remain to be seen, and the regime continues to imprison and repress dissident monks.

Theravada Buddhism arrived in Thailand in the sixth century and was embraced as the religion of the state in the thirteenth. Buddhism provided religious support to the Thai monarchy, which in turn gave material support to the *sangha*. Even so, Buddhist monks in general remained apolitical until the twentieth century. The erosion of absolute monarchy in the 1930s led to a series of conservative nationalist regimes, most of which cultivated Buddhist resistance to Communism as a bulwark of the Thai regime. Since that time successive regimes, democratic or military, have provided support to the *sangha*, which has taken on a number of developmental projects funded by the government. Somboon Suksamran (1982) describes how Thai monks were politicized when economic boom and modernization arrived amid

Thousands of Buddhist monks marched in an unprecedented show of opposition to the repressive military regime in Burma in September 2007. The demonstrations, dubbed the 'Saffron Revolution' in honour of the monks' robes, resulted in a military crackdown on the *sangha*.
Source: AFP/Getty Images

the ideological polarization of the Cold War. On the left, organizations such as the Federation of Buddhists of Thailand, the Monks and Novices' Centre of Thailand, and the Young Monks' Front of Thailand agitated for social change commensurate with the expansion of the economy. On the other hand, conservative Buddhists championed the anti-Communist message, most prominently Kitthiwuttho, a popular preacher, and his Program for Spiritual Development. Suksamran concluded that the mixture of Buddhism and public life was poisonous.

Buddhist doctrines surrounding the *chakravartin* have provided ample support to an extreme cult of royal authority in Thailand. As a result, laws forbidding criticism of the ruling monarch, a crime known as *lèse-majesté*, are strictly enforced and regularly used as political weapons. One prominent political monk of the left is Sulak Sivaraksa, the founder of several social movements, whose criticism of nationalistic religion, military rule, and the regime of former Prime Minister Thaksin Shinawatra have led to two different prosecutions for *lèse-majesté*. Members of the royal family continue to figure as important patrons of state Buddhism. Meanwhile, the increasing salience of religion as a political force at the global level since 2001 has had an important effect in Thailand as well. McCargo (2009) argues that a harder-edged nationalistic Buddhism is replacing benign Buddhist civil religion as religious revivalism takes hold in Thai society. In the southern region of Thailand where Muslims form a majority, this movement has contributed to growing tensions and occasional violence between Muslim and Buddhist vigilantes over the numerous shrines maintained by the minority Buddhist population. The violence has contributed to an increasing blurring of the lines between religion, the state, and the military. Jerryson and Juergensmeyer (2010: 179–209) explore the phenomenon of monks in southern Thailand engaging directly in military activities in defence of the country's religious identity.

Buddhism was introduced in Cambodia about the same time that it arrived in Thailand, and from the thirteenth century the Theravada tradition was embraced as the official religion of the Khmer people. As in other Southeast Asian countries, members of the Khmer royal family habitually patronized the *sangha* and Buddhist institutions, but the relationship was disrupted during the colonial period, and the Communist Khmer Rouge regime (1975–9) identified monks along with other intellectual and professional leaders as obstacles to revolutionary change. The *sangha* was decimated as thousands of monks were defrocked, sent into internal exile, or put to death. Nonetheless, Buddhism remained an important source of national identity (Marston and Guthrie 2004: 60-61). The revivification of the *sangha* continues in Cambodia today, and Buddhist imagery has increasingly been taken up by the various factions as a means of legitimating authority and calling for national unity (Marston and Guthrie 2004: 35). A central figure in this process was the late monk Maha Ghosananda, who began the annual tradition of *dharmayatra*, a walking pilgrimage for peace through the nation of Cambodia.

Tibetan Nationalism: Unattainable Nirvana?

It is in Tibet that Buddhism is most eminently political, since the history of Tibet has provided a uniquely political role to the leading lama, known as the Dalai Lama. The origins of the Dalai Lama's role as the guardian of the people of Tibet date back to the thirteenth century, when the Mongols invaded and defeated the Tibetans in war. A Tibetan Buddhist monk, Kunga Gyaltsen (1182–1251), went to the court of Godan Khan, the Mongol king, and negotiated a special place as the protector of the Buddhist religion in Tibet. According to Olson (2005), the agreement 'was to have enormous importance for Tibetan history because it began the custom of monastic leaders assuming responsibility for the social and political welfare of the Tibetans' (205). Since that time Tibetan political thinking has fused religion and politics in a way that Tibetans find 'perfectly appropriate' (Tuttle 2005: 18). The combination of religious and sacred authority is virtually unmatched outside the Holy See. The special role of the lamas in governing Tibet was recognized by successive Chinese imperial administrations that considered Tibet a vassal state.

Almost three hundred years later, a revival of Buddhist practice took place in Tibet. Central authority was always difficult to enforce on the Tibetan plateau because of its remote location, sparse population, and harsh climate. In the absence of tight central administration, religious centres became the locus of political power. During the middle ages, a feudal system developed that gave a special place to the monasteries, which became the centre of the Tibetan economy and political life. The religious leaders of the monasteries, the lamas, became important political leaders. They constructed several large monastic strongholds that served as the focal points of their power. In the fifteenth century, the Gelugpa sect challenged its rivals for dominance, leading to a violent conflict between the monastic houses. A Gelugpa monk named Sonam Gyatso (1543–88) was recognized as the reincarnation of two prior monastic leaders and became the leading religious and political figure in Tibet. Sonam Gyatso was summoned to the court of the Mongol Altan Khan, who interpreted his surname (meaning 'ocean') as an epithet. Since that time, this religious leader has been known by the Mongol word *dalai*, meaning 'ocean', hence Dalai Lama (Laird 2006: 142–3). Since he was held to be the reincarnation of prior religious leaders, Sonam Gyatso was recognized officially as the third Dalai Lama. Over the following centuries, the Gelugpa sect maintained and consolidated its place as the dominant religious force in Tibet.

By the early 1900s, Tibet was governed under a unique political system in which the monasteries claimed significant political power as landholders. In addition, with large numbers of the country's men attached to them as novices and monks, the monasteries

The Potala Palace in Lhasa is the traditional home of the Tibetan Dalai Lamas. It was originally constructed between 1645 and 1694, in the time of the fifth Dalai Lama, Lozang Gyatso, and served as the winter palace of the Dalai Lamas until the fourteenth Dalai Lama was forced into exile in India in 1959. Today the Palace is maintained as a museum by the People's Republic of China.
Source: Yin Shichang/ChinaFotoPress/Getty Images

had the manpower to challenge the government in the capital of Lhasa if they so wished. The succession of Dalai Lamas also created a unique pattern of authority. It was assumed that the first Dalai Lama was a *bodhisattva*, a living incarnation of the legendary Avalokiteshvara, who had chosen to remain on earth to guide, protect, and help his people reach enlightenment. By tradition, each of the Dalai Lamas is considered to be the reincarnation of his predecessor, and has been selected on the basis of signs indicating the presence of the latter's soul within him. Typically, the new Dalai Lama would be discovered as a child living in a poor family. He would then be brought to the Potala Palace, the official seat of the Dalai Lama, and raised as the new religious and temporal leader of Tibet.

The Gelugpa religious order thus became a sort of hereditary royalty in Tibet. However, it is important to note that, since the Dalai Lamas were not a family dynasty, there was typically a period of several years during the childhood and adolescence of each new incarnation when secular elites had the opportunity to consolidate power behind the monastic throne. One scholar notes that as a result of this 'time lag . . . during most of the Gelugpa hegemony, regents ruled the country' (Florida 2005: 191). In the first half of the twentieth century, Tibet remained a traditional feudal society, governed by the lamas and aristocrats, that maintained a sort of caste system of privilege. Most Tibetans were effectively peasant farmers who worked under the management of the monasteries.

From the 1940s on, attempts by the government to restrain the power of rival monasteries led to violent strife throughout Tibetan society. When the current Dalai Lama, Tenzin Gyatso, was officially enthroned at the age of 15, in 1950, he wanted to bring modern innovations and change the constitutional order. However, at the same time, the People's Republic of China in 1949, was threatening to overturn his authority and bring modernization to Tibet under Chinese rule. In August 1950, the Chinese People's Liberation Army invaded and occupied Tibet, compelling representatives of the Tibetan government to sign a treaty granting Chinese sovereignty over the territory in 1951. A growing Tibetan revolt against the Chinese occupation forces was put down by force. When the Chinese authorities demanded the Dalai Lama's cooperation, ordinary Tibetans staged demonstrations and surrounded the palace where he was staying, in an effort to protect him. The Dalai Lama fled Lhasa on 17 March 1959, taking a secretive route across the Himalayas to India (Barber 1960).

After the invasion, the Chinese authorities enforced cultural homogenization on Tibet, a process that intensified after 1959. Chinese authority was consolidated through brutal suppression of Tibetan attempts at revolt (McCarthy 1997). Chinese settlers were moved in huge numbers to Tibet, changing the ethnic makeup of the population. Buddhism came under strict regulation. During the Cultural Revolution of the late 1960s and early 1970s, more than 6000 monasteries and temples were destroyed (Laird 2006: 345). Today the Chinese government limits the size of Tibetan monasteries to 500 monks in order to control their power (Iyer 2008: 248).

When the Dalai Lama arrived in India in 1959, the Indian government extended asylum to the him and he established a government in exile in the northern city of Dharamsala. Since that time Tibetan refugees have formed a large enclave there in which Tibetan customs, language, and ways of life are preserved. The Dalai Lama himself has rejected the Tibetan tradition of absolutism and developed a democratic form of governance for the community in exile, despite resistance among traditionally minded Tibetans (Boyd 2004: 29). The first prime minister and leader of the Assembly of Tibetan People's Deputies, elected in 2001 by members of the worldwide diaspora, was another lama, Samdhong Rinpoche (Iyer 2008: 177–8). However, his successor, Lobsang Sangay, is not a religious figure but a Harvard-educated legal scholar and exile elected to the position in 2011. The Dalai Lama's insistence on democracy reflects his understanding of the Buddhist *dharma* that respects the dignity of the human person.

The Dalai Lama has also resisted calls for a revolutionary movement to restore Tibetan home rule, and in 1987 he announced his support for a negotiated solution that would grant Tibet autonomy within the People's Republic of China. He has thus become one of the world's leading proponents of non-violent resistance and serves as the spokesman for the national aspirations of the Tibetan people. His efforts won him the Nobel Peace Prize in 1989, and he has become a global celebrity, regularly travelling the world not as a political figure but as a spiritual leader and guru—a role that reduces political difficulties for the states that deal with him. These difficulties arise because Chinese leaders continue to see the Dalai Lama as a separatist leader who threatens to subvert Chinese unity, often referring to him as a 'splittist'. The People's Republic has frequently reiterated its view of the Dalai Lama's movement as reactionary, rooted in atavistic religious practices (Laird 2006: 302). Foreign governments that extend an official welcome to the Dalai Lama are viewed extremely negatively by the Chinese government, which sees such gestures as interference in internal Chinese affairs. The Chinese government actively seeks to undermine the authority of the Dalai Lama. In one notable incident, the Chinese government in 1995 placed the candidate identified by the Dalai Lama as the eleventh reincarnation of the Panchen Lama (a close associate of the Dalai Lama) under house arrest, where he has remained ever since; it then selected its own rival candidate and imposed him on the home monastery of the Panchen Lama.

In March 2008, amid preparations for the Beijing Summer Olympic Games, widespread protests erupted in Tibet against Chinese rule and were put down by force. To the Chinese, the riots only served to bolster their case that the return of the Dalai Lama would be destabilizing. The Tibetan Youth Congress, created by the Tibetan government in exile, is more strident than the Dalai Lama in its calls for independence. The Congress has become a rival pole of authority in the Tibetan community and as a result the Dalai Lama has become somewhat less influential. Boyd (2004) traces the decline of the Dalai Lama's traditional authority to the dramatic decline in the numbers of young men entering the monastic tradition (102). The youth movement has numerous supporters throughout the world who regularly engage in demonstrations against Chinese rule in Tibet at embassies and public events in various countries. As it continues to add fuel to demands for independence, it complicates the Dalai Lama's efforts to mediate his return and the restoration of autonomy to Tibet. In March 2011 the Dalai Lama publicly announced his desire to resign from his position as the head of the Tibetan government but given the traditional importance of his position, he will most certainly remain symbolic of Tibetan nationalism even if he lays aside most temporal duties.

Since the end of the Maoist era, China has taken a more tolerant attitude toward Buddhist practice in Tibet even though it has continued to follow a wider policy of cultural modernization and homogenization. Makley (2007) argues that China's centralized regulation of participation in the monastic orders has only served to strengthen the way in which traditional religious practice helps to masculinize nationalism for both Chinese and Tibetans alike, meaning that the images of the nation and its defenders remain male. Tuttle (2005) argues that Chinese efforts to maintain control over Tibet are linked directly to the Chinese ability to cultivate the link between Chinese Buddhism and Tibetan Buddhism. Far from eliminating Tibetan nationalism, the policies that China imposed on Tibet during the Cultural Revolution only served to deepen the feelings of difference between Chinese and Tibetans. He believes that cultivating the cultural bonds between China and Tibet through support of Tibetan Buddhism is a promising way for the People's Republic to stabilize political relations with Tibet and reduce its demands for independence.

The particular Buddhist tradition practised in Tibet is thus an ongoing challenge to Chinese leaders who seek to consolidate one-China rule throughout the territory of the People's Republic. The legacy of ethnic strife and the desire of the People's Republic to control domestic religious practice have led to a combustible situation. It remains to be seen whether Chinese efforts to manage ethno-religious traditions in Tibet will succeed amid continued agitation by the Tibetan community at home and abroad.

Conclusions

Buddhism is an ancient philosophy rooted in Hinduism. Its gradual spread in the first few centuries of the Common Era led to the development of Buddhist cultures across Asia. Three distinct 'vehicles' reflect different understandings of the Buddha's teachings. The oldest surviving tradition, the Theravada vehicle of Sri Lanka and Southeast Asia, is characterized by a strong attachment to the Buddha's own teachings in the Pali Canon regarding the application of *dharma* in government. It has led to the close association of Buddhist practice with the idea of the nation and, as a result, to identifying defence of the shrines and community of Buddhists with defence of the nation. The Mahayana vehicle that spread to East Asia created a cultural Buddhist tradition that combined with indigenous social thought to shape the political cultures of both China and Japan. On the other hand, the overall secularization of those societies means that Buddhism has relatively little political influence there today. Finally, the unique Vajrayana philosophy that developed in the Himalayan regions of India, Bhutan, and Tibet emphasizes mystical practices and monasticism. As a result, the traditional recognition of reincarnation and respect for the historic role of the *bodhisattva* gives a special place to the Vajrayana lamas, most notably the Dalai Lama.

Review Questions

1. How has Buddhist philosophy, which teaches detachment from the things of the world, been applied as a political religion?
2. What are the major vehicles of Buddhism? Where have they become dominant religious traditions? What are some of the differences in the ways they apply the teachings of Buddhism?
3. In what ways has Buddhism been used to promote political nationalism in Sri Lanka?
4. How has Buddhism been used to promote national solidarity and protest against ruling authorities in areas of Southeast Asia?
5. What are the unique features of Tibetan Buddhism and how do they apply in the political realm?

Sources and Further Reading

Barber, Noel (1960). *The Flight of the Dalai Lama*. London: Hodder & Stoughton.

Boyd, Helen R. (2004). *The Future of Tibet*. New York: Peter Lang.

Chandler, Stuart (2004). *Establishing a Pure Land on Earth: The Foguang Buddhist Perspective on Modernization and Globalization*. Honolulu: University of Hawaii Press.

Florida, Robert E. (2005). *Human Rights in the World's Major Religions: The Buddhist Tradition*. Westport, CT: Praeger.

Harris, Ian, ed. (1999). *Buddhism and Politics in Twentieth-Century Asia*. London: Pinter.

——— (2005). *Cambodian Buddhism: History and Practice*. Honolulu: University of Hawaii Press.

———, ed. (2007). *Buddhism, Power, and Political Order*. New York: Routledge.

Iyer, Pico (2008). *The Open Road: The Global Journey of the Fourteenth Dalai Lama*. London: Bloomsbury.

Jerryson, Michael K., and Mark Juergensmeyer, eds. (2010). *Buddhist Warfare*. Oxford: Oxford University Press.

Kent, Daniel (2010). 'Onward Buddhist Soldiers: Preaching to the Sri Lankan Army'. Pp. 157–77 in Jerryson and Juergensmeyer (2010).

Kraft, Kenneth, ed. (1992). *Inner Peace, World Peace: Essays on Buddhism and Nonviolence*. Albany: State University of New York Press.

Laird, Thomas (2006). *The Story of Tibet*. New York: Grove Press.

Laliberté, André (2004). *The Politics of Buddhist Organizations in Taiwan*. New York: Routledge.

Little, David (1994). *Sri Lanka: The Invention of Enmity*. Washington, DC: United States Institute of Peace Press.

McCargo, Duncan (2009). 'The Politics of Buddhist Identity in Thailand's Deep South: The Demise of Civil Religion?' *Journal of Southeast Asian Studies* 40, 1: 11-32.

McCarthy, Roger (1997). *Tears of the Lotus: Accounts of the Tibetan Resistance to the Chinese Invasion, 1950–1962*. Jefferson, NC: McFarland & Company.

Maguire, Jack (2001). *Essential Buddhism*. New York: Pocket Books.

Makley, Charlene (2007). *The Violence of Liberation: Gender and Tibetan Buddhist Revival in Post-Mao China*. Berkeley: University of California Press.

Marston, John, and Elizabeth Guthrie, eds. (2004). *History, Buddhism and New Religious Movements in Cambodia*. Honolulu: University of Hawai'i Press.

Olson, Carl (2005). *The Different Paths of Buddhism: A Narrative-Historical Introduction*. New Brunswick, NJ: Rutgers University Press.

Queen, Christopher S. and Sallie B. King, eds. (1996). *Engaged Buddhism: Buddhist Liberation Movements in Asia*. Albany: State University of New York Press.

Rogers, Benedict (2008). 'The Saffron Revolution: The Role of Religion in Burma's Movement for Peace and Democracy'. *Totalitarian Movements and Political Religions* 9, 1: 115–118.

Suksamran, Somboon (1982). *Buddhism and Politics in Thailand*. Singapore: Institute of Southeast Asian Studies, 1982.

Swearer, Donald K. (1995). *The Buddhist World of Southeast Asia*. Albany: State University of New York Press.

Tambiah, Stanley (1992). *Buddhism Betrayed? Religion, Politics, and Violence in Sri Lanka*. Chicago: University of Chicago Press.

Tuttle, Gray (2005). *Tibetan Buddhists in the Making of Modern China*. New York: Columbia University Press.

Victoria, Brian A. (1997). *Zen at War*. New York: Weatherhill.

Web Resources

www.sgi.org – Soka Gakkai: Buddhist activism from the perspective of engaged Buddhism.

www.buddhanet.net – Buddhanet: information on worldwide Buddhism.

www.dharmanet.org – Dharmanet: study, practice, and action in Buddhism.

Part II

Religion and
Global Order

Chapter 8

Religion, Democracy, and Human Rights

Religion has had an important part in shaping both the modern system of liberal democracy and contemporary debates over human rights. It has stood on both sides of the debates that have contributed to the spread of democracy and human rights. For example, the institution of slavery was rarely challenged in the classic texts of any of the major world religions. Some antebellum slave owners in the United States even defended slavery as a means of imparting Western ideals and religion to 'heathen' Africans—the 'white man's burden'. On the other hand, the most prominent opponents of slavery and advocates of civil rights for African-Americans were all men and women with strong religious commitments, such as William Wilberforce (1759–1833), Harriet Beecher Stowe (1811–96), and the Reverend Dr Martin Luther King, Jr. Try as one might either to condemn religion or to commend it for its influence on the development of democratic institutions and the expansion of human rights, it is difficult to argue the point.

The historical development of liberal democratic government and respect for human rights was widely held to attend modernization until recent times. As we shall see, the Western model of democracy has come to be more and more widely emulated. There have been times when the progress of democracy was considered the end result of a process of refinement of representative government institutions. This perspective was perhaps most famously evoked in Francis Fukuyama's book *The End of History and the Last Man*, which argued that modern liberal democratic government was the end stage of the evolution of governing systems (Fukuyama 1992). However, since that time the applicability of democracy to the vast array of cultures around the world has continued to be a subject of debate, even among those with a religious perspective. How we define the modern concept of human rights is also subject to argument. Nevertheless, over time a number of basic rights (to privacy, due process, democratic participation, etc.) and freedoms (of religion, conscience, belief, expression, assembly, etc.) have become the bedrock of liberal democratic systems of governance, and individual societies may also recognize a number of additional economic and cultural rights. In this chapter we will consider the relationship between religion, democracy, and human rights.

We will find that religion is by no means entirely opposed to international standards of human rights; but neither is it entirely supportive of them. The earliest statements of human rights—the French Declaration of the Rights of Man and the Citizen (1789) and the US Bill of Rights (the first ten amendments to the Constitution, drafted in 1789 and ratified in 1791)—were both products of secularist movements opposed to the establishment of any religion. But their authors also sought to foster the free pursuit of intellectual curiosity, including curiosity of a religious nature. Thus even though there was a strong anticlerical streak in the revolutionary movements that established the rights-based tradition, those movements did not necessarily take a negative view of religion as pursuit of eternal truth, although they did challenge religious authority in the name of protecting secular freedoms. However, it is equally true that some of the major reform movements in the history of liberal democracy have been associated with movements for religious reform—revivals or 'awakenings' of religious fervour that have challenged the hierarchies and doctrines of state churches and official religions. Today demands for religious liberty have become a significant theme in the discourse over human rights. Often these demands come from new groups that trace their roots to those historic movements for religious reform.

Religion and the Expansion of Liberal Democracy

Democratic modernists maintained that modernization would bring with it expansion of the democratic franchise and liberalization of the rules governing public order. Political scientists writing over the past century believed that as a country modernized and developed economically, its educational system would improve and democratization would naturally take place as people demanded the political influence and rights they needed to pursue the good life. At the same time, the early modernization theorists expected democratization to proceed hand in hand with secularization of public life. Religion would recede as a defining feature of public order and demands for citizens' rights would increasingly be articulated in secular forms. Where religion did not recede in its public importance, religions themselves would modernize by developing more sophisticated ways to understand those rights and freedoms.

One of the foremost defenders of democratic modernization was the political scientist Samuel Huntington (1927–2008). In one often-cited work, Huntington described what he called three 'waves' of democratization corresponding to the expansion of the democratic franchise in the periods 1828–1926, 1943–62, and 1974–90 (Huntington 1991). John Witte, Jr, associates each of those major democratic movements with a period of religious reform (1993: 4–14). Long before the first wave of democratization began in Western Europe (notably in Britain, the Netherlands, and France), the Protestant Reformation had transformed the culture of Europe, leading the people to demand greater responsibility of their political elites and more representative government. The Reformation also demanded stronger lines of division between government and Church as some Reform movements challenged state churches and others broke away to form their own states. Anabaptist and non-conformist groups developed formal critiques of the state in both its coercive and administrative roles. In the Netherlands, the Reformation helped to delegitimize the Hapsburg empire's rule over the United Provinces. In Britain, the legacy of the Reformation fuelled the fire of Roundhead opposition to the monarchy during the Civil War of the 1640s, and eventually led to the rejection of a Roman Catholic king in the 'Glorious Revolution' of 1688–9. In France, the monarchy recognized the Protestant challenge to the Roman Catholic state and attempted to eliminate it throughout the 1600s and 1700s, only to fall to revolutionaries inspired by the Enlightenment.

The long first wave of democratization in Western Europe was thus arguably rooted in developments in the world of religion. The gradual evolution of modern liberalism out of religion was presaged by Thomas Hobbes (1588–1679), but establishing a secular democratic system was a long process (Lilla 2007). Early luminaries of the liberal democratic tradition such as John Locke (1632–1704) debated how religious minorities could be allowed to practise their faith freely without disturbing the proper order of society. They concluded that the expansion of 'negative' liberties, allowing individuals to pursue their desires without hindrance, was a key democratic principle. Newly forming democracies such as the United States thus embraced religious freedom as a founding principle and regarded the establishment of religion (i.e., state recognition of any denomination as the official state church) as a constraint on liberty.

Huntington's second wave of democratization began in the post-fascist states with the end of the Second World War and continued through the 1960s as nations throughout the developing world gained their independence. Witte argues that the processes of democratization and decolonization in many of these countries were associated with nationalist movements strongly influenced by Christian missions. Major Christian institutions had been founded in many of the newly democratizing states, importing Western ideas (of nationhood, individual liberty, fraternity, etc.) as well as Western science and technology to the developing world, for good and for ill. Nor was this process limited to those parts of the developing world where Christian missionaries were active. Early Muslim nationalists such as Jalal al-Din al-Afghani, Muhammad Abduh, and Muhammad Ali Jinnah clearly sought to extend the benefits of the Western democratic tradition to their own communities.

In many cases, anti-colonial leaders drew on intellectual traditions that were first introduced to them by Western missionaries (Diamond et al. 2005: 117–31). Such leaders often combined Western democratic principles with indigenous ideas to argue for the expansion of democracy. *Swaraj* (self-rule) was a central principle developed by Mahatma Gandhi as part of the moral responsibility of the nation. Advocates of political Islam contended that the Islamic concept of **shura**, or consultation, provided support for Western notions of democratic participation in their societies.

Paradoxically, many of the mission-educated nationalists of the 1900s went on to embrace philosophies (e.g., communism) that led them to reject most of the religious traditions purveyed by their missionary teachers. In post-fascist Germany and Italy, however, the effect was quite different. With fascism defeated and discredited, the Christian democratic governments of those countries typically drew on their traditional religious and cultural norms while embracing the democratic system.

The third (or 'Roman Catholic') wave began to break ten years after the Second Vatican Council of 1962–5 had called for a renewal of Roman Catholicism. In its wake, democratization spread from Portugal to Spain to Latin America, and finally to the states of Eastern Europe with the disintegration of the Communist bloc. The association of the third wave with Roman Catholicism was a reflection of the fact that most of the newly democratizing countries in this period were predominantly Catholic. Daniel Philpott argues that major changes in the Vatican helped to speed the process along (Philpott 2005: 102–16). Many of the major reformist movements in Iberian Europe (Spain and Portugal), most of the Latin American states, and post-Communist states such as Poland shared the new ideology that had shaped Vatican II and liberation theology. Some of these movements were conservative, some progressive, and their motivations differed widely, but all of them favoured the expansion of democracy. The appointment of the Polish bishop Karol Wojtyla to the papacy as John Paul II saw a deepening of his Church's commitment to democracy at the highest levels.

Clearly religious reform did play an important role in the process of democratization. To the extent that expansion of the franchise represented expansion of liberal standards of human rights, religion was often supportive. The North American women's suffrage movement developed out of the temperance and prohibition movements—social reform movements whose most influential supporters were progressive churches. The same churches supported the progressive movements of the 1930s that gave rise to human rights activism. By the 1960s, religious activists were lining up on both sides of the debate over the extension of civil rights to African-Americans. However, today it is the Reverend Dr Martin Luther King, Jr, a Baptist clergyman, who is best known for the championing of civil rights in the United States. Throughout history, the expansion of respect for human rights has often gone hand in hand with religious revivalism.

Box 8.1: Religion, Communism, and Post-Communism

Western societies confronting the Communist Soviet Union and its satellites during the Cold War of 1945–90 believed them to be militantly atheistic societies in which religion was entirely repressed. In large part this was true: religious leaders in the Communist world were regularly defamed and marginalized by governments seeking to replace religion with Communist ideology. Communist authorities did allow the practice of religion, but only under strict controls, and they used the Eastern Orthodox Churches in particular as extensions of state authority. Leustean (2009) points out that the early Romanian Communist regimes 'enjoyed good relations with the hierarchy [of the Romanian Orthodox Church] and ensured that those who were suspected of conducting anti-communist activities were replaced' (189). The collaboration of the Orthodox clergy weakened the Romanian Church's credibility as a force in opposition to the state and put it in disrepute among foreign opponents of Communism.

Nevertheless, historians and scholars of religion and politics today are questioning the popular notion that only the Roman Catholic and Protestant churches were involved in the transition from Communist authoritarianism. They note that some lower-level Eastern Orthodox leaders posed significant challenges to Soviet Communism. Some churches operated underground in Soviet society and many members of the Russian Orthodox Church, clergy and laity, refused to cooperate with the Soviet authorities. One leading dissident was the reformist priest Alexander Men, whose evangelical and literary work is widely thought to have helped accelerate change during the period of liberalization in the late 1980s. Men was assassinated in September 1990 and the identity of his murderer has never been discovered. Nonetheless, his superiors in the Russian Orthodox hierarchy had an important role to play in the initial movement toward *glasnost* (openness). Daniel (2006) argues that the strength of Russian Orthodoxy as a bulwark of Russian national identity was an important force in the movement toward a more liberal state in the years following the end of the Cold War.

On the other hand, some national churches have consolidated their dominance by supporting restrictions on other religious organizations (for example, draconian religious registration laws). Svetlana Ryzhova (2005) argues that while religious hierarchs in post-Communist Russia have spoken in favour of religious tolerance, they have also contributed to the spread of nationalist intolerance, which has threatened religious freedom in modern Russia. Overall, then, the role of religion in the promotion of democracy and human rights in post-Communist states has been mixed.

One of the most famous religious proponents of human rights, the Reverend Martin Luther King, Jr, led African-Americans and their supporters in the struggle to end legal discrimination and gain the right to full participation in US public life. From the 1950s until his assassination in 1968, Dr King's powerful speaking style, commitment to non-violent resistance, and grounding in Christian theology were the bedrock of the civil rights movement. Source: © Bob Adelman/Corbis

Human Rights and Constraints on Religious Freedom

While religion was often associated with the expansion of democracy, there was also widespread concern that it was an inherently conservative force that denied the authority of liberal democratic principles or subordinated them to its own tenets. The earliest treatises on human rights often took an anticlerical tone in their efforts to limit the powers of monarchs, state churches, and clergymen in temporal office. On occasion, anticlericalism also implied that the rights of citizens and governments might override those of religions. The suspicion that banning religion would hamper the free pursuit of ideas led the intellectuals of the American and French Revolution to focus instead on limiting its ability to control the life of the citizen.

The Declaration of the Rights of Man and the Citizen stated in article 10: 'No one shall be disquieted on account of his opinions, including his religious views, provided their manifestation does not disturb the public order established by law.' Clearly the French revolutionaries favoured the exercise of religious freedom in a broad sense, but the declaration gave the state considerable leeway to control that exercise using the justification of preserving public order. Over the following two centuries defenders of the principle *laïcisme* ('secularism') worked to eliminate all religious influences from the public space.

In the same year, the United States Constitution was amended to reflect similar thinking. Its first amendment stated that 'Congress shall make no law respecting an establishment of religion, or prohibiting the free exercise thereof.' The intent of the amendment is clear: the American republic was to avoid the establishment of religion that had driven so many of its early settlers to leave their homelands. The descendants of those puritans and non-conformists had become further accustomed to religious innovation and free choice amid the first 'great awakening' of the 1740s and 1750s. Added to the French anticlerical tradition, then, was an American tradition that saw freedom of religion as a basic human right.

As we have seen, the founders of the rights-based liberal-democratic tradition did not always attempt to eliminate religion, despite their anticlerical leanings. Rather, they concentrated on containing religion's power to override secular freedoms. As a consequence, there is a fundamental tension between religion and human rights, centring on the assumed responsibility of religious authorities and hierarchies to define the principles by which a human society will be governed and the right of individuals to engage in the pursuit of truth and exploration of religious and philosophic convictions.

This tension reflects the existence of two conflicting desires in modern liberal democracy. On one side is the desire for freedom of religious faith, based in part on the demands of religious minorities and reformers. On the other is the desire to ensure that religious faith itself does not become an impediment to freedom. According to the noted political scientist Alfred Stepan, this tension means that democratic systems have developed an ongoing process to negotiate the place of religion in public life through 'twin tolerations' (Diamond et al. 2005: 3–23): religious organizations must accept the primary authority of democratic institutions, and democratic institutions must accept the free practice of religion.

Religions, Human Rights, and Democracy

Is democratic respect for human rights a universally accepted notion? Moral relativists argue that not all cultures share the same values. A common argument against moral relativism is the idea that all religions share a common moral compass with regard to matters of basic human rights. The Universal Declaration of Human Rights was so named because the underpinning of human rights as a legal principle holds that all rights are universal in conception and application. That rights are self-evident is thus an important reason to accept that they exist. Our ability to gather together in discussion and agree to express our primary values in the form of rights belonging to all people is sufficient proof that 'human rights are relatively universal', in the words of Jack Donnelly (2003: 106). Yet there are important differences between religious traditions (Reinders 1995: 3–23). The extent to which religious beliefs promote tolerance of liberal democracy continues to fuel debate over the role of religion in public life. To what extent is a particular religious tradition conducive to democracy? Are some traditions less 'democratic' than others? Do all religions truly take it as a basic premise that all human beings are born with the same inherent rights?

On the surface, the modern discourse surrounding human rights is part of a Western tradition that is rooted in Judaism and Christianity, though many would say that these ideas are shared in other traditions. The medieval scholastics and humanist scholars who laid the foundations of the modern legal system were Christians. They created a corpus of Christian thought surrounding the ethical and moral constraints on government that eventually contributed to the 'natural law' view of rights as part of a created moral order. Christian theological and legal reasoning thus embraced the idea of religious pluralism even as Christians fought over the proper role of faith in the public realm. As Brian Tierney put it, 'The peoples of Western Europe slowly learned, through centuries of cruel experience, to acknowledge at least the practical necessity of tolerating religious differences among Christians; and, at best, they came to see religious freedom as an ideal inherent in their traditional faith' (Tierney 1996: 43). Contemporary legal scholars work on the basis of legal precedents and secular reasoning that originated in Christian Europe.

Human-rights reasoning in the Christian tradition shares a great deal with the Jewish tradition out of which it developed. A focal point is the creation narrative in *Genesis* 1, in which God creates human beings with a unique nature in the image of God. In the Christian tradition, this vision is often articulated as a principle in the Latin phrase **imago dei**. Humans are therefore considered beings superior in nature to animals, and over the course of the Jewish scripture, the Hebrews' covenant relationship with God leads to the creation of legal codes protecting the life and rights of the person (Brackney 2005: 7). In addition, the classical Jewish tradition identified several categories of people who were to be afforded special protection, including orphans, widows, 'sojourners' (analogous to foreign residents), and 'strangers' (foreigners) (Haas 2005: 10–12). Acceptance of people outside the regular fold of citizenship was clearly a value in biblical times, even if it was not consistently practised.

That the rule of acceptance was unevenly applied is clear from the historical record. Brackney (2005) draws attention to many episodes in the history of Christianity when the premises of freedom of speech and belief were violated: the early Church's anathematization or silencing of dissident clerics; the Crusades, which were originally directed against the Muslim occupants of the Holy Land but eventually targeted Orthodox Christians as well; the violent takeover of the Americas; not to mention the persecution of religious minorities, including non-conforming Christians and, above all, Jews (32–53). More recently, issues such as the right to abortion or same-sex marriage have pitted conservative religious movements against human-rights activists, particularly in the case of Christianity (though it is important to bear in mind that opinions on issues such as these can differ widely, even within a single faith tradition).

The treatment of human rights in other religions varies. Coward (2005) surveys the arguments for and against the idea that Hinduism supports the concept of guarantees on human rights. At first glance, Hinduism seems far more likely than most other religions to uphold the fundamental importance of duty. For example, the *dharma* concerning the various castes and their roles in Indian society focuses more on the responsibilities that each caste owes to the whole of society than on the rights it enjoys. On the other hand, the fact that the *dharma* of rulers requires them to preserve justice and order for all citizens of the state implies that justice and order are fundamental rights of citizenship.

In the twentieth century, when India was preparing to become a modern democracy, one of the questions that had to be addressed was how to ensure respect for the rights of the Dalits—the people, formerly referred to as 'untouchables', who were excluded from even the lowest of the four castes. Gandhi referred to them as 'children of God' and called for an end to untouchability, but insisted that their rights could be protected without any change to traditional caste system. By contrast, Dr B.R. Ambedkar (1891–1956), the Dalit leader who became the chief architect of the Indian constitution, called for formal constitutional means to empower them. By the early 1950s, he had come to believe that the effort to end Hindu caste discrimination was futile, and he advised the Dalits to convert to Buddhism (Coward 2005: 109–30). Nevertheless, the constitution he drafted embraced the Western concept of rights guarantees to the point that it provides one of the most detailed lists of rights found anywhere in the world.

Although Buddhism rejected the Hindu tradition of caste divisions, its understanding of *dharma* shares a great deal in common with the Hindu understanding in its emphasis on the individual's responsibility to the community, as opposed to the rights of the individual. The basic teaching of *anatman* (self-abnegation), which is at the core of Buddhism, militates against any demand that others respect one's rights; thus human-rights language is largely foreign to Buddhism (Florida 2005: 11). It is possible to interpret the duty to disavow selfish desires as a duty to respect the rights of others. However, the Buddhist affirmation that all individuals are engaged in a personal search for awakening and perfection is more obviously fertile ground for the pursuit of a human-rights agenda. In the words of the Dalai Lama, 'not only are Buddhism and democracy compatible, they are rooted in a common understanding of the equality and potential of every individual' (Diamond et al. 2005: 71).

By far the most controversial of the debates about religion and human rights surrounds the Islamic faith. The limitation of the public role of religious faith in the liberal democratic tradition is a consequence of the demand that the state take no role in enforcing religious orthodoxy. To do so would mean ipso facto that the state does not support the exercise of religious freedom. For this reason, the separation of church and state is typically considered a pillar of the liberal democratic tradition. The situation is very different with Islam. As the prominent historian Bernard Lewis, among others, has pointed out, Islam fuses the sacred and the political in such a way that it is impossible to separate them. Islam is thus a political religion that demands establishment of religion and must borrow the idea of secularism from Western traditions that are otherwise foreign to it (Lewis 1996: 62). Some might therefore assert that Islam has no inherent discussion of secular forms of human rights. Given its demand that all Muslims submit to the dictates of the Shari'a, Islam appears to be ambiguous at best about the expansion of freedom within an Islamic state. The behaviour of Islamist activists only serves to reinforce this impression. The Islamic Republic of Iran is harshly critical of Western-style democracy, while prominent Islamist movements such as the Muslim Brotherhood have shown only lukewarm support for participation in liberal democratic politics (Diamond et al. 2003: 13–27, 130–44). Islamists themselves are divided on the utility of democracy and human rights, typically preferring the dictates of an Islamic state over the assurance of individual rights and liberties, whether or not such an Islamic state comes with Western-style protection of human rights.

On the other hand, the basic principles of Islam assert the dignity of the human being in much the same way that the Jewish and Christian traditions do. For this reason, many Muslim philosophers affirm the bond between Islam and democracy. For example, Iranian theorist Abdolkarim Soroush writes that 'Observing human rights (such as justice, freedom, and so on) guarantees not only the democratic character of a government, but also its religious character' (Soroush 2000: 129). Khaled Abou el-Fadl, an Arab-American authority on Islamic law, argues that justice is at the heart of the Shari'a and that resistance to human rights discourse among Muslims reflects rejection of colonialism rather than rejection of human rights per se (2003): 301–64).

The Qur'an reaffirms the unique nature of human beings as against other created beings and teaches that the freedom of choice afforded to humans gives them both rights and responsibilities (Abd al-Rahim 2005: 20–4). It is this latter observation that reveals the distinctiveness of the Islamic worldview with regard to rights. While a well-known passage from the Qur'an insists that 'there is no compulsion in religion' (2:256), in other passages Islam requires submission to the community's interest in security and serenity in ways that might threaten the absolute freedom of belief. Muddathir Abd al-Rahim argues that Muslims 'have throughout history seen and experienced their faith as a sociopolitical bond as well as a system of ethics and spiritual teachings and beliefs' (2005: 10). For this reason, apostasy in particular is regarded as a form of treason and Western notions of absolute freedom of belief are sometimes construed as unjustifiably subversive. Therefore while non-Muslims are tolerated under classical Islamic jurisprudence, conversion away from Islam is generally forbidden and heresy is considered a severe crime.

The determination of Muslims to preserve order in the community has also given rise to problems with respect to human rights for women. Most Muslims hold that Islam is an empowering force for women, whose welfare is a significant preoccupation of Islamic teaching. On the other hand, many Muslims and non-Muslims share the concern that cultural influences over the centuries have 'undermined the intent of the Qur'an to liberate women from the status of chattels or inferior creatures and make them free and equal to men' (Witte and van der Vyver 1996: 380–1). Practices grounded in interpretations of the Shari'a, including the inferior weight accorded to female testimony in court, the practice of polygamy, and harsh sentences for adultery, have combined with more local cultural practices such as female genital mutilation and honour killing to tarnish the reputation of Islamic attitudes toward women's rights. Even so, the centrality of such practices to Islamic teaching is widely debated.

Amina Wadud, a prominent American feminist and convert to Islam, argues that Muslims need to make the case for women's rights as a matter of authenticity and commitment to the Muslim tradition. In fact, she argues that the more Muslim women act to challenge male dominance in traditional Muslim communities, the more individual Muslims will see past the rhetoric of female subordination toward the goals of justice that are essential to Islam. When these underlying values come to the forefront, attitudes toward both women's and human rights will change significantly and there will be no need for Muslims to distance themselves from their own religion (Wadud 2006: 216). Other feminists, however, contend that the depth of the divide between Islam and the two other Western traditions is too great, and counsel against rooting Muslim women's emancipation in the Islamic Shari'a, instead preferring to embrace a growing worldwide consensus in favour of universal human rights.

A common theme in discussions of human rights in the various religious traditions is the necessity of understanding the contingent and discursive nature of religious arguments about rights. Religious teachings do not directly address the issue of human rights, but their implications have often provided foundational principles for the conceptualization of universal human rights. Therefore the preceding discussion of religious attitudes toward human rights should be understood in the light of both the variation in orthodoxies and interpretations within religious traditions and the inconsistent application of religious values in practice. As we have seen, all religions accept the importance of guaranteeing human dignity, whether as a collective responsibility or as an individual human right. Yet there is often a wide gap between theory and reality on the ground.

Religion in International Human Rights

Debates over cultural standards of toleration for disputes involving religion have played out in various cases around the world. Modern international standards of human rights were developed largely on the basis of the Western rationalist tradition, which has prioritized political rights of freedom of speech, assembly, and conscience over collectivist rights such as the right to economic well-being and development or to positive cultural affirmation. At the level of international discussions, conflicts have often arisen over the social demands of religion. On one side are those who argue that religion entails responsibility to social order over personal freedom. On the other are those who seek to maximize religious liberty against the demands of the community.

The Universal Declaration of Human Rights (UDHR), adopted by the United Nations General Assembly in December 1948, declares in Article 18 that

> Everyone has the right to freedom of thought, conscience, and religion; this right includes freedom to change his religion or belief, and freedom, either alone or in community with others and in public or private, to manifest his religion or belief in teaching, practice, worship and observance.

The Universal Declaration was adopted when the United Nations was in its infancy and reflected in large measure the arguments of the Western powers that dominated the General Assembly at the time. The UDHR was passed unanimously by 48 states, but eight chose to abstain. Six of those eight were Communist states that objected to the document's emphasis on political rights over economic rights; the other two were Saudi Arabia and apartheid South Africa. The Saudis abstained because Western nations had insisted that freedom of religion must include the freedom to change one's religion, which the Saudi foreign minister argued was foreign to the strictures of Shari'a (Abd al-Rahim 2005: 9). As an international declaration, the UDHR had little immediate impact; essentially, it set the stage for later debates over the nature of the freedom of religion under international standards of human rights.

The process of elaborating rights to freedom of religion has passed through several stages. Natan Lerner (2000) points to the role played by Indian academic Arcot Krishnaswami in a report (published in 1959) on the ramifications of state discrimination against religious minorities. Krishnaswami found that certain minority religious practices might need to be limited under article 29 of the UDHR. In addition to affirming that everyone has duties to society, article 29 suggests that limitations on religious freedom could be justified 'for the purpose of . . . meeting the just requirements of morality, public order and the general welfare in a democratic society'. In the interest of basic public order, as well as the more malleable concepts of morality and general welfare, governments could seek to impose limitations on religious freedom.

The application of this principle has sparked many serious disputes over the place of religious practice in the public sphere. In France, it has been used to justify a ban on all religious paraphernalia. In Canada, it has been used to override the parental rights of Jehovah's Witnesses who refuse to permit blood transfusions for their children. In China, it has been used to justify government crackdowns on practitioners of the spiritual discipline known as Falun Gong or Falun Dafa, who are held to present a threat to societal order. In these cases, what the state seeks to limit is not so much religious belief but the freedom of devotees to engage in practices that they believe to be sacred. Is it possible to respect the freedom of religious belief while limiting the freedom to engage in sacred practices? Krishnaswami argued that freedom of religious practice was no less important than freedom of belief, but that freedom of practice was more difficult to guarantee because it might well offend other members of society. In elucidating the extent to which religion entails both belief and practice, Krishnaswami extended the basic understanding of the right to freedom of religion. However, he also suggested that there could be limitations on the full freedom of religious practice (Lerner 2000: 11).

Finally, the Krishnaswami report pointed out that freedom of religion is part of a broader freedom of belief. As such it includes the freedom to embrace beliefs such as agnosticism, atheism, or rationalism. Krishnaswami's report suggests that non-religious belief is in fact analogous to religious belief, a notion that believers and non-believers alike would reject, though for different reasons.

Some of these points were raised in a series of discussions that came to an end in 1966 with the International Covenant on Economic, Social, and Cultural Rights (ICESCR) and the International Covenant on Civil and Political Rights (ICCPR). Together with the Universal Declaration of Human Rights, these covenants form what is known as the International Bill of Human Rights. The 1966 Covenants represented an attempt to address some of the issues raised by developing nations, in particular the fact that advanced political freedoms are difficult to guarantee in societies that cannot guarantee

Box 8.2: Religion by Statute

Most modern states have constitutional documents that make some reference to the right of religious freedom. However, each of these references is phrased in slightly different terms. In the US, religious freedom is asserted against the establishment of any religion. In Egypt, the constitution declares Islam to be the official religion but states that all citizens are equal regardless of religion. In the People's Republic of China, religious freedom is framed in the context of resisting foreign dominance. In both the European Convention on Human Rights and the Canadian Charter of Rights and Freedoms, the guarantee of religious freedom is accompanied by a provision that leaves open the possibility of limiting it if necessary for the public good.

Constitutional guarantees of religious freedom must be read in context. Their relative weight in case law is subject to interpretation and precedent, and the extent to which a government respects constitutional guarantees varies significantly from country to country. Here are some constitutional provisions on the subject of religion:

'Congress shall make no law respecting an establishment of religion, or prohibiting the free exercise thereof; or abridging the freedom of speech, or of the press; or the right of the people peaceably to assemble, and to petition the Government for a redress of grievances.'

—First Amendment, US Constitution (1789)

'The State shall not discriminate against any citizen on grounds only of religion, race, caste, sex, place of birth or any of them.'

—Article 15 (1), Indian Constitution (1949)

'France is an indivisible, secular, democratic, and social republic. It ensures equality before the law of all citizens, without distinction based on origin, race, or religion. It respects all beliefs.'

—First Article, Constitution of the Fifth French Republic (1958)

1. 'Everyone has the right to freedom of thought, conscience and religion; this right includes freedom to change his religion or belief, and freedom, either alone or in community with others and in public or private, to manifest his religion or belief, in worship, teaching, practice and observance.
2. Freedom to manifest one's religion or beliefs shall be subject only to such limitations as are prescribed by law and are necessary in a democratic society in the interest of public safety, for the protection of public order, health or morals, or the protection of the rights and freedoms of others.'

—Article 9, European Convention on Human Rights (1950)

2. 'Islam is the religion of the state and Arabic its official language. Islamic jurisprudence (Shari'a) is the principal source of legislation.'
40. 'All citizens are equal before the law. They have equal public rights and duties without discrimination between them due to race, ethnic origin, language, religion, or creed.'

—Articles 2 and 40, Egyptian Constitution (1980)

'Citizens of the People's Republic of China enjoy freedom of religious belief. No state organ, public organization or individual may compel citizens to believe in, or not to believe in, any religion. The state protects normal religious activities. No one may make use of religion to engage in activities that disrupt public order, impair the health of citizens

> or interfere with the educational system of the state. Religious bodies and religious affairs are not subject to any foreign domination.'
> —Article 36, Constitution of the People's Republic of China (1982)
>
> 'Preamble: Whereas Canada is founded upon the principles that recognize the supremacy of God and the rule of law:
> 1. The Canadian Charter of Rights and Freedoms guarantees the rights and freedoms set out in it subject only to such reasonable limits prescribed by law as can be demonstrably justified in a free and democratic society.
> 2. Everyone has the following fundamental freedoms: (a) freedom of conscience and religion (b) freedom of thought, belief, opinion, and expression, including freedom of the press and other means of communication (c) freedom of peaceful assembly; and (d) freedom of association.'
> —Preamble and Articles 1–2, Canadian Charter of Rights and Freedoms (Constitution Act 1982)

their citizens access to the basic necessities of life. In such places, public order was important not simply to permit the free pursuit of ideas, but to permit the economic development required for internal security. For many countries, the right to political freedom could not be separated from the right to economic development.

In the debates surrounding the 1966 Covenants, several developing countries expressed concern that the decision to convert to another religion might in some cases be compelled through relationships of dominance or colonialism. In such cases it might be difficult to separate religious conversions made for reasons of conscience from those made for reasons of political pressure. Therefore, one of the compromises made to gain acceptance of the ICCPR in many developing countries was the exclusion of an explicit right to change one's religion, although Lerner is of the opinion that such a right is implied by the text (2000: 15). Since the objection to the right to convert was closely associated with the ability of powerful actors to dominate weaker actors, another point that was raised was the need to protect against coercion in matters of religion. The ICCPR also sought to secure the right of parents to educate their children in a manner consistent with their religious beliefs.

Nevertheless, it is important to note that when religious freedom was raised as an issue in international human-rights forums, it tended to be dealt with in the broader framework of political and developmental human rights rather than as a topic in its own right. Until 1981, there was no particular corpus of international law that dealt in depth with the matter of religious discrimination. The passage of a long-awaited Declaration on the Elimination of All Forms of Intolerance and Discrimination Based on Religion or Belief (1981) was meant to fill the void. In the midst of discussions on the convention, the same dispute over the definitions of religious freedom arose. The primary dispute pitted Muslim countries and others against Western states over the right to change one's religion. In the end, the declaration did not refer to this issue but instead made an oblique reference to the fact that previous texts were not overridden by the current text, leaving the ICCPR to stand as the last word on the matter.

This enduring polarization between Western and Islamic states was heightened with the signing of the Cairo Declaration of 1990 at the Conference of Foreign Ministers of the Organization of the Islamic Conference (OIC). The OIC is an intergovernmental organization formed in 1969 that represents the Muslim world. The 1990 Cairo Declaration was signed by 45 states hoping to present a united front on Islamic standards of human rights. Among other things, it expressed the wish 'to contribute to the efforts of mankind to assert human rights, to protect man from exploitation and persecution, and to affirm his freedom and right to a dignified life in accordance with the Islamic Shari'a' (preamble). The text proceeded to deal with common topics in human rights, such as right to life, gender equality, education, and movement. However, it also included numerous qualifications on the application of those rights under the Shari'a. It also confirmed conservative positions based on traditional Islamic law, such as the prohibition of usury. As regards freedom of religious belief, article 10 upheld the Islamic teaching that 'Islam is the religion of unspoiled nature. It is prohibited to exercise any form of pressure on man or to exploit his poverty or ignorance in order to force him to change his religion to another religion or to atheism.'

Ongoing disputes over freedom of religious belief seem likely to forestall further action on that particular aspect of human rights. Several states within the Indian federation have joined Islamic nations in legislating against the use of coercion to compel religious conversion. A court in the late 1970s ruled against the right to promote conversion in India, and individual state governments have taken steps to limit proselytization in an effort to prevent the destabilizing social effects of mass conversion (Sen 2010: 116–21). Disputes over the reliability of Western guarantees of religious rights persist in spite of widespread acceptance of the terminology used in the Universal Declaration. For example, the European Convention on Human Rights protects religious freedom in article 9 using language almost identical to the UDHR. However, its effectiveness may be limited by a subsection that permits exceptions in the interest of 'public safety, for the protection of public order, health or morals, or for the protection of the rights and freedoms of others'. Some scholars argue that this article, combined with the courts' generally limited sympathy for religious rights, may constrain the ability of religious minorities to defend their rights (Evans 1997: 281–314; Evans 2001: 208).

Religion and Human Rights in Practice

As John Witte points out, the definition of religious human rights has been contentious. Religious belief itself is difficult to define, including as it does everything from theistic to non-theistic to atheistic perspectives. In his assessment, the 'capacious definition of religion in international law has left it largely to individual states and individual claimants to define the boundaries of the regime of religious rights' (Witte and van der Vyver 1996: xxiv). In Western societies, it is relatively rare that legal claims for religious rights are simply demanding freedom to believe or worship in the face of a discriminatory ban on such activities. Instead they seek freedom to practise certain rites or engage in public demonstrations of belief. Constitutional guarantees of religious freedom commonly require balancing the right of a religious community to believe and practise as they wish against the state's need to preserve order and maintain common standards. Religious believers often expect the state to provide 'reasonable accommodation' for them: that is, to make exceptions in the face of state regulations, in recognition of their right to express religious devotion.

Cases involving demands for reasonable accommodation of religious preferences in the Western world have been dealt with in various ways. An ongoing controversy in France surrounds the head covering or **hijab** worn by many Muslim women. Since the early 1990s, growing numbers of Muslim students had been suspended from school for wearing the *hijab* to class in contravention of school rules, based on the long-standing principle of *laïcité*. Concern that the *hijab* ban unfairly targeted Muslims led the administrative court known as the *Conseil d'état* to clarify in 2007 that the principle applied to any conspicuous religious paraphernalia, regardless of faith.

In Canada, several high-profile cases of religious accommodation for Sikhs, Jews, and Muslims in the province of Quebec led to the convening of a Consultation Commission on Accommodation Practices Related to Cultural Differences (the Bouchard–Taylor Commission) in 2007. The Commission's final report took a middle way, offering guidelines for preserving what it called an 'intercultural' identity, somewhere between cultural separatism and the enforcement of a specific set of cultural norms. It was expected that these guidelines could be applied without mandating a wide degree of accommodation. In effect, the report did little more than define the nature of the issue for courts and governments to decide. Other countries have experienced controversies centred on religious buildings. In November 2009, for example, a Swiss referendum vote banned the construction of minarets. And in 2010, opponents of a plan to build an Islamic Center near the site of the former World Trade Center in New York demanded that the project be shelved.

Elsewhere in the world religious freedom remains an existential concern. Since the 1990s (see below), the US government's International Religious Freedom Commission has published reports based on continued monitoring of religious freedom around the world. In a survey published in 2000, Paul Marshall reported that violation of basic religious freedom had been increasing. In particular, he found that 'the most intensely persecuted' groups were 'Christians and animists in Sudan, Baha'is in Iran, Ahmadiyas in Pakistan, Buddhists in Tibet, and Falun Gong in China', and that 'Christians [were] the most widely persecuted group' (Marshall 2000: 18).

Religious persecution today takes many different forms and is often combined with ethnic, economic, and political persecution. In many cases, religious discrimination, intolerance, and persecution are part of a broader culture of disregard for human rights. For example, one of the worst violators of religious human rights is the People's Democratic Republic of Korea (North Korea), where state Communism has been enforced through the official state cult of reverence for the family of founder Kim Il-Sung and his philosophy of *juche* (self-reliance). All other varieties of religious observance are banned as threats to the regime.

In Myanmar (Burma), the military regime has controlled all public gatherings in order to prevent opposition and to disseminate its own version of the Buddhist religion. In Turkmenistan, the government does not respect its own paper guarantees of religious freedom, and engages in public intimidation of those who try to take advantage of their freedom to worship (Marshall 2000). Like North Korea, both of these states are broadly repressive, and the restrictions they impose on religion are reflective of a wider array of restrictions on civil society activity and political freedom.

In other cases, religion has been singled out as a particular concern of the state. Chinese policy since 1949 has been to constrain and control religious groups through the centralization of religion in groups controlled by the state. Independent religious movements were repressed through imprisonment and internal exile of their leadership. Since the end of the Cultural Revolution in 1976, China has taken a more moderate approach to controlling religious dissent and the underground Christian church in particular has grown in large numbers (Aikman 2003). Still, periodic repression of Christian leaders is common. Furthermore, the Chinese government continues to forbid the practice of Falun Gong, a spiritual discipline based on traditional religious practices, and has engaged in ongoing persecution of its leadership (Marshall 2000: 99–106). Buddhists and Muslims are also carefully monitored because of their association with separatist movements in Tibet and Xinjiang. Fear that expanding the scope of religious freedom might undermine public order is used by the government to justify heavy constraints on religious freedom.

Established religions or religions that have close links with the governing authorities can also be major instigators of religious repression. The official religion of Saudi Arabia is the Wahhabi school of Islam, the product of a firm alliance between the religious constituency and the Saudi monarchy in place since the eighteenth century. Conformity with the Islamic law is enforced by the 'religious police' of the Society for the Preservation of Virtue and the Prevention of Vice, who have wide arbitrary powers. Freedom to engage in worship outside strict Islamic forms is not respected. Russia is another case in point. The religious freedom enjoyed since the collapse of the Soviet Union has in recent years been constrained. In 1997 a law governing the registration of religious groups recognized four major religions: Russian Orthodoxy, Islam, Judaism, and Buddhism. But in practice Russian Orthodoxy has privileged status and non-Orthodox groups are subject to various forms of repression. The 1997 law has been used to limit the registration of newer religious movements, including various Protestant groups, the Church of Scientology, and the Church of Jesus Christ of Latter-day Saints, or Mormons (USCIRF 2010).

Freedom of religion remains a controversial topic. In every case, the regime must choose between preserving a certain form of order, including a religious order, and the free expression and enjoyment of religious belief. Philosopher John Clayton suggests that it is more helpful to treat 'disputes over priorities as differences *within the discourse of rights*, than to regard them as conflicts between those who are committed to human rights and those who are not' (1995: 166; emphasis in original). When dealing with the most egregious cases of indifference toward religious freedom, however, many would assert that debates over the nature of human rights are little more than attempts to camouflage bigotry.

Practitioners of Falun Gong have sought official toleration in China since the mid-1990s. The government's refusal to recognize the organization as anything more than a divisive cult has sparked widespread global protest.
Source: Scott Oslon/Getty Images

Religious Freedom and the Politics of Human Rights

With the increasing volume of debate over world divisions that take cultural or 'civilizational' forms, it should come as little surprise that culture and religion have emerged as key features of the debate over human rights as well. Since 1981, when the Banjul Charter introduced the concept of 'peoples' rights', the expansion of human-rights discourse to include collective rights for aboriginal, ethnic, and other minorities has broadened the conception of religious rights even as it has complicated the tasks of defining and judging competing claims. Lerner (2006) discusses how international covenants and regulations that touch on human rights have become ongoing forums for the development of conventional ideas about religious freedom.

Disapproval of the suppression of religious freedom was always an important component of the American opposition to Soviet dominance in world politics, but the primary component was a more universal distaste for the totalitarian and non-democratic character of Soviet Communism. With the collapse of the Communist bloc, human-rights concerns were detached from the fear of worldwide Communism and the international system turned its attention to the rights of ethnic minorities, including the right to self-determination. As various post-Communist states dissolved into ethnic factions contending with one another for land and power, the primary concern was to protect the groups targeted for 'ethnic cleansing' and genocidal purges in places such as the former Yugoslavia, Rwanda, and Sudan. By the end of the 1990s, however, divisions based on ethnicity were becoming less of a problem than divisions based on religious differences.

The human-rights community had internalized much of the criticism from developing states to the effect that it focused too much on political and civic rights, to the detriment of broader concerns such as well-being, human development, security, and deference to family. In particular, Asian and Southeast Asian states argued that values such as filial piety, order, and respect for elders were more important to Asian societies than were the traditional political rights to free speech, organization, and assembly (Jacobsen and Bruun 2000). The gist of their argument tended to be summed up as a dispute over the nature of 'Asian values'. This argument was often marshalled in support of authoritarianism in states such as Singapore and South Korea. Critiques from more collectivist states such as China suggested that Western societies might be just as guilty of human-rights abuses of a different kind: for example, assaults on equity, social justice, or social morality. As a result, mainstream human-rights groups had come to criticize Western nations for their apparent hypocrisy, and occasionally to be criticized for treating Western human-rights abuses as if they were on a par with the abuses committed by dictatorial states.

By the late 1990s the human-rights community had begun to address the perception of Western blindness in the face of human rights. At the same time, many religious believers were becoming aware of global social concerns such as human trafficking, gender violence, and depredations in zones of conflict. Among these new activists, this awareness combined with an increasing interest in cycles of religious violence and repression of religious freedom. Allen Hertzke (2004) describes how human-rights and religious activists together drew attention to the politics of human rights in response to each of these causes. He also explains how the renewed interest in human rights led to the development of organizations such as the International Justice Mission, a human-rights activist group with Christian roots that lobbies and intervenes worldwide against illegal activities such as indentured servitude, prostitution, and human trafficking.

A central concern for the religious groups focusing on human rights was religious freedom, both for their co-religionists and for others around the world. Individual activists associated with US-based Freedom House, a pro-democracy think tank based in Washington, DC, were at the forefront of the religious freedom movement. The expansion of Christian religious networks and their success in influencing Congressional elections in the US led to the establishment of several human-rights groups specifically concerned with religious freedom abroad. A frequent foreign policy concern among Christian conservatives was religious persecution, a topic on which they often formed political alliances with people of other faiths, including Jews. One widely hailed success of the religious human-rights lobby was the passage in 1998 of the US International Religious Freedom Act, which created a permanent secretariat in the US Department of State dedicated to oversight of religious freedom around the world. The US Commission on International Religious Freedom (USCIRF) issues an annual report on religious human-rights practices in states around the world, and recommends actions to the office of the American President.

Among the other major issues involving religious freedom that mobilize large numbers of people, in the US and around the world, in rallies, letter-writing campaigns, and other forms of activism are the Chinese government's policies with regard to Falun Gong and the cultural freedom of Buddhists in Tibet. Major Jewish lobbies such as B'nai B'rith and the Anti-Defamation League work to prevent and fight anti-Semitism, while Muslim organizations such as the Council on American-Islamic Relations defend both the rights of Muslims specifically and the freedom of religion in general. Numerous other religious and denominational councils work to publicize human-rights issues and lobby governments in favour of human rights.

Persistent questions about the political and cultural role of human-rights activism and practice remain. To what extent do the various religions support the growing corpus of law, both domestic and international, with regard to human rights? Have Western dominance and the legacy of colonialism played any role in limiting the expansion of human rights in other cultures? How do normal political conflicts, the dominance of the market economy, and Western cultural norms all play into the global politics of religious human rights? These issues, as much as the religious values that divide peoples, continue to affect the development of global standards of democracy and human rights.

Conclusions

The moral and ethical norms that are the foundations of legal principles in all societies are usually strongly influenced by religious traditions. Thus it should come as no surprise that religion has been closely associated with the development of the democratic system ever since the Enlightenment, even though law has typically been considered religiously neutral. Religion played a significant role in the three waves of democratization identified by Huntington. At the same time, constraints on the public role of religion were an important theme in the development of human rights throughout the period. Religion's role in promoting and challenging the expansion of human rights translates today into both civil society activism for human rights and critical attitudes toward human rights among religious people. The right to religious freedom, enshrined in human-rights law as early as 1948 in the Universal Declaration of Human Rights, has been addressed in international law over the years in different and sometimes controversial ways. The inherent difficulty of forming a united front at the global level when it comes to standards of religious freedom is illustrated by the uneven respect given to religious rights around the world. The plight of religious minorities under persecution and the active part that religious organizations play in the global human-rights discourse remain important topics in global politics.

Review Questions

1. In what ways did religion contribute to the expansion of liberal democratic principles during the three 'waves' of democratization?
2. How was religious power deliberately limited during the same period?
3. What principles can be said to support democracy and human rights in the major world religions? What principles seem to argue that democracy and human rights should be limited?
4. What are the key stages in the development of international law with regard to religious freedom?
5. How and where is religious freedom limited in contemporary global politics?
6. How has religious interest in human rights become enshrined as a significant focus of the human-rights community?

Sources and Further Reading

Abd al-Rahim, Muddathir (2005). *Human Rights and the World's Major Religious Traditions*. Vol. 3. *The Islamic Tradition*. Westport, CT: Praeger.

Aikman, David (2003). *Jesus in Beijing: How Christianity Is Transforming China and Changing the Global Balance of Power*. Washington, DC: Regnery.

An-Na'im, Abdullahi Ahmed, Jerald D. Gort, Henry Jansen, and Hendrik M. Vroom, eds. (1995). *Human Rights and Religious Values: An Uneasy Relationship?* Grand Rapids, MI: Eerdmans.

Brackney, William H. (2005). *Human Rights and the World's Major Religious Traditions*. Vol. 2. *The Christian Tradition*. Westport, CT: Praeger.

Clayton, John (1995). 'Religions and Rights: Local Values and Universal Declarations'. Pp. 259–66 in An-Na'im et al. (1995).

Coward, Harold (2005). *Human Rights and the World's Major Religious Traditions*. Vol. 4. *The Hindu Tradition*. Westport, CT: Praeger.

Daniel, Wallace (2006). *The Orthodox Church and Civil Society in Russia*. College Station: Texas A&M University Press.

Diamond, Larry, Marc F. Plattner, and Daniel Brumberg, eds (2003). *Islam and Democracy in the Middle East*. Baltimore: Johns Hopkins University Press.

Diamond, Larry, Marc F. Plattner, and Philip J. Costopoulos, eds (2005). *World Religions and Democracy*. Baltimore: Johns Hopkins University Press.

Donnelly, Jack (2003). *Universal Human Rights in Theory and Practice*. 2nd edition. Ithaca: Cornell University Press.

El-Fadl, Khaled Abou (2003). 'The Human Rights Commitment in Modern Islam'. Pp. 301–64 in Runzo et al. (2003).

Evans, Carolyn (2001). *Freedom of Religion under the European Convention on Human Rights*. Oxford: Oxford University Press.

Evans, Malcolm D. (1997). *Religious Liberty and International Law in Europe*. Cambridge: Cambridge University Press.

Florida, Robert E. (2005). *Human Rights and the World's Major Religious Traditions*. Vol. 5. *The Buddhist Tradition*. Westport, CT: Praeger.

Fukuyama, Francis (1992). *The End of History and the Last Man*. New York: Free Press.

Gearon, Liam, ed. (2002). *Human Rights and Religion: A Reader*. Brighton: Sussex Academic Press.

Ghanea, Nazila, Alan Stephens, and Raphael Walden, eds. (2007). *Does God Believe in Human Rights?* Leiden: Martinus Nijhoff Publishers.

Haas, Peter J. (2005). *Human Rights and the World's Major Religions, Vol. 1. The Jewish Tradition*. Westport, CT: Praeger.

Hertzke, Allen D. (2004). *Freeing God's Children: The Unlikely Alliance for Global Human Rights*. Lanham, MD: Rowman & Littlefield.

Huntington, Samuel (1991). *The Third Wave: Democratization in the Late Twentieth Century*. Norman: University of Oklahoma Press.

Keown, Damien, Charles S. Prebish, and Wayne Rollen Husted, eds (1998). *Buddhism and Human Rights*. Richmond, Surrey: Curzon.

Johnson, Juliet, Marietta Stepaniants, and Benjamin Forest, eds (2005). *Religion and Identity in Modern Russia: The Revival of Orthodoxy and Islam*. Aldershot: Ashgate.

Jacobsen, Michael, and Ole Bruun, eds (2000). *Human Rights and Asian Values: Contesting National Identities and Cultural Representations in Asia*. Richmond: Curzon.

Lerner, Natan (2000). *Religion, Beliefs, and International Human Rights*, Maryknoll, NY: Orbis Books.

—— (2006). *Religion, Secular Beliefs and Human Rights: 25 Years after the 1981 Declaration*. Leiden: Martinus Nijhoff Publishers.

Leustean, Lucian (2009). *Orthodoxy and the Cold War: Religion and Political Power in Romania, 1947–65*. London: Palgrave Macmillan.

Lewis, Bernard (1996). 'Islam and Liberal Democracy: A Historical Overview', *Journal of Democracy* 7, 2: 52–63.

Lilla, Mark (2007). *The Stillborn God: Religion, Politics, and the Modern West*. New York: Knopf.

Marshall, Paul, ed. (2000). *Religious Freedom in the World: A Global Report on Freedom and Persecution*. Nashville, TN: Broadman & Holman.

Philpott, Daniel (2005). 'The Catholic Wave'. Pp.102–16 in Diamond et al. (2005).

Reinders, Johannes S. (1995). 'Human Rights from the Perspective of a Narrow Conception of Religious Morality'. Pp. 3–23 in Naim et al. (1995).

Ryzhova, Svetlana (2005). 'Tolerance and Extremism: Russian Ethnicity in the Orthodox Discourse of the 1990s'. Pp. 65–90 in Johnson et al. (2005).

Runzo, Joseph, Nancy M. Martin, and Arvind Sharma, eds (2003). *Human Rights and Responsibilities in the World Religions*. Oxford: Oneworld.

Sachedina, Abdulaziz (2001). *The Islamic Roots of Democratic Pluralism*. New York: Oxford University Press.

—— (2009). *Islam and the Challenge of Human Rights*. Oxford: Oxford University Press.

Sen, Ronojoy (2010). *Articles of Faith: Religion, Secularism, and the Indian Supreme Court*. New Delhi: Oxford University Press.

Soroush, Abdolkarim (2000). *Reason, Freedom and Democracy in Islam: Essential Writings of Abdolkarim Soroush*. Mahmoud Sadri and Ahmad Sadri, eds. Oxford: Oxford University Press.

Stepan, Alfred (2005). 'Religion, Democracy, and the "Twin Tolerations"'. Pp. 3–25 in Diamond et al. (2005).

Tierney, Brian (1996). 'Religious Rights: An Historical Perspective'. Pp. 17–45 in Witte and van der Vyver (1996).

USCIRF (United States Commission on International Religious Freedom) (2010). *Annual Report*. Washington, DC: United States Commission on International Religious Freedom.

van der Vyver, Johan D., and John Witte, Jr, eds (1996). *Religious Human Rights in Global Perspective: Legal Perspectives*. The Hague: Martinus Nijhoff Publishers.

Wadud, Amina (2006). *Inside the Gender Jihad*. Oxford: Oneworld.

Witte, John, Jr, ed. (1993). *Christianity and Democracy in Global Context*. Boulder: Westview Press.

———, and Johan D. van der Vyver, eds (1996). *Religious Human Rights in Global Perspective: Religious Perspectives*. The Hague: Martinus Nijhoff Publishers.

Web Resource

www.uscirf.gov – The United States Commission on International Religious Freedom.

Chapter 9

Religion and War

In 2007, curmudgeonly journalist Christopher Hitchens published a book-length diatribe against religion as a divisive and often violent social force. One memorable passage describes a conversation he had with an interviewer approximately a week before 11 September 2001. The interviewer had challenged him with a question:

> I was to imagine myself in a strange city as the evening was coming on. Toward me I was to imagine that I saw a large group of men approaching. Now—would I feel safer, or less safe, if I was to learn that they were just coming from a prayer meeting?
>
> . . . I have actually had that experience in Belfast, Beirut, Bombay, Belgrade, Bethlehem, and Baghdad. In each case I can say absolutely, and can give my reasons, why I would feel immediately threatened if I thought that the group of men approaching me in the dusk were coming from a religious observance (Hitchens 2007: 18).

Hitchens is one of several commentators in the past decade who have commented on the apparently common association of religion with violence.

For example, Hector Avalos (2005) has theorized that people fight over religion for the same reason they fight over resources, territory, and power: because it represents assets (spiritual teachings, sacred places, privileges, assurance of salvation) that are scarce and hence highly valued. He also suggests that religion is particularly prone to violence because its premises are 'unverifiable': therefore competing claims cannot be adjudicated by any 'objective means' (2005: 381).

Is religion inherently violent? Is it as likely to contribute to conflict as other polarizing political phenomena like ideology, class, nationalism, or the capitalist system? Very few scholars would castigate religion in the way that Hitchens does, but its potential to spark conflict cannot be denied. Religion has such a great deal to say about what is important that it fuels passions and sets hearts aflame. Selengut (2003) argues that religion gives rise to violence because it creates 'self-legitimating' ideals that must be followed over and above any other contending belief, because it promises other-worldly rewards that transcend the mortal life, and because it helps to make sense of suffering (7–8). In the words of one philosopher, the very concept of violence is at least partly 'transcendental or metaphysical, belonging to the realm traditionally ascribed . . . to the intelligible or the noumenal' (De Vries 2002: 1).

To put it more simply, violence has spiritual implications. The sacrifices demanded by war are so great that they require otherworldly justification. As Chris Hedges notes, 'armed movements seek divine sanction [for their aims] and the messianic certitude of absolute truth' (2002: 14). Therefore it should come as little surprise that religion and war have often been associated throughout history. Religion has a great deal to say about the regulation of our moral and social lives, about ethics, and about matters of life and death. What human behaviour arouses more profound questions than armed conflict?

'Religious' Wars of the Past

For many, the history and development of our modern religions is closely associated with the wars of the past. War and religion have gone hand in glove throughout world history. For two millennia, one of the most important sources of Hindu philosophy has been the *Mahabarata*—the story of an ancient war. The Sikh Khalsa was created in 1699 to defend the Sikh community against violent persecution. The Jewish scriptures describe wars between the people of ancient Israel and their neighbours, justified by divine sanction. Islam was spread through wars of conquest in the seventh and eighth centuries. Christians responded to the erosion of Western power in the Middle East by volunteering for the Crusades—a 'holy war' that continued at intervals from the eleventh century to the fourteenth.

Wellman (2007) makes the point that religion has always been associated with political violence because politics and religion compete for the same basic loyalties. His contributors cite case studies from the ancient Near East and the Roman world all the way through to modern America to make the point. It is frequently noted that the international system was founded in 1648 in the wake of the wars of religion that had pitted the Roman Catholic states of southern Europe against their Protestant rivals to the north. At Westphalia in 1648 world leaders agreed that religion should be laid aside as a reason for war. But in fact religion remained an important factor both as a justification for war and as a rallying point in the midst of it.

Despite the presumed secularity of state purposes, political leaders were never averse to depicting their opponents as godless barbarians or appealing to concerns over religious freedom. For example, throughout the eighteenth century, British efforts to prevent a return of pretenders to the English throne took the form of anti-Catholic policy and rhetoric. Even more notably, a dispute over the custody of holy sites in the Middle East ignited a crisis over Russian ambitions in the eastern Mediterranean in 1854. The result was the bloody Crimean War of 1854–6.

The intimate relationship between religion and nationalism has been observed frequently. For example, Anthony D. Smith, a renowned scholar of the history of nationalism, argues in a recent work that nationalism itself can become a sort of 'religion surrogate':

> the nation state replaces the deity, history assumes the role of divine providence, the leader becomes the prophet, his writings and speeches form the sacred texts, the national movement becomes the new church, and its celebratory and commemorative rites take the place of religious ceremonies (Smith 2003: 17).

At the same time, religion may serve to back up the politics of nationalism, providing a sacred canopy for the actions of the nation-state. The combination of religion and national foreign policy in the major wars of the period after 1815 reached a critical point with the expansion of citizen armies and the pursuit of total war. Colonial resistance against imperial rule often expressed itself in religious nationalism, for example in Sudan from 1881 to 1885 under Muhammad Ahmad ('the Mahdi') or in the Caucasus from 1834 to 1859 under Imam Shamil.

Box 9.1: Faith at War

Some religious leaders have also gained fame as political and military figures. Here are some examples of figures who have been honoured as both warriors and religious leaders:

Ram (Rama) The hero of the Hindu epic *Ramayana*, an avatar of the god Vishnu, Ram, is forced into battle when his wife Sita is abducted by the demon-king Ravana. Ram is a legendary figure with roots dating back to the Vedic period (fifth century BCE) but Hindus revere his supposed birthplace in Ayodhya to this day.

King David (c. 1000 BCE) David, the shepherd boy said to have killed the Philistine giant Goliath, became the founder of a royal dynasty as well as a warrior who led his people in battle against many enemies. He is also traditionally reputed to be the author of numerous psalms in the Hebrew Bible.

Muhammad (c. 570–632) The Prophet of Islam was not just a religious reformer but a political leader who established his authority first in Medina (Yathrib) in 622. He led his followers in several battles over the next decade in an attempt to defend the community of Muslims, finally returning in victory to his home city of Mecca in 630. After his death in 632, his followers turned the community he founded into an empire through military conquest.

Pope Urban II (c. 1042–99) It was in hope of ending the squabbles among the European nobility and restoring the influence of the Roman Catholic Church in the eastern Mediterranean, that Pope Urban II called for the first Crusade against the Turks and Arabs in a sermon at Clermont, France, in 1095. Uttering the words 'Christ commands it' and promising absolution of sins to knights who died on Crusade, Urban laid the foundation for centuries of warfare.

Rashid al-Din Sinan (c. 1132–92) A leader of the Nizari Ismaili sect of Shi'i Islam during the Crusades, Sinan had a reputation for military cunning and intrigue. His followers, known as the Assassins, were legendary for their willingness to give their lives in support of their missions, and in time their name was adopted by several European languages as the term for those who commit strategic murder.

Pope Julius II (1443–1513) Known as the 'warrior pope', Julius II won the papacy in 1503, likely through bribery and intrigue. He spent his time as pope conducting military campaigns to consolidate the Papal States in Italy against the French Bourbons and Austrian Hapsburgs. He formed the 'Holy League' of states with Spain, Venice, and England to support his foreign policy, eventually forcing the French out of Italy.

Guru Gobind Singh (1666–1708) The tenth and final human Guru of the Sikhs, Gobind Singh is best known for his creation of the Khalsa as a special military order dedicated to the protection of the faith in 1699. Over the next few years, Gobind Singh led the Khalsa in a war for the independence of the Sikhs against the Muslim Mughal Emperors of India. He died following an assassination attempt during a later military campaign.

Muhammad Ahmad (1844–85) Originally a Sufi mystic, Muhammad Ahmad claimed to be the 'Mahdi', the Islamic messiah. From 1881 to 1885 he fought Egyptian and British forces to establish an independent state in Sudan. His victory against the British General George Gordon allowed him to declare a mahdiyya (Mahdi state). After his death in 1885, British and Egyptian forces managed to recolonize Sudan, but Muhammad Ahmad remained a symbol of colonial resistance.

By the twentieth century, religion was often used by state authorities to mobilize public support, with or without the cooperation of clergy or religious leaders. Hoover (1989) describes how clerical leaders helped to gain popular support for the nationalist war efforts in Germany and Britain during the First World War. Victoria (1997) describes how Japanese Buddhists came to embrace the project of foreign conquest in the 1920s and 1930s as a fusion of Buddhist self-denial with the traditional Japanese Bushido warrior code; and Skya (2009) relates how Shinto ultra-nationalists spearheaded the effort. Miner (2003) considers the way that religious nationalism was cultivated to defend the Stalinist Soviet regime during the Second World War. Cornwell (1999) asserts that the Vatican cooperated with Hitler's regime. While his work remains deeply controversial, it is clear that a majority of the churches in Germany posed little opposition to Nazi aggression.

On the other hand, religion was also the context out of which secular modernity developed, often with violent results. William Cavanaugh argues that the 'wars of religion' of the 1500s and 1600s had more to do with the violence of the modern secular state than with religion, and that since then the assertion of state power has always come at the cost of both religion and peace (Cavanaugh 1995). Radical secular ideological movements of all sorts—Jacobinism, Marxism, communism, fascism—have usually opposed the established religions and churches of their day. Anticlericalism contributed to the deaths of numerous religious leaders in the midst of revolutions and political violence throughout the past centuries. One of the first acts of the French revolutionaries was to limit the power of the Roman Catholic Church in the Civil Constitution of the Clergy (1790). Many of the clergy were later executed in the Terror. Napoleon Bonaparte also challenged the Church by invading the Papal States a few years later.

The Communist revolutions of the twentieth century resulted in the marginalization of religious institutions and movements, often through violent repression. National socialist and fascist groups sometimes forced religious groups to accept the primacy of the state and nationalist ideology. This was accomplished by forcing the nationalization of the Protestant church hierarchy in Nazi Germany. In addition, fascist movements targeted religious minorities. The most notorious example was of course the attempted genocide of Europe's Jews. However, the German and Japanese wartime military regimes also imprisoned and persecuted other religious opponents of the state, including Christian clergy and missionaries as well as dissident Buddhist monks. Historian Michael Burleigh has made the point that in the past few centuries religion has been at least as likely to be the target of violence as it has been to support the use of military force (Burleigh 2005: 2007). Thus the contentious relationship between religion and politics can also be understood as a product of the movement from traditional conceptions of human identity toward newer and more revolutionary forms.

Religion and War in the Modern World

In his widely cited 1996 work, Samuel Huntington argued that the major conflicts of the future would fall along the lines separating the world's major civilizations, and that religion 'was a central defining characteristic of civilizations' (1996: 47). In fact, as we have seen, religious conflicts had already raged for several years prior to Huntington's pronouncement. Religious rifts merged with ideological ones throughout the Cold War and ethnic conflicts arose in its wake. Thus religion has played an important role in defining the groups that fought the wars of the twentieth century.

Understood in this way, religion 'functions as an identity-forming mechanism that constructs and mobilizes individuals and groups, both to violence as well as peace' (Wellman 2007: 1). Religion tends to stand with other markers such as language, phenotypical features (skin tone, hair and eye colour), cultural practices, and name as indicators of ethnic belonging. Religion thus helps to provide a sort of social glue that binds people together in group solidarity and dedication to shared purposes (Smith 2003). In fact, the English word 'religion' derives from a Latin root meaning 'to bind'.

Religion's social role in reinforcing ethnic belonging contributed to its wide identification with ethnic conflict both historically and in the period that followed the end of the Cold War in the 1990s. As a consequence, many social theorists have identified a strong link between religious belonging and ethnic conflict. For example, Seul (1999) concludes that '[t]he peculiar ability of religion to support the development of individual and group identity is the hidden logic of the link between religion and intergroup conflict.' For most observers of ethnic conflict, religion offered a useful way to categorize 'in-groups' against 'out-groups'. It served as an ordering principle to define 'us' versus 'them'. According to an instrumentalist understanding of these conflicts, religion helped to create groups that would then compete with others for tangible assets such as territory, wealth, and state power.

Indeed religion had an important role to play in several conflicts that developed toward the end of the Cold War and in its immediate aftermath. The breakdown of state authority in Lebanon in the mid-1970s was the first. Lebanon had been created following World War II under French supervision as a country with a bare Christian majority. When it gained its independence in 1943, the government was forged under a pact that maintained Christian dominance. Government power was shared between Christians, Sunni Muslims, Shi'i Muslims, and Druze, based on a set of rules. The rules of the game ensured that the president would always be a Maronite Christian and that Christians would always maintain a majority in the National Assembly. They also gave a high degree of power to the Sunni Muslim minority. Over the following decades the relative numbers of Christians declined and a large number of Palestinian refugees arrived to upset the balance of power between the communities. Finally, the proportion of Shi'i Muslims increased to the point where they formed the largest single sectarian grouping.

However, the Christians and Sunni Muslims were reluctant to alter the system to reflect these demographic changes. After 1982, when Israeli forces invaded south Lebanon to eliminate the PLO, the Lebanese sects fell into open civil war (Khazen 2000). The war forced the Lebanese even further into sectarian enclaves. Between 1982 and 1990 the country fell apart and the various religious groups remained at war with one another. Sectarian belonging became the chief way in which each side was identified in the conflict over Lebanon. Although the civil war came to an end in 1990, Lebanese politics is still sharply divided between the various sectarian groups.

In other cases religion may contribute to the cultural and ethnic cleavages that fuel civil conflict. In Sri Lanka, for example, civil war pitted the Sinhalese majority, who are primarily Buddhist, against the Tamil minority, who are mostly Hindu, from the early 1970s until 2009. Although the conflict itself was over the status of Tamil culture in a predominantly Sinhalese society, religion was used to promote military imagery and to help define the other side. Similarly in Sudan, civil conflict raged between North and South Sudanese for most of the period from the early 1980s until a Comprehensive Peace Agreement was signed in 2005. The distinctions between northern and southern Sudanese fell along numerous ethnic, clan, and racial lines. However, after President Omar al-Bashir came to power at the head of the National Islamic Front in 1989, the government increased its efforts to impose an Islamic state on the predominantly Christian and animist people of the south. The religious dimension further polarized the population and deepened the divisions at the root of the civil war.

The religious dimension of ethnic conflict was further highlighted by the conflict over the former Yugoslavia from 1991 to 1995. After the end of the Cold War, political divisions among the ethnic groups that formed the republic of Yugoslavia led to the breakup of the state into several constituent republics. The process began with Slovenia and Croatia in 1991. In 1992, Bosnia-Herzegovina declared its independence of Yugoslavia. The independence of Croatia and Bosnia-Herzegovina in particular led to the eruption of hostilities between ethnic Serbs who opposed independence and ethnic Croats and Bosnians who generally favoured it. Contributing to the ethnic divide was a religious one: Croats were primarily Roman Catholic, ethnic Bosnians were defined by their Muslim faith, and Serbs were mostly Greek Orthodox. Struggles over religion had helped to define the history of this part of the Balkans since the invasion of the Ottoman Turks in the fourteenth century, as Croats, Muslims, and Serbs had contended for power and their own religious freedoms, both with one another and with regional powers.

In the 1990s, religion played an important role in defining group belonging and in framing the various groups' understanding of history and tradition. Perica (2002) argues that the new state elites emerging from the former Yugoslavia gave religious leaders a free hand in helping to define the ethnic demands of the nation, a role they took up with some relish. Amid the descent into civil war, religious authorities in the Balkan states linked the notion of a national church to the activities of radical clergymen in a model that Perica calls 'ethnoclericalism' (214–15). As a result, religion became a central element in the Yugoslav civil war even though there was no particular revival of interest in religion among the peoples involved.

In the wake of the American invasion of Iraq in 2003, divisions among Iraqis fell in part along sectarian lines. The population of Iraq is divided among three ethnic and sectarian groups: Kurds in the north, Sunni Arabs in the central regions, and Shi'i Arabs in the south. In the chaos of the occupation, some opponents of the American presence sought to deepen the violence by instigating a civil war among the factions. A letter attributed to an al-Qaeda–linked militant named Abu Musab al-Zarqawi, discovered in January 2004, revealed his plans to foment a religious civil war. Attacks on symbolic Shi'i targets, perhaps most notably the 2006 and 2007 bombings of the Askari Mosque in Samarra, were apparently designed to spark intersectarian fighting. Indeed a large number of the attacks and kidnappings that took place between 2003 and 2008 were aimed at deepening the violence between Sunni and Shi'i Arabs. Factional divisions in Iraq continue to threaten further sectarian conflict.

In other regions, religion has helped to define the contending interests that led to conflict between states. Where religion is an important component of national identity, it is common for international disputes to take on a sectarian character, particularly in cases where neighbouring groups are of different faiths. At the heart of the dispute over Kashmir, for instance, is the question whether Kashmiri Muslims should be ruled by a majority Muslim state (Pakistan) or by the secular Indian state. As elaborated in chapter 6, the southern portion of Kashmir went to India as a result of a decision made by its former maharaja. Since 1947, Kashmir has been divided between Pakistan and India, and the tensions between the two states have led not only to communal violence in Kashmir itself but to attacks on the Indian state by Pakistan-based terrorists.

In numerous other cases, religion and nationalism have combined to form a platform for jingoism and to justify expansionistic foreign policies. In earlier chapters, we have seen the association of religion with assertive foreign policies in countries as diverse as the United States, Iran, India, and Israel. A sense of divine chosenness, the notion that one's country has a role in a divine plan can be used to justify violent actions that would otherwise be unacceptable.

Juergensmeyer (1993) points out that religion has provided a strong platform for colonial and postmodern reactionary movements against the modern state system. When modern secularism was found wanting in various parts of the developing world, many formerly colonized people turned to reactionary religious movements as alternatives. For many, religious fundamentalism provided a potent ideological challenge to Western civilization. Following the collapse of the Cold War and the triumph of the modern capitalist West, discontent with the neoliberal world order has increasingly been expressed by religious movements. Thus rebellion against Western modernity, the global economic system, and the international state system itself has been taken up by religious radicals (Philpott 2002). Radicals' use of violence helps to demonstrate their perception of the system as fundamentally illegitimate.

Since 1990 numerous well-publicized violent incidents have drawn attention to the connection between religious radicalism and rebellion against the modern secular state. In April 1993, a US government police action against the compound occupied by the Branch Davidians—a millenarian sect that had been illegally stockpiling weapons in preparation for an expected apocalypse—ended in the fiery destruction of the compound and the deaths of 76 sect members. Among the dead was the sect's leader, David Koresh, who had taught that such a conflagration would bring about the end of the world and the group's vindication as the true disciples of God. The police raid was later cited by Oklahoma City bomber Timothy McVeigh as a motivation for his attack against the United States government in April 1995. On 20 March 1995, another apocalyptic group, the Japanese Aum Shinrikyo, released poisonous sarin gas in the Tokyo metro system, killing 13 people and harming numerous others. Once again, the group believed its action to be the first step in a final reckoning that would bring the secular Japanese state to an end and help to enthrone their religious leader, a man named Shoko Asahara.

The Askari Mosque in Samarra, Iraq, built in 944 and venerated by Shi'i Muslims as the tomb of two of the twelve Imams, was severely damaged by bombing in 2006 and 2007. The apparent intent of the bombers was to instigate civil conflict between Sunni and Shi'i.
Source: Getty Images

At the same time, attacks against secular and Western targets by various radical Islamist groups were increasing. Following their apparent victory in the Afghan civil war of the 1980s, they were convinced that the next step must be to confront both Western secular governments and *jahili* (corrupt) Muslim governments in their home countries. Among the symbols of power in contemporary global society they targeted were the World Trade Center in New York (1993), the American military presence in Saudi Arabia (1996), American embassies in Africa (1998), and the American Navy destroyer USS *Cole* (2000). By the late 1990s it was clear that all these attacks were attributable to a global movement spearheaded by Osama bin Laden's al-Qaeda network, the organization that was to carry out the dramatic attacks of 11 September 2001. Since that time, growing numbers of groups from West Africa to Somalia to the Philippines have presented ideological challenges to the secular and Western international system.

However, religion is not simply an ordering principle or an ideological construct that serves to justify violence against others. Religions also provide moral guidance and clarify our values with respect to violence. Most religions decry violence as a matter of course. The commandment 'Thou shalt not kill' is a fundamental part of the Judeo-Christian tradition. Violence is viewed as a part of humanity's disorder in most eastern religions. Even so, over the centuries the followers of the major religious traditions have found that they had to justify the use of force over the centuries. If religion reviles violence, how is it possible to justify warfare and resort to force on religious grounds?

Most of the major faiths have developed complex understandings around the relative importance of injunctions against violence and injunctions demanding justice. These complex understandings are rooted in interpretive decisions, developed by religious experts, that we may call 'hermeneutic' frameworks. We will consider some of these frameworks in reflection on a few major religious traditions.

The Just War Tradition

Jesus Christ publicly disavowed violence against one's enemies, and the earliest Christians largely followed his example. Early Christians were often persecuted by ruling authorities and by and large Christians resisted Roman militarism. Until the faith began to spread beyond the Jewish community, it did not typically appeal to those in political or military authority. However, as it was embraced by a wider segment of the population, Christians began to develop justifications for the defence of their own society. After their faith became the official religion of Rome in the fourth century, Christians came to be the most prominent defenders of order in the Empire. Christian theology regarded secular authority as an extension of the sovereignty of God, and the earliest Christian philosophers of politics drew on Greek and Roman philosophies that defended the work of political authorities in punishing wrongdoers and defending the community. If the Roman Empire was a tool that God could use to preserve order, the state must have some authority to compel that order—and to use force to that end.

Thus Christianity developed numerous perspectives on the acceptability of warfare. Some held that war was never justified; minorities in both the Eastern and Western churches throughout history were pacifists, as were non-conformists and Anabaptists, particularly on the continent of Europe, after the Protestant Reformation. On the opposite side, some occasionally argued that Christendom itself must be defended by armed force. The idea of 'holy war' provided some justification for the extension of Western temporal power via the Crusades of the eleventh to the fourteenth century. In later years, war also came to be relativized: however regrettable it might be as a symptom of a fallen humanity, as a behaviour of states war was considered essentially amoral; this is the position called Christian Realism (Clough and Stiltner 2007: 6-9). Historically, however, the more common Christian position has been that war is a sinful if occasionally necessary activity and therefore must be subject to strict regulation.

For this reason Christians over the centuries developed a set of principles regarding the use of force that helped them to identify situations in which violence was justified (Schmidt-Leukel 2004: 99–147). Together, these principles came to be known as '**Just War** Theory', or the 'Just War Tradition'. According to Stiltner, 'Just War emerges as a corollary to the Christian call to political participation; it is a rare but sometimes necessary extension of the activities that Christians are always doing as citizens or allowing leaders to do in their name' (Clough and Stiltner 2007: 51). Just War was a Christian attempt to condemn the evils of war while accepting that good citizens must sometimes use force to deal with chaos and injustice. It rejects the notion that war should be used in the defence of the Christian faith. It also parts company with both the Realist idea that war is amoral and the pacifist idea that it is never justified. Its use by the philosophers and moralists who established the earliest bases of international law has made the Just War tradition very influential in modern understandings of international conflict since the seventeenth century, moving it from Just War 'doctrine' to Just War 'theory', in the words of J. B. Elshtain (1992: 324).

The Just War tradition has its roots in ancient Christian scholarship. Ambrose, Bishop of Milan (339–397), and his disciple Augustine of Hippo (354–430) are credited as the first philosophers to create a Christian defence of statecraft, including the use of force in war. Neither of these two composed a treatise on Just War as such, but they did write in defence of Christian uses of force to preserve order and justice. In addition, in Book XIX of his work *City of God* Augustine began to discuss the conditions required for war to be considered ethical, including that it be pursued in a just cause, that it be declared by a proper authority, and that the motivation behind it be appropriate. These ideas were taken up by later authorities within the Christian tradition, the most important of whom was the thirteenth-century philosopher Thomas Aquinas. His *Summa Theologica* is a foundational work in the elucidation of Christian theological principles, structured in the form of answers to questions about theological problems. On the subject of war (Question 40, Part II) Aquinas reiterated Augustine's principles (just cause, proper authority, right intentions) and added two more: the degree of force used in war should be proportionate to the ends sought, and war fought in the defence of life was justifiable (Clough and Stiltner 2007: 53–5). Aquinas's text is still considered foundational in Roman Catholic theology, although the justifications for war are now more narrowly defined and many Roman Catholic

Thomas Aquinas, portrayed here by the fifteenth-century artist Justus van Gent, was a central figure in Christian theology. He laid down the basic ethical premises behind the Christian justifications of war, now known as the Just War tradition.
Source: Portrait of St. Thomas Aquinas (1225-74) c. 1475 (oil on panel). Joos van Gent (fl. 1460-75) and Berruguete, P. (c. 1450-1504)/Louvre, Paris, France/The Bridgement Art Library International

theologians today consider the use of force in modern warfare to have escalated to unjustifiable levels.

Eastern Orthodox Christians, who have their own theological traditions and reflections regarding the use of force, have also moved toward a more narrow definition of the grounds on which war is justified. Protestants are widely divided: continental Anabaptists such as the Mennonites condemn the use of force entirely, while Calvinists and Lutherans are more conservative and tend to embrace the Just War tradition of their Roman Catholic predecessors (Popovski, Reichberg, and Turner 2009: 142–254).

The Christian tradition had a formative influence on the pioneers of international legal thinking, most notably Hugo Grotius. In time, as it became the basis for wider ethical and legal thinking about the use of force in war, Just War Theory developed two sets of ethical criteria, the first relating to the decision to go to war (***jus ad bellum***), and the second to the use of force in war (*jus in bello*). ***Jus ad bellum*** principles include the idea that war should be a last resort, when all other attempts to resolve a dispute have failed, that it should be waged to redress wrongs or in pursuit of a just objective, that it should be declared by properly constituted authority, and that there must be good reason to believe it will be successful. *Jus in bello* criteria govern the conduct of war: for example, requiring differentiation between combatants and non-combatants and demanding that the means used to accomplish individual goals in war must be proportionate to the overall goal. These criteria have been widely debated and now form the basis of philosophic and ethical thinking about war (Walzer 1977; Elshtain 1992; Brough, Lango, and van der Linden 2007).

The Tradition of War in Islam

The fact that Islam initially established itself through military conquest means that it has a very different perspective on war than Christianity does. Islam has no equivalent to the Just War tradition as it developed in the Christian world. Muhammad's successors did not hesitate to use force to extend Islamic civilization through promotion of the Prophet's message and to defend the faith. For this reason, James Turner Johnson argues that the idea of violence in the name of a holy cause is more easily embraced in Islam than it is in Christianity: 'While for the West war for religion is divisive and terrible, for Islam jihad as a war for religion is not divisive but unifying, and what is terrible is the world of strife jihad seeks to bring to an end' (Johnson 1997: 18). At the same time, war was justified not in its own right but only a means towards an ultimate good. For this reason, scholars have noted significant similarities between Muslim and Christian thinking about when war can be justified (Silverman 2002). Kelsay (2007) argues that to understand Just War thinking in Islam it is necessary to look at it through the lens of the Islamic tradition of jurisprudence (*fiqh*). Muhammad's call to all nations to receive Islam meant that conquest constituted an opening for the wider acceptance of Islam—an idea reinforced by the fact that the Arabic words for 'conquest' and 'opening' are homonyms (Kelsay 2007: 38). For this reason, the call to Muslims to engage, personally and collectively, in spreading and practising the faith was a call to engage in personal and collective *jihad* (struggle).

One should distinguish the word *jihad* from the Arabic word **qital** which is used for fighting in war. There are two kinds of *jihad*, 'greater' and 'lesser'. The greater *jihad* is the inner struggle to affirm Islam in one's life, while the lesser is the struggle to establish Islam throughout the world and to defend it by force if necessary. Amira Sonbol argues that it was in the 'greater' sense that Muhammad generally used the word, and that the 'lesser' sense developed as a justification for warfare over the centuries that followed (Popovski, Reichberg and Turner 2009: 282–302).

In the first several centuries after the death of Muhammad, *jihad* came to be associated with the Muslim community's efforts to expand and defend itself through warfare. Muslims followed the injunctions in the Qur'an and Hadith that taught them to fight unbelievers until a peace treaty was negotiated. Islamic tradition, as we have seen, divided the world into two parts, the *dar al-Islam* (household of Islam), which had accepted the authority of Islam, and the *dar al-Harb* (abode of war), which had not. Thus the Muslim worldview assumed that war would persist as long as any part of the world remained outside the community of believers.

Even so, combat in the name of God was limited by specific requirements laid down by various Islamic scholars. One notable example was Muhammad al-Shaybani (c. 750–805), a leading figure in the Hanafi school of Islamic jurisprudence. Shaybani articulated the rules of military *jihad*: war could be justified only for the purpose of spreading the Islamic faith; warriors must not mutilate their enemies or target children; and non-believers conquered in war should not be forced to convert as long as they paid a tax called the *jizya* (Schmidt-Leukel 2004: 152).

Early on, divisions within the *umma* led to civil strife (*fitna*). Among the Sunni scholars who condemned *fitna* was Abu Hasan al-Mawardi (972–1058), who demanded that any resort to warfare be supported by the correct authority in order to prevent arbitrary fighting among Muslims (Kelsay 2007: 110). However, the necessity of *jihad* for the expansion of Islam was a controversial topic. One concept that came to be important to the scholars was the differentiation between the offensive *jihad* to spread the faith of Islam and *jihad* conducted in defence of the community. While mainstream and Sufi thinking emphasized the 'greater' internal *jihad* into the eleventh century, threats to the community such as the Crusades and the Mongol invasions led to a renewal of calls for the 'lesser' military *jihad* thereafter. It was in this context that Ibn Taymiyya instructed Muslims to understand military *jihad* as a religious obligation. To Ibn Taymiyya, offensive *jihad* was the duty of the community of Muslims as a whole, while defensive *jihad* was the duty of every individual Muslim.

As in the Christian tradition, there is no single authoritative position in Islam on the justifiability of violence in war. Modern Muslim theologians and philosophers have many reasons to debate the ways in which Islamic teachings on conflict may be applied to modern warfare. For example, the dissolution of the caliphate almost a century ago makes it difficult to establish who would have the authority to declare a modern-day collective *jihad*. Although Sunni and Shi'i interpretations of the principles governing the conduct of war are similar, Shi'i scholars argue that, in the absence of a properly constituted religious authority, the *umma* has no mandate to engage in offensive *jihad* at all (Popovski, Reichberg, and Turner 2009: 276). Furthermore, Muslims of different sects disagree on what would constitute an offensive *jihad*. The tradition of *ijtihad*, or independent reasoning, allows Islamic scholars to debate the use of force. Although there are Muslims who maintain that the tradition of military *jihad* interpreted by the early scholars applies today, there are at least equal numbers who would consider Western-style Just War criteria acceptable standards for judging the ethics of the use of force.

Himsa and *Ahimsa* in Hinduism and Buddhism

Hindu teachings about the proper conduct of war are as diverse as Hinduism itself. From the beginning, warfare was a common theme of the Vedic and epic literature, which taught that it was the *dharma* of rulers to defend their people and bring order to a universe of disorder. At the same time, *ahimsa* (avoidance of harm to any sentient being) was a basic value, though less central to Hinduism itself than to the ascetic traditions that developed out of it.

Hindu philosophy originated in the so-called Indo-Aryan culture that dominated northern India from roughly 1700 BCE on. The Vedas, the earliest Hindu scriptures, indicate that war was a common occurrence, whether among Indo-Aryan groups or with their neighbours, and that norms of warfare were developing in India at roughly the same time as in the ancient Greek world.

Kaushik Roy explains how the early tradition of warfare laid out the basic expectations of what we might call a just war (*dharmayuddha*) (Roy 2009: 31). The justice of a war was determined primarily by the chivalry and professionalism of the soldier; war should be declared openly and pursued with martial ardour. But the Hindu tradition accepted that rulers might fight primarily for their own ends: for example, the *Arthashastra*, a book written by a court official named Kautilya (c. 300 BCE) offers counsel for conquerors engaging in battle with local rivals. This text suggests that unjust war (*kutayuddha*) was common. By the first few centuries of this era, however, Brahminic texts were refining these rules. For example, the *Laws of Manu* describe the proper organization of society and the roles of the various castes, including the Kshatriya, the caste of warriors and kings. The fact that *Manu's* guidance regarding war is directed specifically to the Kshatriyas, the defenders of the realm, suggests that warfare was not acceptable for any other caste. Certain tactics are ruled unacceptable, although the warrior must be bold to achieve his ends. These rules remain the foundations of the Hindu understanding of war to this day.

War is a major theme of both the great Hindu epics. The central figure in the *Ramayana*, the god-man Ram, is a king who engages in warfare as a matter of course. And the *Mahabharata*—the story of a war between two related clans—suggests that humans are prone to conflict because of their greed and lust, suggesting that war is something to be avoided (Schmidt-Leukel 2004: 19). Its best-known section, the *Bhagavad Gita*, presents a lengthy discussion between Krishna, an avatar of Vishnu, and Arjuna, a warrior prince who is reluctant to go into battle against his kinsmen. Krishna explains why it is Arjuna's duty—his *dharma*—to fight in defence of the social order.

The *Bhagavad Gita*, the most celebrated section of the *Mahabharata* epic, describes how Lord Krishna persuades Arjuna, who wants to lay down his arms, that it is his duty as a warrior prince to proceed with the battle.
Source: bpk, Berlin/Museum fuer Asiatische Kunst, Staatliche Museen/Iris Papadopoulos/Art Resource, NY

The meaning of these epics is ambiguous and has led to diverse *himsa* traditions in Indian religion. The mainstream interpretation is that the epics justify *himsa* in pursuit of the warrior prince's *dharma*. That is, they explain why war is justified in defence of the community, order, and justice, and are critical of war that is not conducted in an ethical manner. However, Mahatma Gandhi saw in the *Gita* a call to self-sacrifice rather than a call to action: therefore he presented a pacifist call to action that favoured suffering in the cause of justice rather than violence. Gandhi's embrace of *ahimsa* was more reminiscent of the Jain or Buddhist than the Hindu tradition.

It is widely held that Buddhism counsels against violence and that the Buddhist tradition was founded on disavowal of the material conditions that lead to violence and discord. Indeed, **shanti** (peace) is a central point of Buddhist teaching. However, the application of that teaching leaves room for a realist interpretation of the necessity of violence in war. The Buddha himself did not engage in war, but he lived in an age when violence was an accepted part of politics and he did not always condemn it. The Mauryan Emperor Ashoka, whose famous disavowal of war is embraced as an expression of the Buddhist ideal, was the first ruler to embrace Buddhist *dharma*.

Yet the virtuous Buddhist leader must accept the moral demand to defend his subjects. The social ethics of Buddhism uphold the ideal of a *chakravartin* (universal ruler) whose righteous concern for his people must sometimes lead to the demonstration of martial power, though the use of that power in war is not generally lauded in Buddhist texts. For example, Mahinda Deegalle mentions the use of a fourfold army under the power of the *chakravartin* in the Theravada text *Cakkavattisihanada Sutta* that would presumably instill a feeling of security for the subjects of his realm. Yet the mere fact that a Buddhist ruler should maintain an army seems to suggest it might be used in combat (Deegalle 2009: 65). Elsewhere, in the Mahayana text known as the Sutra of Golden Light, the use of force by a king is justified as a means of demonstrating 'the basic karmic law that good deeds will bear good fruits while bad deeds will have bad consequences' (Schmidt-Leukel 2004: 44).

There is therefore a significant dichotomy between the philosophic teachings of Buddhism and the practices of Buddhists, which reflects the important distinction between the masses of Buddhist laypeople and the members of the monastic *sangha*. Quite simply, the Buddhist monk in his search for peace is far removed from the demands of daily life and ordinary society and depends on the lay community for his livelihood. This distinction provides a justification for a sort of Buddhist realpolitik that accepts war when it is moderate and characterized by 'right intention' (Schmidt-Leukel 2004: 45–7). With this in mind, according to Michael Jerryson, Buddhists have accepted and even embraced war for numerous reasons, including settling doctrinal differences, defending the faith, and bringing about a future golden age. Jerryson also suggests that the Buddhist doctrine of reincarnation (also embraced in Hinduism) helps to downplay the gravity of killing, given that the individual killed in warfare may be better able to embrace Buddhist *dharma* in the next life (Jerryson and Juergensmeyer 2010: 8–9).

Religion and Terrorism

The ethical bases of legitimacy described above, in particular the Just War tradition, have laid the groundwork for international law with regard to the use of force. But what happens when religious principles that contributed to the development of our ethical understandings of war are themselves used as reasons to question international law? Terrorism is the use of violence and intimidation in ways judged illegitimate by the international community. Such violence may include open assaults on innocent civilians, hijackings, kidnappings, and suicide bombings. It is important to understand that terrorism is neither an ideology nor a unified global phenomenon: it is simply a tool that can be used in many different ways by a wide variety of actors. Religion may serve as a way to justify these actions and help to legitimize them. As Rapoport (1984) noted, many religious traditions in the past have turned to terrorism. A common list includes the Jewish zealots who resisted Roman occupation in first-century Palestine; the Nizari Ismailis known as Assassins who are said to have carried out targeted assassination in the twelfth century; and the Hindu Thuggee cult, which engaged in ritualized robbery and murder as recently as the nineteenth century.

As we have seen, religious movements can present direct challenges to the modern secular state and state system. A particular concern of the past two decades has been the rise in religious radicalism as a justification for violent action against symbols of

Western power. Bruce Hoffman notes that groups with a religious motivation have increased significantly as a proportion of terrorist movements worldwide since the 1960s. Terrorism used to be organized on nationalist and radical ideological bases, but by the mid-1990s roughly half of all terrorist movements had some sort of a religious underpinning (Hoffman quoted in Cromartie 2005: 30). Religious radicalism has been marshalled to frame violent action as a spiritual obligation. This phenomenon takes several forms and can be interpreted in various ways.

Box 9.2: Religion and Modern Terrorism: a Timeline

22 July 1946 Jewish extremists from the Irgun Tsvai Leumi (Etzel) bomb the King David Hotel in Jerusalem.

21 August 1969 An Australian tourist tries to burn down the al Aqsa Mosque in Jerusalem.

20 November 1979 Saudi radicals stage armed takeover of the Holy Mosque in Mecca. After a two-week siege, a pitched battle claims the lives of at least 255 insurgents, pilgrims, and military.

23 October 1983 Two suicide truck bomb blasts at US and French barracks in Beirut kill 299. An organization named Islamic Jihad, likely a precursor of Hezbollah, claims responsibility.

23 June 1985 Air India flight 182 is destroyed in the air over the Atlantic Ocean by a bomb placed by Sikh separatists; 329 people, most of them Canadian citizens, are killed.

25 February 1994 Baruch Goldstein, a radical Israeli settler, opens fire on Muslims at prayer in the Ibrahimi Mosque in Hebron, West Bank, killing 29 before he is apprehended and killed.

20 March 1995 Aum Shinrikyo, an extremist Japanese religious sect, releases poisonous sarin gas in the Tokyo subway, killing 13.

25 June 1996 The Hezbollah al-Hejaz, a radical Saudi opposition group, bombs the Khobar Towers in Khobar, Saudi Arabia, killing 20.

7 August 1998 US embassies in Nairobi, Kenya, and Dar es Salaam, Tanzania, are attacked by suicide bombers linked to the al-Qaeda network. At least 223 people killed in the two attacks.

12 October 2000 A suicide bomber attacks the USS *Cole*, an American navy destroyer, in the port of Aden, Yemen, killing 17 American sailors.

11 September 2001 Hijackers linked to al-Qaeda take over four planes, three of which are used to destroy the World Trade Center towers in New York City and portions of the Pentagon in Arlington, Virginia; 2995 people are killed, including the hijackers.

15–20 November 2003 Bomb attacks against Jewish and international targets in Istanbul, Turkey, kill 57. Al-Qaeda–inspired radicals are later found responsible.

11 March 2004 A series of coordinated bomb attacks in the subway system of Madrid, Spain, kill 191 people. Independent Islamist extremists are determined to be responsible.

7 July 2005 Four suicide bombers inspired by al-Qaeda target the London transit system, killing 52.

26–29 November 2008 Several Islamist radicals linked to Pakistani extremist groups stage a series of bombing and shooting attacks in Mumbai, India, killing 173.

12 July 2010 More than 70 are killed in two bombings in a restaurant and club in Kampala, Uganda. Militants linked to the Somali Islamist Shabab militia take responsibility.

In many cases, religious movements use violence as a catalyst to bring about their apocalyptic visions. Religious movements with a linear understanding of history often expect the divine to bring the world to an end amid some sort of spectacular event or cataclysm. Most conservative and evangelical Christians believe that the last days will unfold according to a divine plan; the same belief is also an essential tenet of Islam. Few Christians or Muslims would seek to bring about the end of history: they assume that such decisions belong to God. Nevertheless, sometimes a religious revivalist movement will develop a conviction that it has a divinely ordained role to play in bringing the world to an end (Stroizer 2007).

A focal point of Jewish and Christian eschatological teaching is the presumed location of the ancient temple in Jerusalem. The presence of Muslim shrines on the traditional site of the temple has made this location an occasional target for terrorist violence. The al Aqsa Mosque was damaged by a religious reactionary arsonist in August 1969 and in the early 1980s a small group of Israeli radicals were arrested in the midst of planning the destruction of the Mosque of Omar (Dome of the Rock). The Aum Shinrikyo cult believed their attacks on the Tokyo subway in 1995 set the stage for the end of the world.

In other cases, violence is used to summon believers to a specific goal or to spark a religious revival. Islamist radicals involved in terrorist activity see themselves as part of a wider effort to revive the jihadist spirit that they associate with the early Islamic community. Osama bin Laden's *fatwas* were designed to summon Muslims around the world to take up the *jihad* that he believed to be an individual duty of every Muslim. American extremists such as John Brown, who sought to create a free black state during a raid in 1859, or James Charles Kopp, an anti-abortion zealot convicted in 1998 of murdering a doctor, saw themselves as standard-bearers for the advancement of a righteous cause.

Religious terrorism might also be understood as a nihilistic reaction against the perceived vices of contemporary Western society. Religious fundamentalists have a deeply rooted animus for the very idea of compromise with competing worldviews. They also tend to feel they are under siege by a secular culture that hinders their pursuit of religious purity. Ranstorp (1996) suggests that '[i]ntrusion of secular values into the extremists' own environment and the visible presence of secular foreign interference provoke self-defensive aggressiveness and hostility against the sources of these evils' (49–50). Feelings of alienation from and superiority to secular society allow terrorists to dehumanize their targets. Some argue that such dehumanization increases the likelihood that the religious terrorist will engage in more extreme levels of violence (Hoffman 2006: 88). At the extreme, the 'underlying motives and urges belong to the realm of psychopathology' (Laqueur 2003: 44).

The ultimate expression of religious fundamentalists' aggressive and misanthropic vision is the suicide operation. Not all suicide operations have been religiously motivated; some have been carried out by secular radicals. However, in her study of such operations, Mia Bloom found that it tends to be easier for religious groups to recruit suicide terrorists, and that the damage they cause tends to be wider (Bloom 2005: 98). In Muslim contexts, the common use of the term *shahid* (martyr) to refer to suicide bombers and the assurance of salvation following death in the name of religious belief contribute to religion's potency as a motivator. The October 1983 suicide bombing of the US Marine Barracks in Beirut, likely carried out by a Hezbollah operative, claimed the lives of 299 American and French servicemen. In 1994, radical Jewish nationalist Baruch Goldstein entered the mosque at the Cave of the Patriarchs and opened fire with the intent of killing as many Muslims as possible before his own death at the hands of his would-be victims. In Israel, the Hamas movement deployed suicide bombers against the civilian population—on buses, at social gatherings, in marketplaces—throughout the 1990s. Since that time, suicide operations have become a strategy of choice for radicalized religious movements.

Finally, religion may also simply follow along relatively traditional lines as a motivating force for terror. Hamas (the name is an acronym for 'Islamic Resistance Movement') uses the rhetoric of political Islam, but its suicide operatives' motivations appear to have been primarily nationalistic. And although only one of the Sikh radicals charged in the bombing of Air India flight 182 was ever convicted, it seems clear that the intent in that case as well was political, related to the anti-Sikh violence that followed the assassination of Indira Gandhi. Though religion can and does provide rationalizations for violence, many terrorist actions are motivated by more worldly issues and concerns.

Conclusions

The deeply rooted convictions at the heart of religion contribute to its association with violence and war. Religion has long been a cause for which nations fight, and in time of war it has often helped to rally national sentiment. It has also helped to draw boundaries, contributing to ethnic conflict, and in modern global society.it has served as a foundation for ideological challenges. Religious traditions have provided the ethical norms required to justify war in spite of what all the major religious creeds understand to be the obvious immorality of killing. A defining feature of the Christian tradition is the use of Just War criteria to defend the resort to war. The Muslim concept of struggle (*jihad*) has often been applied to war. Hindus and Buddhists have affirmed the necessity of war in defence of order and social stability. Finally, religious radicals have occasionally used religion to support violent actions that the international community would otherwise condemn as terrorism. As we will see in the next chapter, however, religion may also have an important role to play in resolving and ending violent conflict.

Review Questions

1. On what grounds do critics argue that religion promotes violence and war?
2. What are some prominent historic examples of the nationalistic use of religion in war?
3. How does religion contribute to conflicts rooted in ethnicity? What are some prominent recent examples of conflict based on differences in religion and ethnicity?
4. How has religion contributed to ideological challenges to the nation-state in the past few decades?

5. What are the roots of Christian Just War thinking?
6. Explain the Islamic doctrine of *jihad*, both inner and outer.
7. What is the place of violence in Hindu and Buddhist philosophy?
8. Why has religion come to be associated with terrorism?

Sources and Further Reading

Avalos, Hector (2005). *Fighting Words: The Origins of Religious Violence*. Amherst, NY: Prometheus Books.

Bloom, Mia (2005). *Dying to Kill: The Allure of Suicide Terror*. New York: Columbia University Press.

Brough, Michael W., John W. Lango, and Henry van der Linden, eds (2007). *Rethinking the Just War Tradition*. Albany: State University of New York Press.

Burleigh, Michael (2005). *Earthly Powers: Religion and Politics in Europe from the Enlightenment to the Great War*. London: Harper Collins.

———— (2007). *Sacred Causes: The Clash of Religion and Politics, from the Great War to the War on Terror*. London: Harper Collins.

Cavanaugh, William T. (1995). "'A Fire Strong Enough to Consume the House": the Wars of Religion and the Rise of the State'. *Modern Theology* 11, 4: 397–420.

Clough, David L. and Brian Stiltner (2007). *Faith and Force: A Christian Debate about War*. Washington, DC: Georgetown University Press.

Cornwell, John (1999). *Hitler's Pope: The Secret History of Pius XII*. New York: Viking.

Cromartie, Michael, ed. (2005). *Religion, Culture, and International Conflict: A Conversation*. Lanham, MD: Rowman & Littlefield.

Deegalle, Mahinda (2009). 'Norms of War in Theravada Buddhism'. Pp. 60–86 in Popovski, Reichberg, and Turner (2009).

De Vries, Hent (2002). *Religion and Violence*. Baltimore, MD: The Johns Hopkins University Press.

Elshtain, Jean Bethke, ed. (1992). *Just War Theory*. New York: New York University Press.

———— (2003). *Just War against Terror*. New York: Basic Books.

Hedges, Chris (2002). *War Is a Force that Gives Us Meaning*. New York: Public Affairs.

Hitchens, Christopher (2007). *God Is Not Great: How Religion Poisons Everything*. New York: Twelve.

Hoffman, Bruce (2006). *Inside Terrorism*. New York: Columbia University Press.

Hoover, A.J. (1989). *God, Germany, and Britain in the Great War*. New York: Praeger.

Jerryson, Michael K. and Mark Juergensmeyer, eds (2010). *Buddhist Warfare*. Oxford: Oxford University Press.

Johnson, James Turner (1997). *The Holy War Idea in Western and Islamic Traditions*. University Park, PA: Penn State University Press.

Juergensmeyer, Mark (1993). *The New Cold War? Religious Nationalism Confronts the Secular State*. Berkeley: University of California Press.

Kelsay, John (2007). *Arguing the Just War in Islam*. Cambridge, MA: Harvard University Press.

————, and James Turner Johnson, eds. (1991). *Just War and Jihad*. Westport, CT: Greenwood Press.

Khazen, Farid el- (2000). *The Breakdown of the State in Lebanon, 1967–1976*. Cambridge, MA: Harvard University Press.

Laqueur, Walter (2003). *No End to War: Terrorism in the Twenty-First Century*. New York: Continuum.

Miner, Steven Merritt (2003). *Stalin's Holy War: Religion, Nationalism, and Alliance Politics, 1941–1945*. Chapel Hill: University of North Carolina Press.

Perica, Vjekoslav (2002). *Balkan Idols: Religion and Nationalism in Yugoslav States*. Oxford: Oxford University Press.

Philpott, Daniel (2002). 'The Challenge of September 11 to Secularism in International Relations'. *World Politics* 55: 66–95.

Popovski, Vesslin, Gregory M. Reichberg, and Nicholas Turner, eds (2009). *World Religions and Norms of War*. Tokyo: United Nations University Press.

Ranstorp, Magnus (1996). 'Terrorism in the Name of Religion'. *Journal of International Affairs* 50, 1: 41–62.

Rapoport, David C. (1984). 'Fear and Trembling: Terrorism in Three Religious Traditions', *American Political Science Review* 78, 3: 658–77.

Reader, Ian (2000). *Religious Violence in Contemporary Japan: The Case of Aum Shinrikyo*. Richmond: Curzon.

Roy, Kaushik (2009). 'Norms of War in Hinduism'. Pp. 30–59 in Popovski, Reichberg, and Turner (2009).

Schmidt-Leukel, Perry, ed. (2004). *War and Peace in World Religions*. London: SCM Press.

Selengut, Charles (2003). *Sacred Fury: Understanding Religious Violence*. Walnut Creek, CA: AltaMira Press.

Seul, Jeffrey R. (1999). 'Religion, Identity, and Intergroup Conflict', *Journal of Peace Research* 36, 5: 553–69.

Silverman, Adam L. (2002). 'Just War, Jihad, and Terrorism', *Journal of Church and State* 44, 1: 73–92.

Skya, Walter A. (2009). *Japan's Holy War: The Ideology of Radical Shinto Ultranationalism*. Durham: Duke University Press.

Smith, Anthony D. (2003). *Chosen Peoples: Sacred Sources of National Identity*. Oxford: Oxford University Press.

Stroizer, Charles B. (2007). 'The Apocalyptic Other: On Fundamentalism and Violence'. *Nova Religio* 11, 1: 84–96.

Victoria, Brian A. (1997). *Zen at War*. New York: Weatherhill.

Walzer, Michael (1977). *Just and Unjust Wars*. New York: Basic Books.

——— (1996). 'War and Peace in the Jewish Tradition'. Pp. 95–114 in Terry Nardin, ed. *The Ethics of War and Peace*. Princeton: Princeton University Press.

Wellman, James K., Jr, ed. (2007). *Belief and Bloodshed: Religion and Violence Across Time and Tradition*. Lanham, MD: Rowman & Littlefield.

Web Resources

www.bbc.co.uk/ethics/war – BBC Guide to the Ethics of War.

www.ppu.org.uk/learn/infodocs/st_religions.html – World Religions: War and Peace.

Chapter 10

Religion and
Conflict Resolution

It is clear that religion contributes to passionate articulation of moral principles and ideas of belonging that have led to conflict over the centuries. Yet most world religions aspire to promote harmony by bringing spiritual ideals to bear on life in society, and peace is highly valued in all religious traditions, whether in the worldly sense of freedom from war or in the spiritual sense of 'inner' peace. The word 'Islam' strictly means submission, but many Muslims feel that the cognate *salaam*, 'peace'—the usual greeting among Muslims—is at the heart of their religion. Christians consider peace central to the saving work of Jesus Christ as a reconciler, and point to his non-violent admonitions in the Sermon on the Mount as foundations of Christian peace activism. One of the most prominent peace activists in history, M.K. Gandhi, mined the traditions of Hinduism as well as other faiths to develop his idea that non-violent resistance could be a means of transforming societies. Clearly there is much in religion to encourage the pursuit of peaceful relationships.

Even so, the study of religion and peace in political science is relatively new. One reason was the low profile that religion held in political science until the 1990s. Insofar as conventional political science thought about religion, it was as an ethnic or communal motivator that made demands on a political system. This instrumentalist view made it difficult for political scientists to see religion as anything other than a contributor to conflict. This perception was only reinforced when a popular book on the 'clash of civilizations' portrayed religion as contributing to conflict (Huntington 1996). At the same time, however, some scholars recognized religious actors' potential to assist in resolving conflict. Religious motivations lurked beneath the surface when particular decision-makers made choices for non-violent resolution of conflicts. Religious actors who were perceived to be politically neutral, or who carried particular moral authority, could be influential mediators and negotiators. In addition, religious images and themes have a resonance that can help to consolidate commitments to peace, although this quality went largely unnoticed in international relations texts until the publication of Douglas Johnston and Cynthia Sampson's edited work *Religion, the Missing Dimension of Statecraft* (1994). Since that time, the study of religion and conflict resolution has burgeoned. Subjects of particular interest include the potential of religious actors as third-party mediators, cultural and religious motivations for peace, and interfaith dialogue.

Religious Resources for Conflict Resolution

That religion has resources for both the instigation and the mitigation of armed conflict has been noted by many scholars of religion and politics. In the words of R. Scott Appleby:

> Rather than a direct translation of the 'mind of God' into human action, religion is a far more ambiguous enterprise, containing *within itself* the authority to kill and to heal, to unleash savagery, or to bless humankind with healing and wholeness' (Appleby 2000: 29).

Appleby goes on to argue that human agency is particularly significant in determining whether a given religious tradition chooses savagery or benevolence. Others stress the way interpretive choices help human beings to navigate between 'hostility and hospitality' (Kearney 2003: 68). Thus the very way in which individual religious people conceive of their religion is held to be important. Just because one group interprets its religious tradition as demanding violence or hostility, this does not mean that all followers of the same religion will interpret it the same way.

Most religions have traditions, stories, and interpretive frameworks that commend peace over conflict within and between societies. However, not all of them value or conceive of peace in the same way (Johnston and Sampson 1994: 266–82; Coward and Smith 2004: 279–301). For example, Buddhists value peace above all things: yet their conception of peace as an emptying of self has little in common with the notion of peace suggested by the Jewish and Muslim words for 'peace', **shalom** and *salaam*, meaning fulfillment, or well-being. Fundamentalist Christians may value peace as the ultimate outcome of a relationship with God, but world history might lead them to question humans' ability to achieve temporal peace on Earth. What's more, individual believers will take different attitudes toward peace if it requires compromise on other moral principles that they consider important. While Sikhs are taught to uphold and preserve peace as a part of their religious duty, they also believe that the Khalsa must be prepared to use violent means when necessary to defend the community. In the same way, most Christians believe that there are times when insisting on peace would mean allowing an injustice to take place: hence many Christian theologians supported the US government's decision to go to war in 1941. Even so, religious believers typically contend that their faiths are committed to earthly peace in one way or another.

Hindu philosophy has a rich tradition of discussion surrounding *dharma* and peace. The Hindu epics enjoin *ahimsa* (non-violence) as a virtue even as they acknowledge its rarity in no uncertain terms (Coward and Smith 2004: 56–8). The value that Hinduism attributes to societal order provides a basis on which to call for the resolution of conflict. Furthermore, the universalism implicit in Hindu theology welcomes all religious perspectives as equals. Therefore Hindus are not likely to bat an eye at contradictory beliefs held by other religions. Though this universalism itself may become a dogma that divides Hinduism from other traditions, it motivates Hindu believers to listen and learn from other traditions. The cognitive dissonance generated by heterodoxy in monotheistic religions is largely absent from Hindu theology. In other words, Hindus are less likely to struggle with contradictory assertions about the world than are those grounded in traditionally rationalistic Western philosophy.

The individual interpretations of Hindu texts surrounding *dharma* and its connection to peaceful relations among people vary widely, but important gurus and spiritual teachers have championed the peace ethic of Hinduisms throughout history. Obviously the most prominent of these was Gandhi, whose dedication to *satyagraha* was grounded in his understanding of Hinduism. At the same time, Gandhi demonstrated Hindu universalism by embracing a broad range of spiritual teachings, including those of Jains (who take extreme measures to avoid doing harm to any living creature) and Jesus Christ. He lived the ascetic life of a Hindu yogi seeking the Truth that would allow him to see God face to face (Gandhi 2002: 50–2). He believed that the solution to interpersonal conflict was the sacrificial commitment to know oneself and others and thereby transform social relationships (Juergensmeyer 2002). Gandhi's approach was emblematic of the Hindu notion that inner peace is closely associated with outer peace.

Gandhi was also influenced by Buddhist thought. The pacifist ethic is widely regarded as a central feature of Buddhism. The Buddha was personally committed to a life of complete non-violence and dismissed the material concerns of the world as distractions that often serve as the driving force behind earthly disputes. Thus Buddhist monks today seek to limit desire of all kinds. To Buddhists, 'nonviolence forms part of a morality of abstention, in which one's own daily behavior is the starting-point of any campaign for peace' (Kraft 1992: 46). Although the Buddhist tradition gives an important place to political power, exemplary leaders follow the example of Ashoka and turn their backs on war as a tool of state policy (Olson 2005: 80). Buddhism teaches a syncretic understanding that embraces people of other faiths as equals, a 'critical tolerance' that gives others the benefit of the doubt (Johnston and Sampson 1994: 272).

Other Eastern traditions such as Confucianism and Shinto, as well as indigenous traditions around the world, have cultivated peace in a variety of senses. Confucianism teaches that peace implies harmony in human relationships, and that just as sustaining harmonious relationships demands continuous effort, so does building and maintaining peace (Coward and Smith 2004: 104). Indigenous spiritual traditions share this relational understanding of peace in the form of reciprocity (Coward and Smith 2004: 40). Indigenous understandings of peace are holistic, encompassing human relations with the environment; Japanese Shinto shares this perspective.

Among the monotheistic faiths, Judaism provides a firm foundation for the construction of peaceful relations in community. Biblical and Talmudic virtues such as *tzedakah* (righteousness) and **hesed** (love or 'loving-kindness') are rooted in the concept of community. Fidelity to and solidarity with the Jewish and human communities are therefore hallmarks of Jewish understandings of peace. Marc Gopin (2003: 102–23) reviews the resources within the Jewish tradition that can help to develop the qualities essential to peace—qualities such as forgiveness, humility, patience, repentance, and reconciliation. *Shalom*, typically translated 'peace', is more than a greeting among Jewish people: it connotes wholeness and well-being and emphasizes that peace means more than a simple cessation of hostilities.

The example of Jesus Christ gives Christianity strong pacifist roots. Christians hold that Jesus eschewed a violent reaction to his own torturers and taught non-violence among his followers. The section of the famous Sermon on the Mount (Matthew 5–7) in which Jesus teaches his followers not to retaliate when they are struck, but to 'turn the other cheek' so that they may be struck again, has been embraced by Christians and non-Christians alike as a foundation of non-violent resistance. The New Testament includes several admonitions for Christians to live in peace with others, to leave vengeance to God (Romans 12:18–19), and to submit to one another (Ephesians 5:21) (Yoder 1972). Teaching reconciliation is widely understood to be a primary purpose of the Christian church (II Corinthians 5:18–20).

Early church leaders such as Tertullian taught that Christians should not participate in acts of violence as soldiers. Although the broad mainstream of Christian doctrine justified war in certain circumstances, many smaller streams, including Mennonites and the Society of Friends (Quakers), have refused to enlist in time of war and have instead demonstrated their commitment to peace through activism, mediation, and the promotion of reconciliation (Driedger and Kraybill 1994, Yarrow 1987). The Sermon on

The medieval cathedral in the industrial town of Coventry, England, was almost entirely destroyed by German bombs in November 1940. Immediately after the bombing, it was decided that a new cathedral would be built alongside the ruins, which would be left standing as a call to the Christian message of reconciliation over vengeance. Recalling the Lord's Prayer, the Provost of the cathedral had the words 'Father Forgive' inscribed above the altar and a small cross was fashioned from nails found amid the ruins. Since that time, the church has been the focal point of the 'Community of the Cross of Nails', a global ministry of peace and reconciliation. Source: Photo supplied couresty of Coventry Cathedral. Photograph by Tim Eccleston.

the Mount was presented by the Russian author Leo Tolstoy as a new form of the Judaic law, deepening the simple admonition 'Thou shalt not kill' to apply to all types of killing, including killing in war (Tolstoy 1987). The same scriptural resources also inspired people such as Gandhi and King to use non-violence as a means of social change.

When the Prophet of Islam, Muhammad, set out to unite the fractious tribes of seventh-century Arabia, his aim was to establish a peaceful society that would operate

Box 10.1: Religious Leaders Discuss Peace

'[Christians] are told that they must not only *have* peace but *make* it. And to that end they renounce all violence and tumult . . . [they] keep the peace by choosing to endure suffering themselves rather than inflict it on others. . . . They renounce all self-assertion, and quietly suffer in the face of hatred and wrong. In so doing they overcome evil with good, and establish the peace of God in the midst of a world of war and hate.'
—Dietrich Bonhoeffer, *The Cost of Discipleship* (1937)

'Truth and nonviolence are not possible without a living belief in God, meaning a self-existent, all-knowing, living Force which inheres in every other force known to the world and which depends on none, and which will live when all other forces may conceivably perish or cease to act. I am unable to account for my life without belief in this all-embracing living Light.'
—Mohandas K. Gandhi, *Non-violence in Peace and War* (1948)

'Christ our Lord did not come to bring peace as a kind of spiritual tranquilizer. He brought to his disciples a vocation and a task: to struggle in the world of violence to establish His peace not only in their own hearts but in society itself.'
—Thomas Merton, *Nuclear War and Christian Responsibility* (1962)

'The Bible knows nothing of peace without justice, for that would be crying 'Peace, peace, where there is no peace.' God's shalom, peace, involves inevitably righteousness, justice, wholeness, fullness of life, participation in decision making, goodness, laughter, joy, compassion, sharing and reconciling.'
—Bishop Desmond Tutu, *Nobel Lecture* (1984)

'Our world is at an impasse. The way of violence has led us to the brink of global annihilation. Desperately, our contemporaries look for alternatives. But they will never find Jesus' way to peace credible unless those of us who have proudly preached it are willing to die for it.'
—Ronald Sider, *God's People Reconciling* (1984)

'A universal humanitarian approach to world problems seems the only sound basis for world peace. What does this mean? We begin from the recognition . . . that all beings cherish happiness and do not want suffering. It then becomes both morally wrong and pragmatically unwise to pursue only one's own happiness oblivious to the feelings and aspirations of all others who surround us as members of the same human family. The wiser course is to think of others also when pursuing our own happiness. This will lead to what I call "wise self-interest", which hopefully will transform itself into "compromised self-interest", or better still, "mutual interest".'
—Tenzin Gyatso, the Fourteenth Dalai Lama, *A Human Approach to World Peace* (1984)

according to the tenets of Islam. Abu-Nimer (2003) discusses how Islamic notions of justice, empowerment, human dignity and equality, patterns of mediation, and respect for rational discussion and forgiveness compel Muslims to seek peaceful solutions in times of conflict. The Qur'an enjoins Muslims to turn to peace when an enemy seeks peace (8:61) and may be understood to affirm religious and cultural pluralism when it discusses the origins of the nations of the world (49:13). Mercy and compassion are central characteristics of Allah, virtues that every Muslim is expected to emulate.

Some Islamic sects reflect the universalism suggested by the Muslim belief that Muhammad, as the 'Seal of the Prophets'—the last in a line that includes the Hebrew prophets as well as Jesus—who sought to unite people of all faiths in final revelation. Sufi mystics following his example seek union with the divine. In these efforts they share much in common with the mystical practices of other traditions, most significantly Hindu *bhakti* and Christian monasticism. Nizari Ismailis make humanitarian initiatives as a focal point of their faith. Finally, although it is an independent religion, the Baha'i Faith shares the Muslim understanding of the unity of the prophetic message, and the Baha'i doctrine of the unity of mankind embraces the diversity of faiths in building peace.

The preceding survey does not exhaust either the spectrum of faiths that cultivate peace or the spectrum of religious responses to the challenges of conflict resolution. However, it does suggest that all religions value and support peace as defined by their own worldviews. It's important to keep in mind that peace is not the only value, and that most religious philosophies also encompass elements that may work against it, such as moral judgments about acceptable and unacceptable behaviours (clean and unclean, encouraged and condemned), differences regarding the propagation of the faith, and rules defining who is and who is not part of their sacred community. Still, it is commonly asserted that religions are united by their shared interest in peace, even though they may disagree significantly on the ultimate sources of it. The diverse motivations of religious ideas are helpful in understanding the motivations that lead religious actors to work for the resolution of conflict.

Religious Activism in Support of Conflict Resolution

Since religion is so often associated with violence in the contemporary world, it may come as a surprise to realize that peace activism was largely invented by religious groups. Modern ecumenical and lay movements in Western Europe and the United States laid the foundations for many peace activist movements worldwide. These included as the Moral Re-armament movement (now Initiatives of Change), the Young Men's Christian Association (YMCA), Gandhian *satyagraha*, Soka Gakkai, and the Student Christian Movement. Issues of war and peace were discussed in religious terms throughout the development of the Idealist movement of the 1920s and 1930s. Religious actors were prominent spokespeople for the pacifist cause. The role of Gandhi in spreading these ideas to the developing world and among eastern religions was also significant (Ramsbotham, Woodhouse, and Miall 2005: 38–41, Weber 2001). Although the modern field of peace and conflict studies was developed by scholars such as the Norwegian Johan Galtung (who has periodically embraced a Buddhist conception of peace), it owes a great deal to early religious activists, and religious groups remain an essential part of efforts to resolve conflict around the world.

Religion's contributions to initiatives seeking the resolution of conflict and construction of peace have been studied by scholars of religion, politics, and peace. Little and Appleby (2004: 1–23) discuss various ways in which religious actors may be involved in peace-building, including conflict management, conflict resolution, and structural reform of social institutions. They may bring public attention to a conflict, stand in solidarity with those involved, mediate between conflicting parties, or work to build a culture of peace through education, publishing, and public campaigns. Religion provides different resources depending on the nature of the involvement. Religious actors may operate as outsiders or be intimately engaged in the environment of the conflict. Religious people may simply have an interest in a conflict because of their wider commitment to peace or they may be directly engaged, whether through diplomatic initiatives with the parties involved or as participants in a conflict themselves.

Complicating matters is the fact that where religious and political notions are concerned, the nature of peace itself is debated. We have already seen that different religions have different ideas of what constitutes peace in an ultimate sense. In addition, peace activists themselves stress the distinction between mere 'negative' peace, which is the cessation of hostilities between people groups, and the much deeper notion of 'positive' peace, which implies restoration of relationships in situations of conflict, reconstruction of war-torn societies, and respect for the demands of social justice. Peace activism today embraces a wide variety of endeavours, from missions to end armed conflict to efforts to redress wrongs through non-violent resistance and global solidarity.

To differentiate the various roles that religious actors play in conflict resolution and peace-building, we will explore four categories of religious involvement. The first, 'religion as interested observer', examines the role of religious actors operating as third-party arbiters or mediators because of their perceived neutrality, balance, and humanitarian and spiritual interest in cultivating peace. Luttwak (1994: 17) suggests that religious parties may be particularly effective as mediators because they carry a certain authority. If the parties to a conflict are able to 'concede assets or claims to that authority . . . rather than to their antagonists', a religious third party may facilitate conflict resolution. In such cases religious peacemakers are most effective when they are neutral as to the outcome and may therefore offer insights as interested but otherwise uninvolved actors. When religious actors are third parties, they have no particular stake in the outcome of a negotiated peace, nor are they likely to promote a return to armed conflict should the process go awry. Third-party religious actors may have some authoritative tie to the groups involved or may be entirely separate, brought into a conflict situation because they have a reputation for balance and general good will.

A second category, 'religion as peacemaker', represents religious actors who are more directly involved in seeking an understanding and resolution of armed conflicts through consciousness-raising and demonstrations of solidarity with the victims. These actors remain external to the dispute itself and therefore neutral except as advocates of peace; they get involved in seeking a formal resolution of the conflict. Instead, their interest is in breaking down the cognitive barriers to peace: lack of understanding, misperceptions, misinformation, and prejudice. Religious peacemakers thus remain neutral with respect to the conflict but seek to understand and live through the suffering of the victims at a deeper level than do simple interested observers. Montville (in Johnston and Sampson 1994: 332) identifies such groups when he describes how '[i]nto the lives of victimized people come religious outsiders, who in varying ways convey a sense of understanding and empathy for their fears and who have established reputations for honesty, discretion, and integrity. They are disinterested in the conflict except for their sadness over the human losses associated with it.'

A third category, 'religion as protagonist' covers situations in which religious groups are directly involved in a conflict and therefore are an indispensable part of the process of negotiating and constructing a formal peace treaty. In fact, the main value of religious actors in such cases is their ability to secure their communities' credible commitment to the terms of an eventual treaty. The religious actor may be one of the parties to a dispute, even directly responsible for acts of violence. When religious actors take responsibility for the perpetuation of a conflict and seek to bring it to an end, they demonstrate the basic principle that it is not friends who need to conclude a peace, but former enemies. Gopin (2003) emphasizes this theme: 'The true, disciplined peacemaker always acts as if he (or she) is the *bridge* between his community and the enemy community . . . the peacemaker must discover a prosocial relationship with the enemy "other" while maintaining a caring relationship with his (or her) own group' (115).   A final category of religious activism reflects the deep-seated commitment to transformative peace that motivates pacifists and supporters of non-violent resistance to injustice, here called 'religion as peace'. For many such people, this commitment constitutes their religion in and of itself. These individuals and groups passionately argue the force of their own moral convictions and seek self-sacrificial engagement in conflict as the key to building peace. They argue that it is insufficient to press for peace: the means used to achieve peace and justice must reflect those goals in themselves. In the words of Martin Luther King, Jr (1967), 'peace is not merely a distant goal that we seek, but a means by which we arrive at that goal'. In the pacifist tradition, religious peace-builders go beyond a simple desire to cajole and steer their side toward peaceful resolution of a conflict. In this sense, religious peace-builders seek peace at all costs, even at the cost of their own life or at least of their comfort within their own community. In such cases religious peace-builders become part of the conflict to the degree that they identify the internal religious journey required as a journey to eliminate conflict in the hearts of those in the midst of conflict. They take on the costs of peace by submitting to injustice both as an example and as a way of ensuring that they do not contribute to the problem of conflict but rather embody its resolution. Neutrality in this case is undesirable. However, the activist's bias has nothing to do with achieving his or her own ends: it is directed entirely towards the interests of peace itself.

Religion as Interested Observer

Religious actors have often served as third-party mediators, arbitrators, or advisors in the midst of conflict. Such assistance is often said to be provided through the 'good offices' of the individual or organization in question. The good offices of religious actors are typically called on when a third party is needed either to provide neutral support or to exercise authority. The fact that religious actors are dedicated to an ultimate authority or a higher calling may be beneficial if it helps them to stand above the temporal concerns of a given conflict. However, it is often the authority of religious actors themselves that is most helpful in resolving conflicts.

Religious actors have on occasion been brought into the middle of a conflict partly because of their own calling to a conflict zone. For example, Christian missionaries in the colonial era were used, willingly and unwillingly, as bridges or mediators between the colonial authorities and indigenous groups. In the early nineteenth century, the American missionary Adoniram Judson was pressed into the service of the Burmese in their conflict with British colonial authorities because of his knowledge of the Burmese language. He eventually composed the text of the Treaty of Yandabo which ended the First Anglo-Burmese War in 1825 (Hunt 2005: 136–44). There are many other historic examples of Muslim, Christian, and Buddhist missionaries and scholars dislocated by circumstances or missionary calling who have facilitated peaceful interaction between various societies.

A more modern case, frequently cited by scholars of religion and conflict resolution, was the intervention of three Quaker peace activists—Adam Curle, John Volkmar, and Walter Martin—in the Biafran conflict of 1967–70 (Yarrow 1987). Southeast Nigeria, an area dominated by the Igbo ethnic group, had been increasingly alienated from the Nigerian central government after independence. In May 1967, General Emeka Ojukwu declared the creation of the independent state of Biafra. Throughout the civil war that followed, Curle, Volkmar, and Martin engaged in shuttle diplomacy between Ojukwu and Nigerian President Gowon. Although their efforts at mediation were not ultimately successful, some credit them for the fact that the retaliatory violence that followed the war was remarkably limited (Sampson in Johnston and Sampson 1994: 88–118).

Perhaps the clearest example of religious mediation is the Vatican's long history of intervening to settle boundary claims among the states of South America, dating back to the earliest days of European exploration. In the Treaty of Tordesillas (1494), the Vatican established the Spanish and Portuguese spheres of influence in the new world. In 1750 the Vatican arbitrated the boundary between Portuguese Brazil and Spanish possessions under the Treaty of Madrid. The process by which the colonial possessions were divided famously provided the background of the 1986 film *The Mission*. By submitting to the authority of the Vatican, the Portuguese and Spanish governments avoided a costly and possibly inconclusive war.

More recently, in 1978, the Vatican intervened in a dispute between Argentina and Chile over islands in the Beagle Channel (Princen 1992). As the dispute escalated, Pope John Paul II dispatched Cardinal Antonio Samoré as his personal representative on a fact-finding and mediation mission to the two states. The authority of the

Cardinal as a 'prince' of the Roman Catholic Church helped to prevent hostilities and persuade the Argentine and Chilean governments to agree to mediation (Princen 1992: 145–6). The process took several years. Defeat in the Falklands War with Britain led to a less aggressive Argentine foreign policy, but the Vatican remained involved throughout. Its long effort was rewarded when the Holy See hosted the final signing of the treaty governing the border in the area of the Beagle Channel in November 1984. As a religious authority with diplomatic standing, the Holy See has frequently promoted negotiated solutions to other international disputes. Other Roman Catholic organizations have also intervened as mediators, perhaps most notably the Sant'Egidio religious community, which has helped to negotiate peace agreements in Mozambique, Guatemala, Kosovo, and Côte d'Ivoire (*The Economist* 2008).

Other religious organizations have dispatched mediators to dangerous environments only to see those individuals become subjects of new disputes. Such was the case with Terry Waite, who served as special envoy of the Archbishop of Canterbury to the Middle East throughout the 1980s. After negotiating the release of numerous hostages held in Lebanon, Waite himself was taken captive by his interlocutors in 1987 on the grounds that his neutrality was compromised by his meetings with American authorities. He was held for more than four years, most of the time in solitary confinement (Waite 1993). Many other individuals who have successfully served as mediators in the past have credited their religious perspectives as important motivators. Two prominent examples are former UN Secretary-General Dag Hammarskjold (1905–61) and former US President Jimmy Carter.

In all these cases, success has typically been measured by the mediator's success in negotiating a resolution, although many religious mediators see their involvement in seeking peace as their primary commitment, whether or not it is noticeably successful. At the same time, intense feelings of solidarity with those in the midst of a conflict zone can make it difficult for a religious mediator to do an effective job. Peace activism in conflict zones often presents the observer with examples of injustice and oppression that a religious activist in particular will feel need to be confronted (a point to which we will return). If impartiality and neutrality are the most important qualities a mediator can have, the way in which religious views impel the religious peace activist can often compromise his or her ability to effectively engage in mediation.

Religion as Peacemaker

Religious individuals and groups for whom promoting peace is part of devotional life often play a more active role in the peaceful resolution of conflicts. In such cases the peacemaker tries to resolve conflicts by facilitating relationship-building between the antagonists or consciousness-raising among other third parties. Religious groups involved in this form of peacemaking look beyond the simple need for a formal resolution to a conflict and concentrate on addressing the cognitive and knowledge deficits or the lack of trust that they believe lead to conflict. This may involve researching and explaining the circumstances behind the antagonists' respective positions, standing between two sides to provide assurances to both in the form of confidence-building measures, or raising public awareness of the issues at stake either through the media or within their own religious constituency.

In addition, religious peacemakers can provide opportunities for the parties to a dispute or armed conflict to meet with one another, or offer active support to the victims of conflict. The ultimate aim is to improve understanding about all sides of a given conflict situation.

The majority of religious actors involved in peace activism fall into this category. Some of the oldest groups of this sort date back to the ecumenical movements of the last century. The World Council of Churches (WCC) advocates for peace in various ways, from providing funding for peace and justice projects to mounting its own campaigns for causes such as the anti-apartheid struggle in South Africa (Warr 1999). Almost all faith traditions have organizations that are involved in peacemaking at some level. For example, following the Second Vatican Council, the Roman Catholic Church established the Pontifical Council for Justice and Peace. Its primary task is to carry out 'action-oriented studies [on] questions related to war, disarmament and the arms trade, international security, and violence in its various and everchanging forms' (Pontifical Council n.d.).

Among less institutionalized religious traditions, peacemaking efforts tend to take the form of independent parallel organizations that respond to the sense of mission that most religions have toward peace. In Japan, the Soka Gakkai organization was founded on the principles of Nichiren Buddhism by two Buddhist activists, Tsunesaburo Makeguchi (1871–44) and Josei Toda (1900–58), who were both imprisoned for their presumed activism against the Japanese military government during the Second World War. The organization was revived after the war and became a leading voice for nuclear disarmament. Since 1975, Soka Gakkai has been an international non-governmental organization, led by Daisaku Ikeda (Seager 2006). It focuses primarily on ritual practice as a means of encouraging peace among its members, who themselves actively promote peace education, interfaith dialogue, and humanitarian assistance.

The pacifist convictions of Christian groups such as the Mennonites and Quakers motivated them to become pioneers in the expansion of peace activism. Organized state violence has always been a challenge to groups whose own core beliefs compel them to resist the use of force. During the First World War, the Quaker commitment to conscientious objection led to the development of the American Friends' Service Committee, a Quaker organization dedicated to relieving human suffering in lieu of performing military service. Since that time, the Friends have remained actively involved as mediators and advocates in several notable conflicts (Gallagher 2007, Le Mare and McCartney 2009). Numerous efforts spearheaded by Mennonite churches and the Mennonite Central Committee have reflected a similar commitment to move beyond simple refusal to take part in war (Sampson and Lederach 2000).

There have also been more assertive efforts at religious peacemaking. For example, Gandhi proposed that peace activists should form a *shanti sena* ('army of peace') that would deliberately seek suffering as a redemptive act. The desire for more active promotion of peace among 'peace churches' such as the Mennonites, Brethren in Christ, and Quakers was articulated famously by Ron Sider, a Brethren in Christ activist who in 1984, in an address to the Mennonite World Conference, called for

Daisaku Ikeda is the central figure in the Nichiren Buddhist Soka Gakkai International movement. The leading disciple of the most prominent Buddhist opponents of Japanese militarism, he promotes peaceful relations between nations.
Source: AP Photo/Xinhua Li Xueren

peace activists to take significant risks in the cause of peace just as those in the military do in the cause of war. In response to his challenge, dedicated activists formed the Christian Peacemaker Teams (CPT), an international non-governmental organization that now operates in conflict zones around the world. Satterwhite (2006) explains that the CPT's holistic social ethic requires members to do more than stand outside conflict zones and demand that violence come to an end. Thus CPT activists operate in the midst of war zones, often standing in solidarity with likely targets of violence (Brown 2005). The organization gained notoriety in November 2005 when four of its activists—Canadians James Loney and Harmeet Singh Sooden, British citizen Norman Kember, and an American, Tom Fox—were taken hostage by militants in Iraq. Fox was killed before the rest were rescued in a military operation in March 2006. Contact with CPT volunteers in the Middle East led Muslim peace activists in Iraq to form a parallel organization called Muslim Peacemaker Teams in 2005.

As we have seen, when individual peacemakers venture into the middle of a war zone, they run the risk of being (or appearing to be) ideologically (or physically) 'captured' by one side or another, even though their role demands impartiality. This risk is especially high for those who believe that peace cannot be embraced without concern for justice. Thus the lines that divide religious peacemakers from those directly involved in conflict may well be blurred. In these cases, the peacemakers may identify with the victims in a conflict to the point of personal suffering, injury, or even death.

Religion as Protagonist

Many wars have been fought, at least in part, to defend a religious community, or to preserve its religious distinctiveness, its doctrines, or its way of life. In such cases, the religious groups in question are typically forced to respond to the realities of the conflict in various ways, from ministering to the people involved to representing their communities in negotiations. In these cases, religions themselves are protagonists, and therefore directly involved in making peace. If believers or the representatives of a religious group are directly involved in a dispute, their authority within the religious community is central to the success of the peace process. Religious protagonists need to be able to deliver peace: that is, they must be able to obtain or provide a credible commitment from the community they represent. Religious leaders' ability to 'sell' peace inside and outside their communities may be based in part on personal charisma, but it may also require the deepening of religious peace through involvement of grassroots activists and laypeople in the religious community.

Two particularly pernicious cases of religious and sectarian strife include the Lebanese civil war of 1976–90 and the 'Troubles' of 1969–98 in Northern Ireland. In both of these cases, populations putatively divided by religion were represented by sectarian parties and militias, supported or paralleled by religious organizations that formed the backbone of communal organization. When it came to negotiating a final peace arrangement, it was the political representatives of the sectarian groups who had to sign on the dotted line.

In the case of Lebanon, the civil war was in part a consequence of the population's inability to agree on changes to the sectarian National Pact of 1943 despite major changes to the demographic balance. By the mid-1980s, Lebanon had devolved into a collection of warring sectarian enclaves, each with its own militia and political party. The end of hostilities came amid significant regional strategic changes that altered the balance of power among the communities in Lebanon. At the same time, leadership within the Christian camp broke down when the Maronite Christian Prime Minister Michel Aoun acted to disarm the various Christian factions. Internal rivalries led to the negotiation of the Ta'if Accord, a peace agreement that committed the various sects to alterations in their representation in the Lebanese government (Norton 1991). While the actual parties to the peace agreement were former members of the Lebanese National Assembly, credible commitment to the accord had to be provided by religious and sectarian leaders, such as the church patriarchs, Shi'i religious scholars, and the leaders of the various sectarian militias.

Northern Ireland's internal conflict, known euphemistically as 'the Troubles', pitted the Royal Ulster Constabulary, the British government represented by the British army, and various loyalist paramilitary groups such as the Ulster Defence Force against the Irish Republican Army (IRA). At its root, however, the conflict was between Protestants (the majority of the population) who wanted to continue the political union with Great Britain and Roman Catholics who wanted to break away and join the Irish republic. Politically, the Catholic vote was split between Sinn Fein, representing the hard-line republicans, and the Social Democratic and Labour Party (SDLP), representing the more moderate nationalists; the main Protestant parties were the Ulster Unionists and the radical Democratic Unionists, led by the fiercely anti-Catholic Rev. Ian Paisley.

After decades of violence, the IRA declared a ceasefire in 1994 and other paramilitary organizations soon followed suit. Although the ceasefire was broken in 1996, peace talks were resumed the following year, and on 10 April 1998 the Belfast Peace Agreement was signed. The Democratic Unionists initially rejected the agreement's power-sharing plan, but it was endorsed in a referendum and became the basis for a new Irish assembly in 1999. Since that time, all four of the major political parties have served in the government of Northern Ireland.

Resolutions to other disputes have involved more direct bargaining between religious sects themselves. One example is the tradition (established by the Ottoman Empire in 1854) of institutionalized bargaining among the established churches in the Middle East to resolve disputes over the control of Christian holy sites. These arrangements formed a part of the peace that concluded the Crimean War of 1854–6 and laid out the privileges and responsibilities of the custodians of the holy sites in the Middle East. Occasional media coverage of these disputes indicates that recognized patterns of authority grant specific church hierarchies control over very particular matters in the churches of the region. Resolution of these disputes requires final agreement between official representatives of the churches involved.

At a broader level, the recognition that religion may contribute to the polarization of communities in conflict has motivated many religious figures and groups to pursue interfaith dialogue (IFD) in the hope of preventing conflict and fostering peaceful interaction between religious communities. The roots of these interactions lay in the connections that many religious leaders have made over the centuries in conversation, debate, and attempts at mutual understanding. Interaction between people of different faiths is hardly a new phenomenon, but the concept of creating opportunities expressly for the purpose of dialogue was bolstered by the growth of the modern ecumenical movement in the years after the Second World War. In the wake of 9/11, when many social activists feared that stereotypes, misperceptions, and ignorance within religious groups might be contributing to conflict worldwide, IFD meetings have become common in Western societies, and increasingly in areas of the developing world, especially in South Asia and the Middle East.

Smock (2002) defines IFD as 'a simple concept: persons of different faiths meeting to have a conversation', but notes that the nature of the conversation and the purposes behind it vary widely (6). Interfaith dialogue in its original form brought religious scholars or experts together to discuss and debate ideas from their own religious traditions as a way of demonstrating civility and interest in one another's beliefs. However, the social usefulness of this form of IFD has been widely questioned, partly because it creates polarizing situations and partly because it does not typically involve the laypeople who make up the religious communities in question. In addition, IFD can tend to ignore the real temporal concerns that contribute to conflict between religious groups. Jane Idleman Smith (2007) outlines a variety of models for IFD that seek to broaden the scope of interfaith conversation, including dialogue in educational environments, formal discussions on issues of ethical concern to the wider community, and exposure to worship practices and rituals, as well as cooperative endeavours to achieve a common goal (63–82). The latter model is reflected in the proliferation of interfaith groups dedicated to addressing issues of social justice at every level from local to global. For example, the Chicago-based Interfaith Youth Core was created as a part of a strategy to bring people of various faith backgrounds together to promote social cohesion and address wider social justice goals (Patel 2007).

The contributions to peace of religious actors whose faiths are directly at issue in a given conflict will typically be measured by the extent to which they are able to ensure their community's commitment to abide by the terms of the peace agreement they have negotiated. When the agreement requires ongoing institutionalized arrangements between the parties, durable interactions between religious groups will be an important part of their success. They may also contribute to the creation of an atmosphere in which all the religious groups concerned want to achieve a self-perpetuating peace. For example, Abu-Nimer, Khoury, and Welty observe that interfaith dialogue in certain contexts 'has become a form of religious expression' (2007: 15). If they are correct, this development represents a potentially transformative approach to conflict resolution.

Religion as Peace

For most faith groups, self-perpetuating peace is an ultimate goal. In this sense, the religious journey itself is a search for peace or transcendence that ends (or transforms) earthly suffering, conflict, and discontent. In some situations of religious activism the practice of faith itself is perceived to be the establishment of peace. Religious actors may seek to transform a conflict through persuasion, self-sacrifice, or reimagination of the conflict itself as a kind of divine or ultimate test. In a sense, as witnesses for peace, offering examples that may help to convert others—if not to their particular religious creed, then to the idea of peace itself, or to a new understanding of the Other not as an enemy but as a fellow human soul. In these cases, religious actors seek to demonstrate through their own behaviour how deeply they value other people, the promotion of harmony, or the preservation of the earth itself.

Most religions seek to serve as peace by transforming the hearts and minds of antagonists. This is perhaps most striking when religious actors deliberately cross lines of communal solidarity and religious sanctity to embrace a putative enemy. They seek to transform the way that people understand others, themselves, their own demands, and the acceptability of armed conflict itself by engaging the antagonists and victims of a conflict with their faith-based critiques of life and relationship with others, by valuing their spiritual journeys, by engaging in dialogue, and by helping them discover new ways to understand their problems, their struggles, and their disagreements.

Examples of religion's commitment to transformative peace range from the everyday to the remarkable. Many faith traditions deliberately seek to break down social barriers and bring disparate individuals together under the canopy of a single entity: the *umma*, the church, the community of Sikhs, or the Buddhist *sangha*, for example. Muslims maintain that all who take part in prayers are recognized as equals, regardless of economic, ethnic, or family background—a statement of both the egalitarianism and the desire for reconciliation at the heart of Islam. A central Islamic tenet is that the purpose of creation is mutual understanding: a passage from the Qur'an (sura 49:11) translates as 'O mankind! We created you from a single (pair) of a male and a female, and made you into nations and tribes, that you may know each other.' Similarly, the Christian Church from the beginning emphasized the erasure of distinctions between believers, one biblical passage teaching that '[t]here is no longer Jew or Greek, there is no longer slave or free, there is no longer male and female; for all of you are one in Christ Jesus' (Galatians 3:28). Indigenous and eastern traditions commonly teach the unity not only of different peoples but of humans and their environment.

More celebrated examples of religion's connection with peace include the Gandhian movement for non-violent resistance. *Satyagraha* or 'truth-seeking' was at once a religious movement seeking to unite people of many spiritual backgrounds and a political movement for recognition of the Indian people's right to self-government. Gandhi would not differentiate between the political and spiritual. He equated his own spiritual quest very deeply with the non-violent resistance to British colonial rule in India, even seeing the lapses of the Indian communities into violence as representative of his own personal spiritual failings (Rudolph and Rudolph 1967: 198). In his view, peaceful resistance to evil was a part of a holistic religion of peace:

> Non-violence is not a garment to be put on and off at will. Its seat is in the heart, and it must be an inseparable part of our very being (cited in Merton 1965: 24)

Gandhi sought to redefine the conflict between his people and the British colonial authorities by uniting oppressor and oppressed. He offered to endure suffering in order to demonstrate Truth to the oppressor and thereby convince the oppressor of the evil of his behaviour. Non-violent resistance was a way of bringing attention to injustice without committing injustice in return. Gandhi's thinking on the subject of peace activism was so well-developed that it has become a philosophic inspiration for many people.

Peace activists who call for transformative solutions to conflict echo Gandhi's insistence on attaining a deeper level of peace. For modern scholars of peace, negotiating formal treaties and developing peaceful institutional arrangements are not enough: peace must be accompanied by justice. John Paul Lederach, a leading

Box 10.2: Religious Leaders and the Nobel Peace Prize

The Nobel Prize for Peace was one of five prizes established under the will of Alfred Nobel, who died in 1896. Nobel was an industrial magnate who had made his fortune from the invention and manufacture of major explosives and armaments, including nitroglycerin and dynamite, and is widely thought to have established the prizes as a sort of counterbalance to the lethal legacy of his inventions. He directed that the prizes were to be awarded to those judged to 'have conferred the greatest benefit on mankind'. The Peace prize was to go to the person 'who shall have done the most or the best work for fraternity between nations, for the abolition or reduction of standing armies and for the holding and promotion of peace congresses'. Over the years, several recipients of the Peace prize have been religious leaders and activists, including:

1930   Lars Olof Nathan Söderblom, Norwegian clergyman, theologian, and pioneer of the ecumenical movement.

1946   John Raleigh Mott, General Secretary of the International Young Men's Christian Association (YMCA)

1947   The Friends Service Council and American Friends Service Committee, Quaker Peace Activists.

1952   Albert Schweitzer, German medical missionary and founder of the Lambaréné Hospital in Gabon.

1958   Georges Piré, French Dominican priest and leader in relief and humanitarian work in Europe and abroad.

1964   Rev. Martin Luther King, Jr, American minister and civil rights activist.

1979   Mother Teresa of Calcutta, Albanian founder of the Missionaries of Charity, humanitarian and relief activist.

1984   Desmond Tutu, Bishop of Johannesburg and South African civil rights activist.

1989   Tenzin Gyatso, His Holiness the Fourteenth Dalai Lama, Tibetan religious leader.

1996   Bishop Carlos Filipe Ximenes Belo, Timorese religious leader and advocate.

1998   John Hume and David Trimble, co-sponsors of the Belfast Agreement in Northern Ireland and representatives of the Roman Catholic and Protestant sectarian communities.

2002   Jimmy Carter, former US President, international negotiator, Baptist layman, founder of the Carter Center that supports peaceful and democratic development around the world.

Source: www.nobelprize.org

figure in religious efforts to cultivate peace, argues that the construction of peace depends on the force of what he calls 'moral imagination'. Among the qualities of that moral imagination is 'a capacity, even in moments of greatest pain, to understand that the welfare of my community is directly related to the welfare of your community' (Lederach 2005: 62). Lederach would explore both cultural and religious sources to transform our understanding of the meaning of conflict.

In short, religion as peace involves nothing less than social transformation. Gandhi's philosophy was not widely embraced in his own country, even if he was viewed as a national hero (Rudolph and Rudolph 1967: 218–19). On the other hand, the spread of non-violent resistance and peace movements throughout the world over the past century could be viewed as a success for religion as peace. Societal transformation of zones of conflict such as South Africa, Northern Ireland, or Uganda may also reflect the extent to which cultures of peace arise among those who have a religious commitment to peace. If societies develop deeper and more complex inquiries into how the popular media, lifestyle, and consumer choices reflect the value of peace, we may see the evidence that religions of peace are having an impact in resolving the problem of armed conflict.

The distinctions between the four categories of religious activity outlined here should not be considered airtight. In fact, most religious actors are engaged in conflict resolution at several or even all levels. What's more, the distinctions between a *religious* peace activist and a peace activist whose motivation is humanitarian rather than religious are often difficult to discern. The quest for peace in the ultimate sense may well form a part of a personal philosophy that is not consciously religious, although the call for social transformation that it implies will inevitably involve basic moral principles of a religious sort.

Conclusions

The desire for peace, resolution of conflict, and reconciliation among people, cultures, and civilizations, is at the heart of many religious beliefs. Almost every religious tradition includes numerous examples and teachings that commend peaceful resolution of conflict. In addition, almost every tradition has produced people willing to offer their services in situations of armed conflict. Religious actors have been employed as third-party mediators and arbitrators. They have brought attention to major conflicts and actively promoted peace by standing in solidarity with those in the midst of conflict zones. They have contributed to conflict resolution as direct representatives of communities and individuals involved in the conflict. Finally, for many people the purpose of religion is to promote peace through personal and social transformation. The potency of religion as a motivating force in conflict resolution should not be overlooked.

Review Questions

1. What are some of the ways in which religious traditions teach the importance of peace?
2. Who are some important religious actors who have been involved in conflict resolution? How have they been involved?
3. In what ways do religious actors become involved as third-party negotiators in the midst of armed conflict?
4. What are some ways in which religious actors have advocated for peace both globally and in the context of active conflict?
5. When do religious actors get involved as principals in conflict resolution?
6. How does religion serve as a form of conflict resolution in and of itself?

Sources and Further Reading:

Abu-Nimer, Mohammed (2003). *Nonviolence and Peace Building in Islam*. Gainesville: University Press of Florida.

————, Amal I. Khoury, and Emily Welty, eds (2007). *Unity in Diversity: Interfaith Dialogue in the Middle East*. Washington, DC: US Institute of Peace.

Appleby, R. Scott (2000). *The Ambivalence of the Sacred*. Lanham, MD: Rowman and Littlefield.

Brown, Tricia Gates, ed. (2005). *Getting in the Way*. Scottsdale PA: Herald Press.

Coward, Harold, and Gordon S. Smith, eds (2004). *Religion and Peacebuilding*. Albany: State University of New York Press.

Driedger, Leo, and Donald B. Kraybill (1994). *Mennonite Peacemaking: From Quietism to Activism*. Scottsdale PA: Herald Press.

Economist, The (2008). 'Not a Sword, but Peace'. 5 July: 72.

Gallagher, Nancy (2007). *Quakers in the Israeli-Palestinian Conflict: The Dilemmas of NGO Humanitarian Activism*. Cairo: American University in Cairo Press.

Gandhi, Mohandas (2002). *Mohandas Gandhi: Essential Writings*. Ed. John Dear. Maryknoll, NY: Orbis.

Gopin, Marc. 'Peacemaking Qualities of Judaism as Revealed in Sacred Scripture'. Pp. 102–23 in Johnston, ed. (2003).

Hunt, Rosalie Hall (2005). *Bless God and Take Courage: the Judson History and Legacy*. Valley Forge, PA: Judson Press.

Huntington, Samuel (1996). *The Clash of Civilizations and the Remaking of World Order*. New York: Simon & Schuster.

Johansen, Robert (1997). 'Radical Islam and Non-violence: A Case Study of Religious Empowerment and Constraint among Pashtuns'. *Journal of Peace Research* 34, 1: 53–71.

Johnston, Douglas, ed. (2003). *Faith-based Diplomacy: Trumping Realpolitik*. Oxford: Oxford University Press.

————, and Cynthia Sampson (1994). *Religion, the Missing Dimension of Statecraft*. Oxford: Oxford University Press.

Juergensmeyer, Mark (2002). *Gandhi's Way: A Handbook of Conflict Resolution*. Berkeley: University of California Press.

Lederach, John Paul (2005). *The Moral Imagination: The Art and Soul of Building Peace*. Oxford: Oxford University Press.

Little, David, ed. (2007). *Peacemakers in Action: Profiles of Religion in Conflict Resolution*. Cambridge: Cambridge University Press.

————, and Scott Appleby (2004). 'A Moment of Opportunity? The Promise of Religious Peacebuilding in an Era of Religious and Ethnic Conflict'. Pp. 1–23 in Coward and Smith (2004).

Kearney, Richard (2003). *Strangers, Gods, and Monsters*. London: Routledge.

King, Martin Luther, Jr (1967). 'The Casualties of the War in Vietnam'. Speech to the Nation Institute, Los Angeles. 25 February.

Kraft, Kenneth, ed. (1992). *Inner Peace, World Peace: Essays on Buddhism and Nonviolence*. Albany: State University of New York Press.

Le Mare, Ann and Felicity McCartney (2009). *Coming from the Silence: Quaker Peacebuilding Initiatives in Northern Ireland, 1969–2007*. York: William Sessions.

Lederach, John Paul (2005). *The Moral Imagination: The Art and Soul of Building Peace*. Oxford: Oxford University Press.

Little, David, ed. (2007). *Peacemakers in Action: Profiles of Religion in Conflict Resolution*. Cambridge: Cambridge University Press.

———, and Scott Appleby (2004). 'A Moment of Opportunity? The Promise of Religious Peacebuilding in an Era of Religious and Ethnic Conflict'. Pp. 1–23 in Coward and Smith (2004).

Luttwak, Edward (1994). 'The Missing Dimension'. Pp. 8–19 in Johnston and Sampson, eds (1994).

Merton, Thomas, ed. (1965). *Gandhi on Non-Violence*. New York: New Directions, 1965.

Norton, August Richard (1991). 'Lebanon after Ta'if: Is the Civil War Over?' *Middle East Journal* 45, 3: 457–73.

Olson, Carl (2005). *The Different Paths of Buddhism*. New Brunswick, NJ: Rutgers University Press.

Patel, Eboo (2007). *Acts of Faith*. Boston: Beacon Press.

Pontifical Council for Justice and Peace (n.d.). Accessed 26 July 2011 at http://www.vatican.va/roman_curia/pontifical_councils/justpeace/documents/rc_pc_justpeace_pro_20011004_en.html

Princen, Thomas (1992). *Intermediaries in International Conflict*. Princeton: Princeton University Press.

Ramsbotham, Oliver, Tom Woodhouse, and Hugh Miall (2005). *Contemporary Conflict Resolution*. 2nd edition. Cambridge: Polity Press.

Rudolph, Lloyd I., and Susanne Hoeber Rudolph (1967). *The Modernity of Tradition*. Chicago: University of Chicago Press.

Sampson, Cynthia, and John Paul Lederach, eds (2000). *From the Ground Up: Mennonite Contributions to International Peacebuilding*. Oxford: Oxford University Press.

Satterwhite, James (2006). 'Christian Peacemaker Teams as an Alternative to "Redemptive Violence"'. *Peace and Change* 31, 2: 222–43.

Seager, Richard Hughes (2006). *Encountering the Dharma: Daisaku Ikeda, Soka Gakkai, and the Globalization of Buddhist Humanism*. Berkeley: University of California Press.

Smith, Jane Idleman (2007). *Muslims, Christians, and the Challenge of Interfaith Dialogue*. New York: Oxford University Press.

Smock, David R. (2002). *Interfaith Dialogue and Peacebuliding*. Washington, DC: US Institute of Peace Press.

Tolstoy, Leo (1987). *Writings on Civil Disobedience and Non-Violence*. Philadelphia: New Society Publishers.

Waite, Terry (1993). *Taken on Trust*. Toronto: Doubleday.

Warr, Kevin (1999). 'The Normative Promise of Religious Organizations in Global Civil Society'. *Journal of Church and State* 41, 3: 499–523.

Weber, Thomas (2001). 'Gandhian Philosophy, Conflict Resolution Theory and Practical Approaches to Negotiation'. *Journal of Peace Research* 38, 4: 493–513.

Yarrow, C.H. (1987). *Quaker Experiences in International Conciliation*. New Haven: Yale University Press.

Yoder, John Howard (1972). *The Politics of Jesus*. Grand Rapids, MI: William B. Eerdmans.

Web Resources

www.religionconflictpeace.org/node/60 – Journal of Religion, Conflict, and Peace.

kroc.nd.edu – Kroc Institute for International Peace Studies (at the University of Notre Dame).

Chapter 11

Transnational Religon, Globalization, and Development

Over the last twenty years or so it has become clear that world politics is no longer organized solely by state authority, but by an increasingly diverse array of intergovernmental organizations, non-governmental organizations (NGOs), people's groups, and individuals. The zone of politics outside the state system in which these entities operate is often labelled 'transnational' or 'global' (as opposed to 'international') politics. Underlying the shift to a more global or transnational pattern in politics is the phenomenon called globalization.

There is no simple or widely accepted definition of globalization. It is a process that has sociological, anthropological, political, and economic dimensions, among many others. Jan Aart Scholte, one of the leading scholars of globalization, suggests that the term is used to refer to at least five distinct phenomena. First is internationalization: the development of cultural connections and methods of production that link an ever-wider diversity of nations around the world. Second is liberalization: the reduction of barriers to the free exchange of goods, services, and ideas. Third is universalization: the development of new global standards in modes of production and convergence with respect to the norms and values respected by the various members of the global community. A fourth phenomenon, recognized by certain members of that community, is modernization or westernization: the triumph at the global level of a very particular way of doing things. Finally, globalization is associated with the reduction of geographic limitations on the things that we do: in other words, the deterritorialization of public life (Scholte 2000: 15–17).

All these aspects of globalization are propelled by the development of new technologies, which have made communication, transportation, and interaction ever faster and more complex global processes. The globalization of business and industry through foreign sourcing in multiple locations contributes to the intensification of global commerce and travel. As people move from one place to another, they alter the nature of one nation's interest in another. Through choice or necessity they establish communities in exile from their home countries. These diasporic communities can have a significant impact on their home societies both economically (through the financial 'remittances' they send to family members) and politically (through global lobbying efforts on behalf of their home communities or direct participation in fomenting change back home).

For political scientists, however, the most important aspects of globalization are the new patterns of authority and power developing with the expansion of the global sphere. For example, increasing connections between previously unrelated states have been reflected in a pattern of interdependence whereby those states now have to contend with one another's vulnerabilities, as well as the feedback effects of increased interrelatedness. At the same time, new institutions and existing institutions empowered to regulate the world economy, such as the International Monetary Fund, the World Bank, the World Trade Organization, and the regular G7/8 and G20 Summits. Recognition of the need to regulate, control, and defend against common threats has also contributed to continued implementation of global responses to violence, environmental degradation, and international justice.

Many of the political and institutional responses to globalization have been controversial, in part because they seem to reflect the concerns and interests of the most powerful social forces in world economics and politics. For this reason, the process of globalization has often been criticized for its tendency to sharpen political divisions such as the one between the advanced capitalist societies of North America, Europe, and East Asia and the developing societies of South and Central Asia, Africa, and Latin America. For decades, the advanced capitalist nations encouraged developing societies to pursue economic and social development through modernization. However, since the 1960s and 1970s critics in both the developing and the developed societies have condemned this model of development on the grounds that it seeks only to bring non-Western societies into a system defined and controlled by Western developed states. Globalization has expanded the forum in which the debates over economic and social development play out.

Another dividing line highlighted by globalization is cultural. With the spread of an increasingly homogenized global culture, many people intent on preserving their cultural identity put a new emphasis on their distinctive traditions (Barber 1995). From the Amazon rain forest to the Hindu Kush, non-Western cultures threatened by the advance of a single Western-based global culture worked to create poles of opposition.

Religion is a key factor at both the economic and the cultural level. A quintessentially transnational phenomenon, religion moves easily across political borders, and that movement is facilitated by globalization. Internationalization and the liberalization of economic and social policy have helped to spread its influence far and wide. Religion has a role to play in constituting the dominant and marginalized cultures that define modern globalization. Religious movements thrive in deterritorialized spaces such as global gatherings, online forums, or virtual communities that exist among co-religionists worldwide. Religious groups extend development assistance and help to define the parameters of development in emerging economies. And religion is at the heart of a world system polarized between traditional cultures and the new global culture. In this chapter we will explore some of the ways in which religion operates as a transnational actor, how it helps to define our interpretation of globalization, and the contributions that religion and religious actors have made to our understanding of social, economic, and political development.

Religion and Globalization

As noted above, globalization is a complex and ongoing process. It has created a new global culture that is rooted in Western traditions but also reflects influences from other traditions. How does religion relate to the new global culture? How does the interaction of Western and non-Western religious forms contribute to the construction of new forms of global culture?

Peter Beyer, a sociologist of religion and globalization, has argued that religion today is a subset of many different social forms that have been evolving since the major cultural developments of the fifteenth and sixteenth centuries. For Europeans, religion had a very particular meaning, reflecting the creeds developed over the first few centuries of Christendom and the notion of a distinct difference between public and religious matters. By the time they began studying the societies of peoples in other parts of the world, they already had a firmly established notion of what religion was and what it offered in terms of organization, worship, and feelings of spiritual meaning. As a consequence, they tried to fit all religions into what Beyer calls a 'distinct function system', an organizational rendering of all peoples by religion (2006: 75). The notion of a function system led moderns to believe that all civilizations must have a set of basic social principles to help people to understand the world at large. When these principles were religious, they would include judgments about good and evil, the role of the divine, and preferences for social organization, among other things. The spread of such ideas about religion hand in hand with globalization meant that religion became a universally recognized social phenomenon even in societies for whom the concept of religion in the European sense was entirely foreign.

The first World's Parliament of Religions, held in Chicago in 1893, marked a watershed in the understanding of religion as a social category. It was also one of the first events to bring together representatives of religious traditions from around the world, and thus could be understood as prototypical of the transformational encounter between religion and globalization. The event was a part of the World Columbian Exposition, a world's fair that featured displays and seminars on a wide range of human endeavour and celebrating a growing American conception of civilization and culture. The Parliament of Religions featured public presentations by a number of influential religious leaders. Particularly noteworthy at the time was the presence of delegates representing eastern religions, such as the Hindu Swami Vivekananda, the Sri Lankan Buddhist Anagarika Dharmapala, and the Jain scholar Virchand Gandhi. The event also highlighted North American Aboriginal spirituality and introduced North Americans to the Baha'i faith. As Seager notes, by the time of the Parliament the process of globalization had already begun, and it created an unprecedented arena for interaction:

> The global dissemination of a stock of general ideas and sentiments in the decades before the Parliament meant that a similarity of outlook existed among many delegates, despite the fact that their religious worldviews were formed in very different cultures and their aspirations were expressed in incompatible theologies and philosophies'. (1995: 96)

From the turn of the last century, the diversity of the world's religions has consistently presented itself as a feature that both characterizes and problematizes the idea of globalization.

Globalization creates an interconnected world and shrinks both the real and the perceived distances between cultures. It forces religious people to deal with daily challenges to the basic underpinnings of their worldviews. In an earlier book (1994) Beyer argued that globalization, to the extent that it implies the emergence of a global consciousness, forces religious people to rethink the way they deal with the moral challenges that they have always seen in the world at large. They are forced to alter the ways in which they classified certain phenomena as evil or judged certain behaviour to be moral or immoral. Most people cope with this challenge in one of

The World's Parliament of Religions held in Chicago in 1893 introduced Americans and the Western world to the diversity of the world's religious traditions. It also established the reputations of Eastern religious leaders such as Swami Vivekananda and Anagarika Dharmapala in the West.

two ways. They may move in a 'liberal' direction where moral evil becomes more abstract and less likely to be attached to any one thing, and where religious cultures converge. Or they may move in a 'conservative' direction where evil becomes more concrete and differences are emphasized, along with the 'holistic commitment and community solidarity' of their particular religious groups (Beyer 1994: 86–90). In this way globalization polarizes believers: moving some toward a universal ethic that helps them accept globalization as a part of their own religious perspective, and some towards resistance in the form of insularity, suspicion of other cultures, and a return to what they believe to be the purest form of their own religious tradition.

The Influence of Transnational Organization: Global Religious Networks

Globalization has facilitated the expansion of religious networks across the world. Information technologies such as the Internet allow religious groups to spread their messages quickly and easily. Internet evangelists are able to subvert official information filters and publishing bans by posting their messages online where travelling expatriates or intrepid information smugglers are able to defeat the controls of national censors. Religious movements that would have had limited reach in the past are now empowered not only by the availability of websites to transmit their messages, but by social media such as Facebook that facilitate expansion of group membership or, for example, the dissemination of sermons via podcasts. The development of translation devices has even begun to make it possible to quickly decipher the meaning of otherwise inaccessible texts. Transportation barriers have fallen away, allowing would-be missionaries to travel wherever they think they are needed to minister to co-religionists or to spread their faith.

The spread of new communications and transportation technologies clearly facilitates globalization. But it is important to realize that this is not the only effect of advances in technology. Technology shapes the culture and organizational structure of societies, and technological change has the power to bring about major changes in both traditional and modern societies. The expansion of our reference points to include new global communities of purpose, for instance, may weaken our existing loyalties if we keep more closely in touch with people we meet through global information networks than we do with people in our own community; our political loyalties may change and new political connections may develop that erode more traditional forms of association.

Transnational networks and globalization have also contributed to the spread of radicalized networks among certain religious groups. Thus globalization contributes to heightened security concerns in law enforcement. The expansion of global transportation links since the 1960s and the availability of affordable air travel in particular have provided terrorist movements of all sorts with a steady supply of soft targets. New information and communications technology has also facilitated the dissemination of literature that foments radicalism or explains how to build improvised explosive devices.

The political implications of these dramatic changes remain a subject of continuous debate. One of the first political theorists to recognize the potential of culture and cultural change to destabilize international relations was the British political theorist Hedley Bull. In his classic work *The Anarchical Society* (1977), Bull surmised that the state system—at that time still the most important organizing feature of international politics—could be undermined by the creation of a new 'system of overlapping authority and multiple loyalty'. He compared this situation to the medieval period, when states and even empires had to compete for political loyalties with both the Roman Catholic Church and various small local communities (Bull 1977: 254–5). Such a system would be characterized as 'neo-medieval'.

As the process of globalization accelerated with the end of the Cold War and the embrace of a neoliberal international economy in the 1990s, a growing number of scholars began to wonder if these developments signalled the end of the traditional state-centred international system. Would neoliberal structural adjustment and the growth of networked global businesses and civil society groups have the effect of eroding state authority and causing a major political shift toward global civil society (Strange 1996)? If so, would a neo-medieval system in fact replace the existing state system?

Religious groups had a central role to play in this discussion. Religion naturally poses a challenge to state authority by attributing ultimate power to an authority—a deity or a universal order—that stands above creation. It also reconstitutes notions of belonging or loyalty. Christians may feel a deeper kinship with other members of the worldwide church than they do with their non-Christian compatriots. Muslims feel themselves to be part of a worldwide *umma* that transcends political boundaries. Buddhists may feel a similar kinship within the worldwide community of *sangha* organizations, or find it easier to communicate with other Buddhists about the problems of life than with people who do not share their faith.

Writing in 1997, Susanne Hoeber Rudolph argued that it is not necessary to assume that religious groups challenge the dominance of the nation-state in order to recognize that they are politically important. She described the politics of transnational religious networks as a sort of 'plastic overlay' placed on top of the more traditional forms of international politics. 'What this suggests is less a waning of states than a more complex set of interrelations in which rival identities and structures jostle the state' (Rudolph and Piscatori 1997: 12). As politics has increasingly played out at the transnational level, religious groups have taken on some of the same roles in global civil society that they have long performed inside the boundaries of the traditional nation-state. This is true of both formal, established networks of religious scholars, clergy, and hierarchies (so-called 'high religion') and of self-constituted, informal, and popular groups ('low religion').

The phenomenon of transnational religion is not entirely new. In chapter 2 we saw that the Roman Catholic Church has been a transnational actor throughout its history, even interacting with the state system as a recognized player in international diplomacy. A variety of other religious groups have operated in multiple states and conducted worldwide diplomacy through emissaries and representatives. For example, the Islamic caliphate—the institutionalized leadership of the *umma* after the death of the Prophet Muhammad—constituted a recognized authority that was referenced throughout the Muslim world for almost fourteen centuries. And Western missionary activism exported European religions to diverse areas of Africa, Asia, and the Middle East throughout the colonial period, with such success that there are now long-established Roman Catholic, Episcopal, Presbyterian, and Baptist churches around the world.

In more recent times, religious networks have been instruments for significant political change at the transnational level. Such networks can be organized from the top down or from the grassroots up. A case could be made that the activities of formal institutions such as the Roman Catholic Church and the Organization of the Islamic Conference (OIC; see below) are the most significant representations of high religion at the international level (Haynes 2001). Warr (1999) details the contributions of the World Council of Churches to the worldwide campaign to end apartheid in South Africa throughout the 1980s. At the less formal level of low religion, religious human-rights activists have drawn international attention to religious persecution, often with the assistance of expatriates who have moved to the West and are concerned for their co-religionists still living in the home country (Rowe 2001). Nussbaum argues that US-based groups linked to the Hindu-nationalist RSS, such as the Hindu Swayamsevak Sangh, Hindu Students Council and the Vishva Hindu Parishad of America, have played an important role in teaching Americans of Indian descent how to think about their own culture. As a result, '[c]onsciousness of being Hindu is already often greater in the United States than in India' (Nussbaum 2007: 305).

We have already noted that diasporic communities are often able to influence the politics of their home states from a distance. Kathryn Poethig (2004) describes how Maha Ghosananda, a leading Cambodian monk forced into exile by years of

> ## Box 11.1: The World Council of Churches
>
> The World Council of Churches (WCC) is an international organization that represents the leadership of 349 different churches in 110 countries around the world. A product of the modern ecumenical movement, it was established in 1948 and its membership encompasses all the major Christian denominations except one. (The Roman Catholic Church maintains that it alone represents the universal church and therefore the authority under which all others should gather; however, it works closely with the WCC and is represented at all major WCC meetings.)
>
> The WCC reflects the ecumenical spirit by seeking united action through faith and communion in worship services and meetings, as well as developmental and political efforts, without eliminating the important differences among the various approaches to faith and worship represented in the movement. The WCC stages global assemblies every seven years or so, at which time a central committee of 150 representatives is chosen to direct the work of the organization. Its administrative offices are located in Geneva and it maintains a presence at the United Nations in New York, in Jerusalem, and leads developmental initiatives in offices in Africa.

civil war, mobilized the worldwide Cambodian community to support the country's reconstruction by establishing an annual peace walk called the Dhammayatra ('Dharma walk'). Similarly, Ismaili Muslims around the world help their co-religionists in central Asia through the Aga Khan Development Network, and Jewish people in North America send support to Zionist initiatives in Israel through the Jewish Federations of North America. Globalization has facilitated the expansion of these networks throughout the world, greatly enhancing the impact of religious philanthropy.

Religion, the Media, and the Global Political Sphere

Developments over the past decade have highlighted the increasingly interrelated arenas of religious organizations, the media, and the rise of a global political sphere. The Organization of the Islamic Conference (OIC) is one of the largest intergovernmental organizations in the world, with 57 member states located on four continents. It is also the only major intergovernmental organization designed to represent adherents of a particular religion. Eickelman and Piscatori (2004) argue that, as a state-based organization, the OIC represents the interests of its member states more than it does those of Muslims. However, more independently constituted groups have worked to spread Islam, mobilize Muslims to help Muslim minorities around the world, and respond to public issues of concern to Muslims (Eickelman and Piscatori 2004, 140–8). Financial support for the expansion of global Muslim civil society has been provided by citizens and governments of Gulf oil states as well as the growing Muslim diaspora.

The overlapping interests of majority-Muslim states and global Muslim movements inspired worldwide headlines in 2006. In September 2005, the Danish newspaper

---

Box 11.2: The Organization of the Islamic Conference

The Organization of the Islamic Conference was founded in the wake of an arson attack on the al Aqsa Mosque in Jerusalem in 1969. Its main goal is to coordinate action and promote cooperation among its member states. However, it has also worked to draw attention to issues of concern to Muslims worldwide. A permanent secretariat was established at a conference of foreign ministers in 1970 and set up in the city of Jeddah in Saudi Arabia.

The OIC holds regular summits every three years, known as the Islamic Summit. Occasional extraordinary summits will also be convened in order to respond to specific issues of the day. The Organization also convenes an annual conference of foreign ministers. The OIC was the champion of the 1990 Cairo Declaration on Human Rights in Islam, a document that continues to be referenced by many Islamic governments as a statement of principles regarding human rights. It regularly responds to issues surrounding the status of Muslims in non-Muslim societies, and speaks out with particular force against Israeli policies (the statements made at OIC summits are often criticized for their apparently anti-Semitic tone). The OIC maintains a permanent delegation at the United Nations in New York, which gives it weight as a voting bloc in the United Nations General Assembly.

Jyllands-Posten had decided to test the limits of public criticism of Islam and public censorship by publishing a number of editorial cartoons depicting Muhammad, the Prophet of Islam, in a negative or whimsical light. The protests of local Muslims that the cartoons were defamatory and deliberately targeted their sensibilities at first went largely unheeded outside Denmark. In December, however, in response to lobbying by European Muslims, the OIC held an Extraordinary Summit in Mecca at which it officially 'condemned the recent incident of desecration of the image of the Holy Prophet Muhammad [peace be upon him] in the media of certain countries' (www.oic-oci.org). By February 2006 the issue had become a *cause célèbre* throughout the Islamic world, sparking riots and violence against Danish and other Western embassies around the world, most significantly in capitals such as Tehran, Cairo, Kabul, and Istanbul. Eight months later, a similarly intense response greeted news of the controversial Regensburg Address, in which Pope Benedict XVI mentioned an ancient quotation that referred to Islam as a religion of violence. Media coverage of the address sparked violent demonstrations by offended Muslims around the world.

As these examples indicate, a new interest in the politics of religion has been reflected in a proliferation of news stories about religion since 2001. Before 9/11 few mainstream media outlets showed any serious interest in religious news; today major publications such as the *The Economist* regularly feature articles about the internal politics of religious groups, the niceties of interfaith dialogue, or the visits of religious leaders to various parts of the world. Nevertheless, critics charge that many media outlets continue to misunderstand or oversimplify religious issues in their haste to produce easily digestible and marketable news stories (Marshall, Gilbert, and Green 2009).

The immediacy of information and communications technology makes it easy to spread religious messages far and wide. This phenomenon was remarked on as early as the 1980s, when the reduced expense of broadcasting, cable television, and later satellite technology made it possible for religious televangelists to exercise significant political sway in the North American market. Simple audio cassette recordings of sermons by the Ayatollah Khomeini had helped to power Iran's Islamic Revolution. By the 1990s, the development of the Internet reduced the cost of entry into the global marketplace of ideas to the point that any religious group could mobilize and disseminate its message around the world.

Today many prominent religious leaders have attracted large followings primarily because of their ability to communicate on media platforms. In many cases, middle-ranking religious scholars and even laypeople have been able to gain greater notoriety than the official leaders and clergy of major religions. For example, Yusuf al-Qaradawi, an Egyptian religious scholar, has become a leading influence on Muslim public and political life around the world through his regular television show *Shari'a and Life*, broadcast in Arabic on al Jazeera, as well as his numerous books. The Indian American doctor Deepak Chopra first attracted attention in the late 1980s through media appearances; since then he has published many books that combine Indian mysticism and spiritual guidance with advice on health and well-being. His notoriety as a public face of eastern philosophy and self-help continues today.

Box 11.3: The World Evangelical Alliance and the Lausanne Movement

Christian Evangelicals belong to a variety of churches and denominations: some mainstream and hierarchical in structure, others egalitarian, non-institutionalized, and independent or non-denominational. They share a commitment to the spread of the Christian gospel through prayer, service, witness, and evangelism that has led to the creation of numerous international fellowships, missions, and joint endeavours over the years. Many of these churches do not embrace the formal and hierarchical approaches to religion that characterize the ecumenical movement. However, they work together in less formal umbrella organizations or groups aimed at achieving specific purposes.

In 1951, a group of evangelicals met in the Netherlands to create what they called the 'World Evangelical Fellowship'. This organization had three stated goals: furtherance of the Christian gospel, defence of the gospel, and fellowship in the gospel. Since that time, national evangelicals have continued to interact under the auspices of the fellowship, which was renamed the World Evangelical Alliance in 2001. With offices in Canada, the United States, and Geneva, the Alliance operates as an umbrella organization of 7 regional and 128 national evangelical alliances, 104 ministry organizations, and 6 specialized ministries.

Another organization with international reach originated in a global congress on world evangelization spearheaded by the Reverend Billy Graham in 1974. The congress was held at Lausanne, Switzerland, at which 2400 delegates from 150 nations signed a document known as the Lausanne Covenant. The document concluded that the Christians gathered in Lausanne should make 'a solemn covenant with God and with each other, to pray, to plan and to work together for the evangelization of the whole world'. The momentum from this meeting led to the formation of the Lausanne Movement and numerous follow-up congresses, most notably in Manila in 1989 and in Cape Town in 2010.

The potency of media reporting on stories that touch on religion was demonstrated in autumn 2007, when Buddhist monks joined public protests against the military regime in Burma. For several days, the international media were full of photographs taken by private citizens using cell phones and cameras and uploaded clandestinely via the Internet for the world to see. In the late summer of 2010, media reports surrounding the threat of Pastor Terry Jones of Gainesville, Florida, to desecrate the Qur'an on 11 September, caused worldwide controversy. The threatened 'International Burn a Koran Day' sparked protests among Muslims and non-Muslims alike, many of whom pled with Jones to relent, which he did amid demands that Muslims reverse plans to construct a mosque near the former World Trade Center site in New York City. His later decision to go through with the plan in March 2011 went largely undetected by the international media but was noticed in Afghanistan, where it sparked riots and a murderous attack on a United Nations compound in which seven expatriates were killed. The decision by US and global media outlets to provide a platform for an otherwise obscure fundamentalist minister underscored the way the new global media have transformed relations between religions around the world.

Migration, Religion, and Integration

Ongoing immigration flows complicate the domestic politics of religious relationships in many Western societies. While Muslim populations across the West are increasing in size, host states have responded with varying degrees of acceptance. Anti-Muslim extremism is a growing problem, especially in countries such as Britain, Norway, France, Germany, and the Netherlands. Established patterns of immigration have created particular ethnic enclaves in each country. In France, former colonial ties are reflected in large numbers of immigrants from Algeria and West Africa. In Germany, historic policies that allowed Turkish citizens to come as 'guest workers' have created large Turkish enclaves. The Netherlands has a wide array of groups from former colonies and elsewhere. In Britain, former colonial ties to South Asia and South America and the Caribbean have contributed to the ethnic makeup of the Muslim community.

Anti-Muslim sentiment often reflects fear that Muslim groups will demand separate privileges or challenge the traditional norms of Western states. Terror attacks over the past decade in Madrid, Istanbul, and London have been linked to the radicalization of Muslim youth in certain community networks and mosques. Journalist Melanie Phillips (2006) has raised the spectre of Muslim radicalism in the mosques of Britain, while Bruce Bawer (2006) and Christopher Caldwell (2009) have argued that the rise of fundamentalism among European Muslims poses a threat to European notions of identity. Others such as the French scholar Olivier Roy (2004) argue that Muslim extremism is a narrower phenomenon, rooted in particularly radical forms of fundamentalism. In his view, the broader Muslim population is able and willing to adapt to the European and Western context.

Still, popular responses to European societies' accommodation of growing communities of Muslims have had significant political implications. Crises have arisen

Ayaan Hirsi Ali, a Somali-born feminist and political activist, arrived in the Netherlands as a refugee in 1992. She was elected to the Dutch legislature in 2003 and became a controversial figure because of her critical attitude toward religion, in particular the Islam of her own heritage. Hirsi Ali went into hiding in 2004 after the murder of Theo Van Gogh, with whom she had collaborated on a short documentary called *Submission*. She published her memoirs in a bestselling book entitled *Infidel* in 2007.
Source: © John Van Hasselt/Corbis

from several high-profile incidents over the past decade, in addition to the global fallout from the Danish cartoon controversy and the Regensburg speech. In November 2009, Swiss citizens voted in a referendum to ban minarets on Muslim places of worship. Conservative politics in the Netherlands has been particularly affected. During the summer of 2004, Dutch filmmaker Theo Van Gogh released a short film entitled *Submission* based on a script written by Somali-born politician Ayaan Hirsi Ali. In November that year, Van Gogh was murdered by an Islamist radical and Hirsi Ali was forced into hiding. Since 2004, Geert Wilders, the leader of the right-wing Dutch Party for Freedom, has consistently defended a hard line on Muslim integration as a central plank in his political platform.

Religion and Development

Several decades ago, the study of social, economic, and political development was dominated by 'modernization' theory, according to which societies moved from backward, traditional, and largely agrarian modes of organization toward more complex, modern, industrialized forms. Modernization became the dominant perspective in the study of international development after the Second World War. While major industrialized states invested in development banks, institutions, and agencies, newly decolonized societies began to build their own domestically run economies and institutions.

As we have noted, a corollary of modernization theory was widely known as the secularization thesis. According to this perspective, the public role of religion becomes increasingly marginalized in modern societies. Traditional societies rely on religion to interpret the world, solve medical problems, provide social services, and so on. In more modern societies, informed by empirical science, the availability of secular answers to questions and technological solutions to problems meant that religion catered to a diminishing sphere of public interest. In short, modern humans would set aside religion as a guiding force in society and instead embrace secular and rationalistic ways of organizing their lives.

In the standard view of a modernizing society, religion would be privatized and would no longer function as a form of public social organization. Government would be in the hands of secular authorities and religious leaders would be consigned to leading the faithful in worship. Institutions would embrace secular and liberal legal systems, complete with written constitutions guaranteeing the religious neutrality of the state. More complex bureaucracies and industrial strategies would be developed by secular public and private institutions, without input from religious groups. These assumptions became an important part of the way people perceived the differences between developed and developing societies. They also informed the ways in which international development programs were implemented. Major world development institutions such as the World Bank and overseas development agencies crafted developmental planning as a secular enterprise based on the assumption that all societies would inevitably follow a similar path toward modernization.

For these reasons, early development strategies were often associated with both modernization and secularization, whether they were carried out by major international agencies or by the governments of countries in the developing world. Numerous political and economic modernizers came to power throughout Asia, Africa, and Latin America in the post-colonial period. Early anticlerical reforms in Latin America could be identified as one of the first turns in post-colonial modernization through secularization. More dramatically, the founder of the modern Turkish state, Mustafa Kemal Ataturk, introduced several initiatives designed to curtail the public power of religion. These included abolition of the Islamic caliphate, banning the Islamic veil for women in public places, and the transformation of the famous Hagia Sophia Mosque into a national museum. Turkey embraced a Western vision for modernization of the economy and development of a Western-style bureaucracy and military. Its example was followed in many other countries.

Following the Second World War, the pace of secularization accelerated in several developing states. In India, Congress Prime Minister Jawaharlal Nehru, who served from 1947 to 1964, set about modernizing the Indian economy through a socialistic form of government intervention and enshrined secularism in the Indian constitution. He oversaw the official dismantling of traditional religious and cultural institutions, most importantly the caste system. In Pakistan, Ayub Khan (1907–74), who seized power in a coup to become President from 1958 to 1969, deliberately sought to limit the power of Muslim clerics and the role of the Islamic religion in Pakistani politics. Throughout the late 1950s and 1960s, Muhammad Reza Pahlavi, the shah (king) of Iran, pursued a 'White Revolution', a widely varied set of strategies to bring Western-style education, economic development, and secularization to his country. In each of these cases and many others, modernization implied the limitation of religion, which was considered atavistic, counter-revolutionary, or simply a throwback to more primitive times. In order to build a more prosperous nation, religion had to be relegated to the sidelines of public policy. Rationalistic and scientific forms of knowledge were prized over traditional religious forms.

However, the implementation of modernization policies sowed the seeds for future revolts against secularization and provided grist for the mills of those who demanded the return of religion to public life. In each of the cases mentioned above, religious movements emerged to challenge the state's secularization policies. In India, the Hindu nationalist movement became the primary beneficiary of the erosion of Congress party power in the 1980s. In Pakistan, a period of instability ended in July 1977 with a coup led by General Muhammad Zia ul-Haq. General Zia developed a close political alliance with the Islamist movement in Pakistan and instituted a range of legal changes designed to Islamize Pakistani society. The Iranian revolution of 1979 brought an end to both the Pahlavi dynasty and the White Revolution, forcefully reversing the former regime's secularizing policies amid the creation of the Islamic Republic.

Meanwhile, religion was making a comeback as a public force in modernized Western societies as well. In Poland, the Roman Catholic Church contributed its voice to the democratic challenge to the Communist model. In the United States, the Moral Majority was cultivating support for the Republican Party. In Israel, Orthodox settlers were establishing new cities in the conquered West Bank. Far from taking a back seat in the process of political and economic development, religion returned as a major force.

As a result, by the 1990s scholars were finding reasons to challenge the basic premises of secularization. José Casanova argued that religious movements throughout the world were 'refusing to accept the marginal and privatized role which theories of modernity as well as theories of secularization had reserved for them'. Instead, religion was being 'deprivatized' (Casanova 1994: 5).

Still, development organizations remained wary of the public role of religion and sometimes blind to its significance in most developing societies. The role of religion in enforcing traditional gender roles and lines of authority, and in defending apparent injustices, led many development activists to view it with suspicion. Tomalin observes that development studies have had 'an uneasy relationship' with religion (2006: 103). She goes on to suggest that this helps to explain why development organizations are wary of working with faith-based agencies and why relatively little research has been done into the role of religion in the field of development. Clarke and Jennings observe that many development organizations trusted as partners only a small group of Christian organizations that offered 'quasi-secular' approaches to development (2008: 4).

Because religious groups had played a role in the colonial project, religion was criticized for reinforcing neo-colonial attitudes. For this reason, many early development efforts improperly conflated the religious calling to assist in development with the imposition of Western cultural norms. Later development groups therefore sought to detach their efforts from religion. But as Ian Linden argues, the very idea that one can separate religious and secular approaches to development assumes an artificial division that has no place in a holistic approach to development (2008: 72–93). Farokh Afshar (2005) notes with regret the extent to which studies of development have traditionally avoided mentioning the cultural contributions of religion and spirituality, preferring to focus on more tangible concerns such as the environment, gender issues, and population growth. He argues that spiritual contributions to happiness and well-being also merit consideration in the study of international development.

In the first decade of the twenty-first century the neglect of religion in development began to be addressed by several scholars of international development. Of particular note is the work of Katherine Marshall and Marisa Van Saanen of the World Bank. They argue that the new interest in religion has had two sources. One is the role that faith organizations have played in voicing concerns about the effects of structural adjustment policies in developing societies. The second was the faith-based Jubilee 2000 movement of the late 1990s which mobilized religious people, mostly Christians in the Western world, to lobby for debt relief at the major global economic summits and was the most enthusiastic participant in the effort to promote the millennium development goals declared in 2000 (2007: 3–4). Marshall and Van Saanen argue that religious actors galvanized opposition and criticism to prevailing patterns of globalization in the 1990s, and that the creation of a 'values for development group' in the World Bank helped to introduce the wider development community to the value of cooperating with religious organizations.

Despite the central role that religious actors have played in international development, however, both scholars and practitioners in the field have tended to keep their distance from the study of religion in development. Today religious and faith-based organizations are among the largest non-governmental institutions involved in development worldwide. They include World Vision, the Salvation Army, Caritas Internationalis, the Aga Khan Foundation, Mennonite Central Committee, Samaritan's Purse, and Compassion International. At the local and community level, churches, mosques, and other religious centres are often focal points for development initiatives as well. Typically, the majority of domestic partners leading, initiating, and organizing development initiatives funded by the major governmental and global development organizations are religious institutions or groups linked to national religious organizations.

The participation of these faith-based organizations in mainstream development initiatives is often controversial, given their conservative attitudes toward gender, sexuality, and authority in developing societies. However, Balchin (2007) argues that the general ignorance of religious ideas and organizations in development circles can also lead to an uncritical embrace of their participation.

Still, Clarke and Jennings maintain that faith-based organizations involved in development possess several unique strengths. They have a distinctive moral and spiritual focus, they tend to be highly networked at the global level, they are typically less dependent than other organizations on donor funding, and they can often provide a high level of relevant and contextual expertise (2008: 272). So while development assistance is distributed and managed by large secular institutions, religion often has an extremely important role to play in the implementation and management of projects on the ground. In addition, globalization itself creates synergies between the developed and developing worlds as exiles, refugees, and immigrants leave their home countries to find new lives in Western societies.

The fact that religion has been harnessed in the service of resistance to modernization and Westernization, as well as the spread of faith-based development initiatives worldwide, may have wider strategic implications in the way religious people relate to one another. Philip Jenkins, a professor of religion, has written widely on the implications of the demographic and cultural growth of Christianity in the developing world. In his book *The Next Christendom* (2002), Jenkins argues that different forms of Christianity are asserting themselves in places such as sub-Saharan Africa, Latin America, and East Asia, with the result that the religion is becoming less Western in character. He predicts that the 'next Christendom' will be far more interested than the old one in mystical and charismatic experience, more paternalistic and patriarchal, and will celebrate a gospel that contextualizes poverty and promises earthly rewards for the faithful. According to Jenkins, the new Christianity is also more likely to take a strong stand in opposition to its perceived rival religions, most notably Islam.

A Divided World? Notions of Division Rooted in Religion and Civilization

Perhaps the most notable theme in recent studies of religion and the transnational politics of globalization has been the polarizing tendencies of religion. Of these studies, Samuel Huntington's 1996 book *The Clash of Civilizations and the Remaking of World Order* has been by far the most influential. Laying out the politics of division in the age of globalization, Huntington's book is not about religion and politics per se, but the differing civilizational identities it refers to are based in large part on religion. 'A civilization is . . . the highest cultural grouping of people and the broadest level of cultural identity people have', short of their identity as human beings (Huntington 1996: 43).

Huntington argued that with the waning of the Cold War, during which global divisions had been based in ideology, flashpoints would develop out of differences based on civilizational identity. Among the eight civilizational groupings that he identified, five were rooted in particular religious traditions: Western Christendom, Eastern Orthodoxy, Islam, Hinduism, and Confucianism. Huntington argued that the major conflicts of the future would pit the leading states of each civilizational grouping against one another. He stopped short of predicting that religious differences would be the spark to light the powder keg of world politics, but he did imply that religious differences would likely be marshalled to justify and support aggressive behaviour on the part of states. He noted with special concern that religious resurgence was likely to deepen the feelings of civilizational identity and intensify violence between civilizations.

The strategic implications of Huntington's book were not lost on those who watched as intense conflicts erupted over the years that followed. Many of these seemed to prove Huntington's point, occurring as they did along the faultlines he had identified. Perhaps the first was the conflict over the Balkans that pitted the Western NATO alliance against Serb nationalists with sympathies in Moscow. Conflict between India and Pakistan led to the Kargil War of 1999. The outbreak of the second Palestinian *intifada* in 2000 illustrated the ongoing potential for conflict between Western and Islamic civilizations. Finally, the attacks of 11 September 2001 were often interpreted as the ultimate expression of an explosive clash between Islam and Western civilization.

Other observers have described religion's contribution to global divisions in other ways. Benjamin Barber wrote that globalization itself had created a new global cosmopolitanism that was unacceptable to traditionalists in most cultures, especially religious fundamentalists, a phenomenon he characterized as *Jihad versus McWorld* (1995). *New York Times* columnist Thomas Friedman similarly argued that the world was increasingly polarized between what he described as *The Lexus and the Olive Tree*: a consumerist, technology-driven culture and a culture devoted to the preservation of values rooted in the past (2000). Mark Juergensmeyer has argued that what unites religious movements in their resistance to globalization is disillusionment with the benefits promised by modernization and Westernization. They are therefore motivated to propose alternative forms, which rise up in rebellion against the symbols of technological progress that represent modern globalization (Juergensmeyer 2008).

The assertion that globalization juxtaposes numerous cultural and religious identities in a polarizing dispute over basic values and loyalties has become a foundational concern of many scholars of global politics. Critics of Huntington have argued that his notion of civilizational clash oversimplifies complex relationships between the world's cultures or that it amounts to an unhelpful self-fulfilling prophecy. Others have focused on the ways in which civilizational and religious norms may also provide unifying contexts for human society.

Conclusions

Modern global politics is characterized by increasingly intimate interaction among people, groups, and movements around the world. It has taken on transnational attributes as a result of the process of globalization. Globalization is a multifarious process that has sociological, economic, and political definitions. It has allowed religious groups to prosper across state and geographic lines and given new political power to ancient religious traditions. New media give religious news stories and events greater resonance at the global level. In the conceptualization and application of international development strategies, the persistence of religion has challenged the long-standing assumption that modernization would put an end to the public role of religion. The very persistence of religion as a worldwide phenomenon has led many to fear that it is likely to polarize the world between spheres of influence or civilizations based on religious identities. Others argue that globalization creates opportunities to mine the world's religious traditions as a means of improving mutual understanding and developing a more inclusive vision for the future.

Review Questions

1. What is meant by the terms 'transnational politics' and 'globalization'? What influence does religion have on transnational politics and globalization?
2. How has our understanding of religion itself been affected by globalization, according to sociologists such as Peter Beyer?
3. In what ways do religious movements influence politics at the global level?
4. How have the media raised the profile of religious figures and religion in general in the age of globalization?
5. What are some of the challenges faced by states with immigrant populations from different religious backgrounds? What are the most common concerns raised about this phenomenon?
6. How have theories of development treated religion in the past? What are some of the new perspectives suggested by more recent theories of development?
7. In what ways might religion serve to deepen the divisions between the world's peoples, according to scholars such as Samuel Huntington? Are these divisions inevitable, or could religion help to bring people together?

Sources and Further Reading:

Afshar, Farokh (2005). 'Exploring the Frontiers of International Development: Countries of the North, Well-being, Spirituality, and Contemplation'. *Canadian Journal of Development Studies* 26, 3: 527–46.

Balchin, Cassandra (2007). 'The F-Word and the S-Word—Too Much of One and Not Enough of the Other'. *Development in Practice* 17, 4–5: 532–8.

Barber, Benjamin R. (1995). *Jihad versus McWorld*. New York: Times Books.

Bawer, Bruce (2006). *While Europe Slept: How Radical Islam Is Destroying the West from Within*. New York: Doubleday.

Beyer, Peter (1994). *Religion and Globalization*. London: Sage.

———— (2006). *Religions in Global Civil Society*. London: Routledge.

Beyer, Peter, and Lori Beaman, eds. (2007). *Religion, Globalization, and Culture*. Leiden: Brill.

Bull, Hedley (1977). *The Anarchical Society*. London: Macmillan.

Caldwell, Christopher (2009). *Reflections on the Revolution in Europe*. New York: Doubleday.

Casanova, José (1994). *Public Religions in the Modern World*. Chicago: University of Chicago Press.

Clarke, Gerard, and Michael Jennings, eds (2008). *Development, Civil Society, and Faith-based Organizations*. New York: Palgrave Macmillan.

Eickelman, Dale, and James Piscatori (2004). *Muslim Politics*. Princeton: Princeton University Press.

Esposito, John L., and Michael Watson, eds (2000). *Religion and Global Order*. Cardiff: University of Wales Press.

Friedman, Thomas (2000). *The Lexus and the Olive Tree: Understanding Globalization.* New York: Anchor Books.

Haynes, Jeffrey (2001). 'Transnational Religious Actors and International Politics'. *Third World Quarterly* 22, 2: 143–58.

———— (2007). *Religion and Development: Conflict or Cooperation?* New York: Palgrave Macmillan.

Huntington, Samuel P. (1996). *The Clash of Civilizations and the Remaking of World Order.* New York: Simon and Schuster.

Linden, Ian (2008). 'The Language of Development: What are International Development Agencies Talking About?' Pp. 72–93 in Clarke and Jennings (2008).

Jenkins, Philip (2002). *The Next Christendom: The Coming of Global Christianity.* Oxford: Oxford University Press.

Juergensmeyer, Mark, ed. (2005). *Religion in Global Civil Society.* Oxford: Oxford University Press.

———— (2008). *Global Rebellion: Religious Challenges to the Secular State from Christian Militias to al Qaeda.* Berkeley: University of California Press.

Marshall, Katherine, and Marisa Van Saanen (2007). *Development and Faith: Where Mind, Heart, and Soul Work Together.* Washington, DC: World Bank.

Marshall, Paul, Lela Gilbert, and Roberta Green (2009). *Blind Spot: When Journalists Don't Get Religion.* Oxford: Oxford University Press.

Nussbaum, Martha C. (2007). *The Clash Within: Democracy, Religious Violence, and India's Future.* Cambridge, MA: Belknap Press.

Phillips, Melanie (2006). *Londonistan.* New York: Encounter Books.

Poethig, Kathryn (2004). 'Locating the Transnational in Cambodia's Dhammayatra'. Pp. 197–212 in John Marston and Elizabeth Guthrie, eds, *History, Buddhism, and New Religious Movements in Cambodia.* Honolulu: University of Hawai'i Press.

Rowe, Paul S. (2001). 'Four Guys and a Fax Machine? Diasporas, New Information Technologies, and the Internationalization of Religion in Egypt'. *Journal of Church and State* 43, 1: 81–92.

Roy, Olivier (2004). *Globalized Islam: The Search for a New Umma.* New York: Columbia University Press.

Rudolph, Susanne Hoeber, and James Piscatori, eds (1997). *Transnational Religion and Fading States.* Boulder: Westview Press.

Sacks, Jonathan (2003). *The Dignity of Difference: How to Avoid the Clash of Civilizations.* Revised edition. London: Continuum.

Seager, Richard Hughes (1995). *The World's Parliament of Religions: The East/West Encounter, Chicago, 1893.* Bloomington, ID: Indiana University Press.

Scholte, Jan Aart (2000). *Globalization: A Critical Introduction.* New York: St. Martin's Press.

Strange, Susan (1996). *The Retreat of the State.* Cambridge: Cambridge University Press.

Tomalin, Emma (2006). 'Religion and a Rights-based Approach to Development'. *Progress in Development Studies* 6, 2: 93–108.

Warr, Kevin (1999). 'The Normative Promise of Religious Organizations in Global Civil Society'. *Journal of Church and State* 41, 3: 499–523.

Web Resources

www.oic-oci.org – The Organization of the Islamic Conference.

www.oikoumene.org – The World Council of Churches.

www.worldevangelicals.org – The World Evangelical Alliance.

faithandglobalization.yale.edu – Faith and Globalization; Yale University's Faith and Globalization initiative.

www.mapsofwar.com/ind/history-of-religion.html – The Global Spread of Religions; a geopolitical representation of religion's global spread.

Chapter 12

Conclusion: Religion in a 'Secular Age'?

Throughout this book we have observed many ways in which religion affects the politics of nation-states and the international or global system at large. Religious movements and organizations continue to play important roles, from the Roman Catholic Church with its global reach to the narrowly focused vigilante organizations that represent Hindu revivalism in India. Religious groups organize in order to have an impact on policy-making, both domestic and foreign, as in the case of the American religious right or the Islamist parties that contest elections in Turkey or Indonesia. They have also come to challenge the very basis of the international system, as in the case of the radical jihadist movement that inspired al-Qaeda and the Taliban movement in Afghanistan.

For many people, the extreme positions taken by religious movements around the world constitute a disturbing phenomenon. The religious resurgence noted in India's Bharatiya Janata Party, the Israeli settler movement, or American right-wing politics seems likely only to divide people and polarize politics in an era when cooperation is so vital. Critics of the religious resurgence argue that global politics must be secular if it is to allow the interaction and cooperation required for human beings to flourish. For others, the growth in interest in religion as a force in politics is not really novel, but a reassertion of more traditional forms of collective action in politics, and therefore a step backward. Still others would argue that if the principle of secularism in political life is under threat, one reason might be that it was never fully respected in the first place.

In this chapter we will briefly consider recent scholarship regarding the past and future of a secular public sphere. Does the resurgence of religion pose an existential threat to international relations as we have known it? Does the notion of a secular state remain viable in a time when growing numbers of people are rediscovering their religious heritage and governments have to defend the legitimacy of state actions in a world of diverse religious cultures? In many ways, the politics of religion as it has developed over the last few decades has forced social scientists to rethink the foundational premises of the secular state system and the boundaries between the religious and the secular in international politics.

The Rise and Decline of the Secular State

The basic parameters of the international states system as we know it today were established in 1648 with the Peace of Westphalia. That treaty brought an end to the Thirty Years' War, which had begun as a struggle between the Roman Catholic Hapsburg Empire and the Protestant states within Europe that were determined to maintain their religious autonomy. It brought to an end more than a century of warfare sparked by the Protestant Reformation. The settlement reached at Westphalia enshrined the principle of *cuius regio, eius religio*, according to which it was the right of every sovereign to determine the religion of his own state. Ever since that time, efforts to develop norms of action and interaction in world affairs have been associated with the process of secularization. Political theorists beginning in the 1600s with Hugo Grotius and Thomas Hobbes and continuing over the centuries with people like John Locke,

Immanuel Kant, and John Stuart Mill (1806–73) sought to lay down rationalistic premises on which international politics might operate. Politicians themselves, from Klemens von Metternich to Otto von Bismarck, Woodrow Wilson to Henry Kissinger, followed their lead in seeking to make foreign policy without reference to religion, or so it was assumed. When questions involving religious issues arose—whether to go to war, to tolerate or punish dissenters, to accept joint stewardship of holy sites—they were generally managed in accordance with state policy, which quickly subordinated the spiritual to the temporal.

It was in this rationalistic context that international relations theory was developed after the Second World War. The dominant perspective in international relations was realism, which assumed that states would make rational calculations based on their own self-interest and behave accordingly. Religion did not enter into their decisions and was considered secondary (or *epiphenomenal*). The liberal and structuralist critiques of realism that were developed starting in the 1960s challenged many of the realists' assumptions but did not challenge the basic principle that religion had no bearing on the decisions made by the leading actors in world politics. From the perspective of liberal pluralists, religious groups had a marginal impact in a world of interdependent economies, rival political movements, and contending ideological, partisan, and ethnic bases of legitimacy. From the perspective of economic structuralists such as neo-Marxists, religious movements developed within a system organized around two opposing social forces—dominant and marginalized—whose power (or lack of it) was usually rooted in class or access either to capital or the levers of military and industrial power.

It would likely be an overstatement to say that religious groups have been entirely ignored by scholars of global politics. However, in most cases such groups became objects of study only as important state actors, political parties, resistance groups, or lobbies operating alongside other groups in society—in other words, operating as if they were not religious at all. The idea that religion itself might be important in understanding the foundations of global politics was almost never broached, except on the odd occasion when religious actors talked about world politics.

This is no longer the case, as we noted in chapter 1. The assumption that religion stands outside international politics has been undermined in the last few decades; as Daniel Philpott (2002) argues, the 'Westphalian synthesis' that excluded religion from discussion in world affairs is increasingly challenged by people, groups, states, and organizations whose notions of legitimacy are firmly rooted in their religious convictions. Increasingly, religious groups are challenging the very legitimacy of international politics as it has been practised for centuries. As we saw in chapter 8, the Organization of the Islamic Conference responded to the Universal Declaration of Human Rights with an Islamic version (the Cairo Declaration of 1990) that sought to curtail many rights in accordance with shari'a. Buddhist *bhikkus* in South Asia have argued against the universality of human rights as a political value. Christian pacifists have long refused to engage in military service and today place themselves directly in the way of armies that claim to be engaged in the preservation of order. In Somalia, the Islamist *shabab* militia stages attacks abroad in opposition to the African Union's support for the Somali government. These challenges take aim at some of the modern

Box 12.1: The Demise of Secularism?

Political theorists of the twenty-first century have been taking aim at the assumptions of secularism. Criticism has been especially trenchant among scholars from the global South:

'If the secularization thesis no longer carries the conviction it once did, this is because the categories of "politics" and "religion" turn out to implicate each other more profoundly than we thought, a discovery that has accompanied our growing understanding of the powers of the modern nation-state. The concept of the secular cannot do without the idea of religion.'

—Talal Asad, *Formations of the Secular* (2003)

'Secularism is the dream of a minority which wants to shape the majority in its own image, which wants to impose its will upon history but lacks the power to do so under a democratically organized polity. In an open society the state will reflect the character of the society. Secularism therefore is a social myth which draws a cover over the failure of this minority to separate politics from religion in the society in which its members live.'

—T.N. Madan, *Images of the World: Essays on Religion, Secularism, and Culture* (2006)

world's basic assumptions about political authority and the way the international system operates.

In some cases, opposition to the secular state has become so great that governments are overturned in favour of theocratic or confessional states. The Iranian revolution of 1979 was perhaps the most dramatic example. Similarly theocratic regimes have been established by the National Islamic Front in Sudan in 1989, the Taliban in Afghanistan (1996–2001), and the various Islamist movements that have held political power in Somalia over the past several years. The very notion of secularity has become a polarizing issue within the international system, with Western industrialized societies on one side, championing limitations on religion in public life, and religious revivalist movements, religious institutions, and states with religious regimes on the other side, asserting their own particular dogmatic principles.

A Secular Age?

For many scholars, the current debate over the place of religion in political life itself constitutes evidence that religion is central to human notions of order. Political philosophers and theorists have been puzzling over the need for religion as a central element in national belonging and identity for a long time. The decline of the public role of Christianity created a vacuum that was filled by a variety of philosophies. When the German philosopher Friedrich Nietzsche (1844–1900) famously observed that 'God is dead', he was marking the conclusion of an era in which religion answered the important questions for global society—questions such as who should rule, what standards of morality the state should obey, and by what processes we should come to such decisions. What would take religion's place? Throughout the twentieth century, many different philosophies, spiritualities, and ideologies presented themselves as candidates. For a time, extreme forms of nationalism mined religion for images and ideas (crosses, martyrdom, moral guidance, self-sacrifice) that would persuade people to accept the nationalists' judgments about which nations were worthy of survival and which should be subordinated or destroyed. Communism also provided a comprehensive ideological answer to the human need for fulfillment in dedication to superhuman goals. Meanwhile, Western liberal democracy and capitalism offered some basic premises on which to order society, many of which remain foundational to global politics today.

Western states have largely accepted the basic principles of secularism. That is, they have agreed that religion should be a private matter with little or no influence on the construction of public policy. Politics that take place in state institutions may be clearly separated from religious teaching and authority, and by divesting itself of religious influence the state becomes a secular institution. Secularism could simply describe the nature of the state, but when it becomes a prescription or a normative assumption about the way the world *should* be, it becomes much more. In other words, secularism can go from being a feature of the way a state chooses to govern itself to a philosophic or ideological demand that the state must be free of religious influences.

Charles Taylor has argued that secularism developed as a way of elucidating our essential values in an age of unbelief. In *Modern Social Imaginaries* (2004) Taylor suggests that today people understand the world through what he calls a 'social imaginary':

the ways people imagine their social existence, how they fit together with others, how things go on between them and their fellows, the expectations that are normally met, and the deeper normative notions and images that underlie these expectations (2004: 23).

Social imaginaries are multiple and they change throughout history. Today, the dominant social imaginary is a secular one in which the place of religion has shifted, but has not been entirely eliminated.

Taylor elaborated on the secularity of the modern social imaginary in a wide-ranging book entitled *A Secular Age* (2007). Here he presents secularism as a sort of replacement for religion in its function as a source of order in human life. He suggests that our contemporary secular age is rooted in the efforts of people in the Christian West to forge meaning in the absence of belief. It is therefore not a product of scientific rationalism or religious neutrality. Rather, 'the modern secular world emerged out of the more and more rule-bound and norm-governed Reform of Latin Christendom' (Taylor 2007: 742). Other philosophers share Taylor's concern that secularism falsely claims the right to override the notion of a transcendent reality beyond earthly politics. Elshtain (2008) explains how secular forms of government run the risk of arrogating the transcendence of divine sovereignty to either the self or the state and losing all sense of limitation or empathy.

In a landmark study of the secular assumption in international politics, Elizabeth Shakman Hurd (2008) argues that secularism is a social and historical construction that has become extremely influential in global politics. As she understands it, secularism has taken two distinct forms. In states such as France, where religion was sidelined as a public force, religious actors and religious justifications are prohibited from entering public discussions. This form of secularism, known as *laicism*, 'works to exclude alternative approaches to the negotiation of the secular that threaten its concept . . . of modern politics,' Hurd argues. 'In attempting to legislate the terms through which the secular and the sacred are defined, laicism rules out in advance linkages between religion and spheres of power and authority such as law, science, and politics within states' (2008: 36).

The second form of secularism she identifies as Judeo-Christian. In this form, church and state are said to be separate, or to perform very different social roles, as they have historically in Western European countries. Forms of religious practice that seek to combine the religious and political spheres are foreign to this tradition. The Judeo-Christian form of secularism helps to define the contours of Western civilization:

> religious history and tradition play a specific and determinative role as the source of particular styles and institutions of governance, forms of civilizational identity, and entrenched and violent clashes between so-called civilizations. Judeo-Christian tradition, in this view, culminated in and contributes to the unique Western achievement of the separation of church and state and forms of liberal democracy. There is solidarity in civilizational consciousness, and religious diversity is dangerous because it threatens this solidarity (Hurd 2008: 42).

Scott M. Thomas writes that while observers continue to express concern over religious challenges to the secular state, the very terms human beings use to describe those challenges underline the extent to which secularism shapes our thinking. The vocabulary we use to refer to religious groups and their activities turns them into spectres: 'extremism, militancy, fundamentalism, terrorism, secularism, political religion, political Islam, Islamism'. However, he goes on to note that 'religious', 'secular' and 'political' 'are not stable, value-neutral concepts or categories but socially and politically constructed (and contested) concepts reflecting particular settings, cultures, and time periods' (2010: 192–3). If this is true, current debates over the role of religion could be moving the world toward a new form of politics, one in which religion itself is debated, discussed, and recognized for the important role that it plays. Hurd believes that religious resurgence should be understood as an attempt to force secularists to rethink their basic presuppositions and engage in debate with those who disagree. She recommends an 'agonistic' or 'agonal' solution that gives both the secular and the religious a role to play in resolving our disagreements at the global level (Hurd 2008: 142–7).

Hostility or Hospitality?

The division in global politics today between the sacred and the secular does not promote friendly relations between religious groups and secular societies. It leaves us with an unfortunate choice between a secular politics that relegates religion to the sidelines and a religious politics that inclines toward the dogmatic. The secular state and the religious fundamentalist demonize one another, in ways that can seem hysterical. Each becomes monstrous in the eyes of the other.

But the truth is that we cannot live or construct politics and meaning without some reference to the eternal truths that these philosophic or religious perspectives give us. This book has been grounded in the idea that we must 'take religion seriously' as a motivator of political action. To simply ignore the reality that human beings come from many different religious traditions, each of which may be interpreted and practised in many different ways, would be unwise. It is inevitable that individual humans will base their interpretations of global politics on the same presuppositions that ground their understanding of life in general, whether those presuppositions be rationalistic or theistic, or some combination of the two. Is it possible to construct a politics that allows the two types to interact? One should not lose sight of the fact that the practice of religion requires ongoing hermeneutic or interpretive choices. All religious traditions have the capacity either to embrace a world full of plural voices or to reject those voices and silence them. But no religious tradition monolithically demands that the believer seek to destroy all others in the path of Truth. When dogmatic interpretations of Truth become all-consuming, believers tend to jettison the complexity of their own religious traditions and respond with hostility to a world that all of a sudden appears hostile to them. In the words of Richard Kearney, a philosopher of public religion:

> there is a deep ambiguity built into religions from the outset. You can kill the Stranger, treating him or her as a threat and the enemy, or you can overcome the initial reaction of fear, responding instead with a gesture of welcome' (Kearney 2010: 16).

It is my hope that this book, by introducing some of the many permutations of religion in global politics, will open up some new opportunities for dialogue in which hostility is replaced with hospitality.

Review Questions

1. In what ways does the politics of religion challenge the politics of secularism at the global level?
2. What are the historical origins of secularism?
3. How has secularism affected global politics in some of the countries we have studied in this book?
4. In what ways is secularism defined in politics today?
5. How have some contemporary scholars criticized the practice of secularism in global politics?

Sources and Further Reading

Asad, Talal (2003). *Formations of the Secular: Christianity, Islam, Modernity*. Stanford: Stanford University Press.

Chaplin, Jonathan, with Robert Joustra, eds (2010). *God and Global Order: The Power of Religion in American Foreign Policy*. Waco, TX: Baylor University Press.

Elshtain, Jean Bethke (2008). *Sovereignty: God, State, and Self*. New York: Basic Books.

Hurd, Elizabeth Shakman (2008). *The Politics of Secularism in International Relations*. Princeton: Princeton University Press.

Kearney, Richard (2010). 'Imagining the Sacred Stranger: Hostility or Hospitality?' In John Dyck, Paul Rowe, and Jens Zimmermann, eds, *Politics and the Religious Imagination*. London: Routledge.

Madan, T.N. (2006). *Images of the World: Essays on Religion, Secularism, and Culture*. New Delhi: Oxford University Press.

Philpott, Daniel (2002). 'The Challenge of September 11 to Secularism in International Relations'. *World Politics* 55: 66–95.

Taylor, Charles (2004). *Modern Social Imaginaries*. Durham: Duke University Press.

——— (2007). *A Secular Age*. Cambridge: Belknap Press.

Thomas, Scott M. (2010). 'Response: Reading Religion Rightly: The "Clash of Rival Apostasies" amidst the Global Resurgence of Religion'. Pp. 187–204 in Chaplin and Joustra (2010).

Warner, Michael, Jonathan VanAntwerpen, and Craig Calhoun, eds. (2010). *Varieties of Secularism in a Secular Age*. Cambridge, MA: Harvard University Press.

Glossary

abhidharma pitaka (Theravada Buddhism) – A series of commentaries on *dharma*; one of the three 'baskets' (*tripitaka*) of sacred texts that make up the Pali Canon.

ahimsa (Hinduism) – Sanskrit word translated as 'non-harm' or 'non-violence'; the guiding philosophy of Mohandas K. Gandhi and an essential principle in Jain and some Hindu traditions.

ahl al dhimma (Islam) – Arabic for 'protected people', referring to the non-Muslim minorities tolerated under Islamic rule.

Aliya (Judaism) – Hebrew word meaning 'ascent', used to refer to the migration of Jews to the land of Israel; since 1880, each wave of Jewish immigrants is referred to as an *Aliya* (pl. *Aliyot*).

anticlericalism – Opposition to the influence of the clergy (or religion in general) in public life, especially politics.

apostles (Christianity) – The earliest leaders of the Christian community, each of whom had personal contact with Jesus of Nazareth; some branches of Christianity also refer to divinely appointed leaders of the church as 'apostles'.

Ashkenazim (Judaism) – Jews of European descent.

atman (Hinduism, Buddhism) – Sanskrit meaning 'self' or 'soul'; refusal to bow to the desires of the self is the Buddhist principle of *anatman*.

autocephalous (Christianity) – 'Self-governing'; an adjective typically used to describe the various independent Orthodox churches, which remain in communion with one another and do not recognize the Roman Catholic pope as the head of a single universal church.

Avodah – The Hebrew word for 'labour'; the original Labour Party of Israel.

Bhagavad Gita (Hinduism) – The 'great song'; the most famous section of the *Mahabharata* epic; a dialogue between the divine Krishna and the warrior-prince Arjuna on war, duty, and self-realization, the *Gita* is considered one of the most important Hindu scriptures.

bhakti (Hinduism) – A Hindu movement that emphasizes devotional practice over ritual adherence.

bhikku (Theravada Buddhism) – The Pali term for a Buddhist monk (*bhikshu* in Sanskrit).

Bible (Judaism, Christianity) – The holy scriptures of Judaism and Christianity; the Christian Bible consists of the Jewish Tanakh (the Old Testament) followed by the scriptures written by the disciples of Jesus, which make up the New Testament.

bodhisattva (Buddhism) – Literally, 'enlightenment being'; in the Theravada tradition the term usually refers to the Buddha himself before his final enlightenment, but in the Mahayana tradition it may be applied to anyone who has taken the vow to become a buddha; Mahayana Buddhism also recognizes numerous celestial *bodhisattvas*.

Brahmin (Hinduism) – A member of the priestly caste, the highest of the four Hindu castes.

Buddha (Buddhism) – Sanskrit for the 'Enlightened One'; usually refers to Siddhartha Gautama, the Indian prince who became the most recent in a succession of buddhas when he attained enlightenment, c. 500 BCE.

caliphs (Islam) – The successors of the Prophet Muhammad. The office of the caliphs, or *caliphate*, designated a leading ruler as 'commander of the faithful' on earth, granting them temporal authority over the worldwide community of Muslims.

caste (Hinduism) – A cultural form of class differentiation based on birth into a particular occupational calling.

chakravartin (Buddhism) – Sanskrit meaning 'wheel-turner'; the ideal Buddhist ruler.

charismatic (Christianity) – A word used to describe a number of movements, mainly Protestant but in recent years Roman Catholic as well, that emphasize experiential participation in miraculous works of God.

Christ (Christianity) – From the Greek meaning 'anointed one', the messiah and central figure of Christianity.

church (Christianity) – Variously, the worldwide community of Christian believers, a particular Christian denomination, a local community of Christian believers, or a place of Christian worship.

Concordat of Worms (Christianity) – The agreement (1122) between the Vatican and the Holy Roman Emperor Henry V that laid out the basis for the separation of the political authority of the church from that of the state.

constructivism – A school of international relations theory focusing on the social and historical development of the images, norms, and ideas that shape our understanding of the world.

Crusades – A series of military campaigns undertaken by Western Christians against Muslims, Jews, pagans, and Eastern Christians in the Middle East and Eastern Europe between the eleventh and fourteenth centuries.

cuius regio, eius religio – Latin phrase meaning 'whose realm, his religion', articulating the principle that the reigning monarch had the right to determine the religion of his or her state. Originally laid down at the Peace of Augsburg of 1555, the principle was taken up in later treaties and became a foundational premise of the Westphalian states system.

Dalits (Hinduism) – The word derived from Sanskrit meaning 'crushed' or 'beaten down' that has become the preferred term for the people formerly known as 'untouchables'.

dar al-harb (Islam) – The 'abode of war'; the areas yet to be subdued to the rule of Islam.

dar al-Islam (Islam) – The 'abode of Islam'; the areas subdued by the rule of Islam.

da'wa (Islam) – Arabic for 'calling', used to refer to mission activity or a divinely inspired vocation

also the name of a leading political movement in Iraq.

dharma (Hinduism, Buddhism) – Sanskrit word variously translated as 'faith', 'duty', 'way of life', 'moral teaching', etc.

dharmayuddha (Buddhism) – The teaching that affirms warfare done according to Buddhist moral precepts.

disestablishmentarianism – A political phenomenon in which the state seeks to ensure that no one religion is recognized as the official religion of the state.

Druze (Islam) – An esoteric sect of Ismaili Shi'ism that arose in the eleventh century, now concentrated in Lebanon and Syria.

Eastern Orthodox Church (Christianity) – The dominant Christian tradition in Eastern Europe and the Middle East, consisting of several autonomous (or 'autocephalous') churches.

Evangelical (Christianity) – A variety of Protestantism characterized by its focus on personal conversion, active propagation of the Christian message, high regard for the authority of scripture, and emphasis on the physical death and resurrection of Jesus Christ.

ex cathedra (Roman Catholicism) – Latin phrase meaning 'from the chair', a designation applied to statements by the pope that carry the full authority of the office; the first Vatican Council (1868) ruled that teachings issued *ex cathedra* are infallible.

fatwa (Islam) – A legal judgment issued by a Muslim judge or religious expert.

fitna (Islam) – Arabic term referring to division or disorder in the Muslim community; most commonly used to refer to the period after the death of the Prophet when the Shi'i broke away from the Sunni.

fundamentalist – A term used to describe an uncompromisingly conservative religious tradition, especially one that insists on a literal reading of traditional scriptures. The term was coined in the United States around the turn of the twentieth century to refer to a Protestant group that rejected textual criticism and liberal interpretation of the Christian scriptures. Application of the term outside this context is contentious.

Great Schism (Christianity) – The formal separation (in 1054) of the eastern (Greek) and western (Latin) branches of Christianity to form what came to be known as the Eastern Orthodox and Roman Catholic churches.

gurudwara (Sikhism) – Punjabi meaning 'gateway to the guru'; a Sikh house of worship.

Hadith (Islam) – The collection of the Prophet's sayings and his companions' accounts of his practices that is considered an authoritative guide to Muslim life.

Hagana – The pre-eminent Jewish militia in Palestine from 1920 until 1948, when the state of Israel was established.

Hajj (Islam) – The pilgrimage to Mecca that is expected of all adult Muslims; one of the five pillars of Islam.

Halakha (Judaism) – The Jewish law, from a Hebrew word meaning a path or a way to walk.

halal (Islam) – 'That which is permitted'; often used to identify food that has been properly prepared according to Islamic strictures.

haram (Islam) – 'That which is forbidden'; behaviour that is prohibited by Islamic practice.

Haredim (Judaism) – 'God fearers'; extremely conservative Jews, sometimes described as 'ultra-orthodox'.

hesed (Judaism) – Hebrew word referring to God's covenantal love, traditionally translated 'loving-kindness'.

hijab (Islam) – The headscarf that some Muslim women wear to cover their hair.

hijra (Islam) – From the Arabic meaning 'migration' or 'flight'; the movement of Muslims, led by Muhammad, from Mecca to Medina in 622 (the year from which the Islamic calendar is dated).

himsa (Hinduism) – Sanskrit word meaning 'violence'; see *ahimsa*.

hindutva (Hinduism) – 'Hinduness'; the ideology of Hindu nationalism in India.

Holy See (Roman Catholicism) – The seat of the bishop of Rome, the pre-eminent bishopric in the Roman Catholic Church.

ijtihad (Islam) – Independent reasoning, carried out by experts in Islamic law.

Ikhwan (Islam) – Arabic meaning 'brothers'; the Ikhwan al-Muslimun is the Muslim Brotherhood, founded in Egypt in 1928.

imago dei (Christianity) – Latin meaning 'image of God'; the tradition that humanity was created in God's own image.

imam, Imam (Islam) – An imam is the person who leads the prayers in a mosque; in Shi'i Islam the Imam is the supreme spiritual leader.

instrumentalism – Interpretive framework in which religion is seen as a tool used by different actors to achieve tangible political ends.

Ismaili (Islam) – A school of Shi'i Islam. Today the term typically refers to Nizari Ismailis, whose Imam (spiritual leader) is the Aga Khan.

jahiliya (Islam) – Arabic, usually translated as 'ignorance', specifically ignorance of the message of Islam. Initially used to describe the pagan culture of Arabia before the life of the Prophet and adapted by twentieth-century salafists, especially Sayyid Qutb, to refer to contemporary societies that ignore the message of Islam.

jihad (Islam) – Arabic for 'struggle'; 'greater *jihad*' is the inner struggle against bad habits and evil; 'lesser *jihad*' is the military or political struggle for the victory of Islam.

jizya (Islam) – The poll-tax traditionally imposed on non-Muslims living in Islamic states.

juche – 'Self-reliance'; the guiding philosophy of the People's Democratic Republic of Korea (North Korea).

jus ad bellum – Latin meaning 'right to wage war'; in Just War theory, refers to criteria that provide the legal justification for war.

jus in bello – Latin meaning 'laws of war'; refers to criteria used to justify actions taken in war in Just War theory.

Just War – The Christian tradition in which war may be considered morally acceptable if it meets certain criteria.

karma (Hinduism, Buddhism) – Sanskrit; the sum of an individual's moral actions, good and bad, as it is believed to affect his or her next life; 'good' *karma* is often translated as 'merit'.

Khalistan (Sikhism) – Punjabi term meaning 'land of the pure', used to refer to a future independent Sikh state.

Khalsa (Sikhism) – The 'pure' Sikhs, established as a military order by Guru Gobind Singh in 1699. Today the Khalsa is the community of baptized Sikhs.

Knesset – The Israeli parliament.

Kshatriya (Hinduism) – The second highest caste, consisting of warriors and rulers.

Lok Sabha – The lower house of the Indian parliament.

Mahabharata (Hinduism) – Indian epic that tells the story of a war between the Kauravas and the Pandavas, two ancient Hindu clans; the *Bhagavad Gita* is a section of the *Mahabharata*.

maharaja – An Indian prince.

Mahavamsa (Theravada Buddhism) – The 'great chronicle', an account of Sri Lanka's ancient history, written down in the sixth century.

Mahayana (Buddhism) – One of the three major vehicles of Buddhism.

mainline churches (Christianity) – The principal denominations in the United States; their more liberal theological perspectives usually set them apart from Evangelical Protestants.

Messiah (Judaism/Christianity) – From the Hebrew meaning 'anointed one', a person specially designated by God to lead the community. In later Hebrew teaching, the messiah is expected to bring deliverance and restoration of the Jewish community. Christians believe Jesus of Nazareth to be the Messiah, or Christ.

Mizrahim (Judaism) – 'Eastern' Jews; Jewish people of non-European descent.

monastic – Relating to a monastery or a community of religious devotees (monks or nuns); the monastic life is typically one of various religious disciplines.

moksha (Hinduism) – Sanskrit for 'liberation' or 'salvation', meaning freedom from the cycle of rebirth.

mujahideen (Islam) – People who engage in *jihad* (sometimes translated 'holy warriors'). Most commonly used to refer to the various Afghan opposition groups that waged war on the Communist-supported government of Afghanistan in the period 1979–91.

mosque (Islam) – A Muslim house of worship.

Muslim (Islam) One who submits to Allah; a follower of Islam.

mysticism – A type of religious practice in which believers seek to become one with the divine, or to apprehend truths beyond human understanding.

nirvana (Hinduism, Buddhism) – The cessation of being or attachment in which the individual becomes one with the universe.

Pali Canon (Theravada Buddhism) – The earliest official collection of Buddhist sacred texts, written down in Sri Lanka, likely in the first century CE.

parinirvana (Buddhism) – The entry of the Buddha into the final nirvana.

personal status laws – Laws governing the familial and personal status of believers in many religious-legal traditions, typically including rules governing divorce, remarriage, and custodial rights.

Peter's Pence – Voluntary donations to the Holy See made by the worldwide Roman Catholic community.

pope (Roman Catholicism) – From the Latin word for 'father'; the presiding bishop of the Roman Catholic Church.

Protestantism (Christianity) – A division of Christianity formed by several religious movements opposed to Roman Catholic authority and doctrine during the sixteenth century, a period known as the Protestant Reformation.

Qur'an (Islam) – The holy scripture of Islam.

raisons d'état – French for 'purposes of state'.

Roman Catholic (Christianity) – The western (Latin) tradition of Christianity, which recognizes the bishop of Rome (the pope) as the head of the worldwide church.

sabras – Native-born Israelis.

salaam – Arabic for 'peace' or 'well-being'.

salat (Islam) – The practice of performing five daily prayers; one of the five pillars of Islam.

samsara (Hinduism, Buddhism) – The cycle of rebirth that leads to reincarnation.

sangh parivar (Hinduism) – The gathering of hindutva movements in contemporary India.

sangha (Buddhism) – The community of Buddhist monks.

Sansad Bhavan – The Indian house of parliament.

satyagraha (Hinduism) – Sanskrit term meaning 'truth-seeking' or 'truth-force'; coined by Gandhi to refer to non-violent resistance as a strategy to effect social and political change.

sawm (Islam) – Fasting from food and drink; refers to the practice of fasting throughout the daylight hours of the month of Ramadan, one of the five pillars of Islam.

secularism – Word used to refer either to a system in which politics and public life are not influenced by religion, or the ideological assertion that there should be a strong distinction between the two. In practice secularism takes many different forms.

Sephardim (Judaism) Literally, 'Spanish', refers to Jews of North African or Arab descent since the fifteenth century expulsion of Jews from Spain.

shahada (Islam) – The confession that there is no god but God and Muhammad is his messenger; one of the five pillars of Islam.

shahid (Islam) – Arabic word for 'martyr'.

shalom (Judaism) – Hebrew, peace and well-being.

shanti (Hinduism, Buddhism) – Peace.

Shari'a (Islam) – The Islamic law, from an Arabic word meaning a way or path.

sheikh (Islam) – A leader in the Islamic community.

Shi'i (Islam) – The minority tradition within Islam, which rejected the rule of the caliphs and believes that the rightful successors of the Prophet are the Imams: descendants of the Prophet's son-in-law Ali.

shirk (Islam) – In Islamic theology, denying the oneness of God by associating something else with the divine; also used to refer to idolatry.

Shoah (Judaism) – The Hebrew word for the Holocaust.

Shudras (Hinduism) – Servants; the lowest of the four Hindu castes.

shura (Islam) – Arabic word usually translated 'consultation'; a principle of governance in Islamic law.

social gospel – A Protestant religious and intellectual movement of the late 1800s and early 1900s that applied Christian ethics to the alleviation of major social problems such as poverty, unjust labour conditions, and abuse of liquor.

stupa (Buddhism) – A mound or structure that contains relics of a Buddhist exemplar; the focal point of Buddhist veneration.

sunna (Islam) – The example set by the Prophet of Islam and recorded in the Hadith; collections of traditional stories of the Prophet and his companions considered by all Muslims to be the authoritative guide to practice and conduct.

Sunni (Islam) – The majority tradition within Islam, differentiated from the Shi'i by their acceptance of leaders (the caliphs) from outside the family of the Prophet Muhammad.

sutra-pitaka (Buddhism) – One of the three 'baskets' (*tripitaka*) of sacred texts in the Pali Canon, containing the teachings of the Buddha.

sutras (Hinduism, Buddhism) – Written religious teachings.

symphonia (Eastern Orthodoxy) – The Orthodox principle of harmony between church and state, in which neither is more authoritative than the other. The principle dates back at least as far as the Roman (Byzantine) Emperor Justinian I in the sixth century.

syncretism – The combination of elements from two or more disparate religious traditions.

Taliban – An extremist Islamic movement founded in Afghanistan in the mid-1990s; the name is derived from the Arabic term for students.

Talmud (Judaism) – The collection of rabbinic writings on the Jewish religious law, collected around the year 500.

Tanakh (Judaism) – The Hebrew scriptures, consisting of the Torah (law), the Neviim (prophetic scriptures) and the Ketuvim (writings).

tawhid (Islam) – The Islamic doctrine of divine unicity or the oneness of God.

Theravada (Buddhism) – The oldest of the three major vehicles of Buddhism.

tripitaka (Buddhism) – The 'three baskets' of sacred texts that make up the Pali Canon.

tzedakah (Judaism) – Hebrew term typically translated as 'righteousness'; showing reverence for the community through good deeds.

ulema (Islam) – The community of Islamic legal scholars; *ulama* is a variant spelling (singular *alim*).

umma (Islam) – The worldwide community of Muslims.

Vaishyas (Hinduism) – The third or merchant caste of Hinduism.

Vajrayana (Buddhism) – The third of the three major vehicles; also known as Tibetan Buddhism.

varna (Hinduism) – Sanskrit for 'colour', used to refer to the castes of Hinduism.

Vedas (Hinduism) – The earliest sacred texts of Hinduism, some of which are conservatively dated c. 1500 BCE.

velayat i-faqih (Shi'i Islam) – Judicial guidance, enshrined as a constitutional principle in the Islamic Republic of Iran.

vinaya-pitaka (Buddhism) – The 'basket' of sacred Buddhist texts that records the rules of order for Buddhist monks.

waqf (Islam) – A religious endowment, whether the inheritance of the Islamic community worldwide or a local inheritance or foundation that supports a Muslim community or mosque.

wat (Buddhism) – A sacred shrine or temple.

westoxication – A term popularized by the Iranian dissident Ali Shari'ati, referring to the corruption of Islamic society by Western influences.

Westphalian system, Westphalian synthesis – The modern international system of states, established in the Peace of Westphalia (1648), in which state sovereignty and territorial authority, equality of status, and the principle of *cuius regio, eius religio* are respected.

yeshiva (Judaism) – A school for Jewish religious education; plural *yeshivot*.

Yishuv – The community of Jews in Palestine prior to the declaration of the state of Israel.

zakat (Islam) – Almsgiving; one of the five pillars of Islam.

Index